THOMSON
SOUTH-WESTERN

MEAN JEANS MANUFACTURING CO.

Student Reference Book

A Business Community Simulation

4e

Marie Weeks

SOUTH-WESTERN

THOMSON LEARNING

Mean Jeans Manufacturing Co.
A Business Community Simulation, 4th Edition
Student Reference Book
by Marie Weeks

Vice VP/Editorial Director
Jack W. Calhoun

VP/Editor-in-Chief
Karen Schmohe

Executive Editor
Eve Lewis

Project Manager
Enid Nagel

Senior Marketing Manager
Nancy Long

Marketing Coordinator
Angela Glassmeyer

Production Manager
Patricia Matthews Boies

Content Project Manager
Darrell Frye

Technology Project Manager
Scott Hamilton

Manufacturing Coordinator
Kevin Kluck

Editorial Assistant
Linda Watkins

Art Director
Tippy McIntosh

Cover Designer
Kathy Krechnyak

Cover Photo Source
Alamy Limited

Development & Electronic Prepress
A.W. Kingston Publishing Services, LLC

Printer
Quebecor World
Dubuque, Iowa

About the Author

Marie Weeks holds an Education Specialist degree from Valdosta State University. She has taught at Lowndes High School in Valdosta, Georgia, since 1982. Mrs. Weeks previously worked for private companies, public organizations, and as the owner of her own business.

For more information about our products, contact us at:

Thomson Higher Education
5191 Natorp Boulevard
Mason, Ohio 45040
USA

REVIEWERS

Sharon Beyer Glenn Mills, PA	Joe B. Crislip Parkersburg, WV	Gen Craft Terre Haute, IN	Kristin Matchey Arcadia, WI	Lisa Perry Blair, WI
Mary Elaine Chaney Ventura, CA	Madge L. Gregg Hoover, AL	Kathleen Leis Alma Center, WI	Carol Milove Mayhopac, NY	Jane Vondracek Kaukauna, WI

TABLE OF CONTENTS

REFERENCE GUIDE

48

PART 4   PRESIMULATION: GROUP ACTIVITY   326

PART 5   PRICE LISTS AND PERSONAL SUPPLIES   350

Doing Business on the 'Net

INTERNET EXPLORATIONS

PART 1

Orientation to a Business Community Simulation

Pettisville Chamber of Commerce
101 Dungaree Drive • Pettisville, Ohio 43553-0178

WELCOME TO PETTISVILLE, OHIO, USA

You are about to become one of many respected businesspersons in this interesting and historic community located in upstate Ohio.

In the early 1800s John Pettis (for whom Pettisville was later named) described the area as "woods, water, friendly Indians, wolves, and black bears." The building of the railroad through Ohio brought with it hardworking men and women who set up places of trade. One of the early industries was the Pettisville Woolen Mills on Front Street. There, satinets, flannels, canvas, cassimeres, and other textiles were manufactured. Today Pettisville is a thriving business community.

Pettisville is the perfect setting for the Mean Jeans Manufacturing Co. simulation. You will be managing one of the 15 businesses which provides goods and services to Mean Jeans Manufacturing Co. and to each other. It will be exciting for you to watch as your classroom is changed into a model business community.

You will be proud to be one of Pettisville's respected businesspersons. It will be your responsibility to manage one of the following businesses:

18 Wheeler Truck Lines	Passports-2-Go
Buckeye Equipment	Pettisville Bank
The Clothes Closet	Pettisville Post Office
Creative Advertising Agency	Popular Designs
The Denim Maker	Taylor Office Supplies
Hollywood & Vine Videos	The Towne Crier
Lee Community Center	United Communications
Nouveau Investment Company	

You will enjoy working in Pettisville and managing your own business. Enclosed for your reference is the Pettisville Business Community Directory. It is with great pleasure that the Pettisville Chamber of Commerce welcomes you to our community.

Jerry A. Sherman, President

Pettisville Business Community Directory

The Model Business Community

18 Wheeler Truck Lines
1208 Oshkosh Blvd.
Pettisville, OH 43553-0177
419-555-0119
(Corporation)

Buckeye Equipment
1313 Olentangy Road
Pettisville, OH 43553-0175
419-555-0178
(Partnership)

The Clothes Closet
61 Dungaree Drive
Pettisville, OH 43553-0178
419-555-0154
(Sole Proprietorship)

Creative Advertising Agency
816 Corduroy Drive
Pettisville, OH 43553-0177
419-555-0188
(Limited Liability Company)

The Denim Maker
752 Gold Mine Lane
Pettisville, OH 43553-0176
419-555-0195
(Corporation)

Hollywood & Vine Videos
2501 Kneepatch Avenue
Pettisville, OH 43553-0175
419-555-0172
(Limited Liability Company)

Lee Community Center
One Vale Stree
Pettisville, OH 43553-0177
419-555-0166
(Corporation, Nonprofit)

Mean Jeans Manufacturing Co.
45 Maple Street
Pettisville, OH 43553-0175
419-555-0100
(Corporation)

Nouveau Investment Company
440 Wall Street
Pettisville, OH 43553-0178
419-555-0134
(Partnership)

Passports-2-Go
728 Blazer Avenue
Pettisville, OH 43553-0177
419-555-0164
(Sole Proprietorship)

Pettisville Bank
101 Greenback Drive
Pettisville, OH 43553-0178
419-555-0101
(Corporation)

Pettisville Post Office
22 Stamp Street
Pettisville, OH 43553-0178
888-555-0133
(Federal Agency)

Popular Designs
2020 Carpenter Road
Pettisville, OH 43553-0176
419-555-0182
(Sole Proprietorship)

Taylor Office Supplies
12 Rivet Street
Pettisville, OH 43553-0177
419-555-0135
(Sole Proprietorship, Franchisee)

The Towne Crier
Information Circle Mall
P. O. Box 276
Pettisville, OH 43553-0176
419-555-0122
(Sole Proprietorship)

United Communications
Information Circle
Pettisville, OH 43553-0176
800-555-0111
(Corporation, Controlled Monopoly)

The model business community is located in Pettisville, Ohio, and is made up of Mean Jeans Manufacturing Co. and 15 other businesses. (Pettisville, Ohio, is a *real place*; Mean Jeans Manufacturing Co. and the 15 other businesses are *imaginary*.) A *business* is an establishment that supplies goods or services. Mean Jeans Manufacturing Co. is the largest company in Pettisville. The other 15 businesses provide Mean Jeans and each other with a variety of goods and services. All of these businesses are typical of those found in communities throughout the country. And all of them interact by doing business with each other and with many businesses outside the model business community.

If you have not already done so, read the letter of welcome from the president of the Pettisville Chamber of Commerce in the front of this *Student Reference Book*. A *chamber of commerce* is a local organization of businesses whose goal is to further the business interests of the community. During the month of July, the Pettisville Chamber of Commerce will sponsor the Western Roundup Days, a very exciting annual event in Pettisville.

Pay special attention to the names of the businesses. A complete mailing address and telephone number for each of the businesses is given in the Pettisville Business Community Directory on the opposite page. Begin thinking now about the business that interests you most. You will find more information about each business in PART 2 of this *Student Reference Book*.

Now look at the map of Pettisville shown on page 7 in this *Student Reference Book*. Notice that all community streets are shown on the map. Can you find Kneepatch Avenue, Dungaree Drive, and Stamp Street? Notice, too, that Clear Lake, Pettisville Community Park, and the Conrail railroad tracks are shown also.

At the bottom of the map, each Pettisville business is listed by identification number and name. Mean Jeans Manufacturing Co. is number 8, for example. Find number 8 on the map. Passports-2-Go is number 10. Find number 10 on the map. Buckeye Equipment is number 2. Find number 2 on the map. Continue in this manner until you have located Mean Jeans Manufacturing Co. and each of the other 15 businesses. Do you see that Nouveau Investment Company and Pettisville Post Office are located across the street from each other?

YOUR PART IN THE BUSINESS COMMUNITY

You will play a very important role in this model business community. As manager of one of the 15 businesses, you will be a respected businessperson. You will see for yourself what it is like to be responsible for the overall success or failure of your own business. You will also have an opportunity to become familiar with a variety of business papers typically used in businesses today.

As manager of a business in the model business community, you will perform activities representative of those performed by managers in the real world of work. These activities include

- preparing business papers for mailing and following through on the actions required by incoming mail (such as letters, purchase orders, sales invoices, contracts, and invoices for services rendered)

- making independent decisions and accepting the consequences of those decisions

- conducting banking activities (such as preparing bank deposits, making rent and mortgage payments, paying federal income and FICA taxes, and reconciling bank statements)

- practicing good human relations skills (such as listening carefully and communicating effectively, being considerate and helpful to customers and clients, and maintaining a positive attitude)

- managing human resources (including advertising job openings, hiring new employees, showing appreciation and respect for employees, and attempting to maintain good morale)

- keeping records neatly and accurately (such as a cashbook, checkbook, stock inventory, and payroll records)

- adjusting to changing work demands

- practicing good public relations with the business community (such as supporting civic groups, participating in community activities, and respecting the rights of other community businesses)

- investing time and money for personal growth, such as buying shares of stock in American corporations, taking classes in money management and CPR (cardiopulmonary resuscitation), and registering for computer workshops

As a manager, you will interact with managers of other Pettisville businesses. Also, you will willingly participate in projects designed to benefit the community. Western Roundup Days, for example, is the biggest, most exciting event of the year!

As manager ...

... of a business in the model business community, you will perform activities representative of those performed by managers in the real world of work.

MAP OF MODEL BUSINESS COMMUNITY PETTISVILLE, OHIO

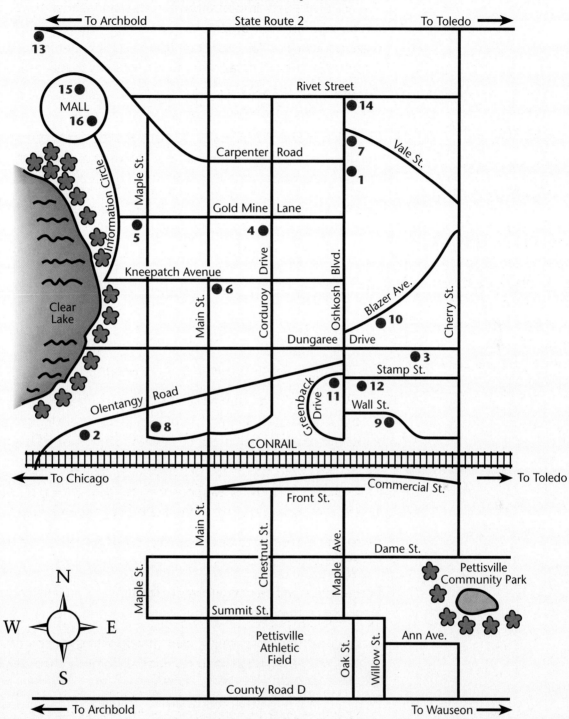

1 18 Wheeler Truck Lines
2 Buckeye Equipment
3 The Clothes Closet
4 Creative Advertising Agency
5 The Denim Maker
6 Hollywood & Vine Videos

7 Lee Community Center
8 Mean Jeans Manufacturing Co.
9 Nouveau Investment Company
10 Passports-2-Go
11 Pettisville Bank
12 Pettisville Post Office

13 Popular Designs
14 Taylor Office Supplies
15 The Towne Crier
16 United Communications

RESPONSIBLITIES OF MANAGERS IN BUSINESS TODAY

Persons of all ages, abilities, and interests manage their own businesses or the businesses of others. The newspaper carrier who brings your paper to your door manages a business. The man or woman who is president of the largest corporation in your city manages a business.

All managers—whether they manage businesses in Pettisville or businesses in your hometown—are responsible for the successful operation of their businesses. A *manager* is a person responsible for the five functions of management—planning, organizing, leading, controlling, and staffing.

- *Planning* involves deciding what has to be done and determining how goals can be met.

- *Organizing* involves making the necessary arrangements to do work that has been planned.

- *Leading* involves guiding employees in doing the work.

- *Controlling* involves checking to see that work has been done as planned.

- *Staffing* involves finding, hiring, training, and evaluating employees.

In today's fast-moving world of business, owners look to managers for help in making businesses successful and profitable. It is important that you remember that managers are made, not born. Making decisions and carrying them through, being dependable, being willing to try any task regardless of how unpleasant or how routine it is, and possessing initiative—these are all qualities that you, as a young person, should strive to develop NOW.

When you accept your assignment as manager of a Pettisville business, you will be on your way to becoming a qualified applicant for a position in tomorrow's exciting business world.

CAREER OPPORTUNITIES FOR PERSONS WITH MANAGEMENT ABILITIES

Want ads like these that follow are typical of ads that appear daily in newspapers all over the country. Notice that the advertised openings are for managers and manager trainees. Men and women who qualify for management positions find challenging, exciting, and well-paying job opportunities available to them.

Salaries for managers vary greatly. Job experience and education affect the salary range most significantly. The size of the company and

---

A manager ...

... is a person responsible for the five functions of management —
- planning
- organizing
- leading
- controlling
- staffing

its geographic location also influence the salaries paid and the career paths available.

Good managers are needed at all levels of employment. The beginning employee who is willing to work hard and who is eager to learn will often get management training on the job. A person who has self confidence and adapts easily to changing work demands is a good candidate for a career in management. It's not too early for you to begin to develop these important qualities.

A key attribute of a good manager is the ability to recognize that a company's most important asset is PEOPLE (the company's employees). Because human relations skills are of critical importance, a self evaluation checklist is provided on *page 307 in this Student Reference Book*. Completing this checklist will help you to determine your strengths and weaknesses in the area of human relations. Everyone has both strengths and weaknesses. But you can strengthen weak areas if you have the desire to improve by setting realistic goals that lead to improved skills.

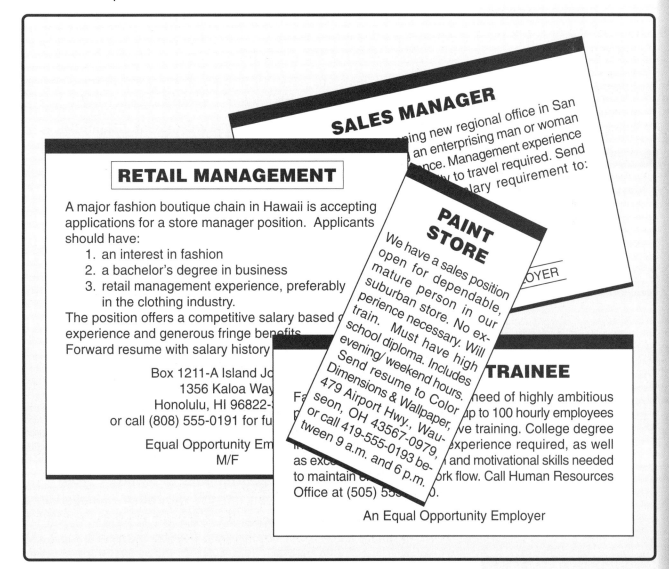

You will ...

... make decisions, accept responsibility, establish priorities, and follow directions.

You will ...

... develop a sense of pride in yourself and your accomplishments.

❖ WHAT WORKING IN THE MODEL BUSINESS COMMUNITY WILL DO FOR YOU

1. You will learn common business procedures, including those relating to banking, payroll, and purchasing.

2. You will make decisions, accept responsibility, establish priorities, and follow directions.

3. You will use basic math skills to verify invoices, pay for goods ordered, keep records of all money coming into or going out of your business, and use postal and freight services.

4. You will use your creativity in composing simple business letters, want ads, and advertising copy.

5. You will experience the thrill of a job well done when your payroll register proves, your bank statement reconciles, and your cashbook balances.

6. You will receive immediate feedback when you practice good human relations skills.

7. You will feel the excitement of cooperating in a community project such as Western Roundup Days.

8. You will learn to deal with the stress caused from having customers or clients wait for you to complete an activity.

9. You will learn how important the organization of materials is to production.

10. You will develop a sense of pride in yourself and your accomplishments.

11. You will make a personal financial investment in an American corporation, and you may participate in the Mean Jeans Annual Stockholders' Meeting.

12. You will see how the operation of one business affects the operation of other businesses in a community.

13. You will see the need for the prompt and accurate processing of business papers.

14. You will see the need for good public relations as you try to accomplish the objectives of your company.

15. You will appreciate the roles of a consumer, worker, and citizen in a free enterprise system.

16. You will have many opportunities to improve your oral communication skills as you interact with other managers in a typical business environment.

Blue jeans are popular and have remained basically unchanged for many, many years. Light, medium, and heavy blue denim jeans are worn by people of all ages, shapes, and sizes. The jeans with the famous trademark on the back pocket are manufactured in Pettisville, Ohio, by Mean Jeans Manufacturing Co.

Look at the map on <u>*page 5 in this Student Reference Book*</u>. Notice that Pettisviile is located in the northwestern corner of Ohio, almost to the Ohio-Michigan border. Interstate Highway 80/90 is near Pettisville, and Conrail runs south of the center of town. Can you find the busy port of Toledo? Notice that it is a short drive from Pettisville.

Mean Jeans Manufacturing Co. is located on a 12-acre tract of land on the western edge of the Pettisville Business District. The factory, located on a street lined with maple trees, contains the administrative offices, production department, and warehousing operations of Mean Jeans.

History of the Company

In December, 1948, Brent Rychener began selling his own creation of denim overalls to the railroad workers who stopped to talk near the barn on his parents' farm. That small barn soon became the original site of Mean Jeans Manufacturing Co.

American Families ... Work and Play in Mean Jeans

All Photos ©NOVA DEVELOPMENT CORPORATION

PART 1: ORIENTATION TO A BUSINESS COMMUNITY SIMULATION

©NOVA DEVELOPMENT CORPORATION

©NOVA DEVELOPMENT CORPORATION

As demand for his overalls grew, Brent continued to design more jeans and to buy sewing machines. Finally, in 1960 he took in a partner, Diane Diener. They moved the business from the original barn where Brent operated for years into a newly constructed factory on Maple Street. In the past, Brent advertised his jeans by painting signs on the back of his barn. With the new location, Mean Jeans made use of the services of Pettisville's own Creative Advertising Agency. Soon the distinctive Mean Jeans trademark was seen on billboards, in newspapers, and in magazines.

But the public soon demanded that additional designs be added to the popular Mean Jeans line. So, Popular Designs (located on Carpenter Road in Pettisville) was contracted to design a special line of denim clothing for the company. It was at this time that Mean Jeans Manufacturing Co. began experimenting with white, red, and black denim.

The Company Today

By 1974 the partnership formed by Brent Rychener and Diane Diener had grown into a corporation, and the facilities on Maple Street were enlarged to their present size. Mean Jeans Manufacturing Co. now employs approximately 1,200 full-time production workers and a sizable office staff. Brent and Diane no longer head the management team as president and secretary-treasurer of the board of directors. They both retired in the 1990's, and other managers were promoted to take their places.

Mean Jeans Manufacturing Co. is a member of the Pettisville Chamber of Commerce and the National Manufacturers Association. The new president, Glenn Copeland, is a member of Lee Community Center, Little Church Around the Corner, and Pettisville Board of Education.

As Mean Jeans grew, new businesses sprang up in Pettisville to meet the needs of this expanding manufacturing corporation. Pettisville today is a thriving business community, and Mean Jeans remains at the center of community operations.

❖ GENERAL INFORMATION ABOUT THE SIMULATION

Mean Jeans Manufacturing Co. (Mean Jeans, for short!) is a business community workflow simulation. It is designed to give you a life-like experience managing your own business. As a manager of a Pettisville business, you will be an important member of the model business community and will gain firsthand knowledge of basic business concepts and procedures. You also will learn to appreciate the roles of a consumer, worker, and citizen in a free enterprise system.

Included in the model business community are five sole proprietorships, two partnerships, one federal agency, six corporations, and two limited liability companies. Two of the corporations (Lee Community Center and United Communications) have special features. Lee Community Center is a nonprofit organization, and United Communications is a utility that is a controlled monopoly.

Workflow

The simulation will operate during the simulated month of July. Business papers flow into and out of your company in an orderly and planned manner. Mail delivery of items (letters, orders, invoices, and so forth) and personal visits from other community businesspersons generate work to be performed by your company. An *Operations Manual* for your business will also provide activities for you to complete. You will see how the daily operation of your business affects the operation of Mean Jeans and other community businesses.

Assignment of Businesses

All 16 businesses are important to the basic community operation. Your Instructor will manage Mean Jeans Manufacturing Co. You will be assigned the position of manager of one of the other 15 businesses. Your Instructor will take into consideration your individual interests and abilities when making these assignments.

General Activities

As manager of a company in the model business community, you will perform a variety of interesting and challenging activities. You will have an opportunity to acquire basic management skills that employers look for when hiring management trainees. These skills include the ability to plan, to organize, to lead, to control, and to staff. You will be preparing yourself for a career in business, developing your self confidence, and expanding your knowledge of basic business concepts and procedures.

Presimulation: Group Activity

Before you begin your duties, you will need to become familiar with the community of Pettisville, with the operation of Mean Jeans Manufacturing Co., and with the operation of the company you will manage. Therefore, your Instructor will ask you to complete the "Presimulation: Group Activity" outlined later in this *Student Reference Book*. Your success as a manager will depend greatly on the accurate completion of this "Presimulation: Group Activity." Complete each step carefully; be sure not to overlook anything. Try to learn as much as you can about the Pettisville community and the company you will manage. Remember that Pettisville is now your community, and the business you manage is your company.

Supplies and Folders for Organizing Work

During the Getting Ready To Do Business activities located in your *Operations Manual*, your Instructor will give each manager files, folders, and supplies for use during the simulation. You will also receive specific instructions for setting up the files and folders for which you are responsible and for organizing your own supplies.

◆ MEAN JEANS BUSINESS COMMUNITY SIMULATION COMPONENTS

Student Reference Book

STUDENT REFERENCE BOOK

Your *Student Reference Book* (which you are reading right now) is a vital resource designed to help you succeed in carrying out your duties as manager of a Pettisville business. It is both a learning tool and a ready reference. <u>The *Student Reference Book* tells you HOW to do things</u>. Pay special attention to the titles of the 10 Units in the Reference Guide (PART 3) of the book so you have a general knowledge of all areas covered.

PART 1, Orientation to a Business Community Simulation, begins with a letter of welcome to the Pettisville business community from the Pettisville Chamber of Commerce. The Pettisville Business Community Directory on page 4 in this *Student Reference Book* lists many of the mailing addresses you will use throughout the simulation. General information about the Pettisville business community, Mean Jeans Manufacturing Co., and the operation of the simulation are also given in this part.

PART 2, Orientation to the 15 Businesses, provides interesting background information about the 15 businesses that provide Mean Jeans Manufacturing Co. with a variety of goods and services. This information will be helpful to you as you decide which business you would most like to manage.

PART 3, Reference Guide, describes and illustrates the various business papers you will use and the procedures you will follow as you conduct daily business transactions. You should look carefully at the illustrations and follow the step-by-step directions each time you complete a new form or perform a new activity.

PART 4, Presimulation: Group Activity, contains specific activities to familarize you with the Mean Jeans Business Community Simulation in general and this *Student Reference Book* in particular. During the course of this group presimulation activity, you will be applying for employment as a manager of one of the businesses. You will also fill out the necessary forms when you are hired. And you will prepare for the managers' meeting.

PART 5, Price Lists and Personal Supplies, includes all of the price lists for the various businesses and certain personal supplies that you will use during the course of the simulation. The price lists need to be referenced during the course of many of the business activities. Included with the supplies is "Mean Jeans" money that you will use to purchase such things as newspapers and shares of stock.

You should refer to your *Student Reference Book* whenever you have a question about procedures, forms, or terminology. Always refer to this *Student Reference Book* before you ask for assistance.

Operations Manuals

There is an *Operations Manual* for each of the 15 businesses. Your *Operations Manual* will provide you with information you'll need to know about your business, including the confidential financial statements for your business. It will tell you how to get your business started. It contains detailed lists of your responsibilities as a manager and *DAILY ACTIVITIES* for you to follow each day during the simulation. You will also find many references to sections of the *Student Reference Book*. Your *Operations Manual* tells you WHAT to do and WHEN to do it. As you complete the *DAILY ACTIVITIES* for your particular business and follow the procedures given in this *Student Reference Book*, you will see how and why businesses must work together to accomplish common objectives.

OPERATIONS MANUAL

Supplies and Resources CD

For students with access to computers, a *Supplies and Resources CD* is available to automate many of the tasks completed by managers. The *Supplies and Resources CD* provides you with the forms and templates WHERE you can record your business transactions. The CD contains a folder for each business with all of the forms and templates needed to run the business. Your Instructor will move these documents onto your workstation. When a template form is used, a manager will be able to key data directly onto the form and then print it. At other times, a manager will print the form first and then complete it by hand. If you do not have a computer, your Instructor will provide your forms for you.

SUPPLIES AND RESOURCES CD

> ### ◆ SIMULATION—AN EXCITING NEW LEARNING EXPERIENCE

Mean Jeans Manufacturing Co.—A Business Community Simulation will provide you with an exciting new learning experience. From the moment the simulation begins, you will be actively involved in the learning process. Each day you will be called upon to perform new and varied activities in a simulated business community environment.

PART 2

Orientation to the 15 Businesses

18-Wheeler Truck Lines
Buckeye Equipment
The Clothes Closet
Creative Advertising Agency
The Denim Maker
Hollywood & Vine Videos
Lee Community Center
Nouveau Investment Company
Passports-2-Go
Pettisville Bank
Pettisville Post Office
Popular Designs
Taylor Office Supplies
The Towne Crier
United Communications

PASSPORTS 2 GO

UNITED COMMUNICATIONS

THE DENIM MAKER

PETTISVILLE BANK

POPULAR DESIGNS

TAYLOR OFFICE SUPPLIES

PETTISVILLE POST OFFICE

CREATIVE ADVERTISING AGENCY

MEAN JEANS MANUFACTURING CO.

The TOWNE CRIER

THE CLOTHES CLOSET

HOLLYWOOD & VINE VIDEOS

LEE COMMUNITY CENTER

BUCKEYE EQUIPMENT

18 WHEELER TRUCK LINES

NOUVEAU INVESTMENT COMPANY

18 WHEELER TRUCK LINES

This rapidly growing truck line was formed to meet the shipping needs of four Pettisville businesses—Buckeye Equipment, The Denim Maker, Taylor Office Supplies, and The Towne Crier. All four businesses were having difficulty shipping goods into and out of Pettisville.

On October 2, 1980, a corporation was formed by the four businesses, and two rigs were purchased. The corporate officers (Lawrence Avery, Samantha Nichols, Carol Myers, and Tom Williams) hired Ben and Rosie O'Riley to drive the newly purchased trucks. For the moment, the transportation problem was solved.

Elmer Murphy had contracted the local deliveries (or agreed to provide this delivery service for a fee) for many Pettisville businesses for forty years. When he died, 18 Wheeler Truck Lines purchased the rights to provide local delivery service from the Murphy heirs. Several vans were added to 18 Wheeler's existing fleet of trucks. These vans were to be used for local deliveries of goods and the U.S. mail. Later, 18 Wheeler was fortunate to be the truck line awarded a contract to haul U.S. mail from distribution centers to local post offices.

©NOVA DEVELOPMENT CORPORATION

The corporation has become a major business in the Pettisville community. The 18 Wheeler vans can be seen on the streets of Pettisville at any hour of the day or night. And the blue and gold 18 Wheeler trucks can be seen moving goods throughout the United States.

Today, much of their success is credited to the quality of the fleet drivers. Each 18 Wheeler driver has over five years of truck driving experience, has passed strict physical examinations, and is a responsible individual. Without a doubt, 18 Wheeler truck drivers are among the best on the road.

Currently, 18 Wheeler Truck Lines is in need of a driver/manager. The driver/manager will supervise local deliveries, complete cash transactions, hire new employees, handle payroll, and prepare freight bills. A *freight bill* is a bill for a shipment of merchandise prepared by the common carrier, such as a trucking company or a ship. The *carrier* is the agent (such as 18 Wheeler Truck Lines) who transports goods from the shipper to the *consignee* (the receiver). The manager of 18 Wheeler Truck Lines also will be expected to handle daily transactions with other businesses.

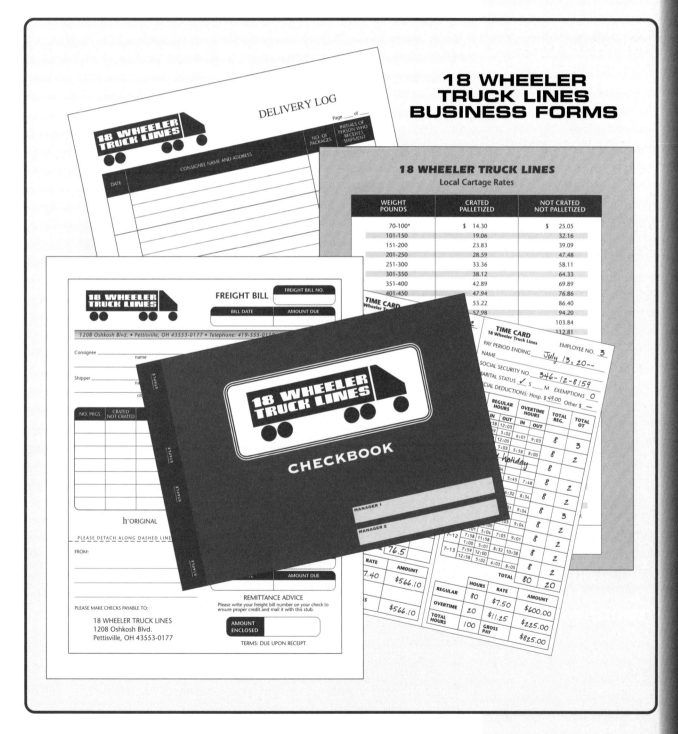

BUCKEYE EQUIPMENT

Larry Avery grew up in downtown Milwaukee where his father was a dockworker. As a boy, Larry used to go down to the waterfront and watch the workers unload freighters. After high school he started working on the docks himself. He soon became familiar with the repair and operation of heavy-duty machinery.

©NOVA DEVELOPMENT CORPORATION

Larry became good friends with Guy Burkholder ("Buck" for short), who operated a big crane on the dock. Seven years later Buck and Larry had saved enough money to buy the big warehouse on Olentangy Road near the Conrail tracks. On June 1, 1988, they began renting front loaders, compressors, grinders, and small cranes. Buckeye sells, rents, and repairs industrial equipment of all kinds, including conveyor belts, hand trucks, sewing machines, assembly line equipment, and forklifts. In 1995, the partnership also began selling custodial supplies.

As new industries come into Pettisville, the demand for more specialized equipment requires Buck to do more steel fabricating. He enjoys designing and building special parts that will provide his customers with greater efficiency in their operations.

Larry enjoys sales work. Given a choice, he would spend all day demonstrating to customers the use of various pieces of equipment. But business has expanded so much that the partners must spend much time "on the road" maintaining their rental equipment. The need for equipment maintenance and repair increases each time they sell or rent another piece of equipment.

During July, Buck and Larry hope to be able to hire a top-notch mechanic to take over some of the maintenance of their rental equipment. This would allow Buck and Larry to spend more time in their equipment shop.

Currently, Buckeye Equipment needs a manager who will hire and supervise employees, keep banking and payroll records, and complete rental and maintenance contracts. A *maintenance contract* is a contract between parties whereby a customer agrees to pay a fee to a business to keep equipment in good operating condition. The manager also will be expected to handle daily transactions with other businesses.

PART 2: ORIENTATION TO THE 15 BUSINESSES

THE
CLOTHES CLOSET

"Satisfaction Guaranteed!" is the motto on the front door of this fashionable retail-clothing store on Dungaree Drive.

Chris Flanagan, a native of Pettisville, took frequent vacations in Hawaii. During her last vacation in Hawaii, she encouraged her friend, Kimo Yonekura, to return to the mainland with her to relocate the Yonekura Retail Clothing Store in Pettisville.

©GETTY IMAGES/PHOTODISC

Kimo finally agreed and on March 3, 2005, she bought a charming old candy shop on Dungaree Drive. It took only a few months to totally redecorate the shop (using a Hawaiian theme, of course!) and turn it into a fashionable retail-clothing store. Kimo made the wise decision to keep the two clerks who had previously worked in the candy shop and who had a lot of selling experience. Soon Kimo was ready to welcome the first customers to her proprietorship, The Clothes Closet.

Business has been very good. The Clothes Closet features sportswear designed by a local designer, Felicia Hernandez. Her clothing designs are recognized all over the country. Kimo believes that the Hernandez-designed fashions are the key to her successful operation.

Although Kimo sells denim wear for the whole family, she specializes in custom orders for western wear. Orders arrive daily for clothes made of white denim and traditional blue denim. Some orders are from entertainers and other celebrities.

Her Hawaiian fashions have also increased in popularity here on the mainland. The fashion shows Kimo has presented at the downtown Maumee River Mall have attracted many Toledo residents to The Clothes Closet.

RETAIL: CLOTHING

Local retail clothing store is looking for a person with management ability. Must have fashion flair and basic record keeping skills. Pleasant surroundings and challenging work. Call 555-0154 between 10 a.m. and 5 p.m.

Last month Kimo's store began offering screen printed T-shirts to the community. She is considering expanding her fashion line, hiring a fashion coordinator, and enlarging her store. However, first she wants to hire a manager to work with her on these plans.

The manager of The Clothes Closet will be expected to keep banking and payroll records and handle returns and allowances. *Returns* are items returned to the store for a refund or exchange. An *allowance* is a reduction in the price of goods sold because the goods have been damaged or the customer is not happy with the product. The manager will also work with customers, supervise the other employees, and handle daily transactions with other businesses.

MANAGER NEEDED

Successful advertising agency is seeking an innovative manager. Computer skills essential; creative ability helpful. Attractive working conditions; duties varied. Call Creative Advertising Agency at 555-0188 immediately.

Creative Advertising Agency was formed by three college friends: Larry Marree was a business administration major, Jose Fernandez was an aspiring writer who majored in English, and Mary Ellen Newman was an art major who specialized in graphic design. On weekends, Mary Ellen worked part-time for College Town Florists. Her dream was to own her own business someday.

Mary Ellen convinced Larry and Jose to help her prepare advertising layouts and brochures for College Town Florists. Soon the creativity and original style of their work caught the attention of other businesspersons. By the time Mary Ellen, Larry, and Jose graduated from college, their ads were reaching a multitude of people. They had more than enough work to go into business for themselves—and they did! On July 1, 1960, the three young businesspersons formed a partnership, bought a building on Corduroy Drive in Pettisville, and began serving the needs of the Pettisville community. In 2001, they changed their form of ownership to a limited liability company.

©JOE HIGGINS

An advertising agency is an exciting place to work because it is involved with many different advertising media—radio, television, newspapers, the Internet, magazines, and billboards. *Advertising media* are the means used to communicate with the general public. Clients pay fees to advertising agencies, which arrange for customers' products to be properly advertised in the various media. Larry lines up advertising clients, Jose writes ads, and Mary Ellen designs the advertising layouts. Creative Advertising recently expanded its services to include designing web pages for its customers.

It comes as no surprise that Mean Jeans Manufacturing Co. is Creative Advertising's most valued customer. Mean Jeans bib overalls (loose trousers of strong material with shoulder straps) have become well known throughout the world. Creative Advertising's newest customer is Felicia Hernandez, owner of Popular Designs. Her creations enjoy worldwide popularity.

Business has been so good that Jose, Larry and Mary Ellen need additional help. They want to hire an advertising manager who can relieve them of some of the responsibilities of running the office. The manager of Creative Advertising Agency will be responsible for handling work that comes into the agency through the regular mail, by e-mail, or over the telephone. He or she will keep banking and payroll records, hire and supervise new employees, and write advertising copy. The manager also will be expected to handle daily transactions with other businesses.

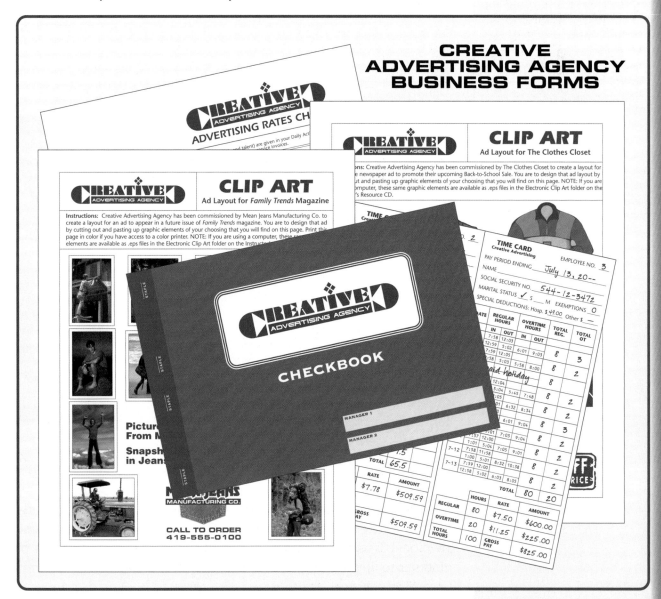

THE DENIM MAKER

It all began during the Great Depression of the 1930's. Three brothers—Jack, Phil, and Walter—owned a small factory on Gold Mine Lane in Pettisville. Unfortunately, they couldn't find anyone interested in leasing the building, so it sat empty for several years. Finally, the brothers convinced a well-known Georgia textile firm to open a new factory in Pettisville. A textile firm is a business that manufactures fabrics or clothing. To make sure the company would go through with the deal, the brothers offered the textile firm a ten-year, rent-free lease on the factory. There was one restriction, however. The company (The Denim Maker) had to hire local people to work in the factory.

©NOVA DEVELOPMENT CORPORATION

The new factory opened on May 1, 1934, and three corporate officers were named: Carol Myers, Meiling Chin, and Mildred Wanamaker. The Denim Maker's main purpose was to manufacture denim fabric according to the specifications of Mean Jeans Manufacturing Co. Mean Jeans was then—and is now—The Denim Maker's main customer.

The small corporation thrived in Pettisville! After the ten-year lease expired, the Georgia-based company purchased the property and enlarged the factory building. At that time The Denim Maker's factory workers decided to form a union.

Today trailers owned by 18 Wheeler Truck Lines bring bales of fluffy Georgia cotton to Pettisville. Often these trailers are carried on Conrail by piggyback (or loaded on flatcars). Bolts of denim in a rainbow of colors are shipped daily from The Denim Maker to manufacturing firms across the country.

Mean Jeans Manufacturing Co. buys in quantity from The Denim Maker and turns the soft, white denim into every type of garment from painter's overalls to evening attire. Mean Jeans buys over 90 percent of the denim made by The Denim Maker.

Twenty years ago, employees voted to join a labor union. Because of the success enjoyed by The Denim Maker, it is not surprising that the employees' labor union has brought many demands to the bargaining table. The current labor contract ends in July.

Since there have been rumors of a possible strike by union workers, a manager is needed to negotiate with the union. A *strike* is a shutdown of the operation of a business caused by employees who refuse to work in an effort to force the employer to pay better wages or improve working conditions. In addition, the manager's duties will include hiring new employees, keeping banking and payroll records, and completing bills of lading. The manager also will be expected to handle daily transactions with other businesses.

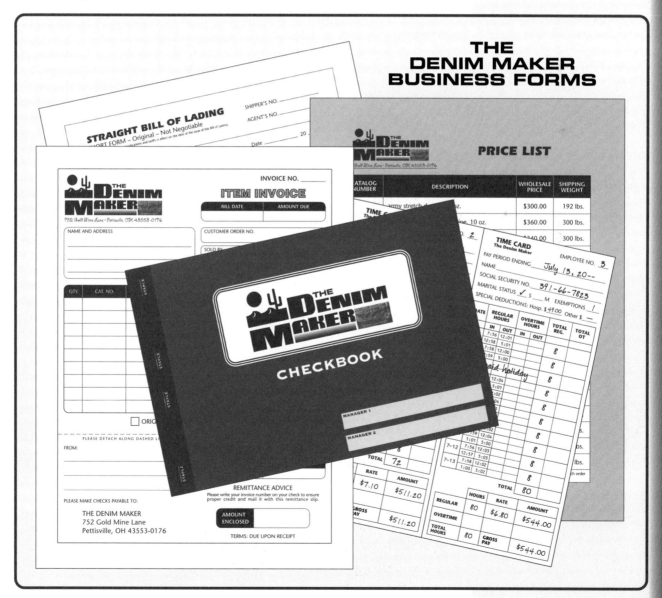

HOLLYWOOD & VINE VIDEOS

Steve and Kathy Ripley grew up in Pettisville, Ohio, were high school sweethearts, and married while they were in college. After graduation they both were hired to teach at Pettisville High School where Steve first taught typewriting and office procedures (and, later, computer applications) in the Business Education Department and Kathy was a math teacher.

©NOVA DEVELOPMENT CORPORATION

Steve asked the president of the Chamber of Commerce to serve on his school's advisory committee. In a conversation with the chamber president, Steve discovered that Pettisville needed a local video store. The closest video distributor was over 20 miles away, and the chamber believed this was a business opportunity being overlooked.

When Steve told Kathy about his discussion with the chamber president, she exclaimed, "I'd love to own a video store!" Steve and Kathy talked over the situation and made the decision for Kathy to leave teaching. Steve would help her set up the business and spend summers and weekends helping out, while their children would have made-to-order jobs after school.

Steve and Kathy convinced many people that their idea was a good one. On June 1, 1992, Hollywood & Vine Videos began as a limited liability company and started serving the community. The store is located at the corner of Kneepatch Avenue and Main Street.

The chamber's prediction proved correct. Pettisville residents were eager to have a video store in their community. Kathy has concentrated on good customer relations. When a customer asks for a video the store doesn't carry, she makes every effort to find it for the customer. She also offers a discount on future rentals when videos are returned to the store within 24 hours. Drop boxes were recently installed outside the store for the convenience of customers.

The business includes a large inventory of videos. *Inventory* is a list of goods maintained by the seller. It is important for the business to maintain an inventory for several reasons. The management needs to have an accurate count of the goods, determine the frequency of the video rentals, and (for tax purposes) place a value on each piece of inventory. Hollywood & Vine's inventory is categorized by type of video. Every video purchased is placed into one of the following categories: New Releases, Classics, Drama, Comedy, Horror, Children's, and Training.

Kathy has realized for some time that she misses teaching. She wants to teach part-time at the high school. If Kathy does this, Hollywood & Vine Videos must hire a manager to run the day-to-day operation of the business.

The manager of Hollywood & Vine Videos will be expected to make all purchases for the company, keep payroll and cash records, and serve customers efficiently. The manager will also be expected to handle daily transactions with other businesses.

STORE MANAGER

Local video store is in need of a manager. This is a unique opportunity for the right individual. Management experience helpful but not required. This position requires someone who can keep accurate financial records, supervise part-time employees, and work well with the public. Call 555-0172 between 9 and 5.

Pettisville has always been a warm, friendly community in which to live and work. This spirit of "togetherness" has existed for many years.

On January 1, 1930, Haywood Lee donated an attractive tract of land for a place to gather for community activities. Today that same five-acre plot of land northeast of the Pettisville business district is the location of a picturesque community center. The structure is appropriately called Lee Community Center.

©NOVA DEVELOPMENT CORPORATION

Many people from the Pettisville community are members of Lee Community Center, which is a nonprofit corporation. Hayrides, recycling project meetings, physical fitness classes, and athletic events are held regularly. The center helps the poor of Pettisville with a soup kitchen and by constructing modest homes for the needy. The center also serves as a collection point for donated items for persons or families who have suffered a tragedy such as a fire, flood, tornado, accident, or illness.

Recently a new program was initiated and is receiving enthusiastic support. Volunteers set aside time to tutor children in foreign languages and various musical instruments. The center offers entertainment programs for teens on Saturday nights. Classes are also available in money management and CPR (cardiopulmonary resuscitation).

Lee Community Center operates entirely on monies donated by the community and from annual membership dues. When revenues (income from donations) are not as high as expenses (money spent to keep the center operating), then it becomes necessary for the center to raise money through other means, such as fundraising letters.

Lee Community Center also prepares and distributes a monthly newsletter to all businesses in the Pettisville community. The monthly newsletter and any fundraising letters written are prepared using desktop publishing. *Desktop publishing* is the use of text and images to produce publications, such as newsletters and brochures, on a computer. Because newsletters are mailed in large quantities, the center pays an annual fee at Pettisville Post Office for a standard mail permit. A discounted postage rate is used when sending bulk mail to a large number of addressees.

A Strawberry Festival has been held each July for the past ten years. Community residents come to the center's grounds to sample homemade ice cream, cakes, cookies, and pies made with local strawberries. In addition to the wide variety of activities offered by the center itself, many organizations hold their meetings in the center's meeting rooms.

Lee Community Center needs a manager who will keep records of all activities, hire and supervise any additional employees, and prepare the newsletter.

NOUVEAU
INVESTMENT COMPANY

The Nouveau children, Sonja and Pierre, grew up in a small town outside Paris, France. They enjoyed listening to their parents' stories about the American soldiers they had met during the war. When Sonja decided to study law, she chose to leave France and attend Yale University in the United States.

Sonja majored in economics and enjoyed her part-time work with an investment firm near the campus. Two years later, Pierre also came to the United States and enrolled in business and finance at Yale.

After her graduation, Sonja's work at the investment firm became full-time. Later when Pierre graduated and was looking for a job, he read a newspaper ad for an investment counselor in Pettisville, Ohio. He was arranging for an interview when Sonja decided to change jobs. They decided to travel together to the Midwest, and both of them were hired by Pettisville Bank.

After several years of working as investment counselors at Pettisville Bank, Sonja and Pierre decided to start their own business. Pierre was 27 years old and Sonja was 29 when they opened their partnership on July 1, 1984. They offer each of their clients an individualized *portfolio* (a list of an investor's stocks and bonds). It is

©GETTY IMAGES/EYEWIRE

important that clients be able to trust their investment counselors with their money. Sonja and Pierre take pride in their high ethical standards. *Business ethics* are rules of right and wrong about how employees and employers behave in the workplace.

In recent years, Nouveau investment Company has added banking services for the convenience of its customers. Clients may also track their financial transactions through Nouveau's national on-line investment services.

Because their investment business has grown and become a financial success, Sonja and Pierre have decided to add a manager to their staff. This person will be expected to handle stock sales transactions, write stock reports for *The Towne Crier* (Pettisville's local newspaper), keep cash and payroll records, hire new personnel, and write correspondence. The manager also will be expected to handle daily transactions with other businesses.

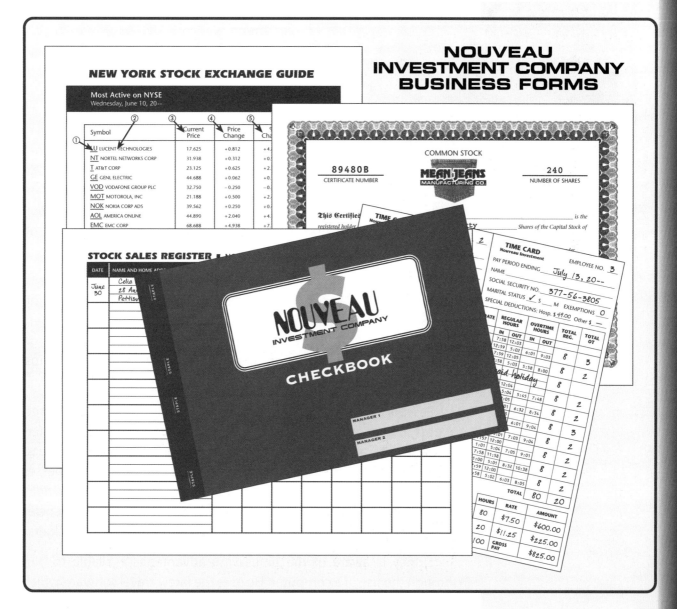

PASSPORTS 2 GO

Sidney Parker started Passports-2-Go as a sole proprietorship on January 1, 1992. At that time it was located in a rustic building near Clear Lake. Today the business occupies space in a small building on Blazer Avenue in downtown Pettisville.

The travel needs of the Pettisville community vary greatly. Passports-2-Go has seen an increase in service to businesses in Pettisville but has experienced a decline in sales from individuals planning travel. The main reason for the decrease in sales to individuals is the availability of travel arrangements made through Internet services. The *Internet* is a worldwide network of users who communicate electronically. Sidney saw this trend early on and concentrated his sales efforts on the business community.

Because of Sidney's careful planning and hard work, his volume of sales has increased, and he has added more staff to accommodate the needs of the business community. Currently, Passports-2-Go offers group and individual travel plans to meet the needs of small and large corporations, senior citizens groups, charity fundraisers, church groups, and meeting planners.

Passports-2-Go arranges for hotel reservations, airline flights, airport and transportation coordination, car rentals, business conferences, off-site activities planning, name badge preparation, and food and beverage service. The agency specializes in helping businesses offer incentive trips for their employees and customers. It also provides an additional service to businesses that few other travel agencies offer—customized reports to help clients control their travel budgets.

Sidney is aware of the timesaving advantages available to him through the use of a computer. He uses the latest travel software, which simplifies the reservations process. He would like to hire an account specialist who is knowledgeable about computers and can access data on-line to provide better service to his clients in less time. This will free him to concentrate on expanding his sales into new territories.

His immediate desire, however, is to hire a manager with a sincere interest in the travel business. Sidney will offer a 10 percent share of the profits to his manager and consider selling the company when he retires to someone who, in his judgment, will provide his clients with quality services offered by his agency.

The manager of Passports-2-Go will be expected to keep banking and payroll records, bill customers for services received, hire new employees, and travel with groups as needed. The manager will also be expected to handle daily transactions with other businesses.

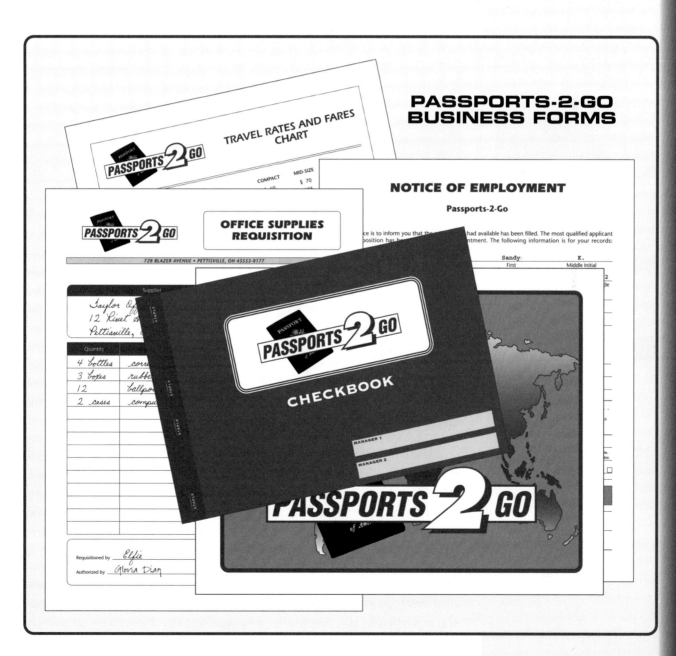

PART 2: ORIENTATION TO THE 15 BUSINESSES

₱PETTISVILLE BANK

Pettisville Bank has been located on the corner of Greenback Drive and Oshkosh Boulevard since it was chartered on August 1, 1920. At that time, the corporate officers were Rita Riegsecker, Douglas Good, and Dallas Schrock. Although the bank still occupies its original historic building, many modern conveniences have been added.

Pettisville Bank is a *commercial bank* (a bank that offers a full range of financial services). Each firm in the business community has a

checking account at the bank. Many Pettisville citizens rent safe deposit boxes from the bank. A *safe deposit box* is a rented space in a bank for storing valuables. The bank holds mortgages on seven of the businesses in the model business community. A *mortgage* is a legal paper giving a lender a claim against real estate if the loan is not repaid. The bank also is a collection point for Pettisville utility bills and is an official depository for the Internal Revenue Service.

©NOVA DEVELOPMENT CORPORATION

Many of Pettisville's residents work at the bank as tellers, secretaries, and accounting clerks. No matter when one enters the bank, it is a scene of constant activity.

The Loan Department occupies a large area to the right of the main entrance to the bank. The bank's executive offices are on the upper floor. Equipment changes at the teller stations have improved banking efficiency. Each teller operates a terminal connected to the bank's central computer. The quiet, efficient equipment has created a modern business-like setting.

Last year Pettisville Bank issued a record number of small business and mortgage loans. In this way the bank has had a direct influence on the growth and development of Pettisville.

Thirty years ago, the Pettisville Bank improved services with the installation of automatic teller machines. In more recent years, it has added electronic funds transfers and Internet banking.

The Board of Directors of Pettisville Bank has decided to hire a manager to assume responsibility for conducting the banking services for the businesses operating in the model business community. A *board of directors* is a group of people elected by the stockholders who make important decisions affecting the company.

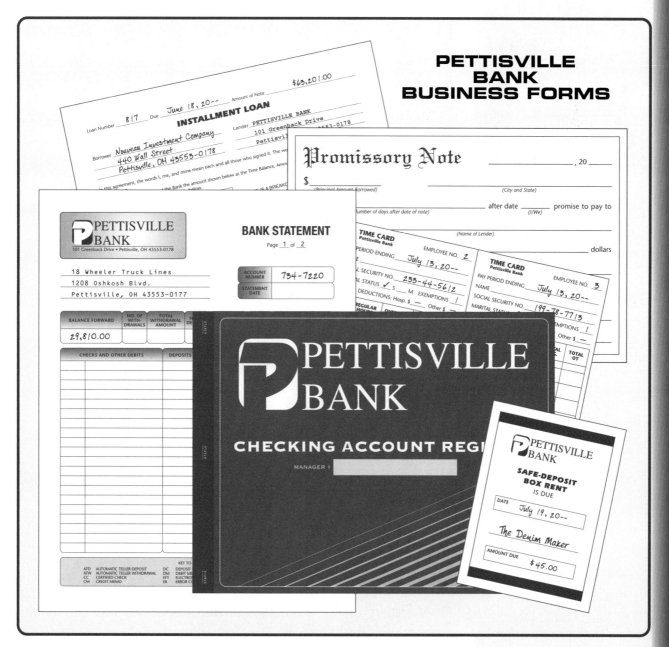

PART 2: ORIENTATION TO THE 15 BUSINESSES

PETTISVILLE POST OFFICE

©GETTY IMAGES/PHOTODISC

The Pettisville Post Office is a *federal agency* (an administrative unit of the U.S. Government). The United States Postal Service is more than 200 years old, and the Pettisville Post Office has been serving the needs of the residents and businesses in the Pettisville area for more than 130 years. Some Pettisville residents can remember when there was no home delivery and postage for a first-class letter cost only five cents!

The use of ZIP Codes, postage vending machines conveniently located around town, mechanized mail sorting, and overnight delivery are some examples of the improved efficiency of the post office. Pettisville Post Office provides all the modern services but with a "personal touch." The postmaster greets most Pettisville residents by name.

Due to the growth of the Pettisville community, it became necessary to open a new post office substation on Stamp Street. This new facility (although small) provides the same efficient, friendly service as the main post office.

©GETTY IMAGES/PHOTODISC

A number of Pettisville's businesses lease (rent) postage meter machines. A *postage meter* machine prints the postmark and amount of postage on each piece of mail and also seals the envelope. This can be a real time saver for companies that process a great deal of mail.

Managers of the businesses in the model business community come to the substation to buy stamps, replenish postage meters, renew standard mail permits, insure mail, rent post office boxes, request change of address cards, and send both domestic and international mail. *Domestic mail* is mail sent to an address within the United States. *International mail* is mail sent to an address outside the United States. A mail carrier from the substation delivers mail to most businesses Monday through Saturday.

POST OFFICE MANAGER

Manager is needed to operate a newly created substation of the main Pettisville post office. Individual should have basic record keeping skills, concern for accuracy, and should enjoy working with the public. Contact Pettisville Post Office at 888-555-0133.

— An Equal Opportunity Employer —

The Pettisville Post Office substation is in need of a manager. The manager will be responsible for sorting and delivering incoming mail, selling stamps, figuring postage fees for packages, and keeping a variety of records. The manager also will be expected to handle daily transactions with other businesses.

POPULAR DESIGNS

Felicia Hernandez is a *fashion designer* (one who designs or makes original sketches or patterns for clothing). She came to Pettisville from Brooklyn, New York, eight years ago. While in New York, she worked as a designer and model for the well-known firm of Klein and Steinberg. She enjoyed the excitement of living and working in a major city, but she had always wanted to become an entrepreneur. An *entrepreneur* is a person who

starts a new business. When she heard that a designer was needed to provide designs for the ever-popular Mean Jeans brand of denim products, she opened her design shop in Pettisville on August 13, 1998.

Felicia's sole proprierorship is small but adequate. Much time and effort goes into her designs, and she is rightfully proud of the jeans and sports clothes she creates. Her creations have been worn by professional golfers, actors, politicians, and by teenagers throughout the world.

It is not uncommon to walk past her shop late at night and see Felicia hard at work at her drawing board or sewing machine. But she creates her best designs when she works at her home overlooking Clear Lake.

Felicia has minor contracts with local businesses, but the majority of her time is spent designing for Mean Jeans Manufacturing Co. Her most popular design is the famous Hernandez Denim Designer Jeans sold only to retailers. She is currently working on designs of denim accessories for Mean Jeans Manufacturing.

Her trips to major cities on special assignments have become more frequent. Therefore, Felicia wants to hire a manager to take responsibility for running the shop. This would allow Felicia to spend the majority of her time doing what she enjoys most—designing a variety of jeans and sports clothes.

The manager of Popular Designs would be expected to supervise and hire personnel, maintain banking and payroll records, and handle daily transactions with other businesses.

TAYLOR
OFFICE SUPPLIES

It came as no surprise to anyone in Pettisville that Tom Williams now owns a sole proprietorship. He runs a successful office supply store that specializes in the sale and repair of office equipment and also sells office supplies and furniture. Part of the secret of Taylor Office Supplies' success has been its emphasis on giving personal service. Tom and his employees are genuinely interested in their customers. Taped onto each cash register is a sign that reads: "The customer is never an interruption—the customer is the reason we are here!"

Taylor Office Supplies, a franchisor, owns and operates a group of supply stores in 27 states. A *franchisor*, or parent company of a franchise agreement, grants a person or group of people the right to sell its product or service. So when Tom opened an office supply store on November 2, 1993, he became a *franchisee*, a person who receives permission from a parent company to sell its products. Taylor Office Supplies provides Tom with quality merchandise, a nationally known name, and *cooperative advertising* (advertising where the cost is shared by both franchisee and franchisor). In exchange for these benefits, Tom agrees to pay Taylor a percentage of his gross (total) sales.

©NOVA DEVELOPMENT CORPORATION

Advances in electronic technology are currently revolutionizing modern offices. The need for more efficient equipment has brought into offices facsimile (fax) machines, copiers, scanners, and personal computers (PC's). A *facsimile* machine transfers text and images over phone lines while a *scanner* transmits text and images onto computer files. Tom encourages his salespersons to learn about this new equipment by paying their way to seminars and training workshops.

One of the store's policies is to sell office supplies only on a cash-and-carry basis. *Cash and carry* means that a customer pays cash for goods and takes them rather than having them shipped and paying for them later.

Taylor Office Supplies offers a computer workshop to the business community from 9 a.m. to 11 a.m. each Saturday morning. Whenever possible, Tom conducts the workshops himself. Local businesspersons enthusiastically participate in these informative workshops.

Because Tom still enjoys repairing equipment, he is much more involved with the service part of the business than with sales. He feels he must now hire a manager who will take full responsibility for managing the store. The manager of Taylor Office Supplies will be expected to monitor sales and inventory, supervise and hire personnel, and maintain cash and payroll records. The manager will also be expected to handle daily transactions with other businesses.

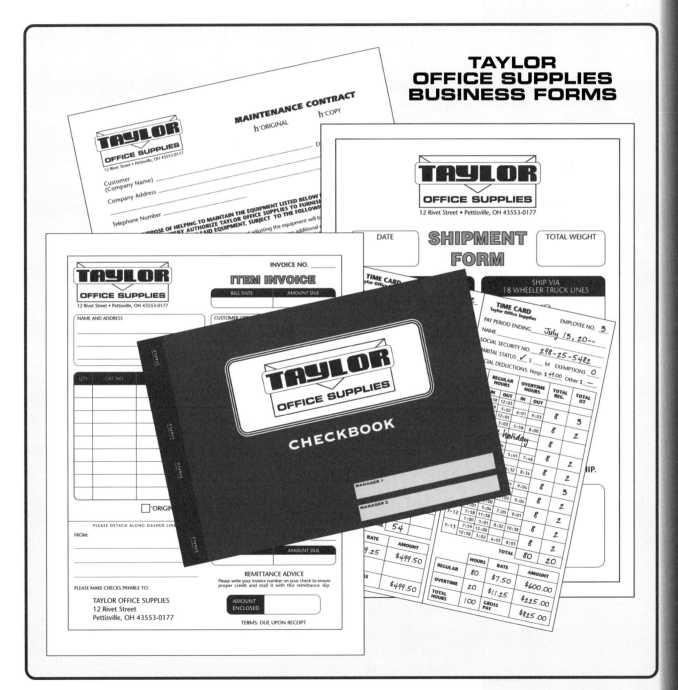

The TOWNE CRIER

©GETTY IMAGES/PHOTODISC

Before she was 17 years old, Samantha Nichols knew she would have a career in the newspaper business. She attended high school in Toledo, Ohio, and worked part-time for the Toledo Chronicle in the Classified Advertising Department selling ads over the telephone. She was also a member of the yearbook staff at her high school. By the time graduation arrived, Samantha knew that journalism would be her major in college. No one was surprised when Samantha became editor of her college newspaper. After college she rejoined the Toledo Chronicle as a reporter covering the city beat and was also responsible for writing a weekly column called "Bits and Pieces." Eventually Samantha's weekly column became so popular that it was syndicated in newspapers in several states. A *syndicate* sells articles or features for publication by many newspapers.

For a long time Samantha had considered owning her own newspaper; and when The Towne Crier in Pettisville went on the market (was put up for sale), she decided to buy it. The Towne Crier had been a family owned business for several generations; but when Darren Strietmann (the owner) died, his heirs sold the newspaper to Samantha Nichols on June 30, 2003.

The Towne Crier receives most of its income from the sale of newspapers and from display and classified advertising. *Display advertising* is advertising that contains both art and words. *Classified advertising* is located in the want ad section of a newspaper or other medium.

The Towne Crier is in the process of acquiring some up-to-date equipment that will reduce the amount of time needed to write the articles, plan the page layouts, and print the paper. Employees include a managing editor, layout editor, city editor, graphic artist, press operator, bookkeeper, and reporters.

Samantha has decided to hire a manager to take over the day-to-day operations of her sole proprietorship and to oversee the financial management of the company. This will give her more time to work on her weekly column and recruit advertisers for the newspaper. The new manager will be expected to hire new employees, keep accurate cash and payroll records, and write correspondence. The manager will also be responsible for coordinating the work between the different departments of the business and handling daily transactions with other businesses.

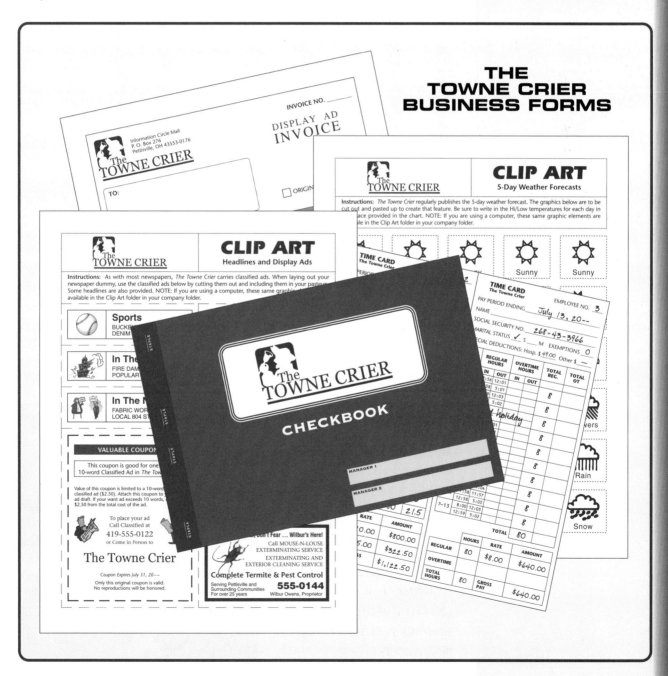

PART 2: ORIENTATION TO THE 15 BUSINESSES

UNITED COMMUNICATIONS

United Communications is rightfully proud of its reputation for reliable service. Years ago when Pettisville was small and telephone service was limited, service was provided by the Pettisville Area Telephone Co. In those days, Pettisville was mostly farm country, and only one home out of six had a telephone. As the community grew, more and more people began to rely on the telephone. Service improved, and additional telephones were installed. Today, United Communications proudly provides its customers with the latest equipment and services.

In addition to billing customers for local and long distance calls, United Communications sells telephones in a variety of styles. For the convenience of customers, a Phone Center Store is located adjacent to the main office. Many customers come to the Phone Center to view the business, mobile, and cell phones on display and to place orders.

A portion of the company's profits comes from *directory advertising* (advertising displayed in the Yellow Pages of the telephone book). The majority of Pettisville businesses take advantage of this service.

On April 1, 1996, Northwest Ohio Telephone Co. became part of United Communications, whose corporate offices are located in Mansfield, Ohio. At the time of the merger, United Communications became a *public corporation* (a business that sells shares on the open market.)

United Communications serves the needs of Pettisville area residents and businesses with modern equipment and highly skilled repair persons. United Communications is a controlled monopoly. A monopoly is a business that has no competitors. A *controlled monopoly* is a business that operates without competition but is regulated by the government.

©CORBIS CORPORATION

Information Circle Mall, located a short distance from the Pettisville business district, opened last year. The mall houses The Towne Crier, a computer center, a television station, and United Communications

United Communications needs a manager. The new manager will be expected to take charge of the office payroll, oversee all billings and services to the model business community, and maintain cash records. The manager also will be expected to handle daily transactions with other businesses.

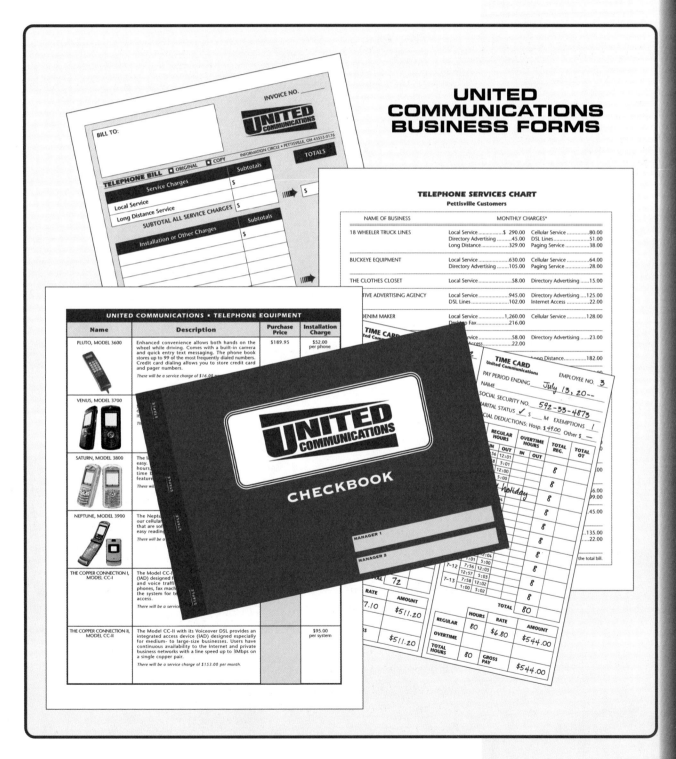

PART 3

Reference Guide

BANKING AND BOOKKEEPING

One of the most important responsibilities of a business manager is keeping accurate financial records for the business. Business managers in small firms may handle their own banking and bookkeeping transactions, hire an experienced bookkeeper or accountant, or use an outside accounting service. Large corporations usually have accounting departments that take care of all financial transactions.

As a manager in the model business community, you will be expected to handle these financial transactions yourself. Your bookkeeping duties include writing checks, making deposits, posting to a cashbook, and reconciling the bank statement monthly.

Unit Lessons

Lesson 1•1	**Writing Checks**
Lesson 1•2	**Posting to a Cashbook**
Lesson 1•3	**Making Bank Deposits**
Lesson 1•4	**Reconciling a Bank Statement**

Unit Activities

Activity 1•1	**Writing Checks**
Activity 1•2	**Posting to a Cashbook**
Activity 1•3	**Writing Checks, Posting to a Cashbook, and Making Bank Deposits**
Activity 1•4	**Reconciling a Bank Statement**

WRITING CHECKS

A **check** is an order written by you, the depositor, directing the bank to pay out money. All your company money will be handled through a checking account with Pettisville Bank. Many businesses prepare their checks electronically and then print them using software such as QuickBooks, Quicken, and MYOB. For the purpose of this simulation, all checks will be written by hand. You may, however, choose to maintain an electronic check register rather than posting to the check register manually (by hand). Your Instructor will tell you which method you will use to record your checks. A **check register** is a separate form on which a depositor keeps a record of deposits and checks.

©GETTY IMAGES/PHOTODISC

Look at the check illustrated below. The drawer on this check is André Sayyah. The **drawer** on a check is the business or person who owns the account. The payee is Pettisville Post Office. The **payee** on a check is the business or person receiving the check. Pettisville Bank is the drawee. The **drawee** on a check is the bank on which the check is drawn.

TAYLOR OFFICE SUPPLIES
Taylor Office Supplies
12 Rivet Street
Pettisville, OH 43553-0177

800

56-25 / 412

DATE July 1, 20--

PAY TO THE ORDER OF Pettisville Post Office $ 35.00

Thirty-five and no/100 ——————————— DOLLARS

FOR SIMULATION USE ONLY

PETTISVILLE BANK
101 Greenback Drive • Pettisville, OH 43553-0178

FOR Postage   André Sayyah   MP

⑈000800⑈ ⑊041200257⑊ 103⑈7943⑈

Checks include a check number, a bank number, and an account number. Look at the illustration again (above). The *check number* is 800. The bank number and account number are usually printed in magnetic ink. These magnetic ink numbers enable banks to sort checks quickly with machines that "read" the numbers. The *bank number*, found between colons, is 041200257, and the *account number* is 103-7943.

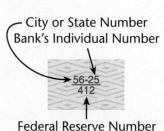

City or State Number
Bank's Individual Number
56-25 / 412
Federal Reserve Number

All checks should be written in ink. You should complete a check

a. When you are told to do so in the *DAILY ACTIVITIES* in your *Operations Manual*

b. When you receive an item invoice

c. When you receive a service invoice or other bill.

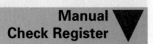

Look at the illustration above. It shows that André Sayyah, manager of Taylor Office Supplies, has written Check No. 801 for $282.45 to Passports-2-Go for an airline ticket.

Check Register

NUMBER	DATE	DESCRIPTION OF TRANSACTION	PAYMENT/DEBIT (−)	✔ C	DEPOSIT/CREDIT (+)	BALANCE	
			BALANCE BROUGHT FORWARD →			24,930	00
800	July 1	Pettisville Post Office	35 00			24,895	00
801	July 2	Passports-2-Go	282 45			24,612	55

Every check must be recorded in a check register, as shown above and on page 53. The manual check register provides columns to record the check number, the date, and the name of the person or business to whom the check is written (DESCRIPTION). The PAYMENT column shows the amount of each check written. The ✔ column is used for recording canceled checks when reconciling the bank statement. The last two columns show the amount of deposits and the balance in the account. Notice the vertical line separating dollars from cents.

CHECKPOINT

Identifying the Parts of a Check

Use the list of terms below to identify the parts of a check. Write your answers on the blanks provided.

■ account number

■ bank number

■ check number

■ drawee

■ drawer

■ payee

TAYLOR OFFICE SUPPLIES

Taylor Office Supplies
12 Rivet Street
Pettisville, OH 43553-0177

801

56-25
412

DATE July 2, 20--

PAY TO THE ORDER OF Passports-2-Go $ 282.45

Two hundred eighty-two and 45/100 ———————— DOLLARS

FOR SIMULATION USE ONLY

PETTISVILLE BANK
101 Greenback Drive • Pettisville, OH 43553-0122

FOR Airline Ticket   André Sayyah   MP

⑈00080⑈ ⑆041200257⑉ ⑈03⑈7943⑈

The electronic check register (shown below) provides the same information as the manual check register. However, it is not necessary to use a calculator to find the balance. When the amount of a check is recorded, the balance is calculated automatically. If you are using an electronic check register, you may want to keep a "paper and pencil" copy, too.

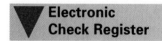

▼ **Electronic Check Register**

Check Register

NUMBER	DATE	DESCRIPTION OF TRANSACTION	PAYMENT/DEBIT (–)	√ C	DEPOSIT/CREDIT (+)	BALANCE
Taylor Office Supplies			**Balance Brought Forward**			$ 24,930.00
800	July 1	Pettisville Post Office	35.00			24,895.00
801	July 2	Passports-2-Go	282.45			24,612.55

Before you prepare a check, first record the information about the check on the check register. Otherwise, you may forget and then not remember the amount of the check or to whom it was written. In that case, you would not know how much money is in your company checking account!

Follow these steps when you prepare a check

1. Remove the checkbook from the Cash File.

2. Complete the record of the check first.

📝 *If you are using a manual check register*

a. Make the entries in pencil.

b. Record the check number under the NUMBER column.

c. Record the July date (given in your *DAILY ACTIVITIES*) under the DATE column.

d. Record the payee's name (the name of the person or business receiving the check) under the DESCRIPTION column.

e. Record the amount of the check under the PAYMENT/DEBIT column.

f. Subtract the amount of the check from the previous balance and record the new balance.

🖱 *If you are using an electronic check register*

a. Open your check register.

b. Record the check number in the NUMBER column.

c. Record the July date (given in your *DAILY ACTIVITIES*) in the DATE column.

d. Record the payee's name (the name of the person or business receiving the check) in the DESCRIPTION column.

e. Record the amount of the check in the PAYMENT/DEBIT column. Your electronic check register will subtract the amount of the check from your previous balance and give you a new balance.

f. Save your work.

---

3. Complete the check in *ink*. Remember that a check is an order to the bank to pay out company money, so fill out the check completely and accurately.

    a. Record the July date (given in your *DAILY ACTIVITIES*) on the date line.

    b. Record the payee's name (the name of the person or business receiving the check) on the line marked PAY TO THE ORDER OF.

    c. Record the amount of the check in figures, close to the dollar sign.

    d. Record the amount in words. Record the cents amount as a fraction of a dollar. Draw a line from the fraction to the word DOLLARS.

    e. Record the purpose of the check on the line marked FOR.

    f. Sign your name on the signature line. You are authorized to sign all checks for your company.

    g. Compare the check you have just written with the illustration. If the check is correctly completed, go to step 4 on the opposite page. If the check is not correctly written, go to the steps on *page 56 in this Student Reference Book* titled *Follow these steps if you ruin or make a mistake on a check.*

4. Your *DAILY ACTIVITIES* will usually tell you whether you are to mail the check or deliver the check in person.

■ *If you are told to mail the check, you should*

a. Use scissors to remove the check.

b. Address an envelope to the person or company to whom the check is being sent. (Refer to *page 99 in this Student Reference Book*.)

c. Put a stamp on the envelope, or use your postage meter. (Refer to *page 186 in this Student Reference Book*.)

d. Place the envelope in the nearest mailbox.

■ *If you are told to deliver the check, you should*

a. Use scissors to remove the check.

b. Walk to the business.

c. Deliver the check to the manager.

---

5. Record the payment in your cashbook. *Turn to page 58 in this Student Reference Book.* Complete the steps titled *Follow these steps when recording cash payments (by check) in the cashbook.*

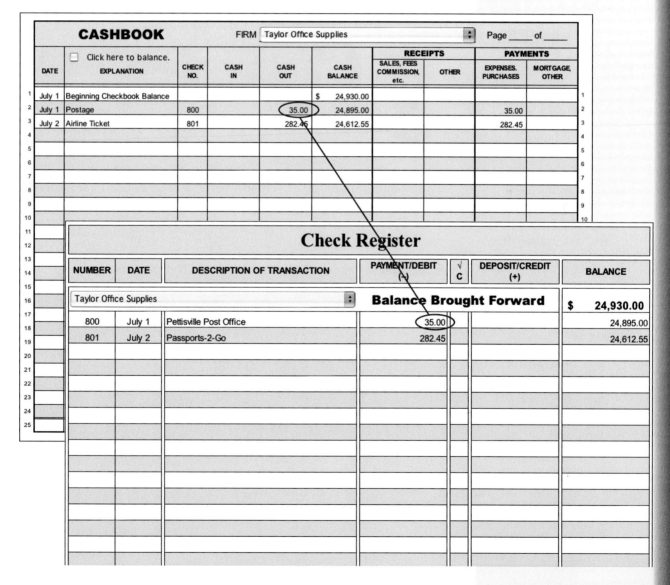

Follow these steps if you ruin or make a mistake on a check

1. Void the record of the check.

 If you are using a manual check register

a. Erase the payee name from the DESCRIPTION column and write *Void* in its place.

b. Erase the check amount in the PAY-MENT/DEBIT column.

c. Erase the total under the BALANCE column. Bring down the total from the previous balance.

If you are using an electronic check register

a. Replace the payee's name in the DESCRIPTION column with the word *Void*.

b. Delete the check amount in the PAYMENT/DEBIT column.

2. Draw a line diagonally across the check and write *VOID* on it.

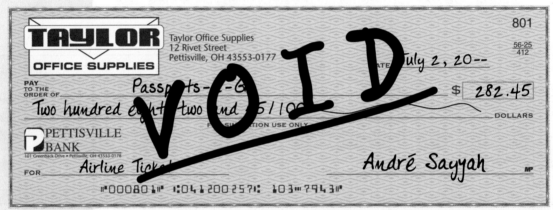

3. Remove the voided check and place it in your Cash File. You are now ready to complete a new check.

4. Rewrite the check correctly (using the next blank check).

5. Complete the check register to record the new check.

CHECKPOINT

Writing the Amount on a Check

Write the following amounts just as you would on a check.

1. $39.45 _____ Dollars

2. $1,522.16 _____ Dollars

3. $89.00 _____ Dollars

4. $2,671.95 _____ Dollars

5. $110.00 _____ Dollars

POSTING TO A CASHBOOK

A **cashbook** is a bookkeeping record used to record all receipts and payments of company money. These receipts or payments can be in the form of paper money, coins, or checks. Each manager of a business (except the managers of Pettisville Bank) will maintain a cashbook. Your cashbook may be maintained manually (by hand) or electronically using software available on your computer. Your Instructor will tell you which method you will use to record entries on your cashbook. If you are using an electronic cashbook, you may want to keep a "paper and pencil" copy, too.

Notice on the illustration below that the cashbook is divided into six columns plus a RECEIPTS section and a PAYMENTS section. Each time money is received or paid out, it must be recorded in the cashbook. Either the *DAILY ACTIVITIES* or a check coming into the company provides the information for each receipt of money to be recorded.

Each entry in the cashbook should be made carefully and accurately. If you are making entries by hand, you should use a *pencil*. If you are making entries electronically and make a mistake, select the entry and replace it. The balance will adjust itself. It is important that an entry be made in the cashbook *immediately* after money is received or paid out.

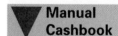

Manual Cashbook

	CASHBOOK						FIRM Taylor Office Supplies			Page 1 of		
							RECEIPTS		PAYMENTS			
	1 DATE	**2** EXPLANATION	**3** CHECK NO.	**4** CASH IN	**5** CASH OUT	**6** CASH BALANCE	SALES, FEES, COMMISSION, etc.	OTHER	EXPENSES, PURCHASES	MORTGAGE, OTHER	
1	July 1	Beginning Checkbook Balance				24 930 00					1
2	July 1	Postage	800		35 00	24 895 00			35 00		2
3	July 2	Airline Ticket	801		282 45	24 612 55			282 45		3
4	July 3	Promissory Note ($2.000)									4
5		plus Interest ($40)	802		2 040 00	22 572 55				2 040 00	5
6	July 5	Cash Sales		2 000 00		24 572 55	2 000 00				6
7	July 6	Sales and Shipping Charge		149 50		24 722 05	144 00	5 50			7
8											8
9											9
10											10
11											11
12											12
13											13
14											14

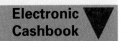

	CASHBOOK		FIRM Taylor Office Supplies					RECEIPTS		PAYMENTS		
1 DATE	☐ Click here to balance. **2** EXPLANATION	**3** CHECK NO.	**4** CASH IN	**5** CASH OUT	**6** CASH BALANCE		SALES, FEES COMMISSION, etc.	OTHER	EXPENSES. PURCHASES	MORTGAGE, OTHER	
1 July 1	Beginning Checkbook Balance				$ 24,930.00						1
2 July 1	Postage	800		35.00	24,895.00				35.00		2
3 July 2	Airline Ticket	801		282.45	24,612.55				282.45		3
4 July 3	Promissory Note ($2,000)										4
5	plus Interest ($40)	802		2,040.00	22,572.55					2,040.00	5
6 July 5	Cash Sales		2,000.00		24,572.55		2,000.00				6
7 July 6	Sales and Shipping Charge		149.50		24,722.05		144.00	5.50			7
8											8
9											9
10											10
11											11
12											12

Page _____ of _____

◆ RECORDING CASH PAYMENTS (PAYMENTS MADE BY CHECK)

Refer to line 2 of the illustration above. Note that on July 1, Check No. 800 was written in the amount of $35.00 to pay for postage. Because the $35.00 is considered an expense of the business, it also is recorded in the EXPENSES, PURCHASES column of the PAYMENTS section of the cashbook. The $35.00 was deducted from the preceding cash balance of $24,930.00 to arrive at a new cash balance of $24,895.00.

Follow these steps when recording cash payments (by check) in the cashbook

1. Open your cashbook.

📓 *If you are posting to a manual cashbook,* remove the cashbook from the Cash File.

🖱 *If you are posting to an electronic cashbook,* open the cashbook. Use the tab key to move from column to column. **NOTE:** Do *not* attempt to make entries in the CASH IN, CASH OUT, or CASH BALANCE columns. These entries are made automatically.

2. Record the July date (given in your *DAILY ACTIVITIES*) in column 1.

3. Record the purpose of the check in the EXPLANATION column (column 2).

4. Record the check number in column 3.

5. Record the amount of the check in the EXPENSES, PURCHASES column of the PAYMENTS section.

6. Record the amount of the check in the CASH OUT column (column 5). *If you are posting to an electronic cashbook,* your software will automatically make the entry in the CASH OUT column.

7. Find the cash balance.

 If you are posting to a manual cashbook

a. Calculate the new cash balance by subtracting the amount in the CASH OUT column from the preceding cash balance.

b. Record the new balance in the CASH BALANCE column (column 6).

c. Return the cashbook to the Cash File.

 If you are posting to an electronic cashbook

a. Look at the cash balance column (column 6). Your software should have automatically subtracted the amount in the CASH OUT column from the preceding cash balance.

b. Save your work.

RECORDING A CHECK WRITTEN IN PAYMENT OF A PROMISSORY NOTE PLUS INTEREST

A *promissory note* is a written promise to repay a specific amount borrowed, usually with some interest, on a certain date. Taylor Office Supplies borrowed $2,000.00 from Farmers & Merchants State Bank. The interest rate is 12 percent, and the date of maturity (or the date on which the note is due) is July 3, 20--.

Refer to lines 4 and 5 of the cashbook illustrated on *page 58 in this Student Reference Book*. Note that on July 3 Taylor Office Supplies wrote Check No. 802 in the amount of $2,040.00 ($2,000.00 to cover the face value of the note and $40.00 to cover the interest on the note). Because the $2,040.00 is a payment on a debt owed by the business, it is recorded in the MORTGAGE, OTHER column of the PAYMENTS section. The $2,040.00 was deducted from the preceding cash balance of $24,612.55 to arrive at a new cash balance of $22,572.55.

Follow these steps when recording a check for a promissory note

1. Open your cashbook.

 If you are posting to a manual cashbook, remove the cashbook from the Cash File.

 If you are posting to an electronic cashbook, open the cashbook. Use the tab key to move from column to column.

2. Record the July date (given in your *DAILY ACTIVITIES*) in column 1.

3. Record the purpose of the check in the EXPLANATION column (column 2).

a. Record on one line that portion of the check that is in payment of the face value of the promissory note.

b. Record on a second line that portion of the check that is in payment of the interest. (Refer to lines 4 and 5 of the illustration on *page 58 in this Student Reference Book*.)

4. Record the check number in column 3.

5. Record the amount of the check in the MORTGAGE, OTHER column of the PAYMENTS section.

6. Record the amount of the check in the CASH OUT column (column 5). *If you are posting to an electronic cashbook*, your software will automatically make the entry in the CASH OUT column.

7. Find the new cash balance.

If you are posting to a manual cashbook
a. Calculate the new cash balance by subtracting the last amount in the CASH OUT column from the preceding cash balance.
b. Record the new balance in the CASH BALANCE column (column 6).
c. Return the cashbook to the Cash File.

If you are posting to an electronic cashbook
a. Look at the cash balance column (column 6). Your software should have automatically subtracted the amount in the CASH OUT column from the preceding cash balance.
b. Save your work.

RECORDING CASH SALES (CASH RECEIPTS)

Each week your *DAILY ACTIVITIES* will give you the dollar amount of cash sales for the week. This figure represents the amount of sales made by your business to persons and companies outside the model community. Refer to line 6 of the illustration on *page 58 in this Student Reference Book*. Note that on July 5 cash sales in the amount of $2,000.00 were recorded. The $2,000.00 is also recorded in the SALES, FEES, COMMISSION, etc. column of the RECEIPTS section of the cashbook. The $2,000.00 was added to the preceding cash balance of $22,572.55 to arrive at a new cash balance of $24,572.55.

Follow these steps when recording cash sales (cash receipts) in the cashbook

1. Open your cashbook.

If you are posting to a manual cashbook, remove the cashbook from the Cash File.

If you are posting to an electronic cashbook, open the cashbook. Use the tab key to move from column to column.

2. Record the July date (given in your *DAILY ACTIVITIES*) in column 1.

3. Record the source of the money (cash sales) in the EXPLANATION column (column 2).

4. Record the amount in the SALES, FEES, COMMISSION, etc. column of the RECEIPTS section.

5. Record the amount in the CASH IN column (column 4). *If you are posting to an electronic cashbook*, your software will automatically make the entry in the CASH IN column.

6. Find the new cash balance.

 If you are posting to a manual cashbook

a. Calculate the new cash balance by adding the amount in the CASH IN column to the preceding cash balance.

b. Record the new balance in the CASH BALANCE column (column 6).

c. Return the cashbook to the Cash File.

 If you are posting to an electronic cashbook

a. Look at the cash balance column (column 6). Your software should have automatically added the amount in the CASH IN column to the preceding cash balance.

b. Save your work.

RECORDING AN INCOMING CHECK (CASH RECEIPTS)

An item invoice in the amount of $149.50 was prepared by Taylor Office Supplies and sent to Buckeye Equipment. On July 6, Taylor received a check in the amount of $149.50 from Buckeye Equipment.

Refer to line 7 of the cashbook illustrated on *page 58 in this Student Reference Book*. Note that it shows that on July 6 a check in the amount of $149.50 was received for sales and shipping charges. Look closely at the RECEIPTS section of the cashbook. Note that the $149.50 recorded in column 4 is now broken down as follows: $144.00 represents sales and is recorded in the SALES, FEES, COMMISSION, etc. column; $5.50 represents shipping charges and is recorded in the column labeled OTHER. The $149.50 was added to the preceding cash balance of $24,572.55 to arrive at a new cash balance of $24,722.05.

Follow these steps when recording incoming checks (cash receipts) in the cashbook

1. Open the cashbook.

 If you are posting to a manual cashbook, remove the cashbook from the Cash File.

 If you are posting to an electronic cashbook, open the cashbook. Use the tab key to move from column to column.

---

2. Record the July date (given in your *DAILY ACTIVITIES*) in column 1.

3. Record the source of the money (sales and/or shipping charge) in the EXPLANATION column (column 2).

4. Record the amount of the check in the proper columns of the RECEIPTS section: record sales, fees, commissions, etc. in the SALES, FEES, COMMISSION, etc. column, and record other receipts (such as money received for shipping charges) in the OTHER column.

5. Record the amount of the check in the CASH IN column (column 4). *If you are posting to an electronic cashbook*, your software will automatically make the entry in the CASH IN column.

6. Find the new cash balance.

📖 *If you are posting to a manual cashbook*

a. Calculate the new cash balance by adding the amount in the CASH IN column to the preceding cash balance.

b. Record the new balance in the CASH BALANCE column (column 6).

c. Return the cashbook to the Cash File.

💻 *If you are posting to an electronic cashbook*

a. Look at the cash balance column (column 6). Your software should have automatically added the amount in the CASH IN column to the preceding cash balance.

b. Save your work.

---

7. Endorse the check for deposit. (Refer to the illustration below.) Place the check in the cash receipts envelope.

NOTE: Incoming checks are recorded in the cashbook when they are received, but you should not record them on the check register until you are told to make a deposit.

When you receive a check, you have the added responsibility of preparing that check for deposit at the bank. As soon as you have completed the entry in the cashbook, you should

1. Turn the check to the back.

2. Endorse the check with a restrictive endorsement. A **restrictive endorsement** includes the words For Deposit Only, in addition to the signature on the back of a check, which transfers ownership of the check to another party. If the check is lost or stolen, the finder cannot cash it. Near the left end of the check, you should write

   a. the words "For Deposit Only."

   b. the name of your company (Taylor Office Supplies is used in the illustration.)

3. Place the check in the cash receipts envelope in the Cash File. The check will remain in this envelope until you are ready to make your next deposit at Pettisville Bank. Refer to Lesson 1•3 for instructions for making deposits.

ENDORSING CHECKS FOR DEPOSIT

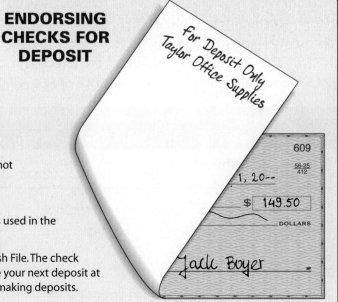

◆ BALANCING AND RULING THE CASHBOOK

Before you can begin keeping cash records for a new month, you must balance the cashbook for the previous month by totaling the columns. By doing this, you will account for all receipts and payments and prove the accuracy of your work. If you are using a manual cashbook, draw two lines under each total to show that the work is complete and accurate. At the end of July, you should have three cash records which all agree: the cashbook, the check register, and the bank reconciliation. Do not total the cashbook until the bank statement has been reconciled and it agrees with your check register.

■ Follow these steps when balancing and ruling a manual cashbook

1. Get a sharp pencil, a ruler, a sheet of scratch paper, and your cashbook sheet.

2. Draw a single line under all amount columns. Refer to line 15 of the illustration below.

3. Total all columns except the CASH BALANCE column. Use a pencil and tiny pencil figures to record the totals. Refer to line 16 of the illustration.

4. Make the following calculations on a sheet of scratch paper.
   a. Add together the totals of the two RECEIPTS columns (SALES, FEES, COMMISSION, etc. and OTHER).
   b. Add together the totals of the two PAYMENTS columns (EXPENSES, PURCHASES and MORTGAGE, OTHER).

CASHBOOK — FIRM Taylor Office Supplies — Page 1 of ___

	DATE	EXPLANATION	CHECK NO.	CASH IN	CASH OUT	CASH BALANCE	RECEIPTS SALES, FEES, COMMISSION, etc.	RECEIPTS OTHER	PAYMENTS EXPENSES, PURCHASES	PAYMENTS MORTGAGE, OTHER	
1	July 1	Beginning Checkbook Balance				24930 00					1
2	July 1	Postage	800		35 00	24895 00			35 00		2
3	July 2	Airline Ticket	801		282 45	24612 55			282 45		3
4	July 3	Promissory Note ($2,000)									4
5		plus interest ($40)	802		2040 00	22572 55				2040 00	5
6	July 5	Cash Sales		2000 00		24572 55	2000 00				6
7	July 6	Sales and Shipping Charge		149 50		24722 05	144 00	5 50			7
8	July 9	Air Compressor	803		1145 83	23576 22			1145 83		8
9	July 12	Cash Sales		8114 22		31690 44	8114 22				9
10	July 16	Display Ad	804		250 00	31440 44			250 00		10
11	July 18	Freight Charges	805		18 00	31422 44			18 00		11
12	July 23	Telephone	806		136 00	31286 44			136 00		12
13	July 27	Cash Sales		2435 00		33721 44	2435 00				13
14	July 31	Insurance	EFT		122 00	33599 44			122 00		14
15	July 31	Bank Service Charge	SC		12 95	33586 49			12 95		15
16	July 31	TOTALS		12698 72 12698 72	4042 23 4042 23		12693 22 12693 22	5 50 5 50	2002 23 2002 23	2040 00 2040 00	16
17											17

5. Check your work. Does the total of the two RECEIPTS columns equal the total of the CASH IN column? Does the total of the two PAYMENTS columns equal the total of the CASH OUT column? If you can answer "yes" to these questions, you may continue to step 6. If you must answer "no," recheck your figures.

6. Complete the last line of the cashbook.
   a. Record today's simulation date in the DATE column.
   b. Record the word *TOTALS* in the EXPLANATION column.
   c. Find the tiny pencil totals you recorded in step 3. Write these totals again. Refer to line 16 of the illustration on the previous page.

7. Double rule the cashbook. Use a pencil and a ruler to draw two lines under all of the amount columns. Refer to line 16 of the illustration.

Follow these steps when balancing an electronic cashbook

1. Open your cashbook.

2. Balance the cashbook. Select the check box titled *Click here to balance*. (The check box is located just above the word *EXPLANATION* in column 2.)

3. Look at the last line on your cashbook. All columns should be totaled. The total of the two RECEIPTS columns should equal the total of the CASH IN column. The total of the two PAYMENTS columns should equal the total of the CASH OUT column.

4. Save your work.

CHECKPOINT

Understanding the Cashbook

Answer the following questions.

1. The cashbook is a _____ record used to record all _____ and _____ of company money.

2. A restrictive endorsement on the back of a check uses the words _____ .

3. At the end of the month, you should have three cash totals which all agree:
   _____

4. The total of the two receipt columns on a cashbook should equal the total of the _____ _____ column.

5. The total of the two payment columns on a cashbook should equal the total of the _____ _____ column.

MAKING BANK DEPOSITS

When you deposit money in your company checking account, you will fill out a **deposit slip**. This is a form on which you list the items you are depositing—coins, paper money, and/or checks. The deposit slip (also called the deposit ticket) shows the date, the depositor's company name and address, the account number, the items deposited, and the total of the deposit.

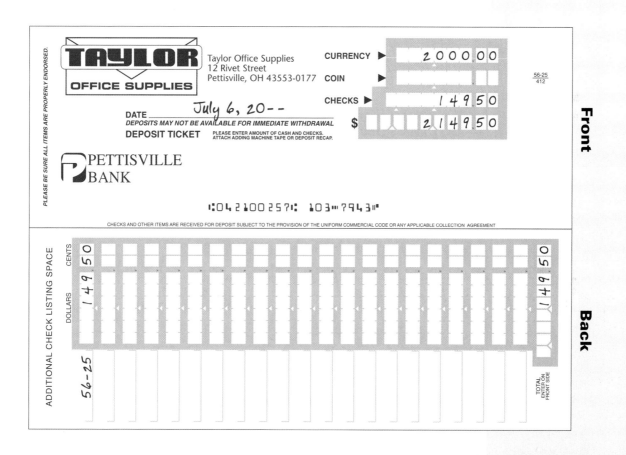

Look at the illustration above. The deposit slip was completed by Taylor Office Supplies on July 6, 20––. The account number assigned to Taylor is 103-7943. The deposit consisted of $2,000.00 in cash and one check for $149.50. The total deposit was $2,149.50.

Each check deposited is identified by the number of the bank on which it is drawn. This number is assigned to each commercial bank by the American Bankers Association. The three parts of this number are identified in the illustration on the right.

American Bankers Association (ABA) Number

City or State Number
Bank's Individual Number

56-25
412

Federal Reserve Number

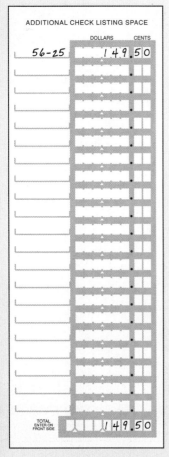

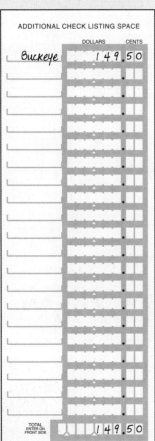

The first part of the number above the line indicates the city or state in which the bank is located. The second part is the number assigned to the individual bank. The number below the line is a Federal Reserve number that banks use in sorting checks.

When listing checks on a deposit slip, you may list either the drawer's name (the name of the business or person who gave you the check) OR the American Bankers Association (ABA) number. Look at the first illustration on the left. The check for $149.50 shows the ABA number 56-25. If you use the ABA number, only the two top numbers are listed on the deposit slip, as shown in the illustration. Now look at the second illustration on the bottom left. The check for $149.50 shows the drawer's name (Buckeye Equipment). Your Instructor will tell you which method to use for listing checks on a deposit slip.

◆ MAKING A DEPOSIT AT PETTISVILLE BANK

You will make a deposit at Pettisville Bank once a week. All deposits should be made at the drive-in window.

Follow these steps when making a deposit at the bank

1. Remove the cash receipts envelope from the Cash File.

2. Remove the incoming cash slip from the cash receipts envelope.

3. Remove cash (if you have any) and incoming checks (if you have any) from the cash receipts envelope.

4. Return the cash receipts envelope to the Cash File.

5. Remove the checkbook from the Cash File. Remove a deposit slip from the checkbook.

6. Complete the deposit slip (refer to the illustration on *page 65 in this Student Reference Book*.
   a. Write the current simulation date.
   b. Add the cash received during the week (if you have any) to the incoming cash slip. Record the total on the CURRENCY line.
   c. List checks (if you have any) on the back of the deposit slip. Record either the name of the drawer (the business or person who gave you the check) OR the American Bankers Association number of each check. List the amount of each check under the DOLLARS and CENTS columns.
   d. Calculate the total of the checks. Turn back to the front of the deposit slip. Record the total on the line marked *CHECKS*.
   e. Add the total of the CURRENCY to the total of the CHECKS. Record the total of the deposit.

7. Check the accuracy of your work.

   a. Open your manual or electronic cashbook.

> 📇 *If you are posting to a manual cashbook,* remove the cashbook from the Cash File.
>
> 🖱 *If you are posting to an electronic cashbook,* open your cashbook.

   b. On a separate sheet of scratch paper, add the amounts recorded in the CASH IN column *during this week* to get a total. This total should equal the total on the deposit slip. (If they do not equal, check your work. If you cannot find your error, ask your Instructor for help.)

   c. Write the word *deposit* on the sheet of scratch paper and put the paper aside for now.

   d. Keep your cashbook open until you have completed step 16.

8. Check to see that each check to be deposited has been endorsed (refer to *page 62 in this Student Reference Book* for instructions for endorsing checks).

9. Arrange your cash, cash slip, and any checks in the order they are listed on the deposit slip. Clip the cash, cash slip, and all checks to the back of the deposit slip.

CASHBOOK — FIRM Taylor Office Supplies — Page 1 of ___

	DATE	EXPLANATION	CHECK NO.	CASH IN	CASH OUT	CASH BALANCE	RECEIPTS: SALES, FEES, COMMISSION, etc.	RECEIPTS: OTHER	PAYMENTS: EXPENSES, PURCHASES	PAYMENTS: MORTGAGE, OTHER	
1	July 1	Beginning Checkbook Balance				24 930 00					1
2	July 1	Postage	800		35 00	24 895 00			35 00		2
3	July 2	Airline Ticket	801		282 45	24 612 55			282 45		3
4	July 3	Promissory Note ($2,000)									4
5		plus interest ($40)	802		2040 00	22 572 55				2040 00	5
6	July 5	Cash Sales		2000 00		24 572 55	2000 00				6
7	July 6	Sales and Shipping Charge		149 50		24 722 05	144 00	5 50			7
8											8
9											9

CASHBOOK — FIRM Taylor Office Supplies — Page ___ of ___

☐ Click here to balance.

	DATE	EXPLANATION	CHECK NO.	CASH IN	CASH OUT	CASH BALANCE	RECEIPTS: SALES, FEES COMMISSION, etc.	RECEIPTS: OTHER	PAYMENTS: EXPENSES, PURCHASES	PAYMENTS: MORTGAGE, OTHER	
1	July 1	Beginning Checkbook Balance				$ 24,930.00					1
2	July 1	Postage	800		35.00	24,895.00			35.00		2
3	July 2	Airline Ticket	801		282.45	24,612.55			282.45		3
4	July 3	Promissory Note ($2,000)									4
5		plus interest ($40)	802		2,040.00	22,572.55				2,040.00	5
6	July 5	Cash Sales		2,000.00		24,572.55	2,000.00				6
7	July 6	Sales and Shipping Charge		149.50		24,722.05	144.00	5.50			7
8											8
9											9

10. Take the deposit slip, cash, and checks to Pettisville Bank. All deposits must be made at the drive-in window. If the window is open, give your deposit directly to the manager. If the window is closed, place your deposit slip and checks in the deposit slot.

©GETTY IMAGES/PHOTODISC

11. You will receive a deposit receipt.
    a. from the bank manager at the time of the deposit, or
    b. from the bank later if you used the deposit slot.

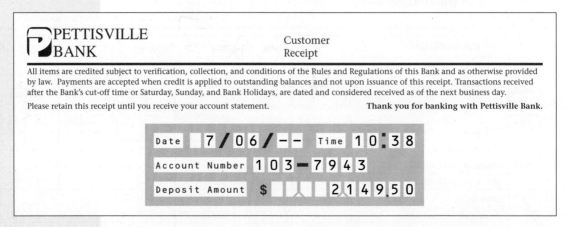

PETTISVILLE BANK

Customer Receipt

All items are credited subject to verification, collection, and conditions of the Rules and Regulations of this Bank and as otherwise provided by law. Payments are accepted when credit is applied to outstanding balances and not upon issuance of this receipt. Transactions received after the Bank's cut-off time or Saturday, Sunday, and Bank Holidays, are dated and considered received as of the next business day.

Please retain this receipt until you receive your account statement.   **Thank you for banking with Pettisville Bank.**

Date 7 / 06 / – –   Time 10 : 38

Account Number 1 0 3 – 7 9 4 3

Deposit Amount $ 2 1 4 9 . 5 0

12. When you receive your deposit receipt, find the sheet of scratch paper. Check to see that the total on the scratch paper agrees with the total on the deposit receipt. If they agree, discard the scratch paper. If they do not agree, notify the bank immediately.

13. Open your check register.

📖 *If you are posting to a manual check register,* remove the check register from the Cash File.

🖱 *If you are posting to an electronic check register,* open your check register.

14. Record the deposit on your check register.

    a. Record the date under the DATE column and the word *Deposit* under the DESCRIPTION column.

    b. Record the total amount of the deposit under the DEPOSIT/CREDIT column.

    c. Find the new balance.

> 📇 *If you are using a manual check register,* add the deposit to the previous total in the BALANCE column and record the new balance.
>
> 🖱 *If you are using an electronic check register,* your new balance will be calculated automatically.

    d. Keep the check register open until you have completed step 16.

15. File the receipt in your Office File.

16. Prove cash after each deposit. (Refer to the illustration below.)

Check Register

NUMBER	DATE	DESCRIPTION OF TRANSACTION	PAYMENT/DEBIT (−)	√ C	DEPOSIT/CREDIT (+)	BALANCE
Taylor Office Supplies ⬍			**Balance Brought Forward**			$ 24,930.00
800	July 1	Pettisville Post Office	35.00			24,895.00
801	July 2	Passports-2-Go	282.45			24,612.55
802	July 3	Farmers & Merchants State Bank	2,040.00			22,572.55
	July 6	Deposit			2,149.50	24,722.05

CASHBOOK

FIRM Taylor Office Supplies ⬍   Page ___ of ___

☐ Click here to balance.

	DATE	EXPLANATION	CHECK NO.	CASH IN	CASH OUT	CASH BALANCE	RECEIPTS SALES, FEES COMMISSION, etc.	OTHER	PAYMENTS EXPENSES. PURCHASES	MORTGAGE, OTHER	
1	July 1	Beginning Checkbook Balance				$ 24,930.00					1
2	July 1	Postage	800		35.00	24,895.00			35.00		2
3	July 2	Airline Ticket	801		282.45	24,612.55			282.45		3
4	July 3	Promissory Note ($2,000)									4
5		plus interest ($40)	802		2,040.00	22,572.55				2,040.00	5
6	July 5	Cash Sales		2,000.00		24,572.55	2,000.00				6
7	July 6	Sales and Shipping Charge		149.50		24,722.05	144.00	5.50			7
8											8
9											9
10											10

    a. Locate the last amount entered in the CASH BALANCE column of the cashbook.

b. Locate the last amount in the BALANCE line of your check register. The last amount in the CASH BALANCE column of the cashbook and the amount written under BALANCE in your check register should be the same. Make no further entries on the check register or cashbook until these two figures equal. (If they are not equal, check the accuracy of your work. If you cannot find your error, ask your Instructor for help.)

c. Close your cashbook and check register.

📓 *If you are using a manual check register or cashbook,* return them to the Cash File.

🖱 *If you are using an electronic check register or cashbook,* save your work.

CHECKPOINT

Making Deposits

Label the parts of the ABA number on a check.

1. _____

2. _____

3. _____

❶ ❷

<u>56-25</u>
412

❸

Answer the following questions.

4. When depositing checks, use a restrictive endorsement. Include your company name and the words _____ .

5. The word _____ is used to distinguish paper money from coins.

---

computational resources

HOW TO COMPUTE INTEREST

Example Banks offer special interest-bearing checking accounts, such as Money Market Accounts, for customers who maintain large balances. What is the interest earned for 1 month on an account with an average daily balance of $60,000.00 if the annual interest rate is 1.44%?

$$\text{Interest} = (\text{Amount} \times \text{Annual Rate}) \div 12 \text{ months}$$

$$x = (60,000.00 \times 0.0144) \div 12$$

$$x = \$72.00$$

Solution Multiply the average daily balance by the annual interest rate. Remember to change the percent to a decimal. The interest for a year would be $864.00. To find the amount earned for 1 month, divide by 12. The interest for 1 month is $72.00.

RECONCILING A BANK STATEMENT

As manager of your own business, you will need to review the record of your account with Pettisville Bank. On July 30 or 31, the bank will send your business a bank statement. A **bank statement** is a report provided by a bank to the depositor showing the condition of the account. *Be sure to save the envelope in which your statement comes. You will need it later.*

◀ Manual
Bank Statement

PETTISVILLE BANK
101 Greenback Drive • Pettisville, OH 43553-0178

BANK STATEMENT

Page 1 of 2

Taylor Office Supplies
12 Rivet Street
Pettisville, OH 43553-0177

ACCOUNT NUMBER	103-7943
STATEMENT DATE	July 31, 20--

BALANCE FORWARD	NO. OF WITH-DRAWALS	TOTAL WITHDRAWAL AMOUNT	NO. OF DEPOSITS	TOTAL DEPOSIT AMOUNT	SERVICE CHARGE	BALANCE THIS STATEMENT
$24,930.00	6	$3,761.28	2	$10,263.72	$12.95	$31,419.49

	CHECKS AND OTHER DEBITS		DEPOSITS AND OTHER CREDITS	DATE	BALANCE
				July 1	$24,930.00
✓	800	35.00		July 3	24,895.00
✓	801	282.45		July 5	24,612.55
			✓ 2,149.50	July 6	26,762.05
✓	802	2,040.00		July 9	24,722.05
✓	803	1,145.83		July 11	23,576.22
			✓ 8,114.22	July 12	31,690.44
✓	806	136.00		July 25	31,554.44
	EFT	122.00		July 31	31,432.44
	SC	12.95		July 31	31,419.49

KEY TO SYMBOLS

ATD	AUTOMATIC TELLER DEPOSIT	DC	DEPOSIT CORRECTION	IE	INTEREST EARNED
ATW	AUTOMATIC TELLER WITHDRAWAL	DM	DEBIT MEMO	OD	OVERDRAFT
CC	CERTIFIED CHECK	EFT	ELECTRONIC FUNDS TRANSFER	RT	RETURNED CHECK
CM	CREDIT MEMO	ER	ERROR CORRECTION	SC	SERVICE CHARGE

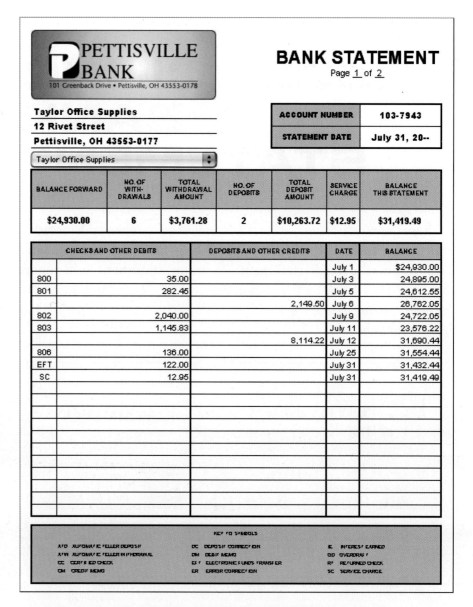

PETTISVILLE BANK
101 Greenback Drive • Pettisville, OH 43553-0178

BANK STATEMENT
Page 1 of 2

Taylor Office Supplies
12 Rivet Street
Pettisville, OH 43553-0177

Taylor Office Supplies

ACCOUNT NUMBER	103-7943
STATEMENT DATE	July 31, 20--

BALANCE FORWARD	NO. OF WITH-DRAWALS	TOTAL WITHDRAWAL AMOUNT	NO. OF DEPOSITS	TOTAL DEPOSIT AMOUNT	SERVICE CHARGE	BALANCE THIS STATEMENT
$24,930.00	6	$3,761.28	2	$10,263.72	$12.95	$31,419.49

CHECKS AND OTHER DEBITS		DEPOSITS AND OTHER CREDITS	DATE	BALANCE
			July 1	$24,930.00
800	35.00		July 3	24,895.00
801	282.45		July 5	24,612.55
		2,149.50	July 6	26,762.05
802	2,040.00		July 9	24,722.05
803	1,145.83		July 11	23,576.22
		8,114.22	July 12	31,690.44
806	136.00		July 25	31,554.44
EFT	122.00		July 31	31,432.44
SC	12.95		July 31	31,419.49

KEY TO SYMBOLS

ATD AUTOMATIC TELLER DEPOSIT	DC DEPOSIT CORRECTION	IE INTEREST EARNED	
ATW AUTOMATIC TELLER WITHDRAWAL	DM DEBIT MEMO	OD OVERDRAFT	
CC CERTIFIED CHECK	EFT ELECTRONIC FUNDS TRANSFER	RT RETURNED CHECK	
CM CREDIT MEMO	ER ERROR CORRECTION	SC SERVICE CHARGE	

Refer to the illustrations. Note that the statements show

1. Your balance at the beginning of the month.

2. The checks paid by the bank during the month.

3. The deposits made during the month.

4. The service charge or other charges for the month, if any.

5. Your balance at the end of the month.

EXAMINING YOUR RETURNED CHECKS AND DEPOSIT SLIPS

The bank will return your canceled checks when it sends you a bank statement. A **canceled check** is a check that has been paid by the bank. Before the bank sends you your paid checks, it cancels each one, usually using a machine that stamps or punches holes in the checks. (Checks returned to you by Pettisville Bank will be canceled by hand. A sample hand-canceled check is shown in the illustration on the right.) Be sure to save your canceled checks. They are valuable records.

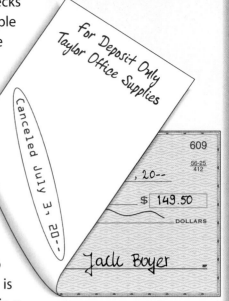

Also included with your paid checks are the deposit slips you completed during the month. The deposit slips should match the deposit receipts in the Office File.

◆◆◆ COMPARING YOUR RECORD WITH THE BANK'S RECORD

As a depositor, you keep a record of your checks and deposits on your check register. The bank statement gives you a copy of the bank's record of your business's account. The balances on the two will almost always differ. Bringing the balances into agreement is known as *reconciling the bank balance*. A **bank reconciliation** is a statement showing how a check register balance and a bank statement balance are brought into agreement. The form for reconciling is printed on page 2 of the bank statement you will receive from Pettisville Bank.

There are several reasons that the balances shown in your records and the bank statement may be different.

1. Some of the checks that you wrote and subtracted from your balance may not have been presented to the bank for payment before the bank statement was prepared. These checks, therefore, have not been deducted from the bank statement balance. Such checks are known as outstanding checks. An **outstanding check** is a check given to the payee but not yet returned to the bank for payment.

2. A **service charge** (a fee charged for checking account services), which you have not yet recorded, may be shown on the bank statement.

3. You may have mailed a deposit to the bank that had not yet been received, or you may have made a deposit at the drive-in window that had not yet been recorded when the statement was prepared.

4. An error may have been made by you or by the bank.

Let's see how a bank reconciliation is made for Taylor Office Supplies On July 31, Taylor received the bank statement shown in the illustration on *page 71 in this Student Reference Book*. The statement balance is $31,419.49. Taylor's check register balance is $33,721.44. The manager of Taylor examined the canceled checks, which were returned with the statement, and found that Check Nos. 804 and 805 were outstanding.

In the bank reconciliation shown below, the manager proved the accuracy of the bank statement and the check register balance by

- adding one outstanding deposit for $2,435.00 (made after the bank statement was mailed)

- subtracting the total of the outstanding checks from the bank statement balance (in this case, two checks—Nos. 804 and 805 were outstanding for a total of $268.00)

- subtracting the $12.95 service charge and the $122.00 electronic payment from his check register balance

In some cases, other additions or subtractions might have to be made in the reconciliation. For example, a charge made for an overdrawn check should be subtracted from the check register balance. A deposit made so late in the month that it did not appear on the bank statement should be added to the balance on the bank statement.

Taylor Office Supplies
12 Rivet Street
Pettisville, OH 43553-0177

BANK STATEMENT

Page _2_ of _2_

RECONCILIATION

YOU CAN EASILY BALANCE YOUR CHECKBOOK
BY FOLLOWING THIS PROCEDURE

FILL IN BELOW THE AMOUNTS FROM YOUR BANK STATEMENT AND CHECKBOOK

BALANCE SHOWN ON BANK STATEMENT	$ 31,419.49		BALANCE SHOWN IN CHECKBOOK	$ 33,721.44
ADD DEPOSITS NOT ON STATEMENT	$ 2,435.00		ADD DEPOSITS NOT ALREADY ENTERED IN CHECKBOOK	$
TOTAL	$ 33,854.49		TOTAL	$ 33,721.44

SUBTRACT CHECKS ISSUED BUT NOT ON STATEMENT

804   $ 250.00
805   18.00

SUBTRACT SERVICE CHARGES AND OTHER BANK CHARGES NOT IN CHECKBOOK

$ 12.95 SC
122.00 EFT

TOTAL $ 268.00		TOTAL $ 134.95
CORRECTED BANK STATEMENT BALANCE $ 33,586.49		CORRECTED CHECKBOOK BALANCE $ 33,586.49

THESE TOTALS REPRESENT THE CORRECT AMOUNT OF MONEY YOU HAVE IN THE BANK AND SHOULD AGREE. DIFFERENCES, IF ANY, SHOULD BE REPORTED TO THE BANK WITHIN 10 DAYS AFTER RECEIPT OF YOUR STATEMENT.

WHAT HAPPENS IF THE BALANCES DON'T AGREE?

If the balances do not agree, it could be a mistake you made or an error the bank made. Mistakes made by the depositor probably are the most frequent causes of differences on the bank reconciliation. Forgetting to record a transaction on the check register is a common error. In any case, you should compare your canceled checks and deposit slips with those listed on the bank statement and with those recorded on your check register. Also, check the mathematical calculations on the bank statement and on the check register. If you do not find an error in your calculations, take up the matter with the bank immediately.

After you have reconciled your bank statement, correct any errors you may have made on the check register. Subtract the service charge and any other payments from the balance so the check register will show the correct balance before you write any more checks.

Follow these steps when you reconcile a bank statement

1. Remove your check register from the Cash File (or open it on your computer).

2. Remove the checks and deposit slips included with the bank statement. Examine each check to make sure it was canceled by the bank.

3. Remove the deposit receipts from your Office File. A deposit receipt should match each deposit slip returned to you by the bank. Staple or clip together each deposit receipt with the deposit slip that matches it.

4. On page 1 of the bank statement, notice the last balance shown. On the bank reconciliation form (page 2 of the bank statement) write that last balance amount on the BALANCE SHOWN ON BANK STATEMENT line. Then write the balance from the last check register entry on the BALANCE SHOWN IN CHECKBOOK line.

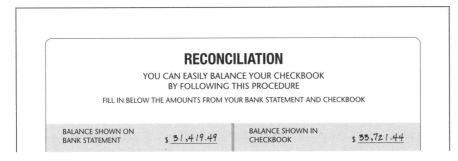

RECONCILIATION

YOU CAN EASILY BALANCE YOUR CHECKBOOK
BY FOLLOWING THIS PROCEDURE

FILL IN BELOW THE AMOUNTS FROM YOUR BANK STATEMENT AND CHECKBOOK

BALANCE SHOWN ON BANK STATEMENT	$ 31,419.49	BALANCE SHOWN IN CHECKBOOK	$ 33,721.44

5. Complete the left side of the form. Refer to the illustration below.
   a. Arrange the deposit slips in chronological order.
   b. Compare the amounts on the deposit slips with the record of your deposits on the check register.
   c. Make a record of deposits that have cleared the bank.

📇 *If you are using a manual check register,* place a checkmark in the ✔/C column for an amount that agrees with an amount on a deposit slip.

🖱 *If you are using an electronic check register,* key the letter "C" (for "cleared") in the ✔/C column for an amount that agrees with an amount on a deposit slip.

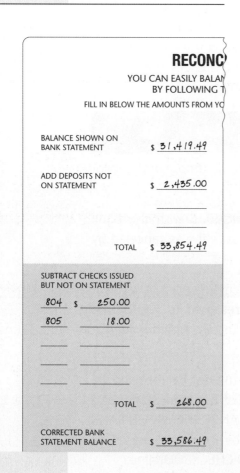

RECONC

YOU CAN EASILY BALA
BY FOLLOWING T

FILL IN BELOW THE AMOUNTS FROM YO

BALANCE SHOWN ON BANK STATEMENT	$ 31,419.49
ADD DEPOSITS NOT ON STATEMENT	$ 2,435.00
	_____
	_____
TOTAL	$ 33,854.49

SUBTRACT CHECKS ISSUED BUT NOT ON STATEMENT

804	$ 250.00
805	18.00
____	_____
____	_____
____	_____
TOTAL	$ 268.00

| CORRECTED BANK STATEMENT BALANCE | $ 33,586.49 |

d. Keep your check register open as you continue to reconcile the bank statement.
e. Turn to the bank reconciliation form (on page 2 of the bank statement). Under ADD DEPOSITS NOT ON STATEMENT, list any deposit that does not appear on the statement. (See the illustration on the left.) Then add the BALANCE SHOWN ON BANK STATEMENT and the amounts listed on the ADD DEPOSITS NOT ON STATEMENT and record that total on the TOTAL line. (If all deposits on the check register have check marks, bring down the amount on the BALANCE SHOWN ON BANK STATEMENT line and record it on the TOTAL line.)
f. Remove any voided checks from the Cash File.
g. Arrange the canceled checks in numeric order including any voided checks. Compare the amount on each check with the amount on the check register showing the same number.
h. Make a record of checks that have cleared the bank.

📇 *If you are using a manual check register,* place a checkmark in the ✔/C column for an amount that agrees with an amount on a check.

🖱 *If you are using an electronic check register,* key the letter "C" (for "cleared") in the ✔/C column for an amount that agrees with an amount on a check.

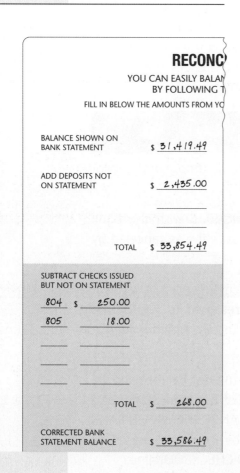

UNIT 1 • BANKING AND BOOKKEEPING

i. Turn back to the bank reconciliation. Complete the section titled SUBTRACT CHECKS ISSUED BUT NOT ON STATEMENT. List the check number and the amount of any checks that do not appear on the statement. Total the amounts and record that figure on the TOTAL line.

j. Determine the CORRECTED BANK STATEMENT BALANCE. Subtract the TOTAL of the section titled SUBTRACT CHECKS ISSUED BUT NOT ON STATEMENT from the TOTAL above to determine the CORRECTED BANK STATEMENT BALANCE. (If all checks cleared the bank, bring down the amount from the TOTAL of the section titled ADD DEPOSITS NOT ON STATEMENT and write that amount as the CORRECTED BANK STATEMENT BALANCE.)

6. Complete the right side of the form.

a. On the lines after ADD DEPOSITS NOT ALREADY ENTERED IN THE CHECKBOOK, list any deposits you have made which you forgot to record on the check register. Or, if you have prepared a deposit but have not yet recorded it on your check register or taken it to the bank, record it here. (If all deposits have been entered on the check register, bring down the amount of the BALANCE SHOWN IN CHECKBOOK line and record it on the TOTAL line.)

b. Complete the section titled SUBTRACT SERVICE CHARGES AND OTHER BANK CHARGES NOT IN CHECK-BOOK. On the first line provided, list the amount of any service charge. On the remaining lines, list any additional bank charges (for example, a charge for an overdraft, an electronic funds transfer, a certified check, or for stopping payment on a check). Total the amounts and record that figure on the TOTAL line.

c. Determine the CORRECTED CHECKBOOK BALANCE. Subtract the TOTAL of the section titled SUBTRACT SERVICE CHARGES AND OTHER BANK CHARGES NOT IN CHECKBOOK from the TOTAL line above. If there were no service or other bank charges, bring down the first total and write that amount as the CORRECTED BANK STATEMENT BALANCE.

...LIATION
...CE YOUR CHECKBOOK
...HIS PROCEDURE
...UR BANK STATEMENT AND CHECKBOOK

BALANCE SHOWN IN CHECKBOOK	$ 33,721.44
ADD DEPOSITS NOT ALREADY ENTERED IN CHECKBOOK	$ _____
	_____
	_____
TOTAL	$ 33,721.44

...LIATION
...CE YOUR CHECKBOOK
...HIS PROCEDURE
...UR BANK STATEMENT AND CHECKBOOK

BALANCE SHOWN IN CHECKBOOK	$ 33,721.44
ADD DEPOSITS NOT ALREADY ENTERED IN CHECKBOOK	$ _____
	_____
	_____
TOTAL	$ 33,721.44

SUBTRACT SERVICE CHARGES AND OTHER BANK CHARGES NOT IN CHECKBOOK	
$ 12.95 SC	
122.00 EFT	
_____	
_____	
TOTAL	$ 134.95
CORRECTED CHECKBOOK BALANCE	$ 33,586.49

| CORRECTED BANK STATEMENT BALANCE | $ 33,586.49 | CORRECTED CHECKBOOK BALANCE | $ 33,586.49 |

THESE TOTALS REPRESENT THE CORRECT AMOUNT OF MONEY YOU HAVE IN THE BANK AND SHOULD AGREE. DIFFERENCES, IF ANY, SHOULD BE REPORTED TO THE BANK WITHIN 10 DAYS AFTER RECEIPT OF YOUR STATEMENT.

7. Compare the CORRECTED BANK STATEMENT BALANCE on the left side of the form with the CORRECTED CHECKBOOK BALANCE on the right side of the form. If they agree, you have successfully reconciled your bank statement. Go to Step 8 below.

NOTE: If the balances do not agree, you should

a. Compare the deposit amounts listed on the check register with the amounts listed under DEPOSITS AND OTHER CREDITS on the bank statement. Place a checkmark beside each amount on the statement that agrees with a deposit listed on the check register.

b. Compare the amounts on the check register with the amounts listed under CHECKS AND OTHER DEBITS on the front of the bank statement. Place a checkmark beside each amount on the statement that agrees with a check that has a checkmark or "C." Refer to the illustration on *page 71 in this Student Reference Book,* if necessary.

c. Go back through your check register and check all math calculations.

d. Go back through the reconciliation form and check all math calculations.

e. Ask the bank for help.

f. Ask your Instructor for help.

8. Record any other charges.

a. If you have an electronic funds transfer not already deducted from your checkbook balance, record the letters EFT under the NUMBER column. Record *July 31* under the DATE column. Record a description of the EFT.

b. Record the amount of the funds transferred under the PAYMENT/DEBIT column.

c. Find the new balance.

Check Register

NUMBER	DATE	DESCRIPTION OF TRANSACTION	PAYMENT/DEBIT (−)	√ C	DEPOSIT/CREDIT (+)	BALANCE
Taylor Office Supplies			**Balance Brought Forward**			$ 24,930.00
800	July 1	Pettisville Post Office	35.00	C		24,895.00
801	July 2	Passports-2-Go	282.45	C		24,612.55
802	July 3	Farmers & Merchants State Bank	2,040.00	C		22,572.55
	July 6	Deposit		C	2,149.50	24,722.05
803	July 9	Buckeye Equipment	1,145.83	C		23,576.22
	July 12	Deposit		C	8,114.22	31,690.44
804	July 16	Creative Advertising	250.00			31,440.44
805	July 18	18 Wheeler Truck Lines	18.00			31,422.44
806	July 23	United Communications	136.00	C		31,286.44
	July 27	Deposit			2,435.00	33,721.44
EFT	July 31	Security Insurance Company	122.00	C		33,599.44
SC	July 31	Service Charge	12.95	C		33,586.49

d. On your next unused line in the check register, record the letters *SC* (service charge) under the NUMBER column. Record *July 31* under the DATE column. Record the words *Service Charge* under the DESCRIPTION column.

e. Record the amount of the service charge under the PAYMENT/DEBIT column.

f. Find the new balance.

📋 *If you are using a manual check register,* subtract the amount of the electronic funds transfer from the previous total in the BALANCE column and record the new balance. Do the same for the service charge.

🖱 *If you are using an electronic check register,* your new balances will be calculated automatically.

---

g. Close your cashbook and check register.

9. Place the bank statement, voided and canceled checks, and deposit slips with deposit receipts attached into the envelope you received from the bank. Place the envelope in the Cash File.

10. Return any deposit receipts without deposit slips to the Office File. These deposits should appear on next month's bank statement.

©GETTY IMAGES/PHOTODISC

CHECKPOINT

Reconciling Bank Statements

Answer the following questions.

1. A monthly report provided by the bank showing the condition of your account is called a/an

   _____ .

2. A/an _____ check is one that has been paid.

3. A/an _____ check is one that has not been paid.

4. A fee charged for checking account services is called a/an _____ .

Doing Business on the 'Net

Online Banking

Today, almost all major banks have a web site where customers can go to conduct much of their banking business online.

Services include

- ❏ Cash Management
- ❏ Certificates of Deposit
- ❏ Checking
- ❏ Credit Cards
- ❏ Direct Deposit of Employees' Payroll
- ❏ Foreign Currency
- ❏ Line of Credit
- ❏ Loans
- ❏ Payments by E-mail
- ❏ Payroll
- ❏ Savings
- ❏ Tax Payments
- ❏ Transfer of Funds

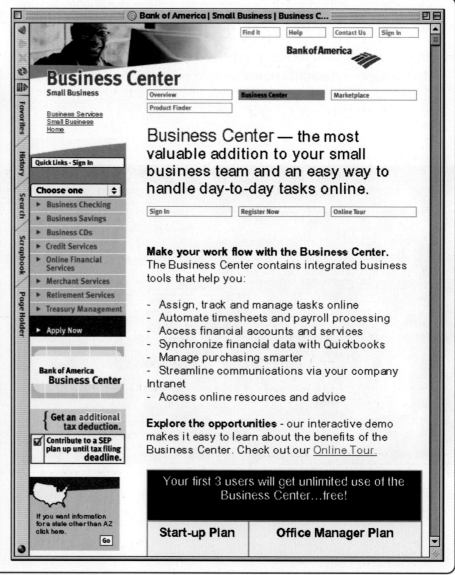

UNIT SUMMARY

1. Checks include a check number, a bank number, and an account number.

2. All checks should be written in ink, but the entries on a check register should be made in pencil or electronically.

3. Before you prepare a check, first record the information about the check on the check register.

4. When you ruin or make a mistake on a check, you should void the record of the check and the check itself.

LESSON 1•1
WRITING CHECKS

5. The EXPLANATION column on a cashbook lists the purpose of a check or source of money received.

6. The CASH IN column on a cashbook should equal the total of the RECEIPTS columns on the cashbook.

7. The CASH OUT column on a cashbook should equal the total of the PAYMENTS columns on the cashbook.

8. At the end of the month, the cashbook should be balanced so that the manager can account for all receipts and payments of company money and prove the accuracy of his or her work.

9. When depositing checks, use a restrictive endorsement, which includes the words *For Deposit Only* and the name of the business depositing the check.

LESSON 1•2
POSTING TO A CASHBOOK

10. When listing checks on a deposit slip, include either the drawer's name or the American Bankers Association number.

11. Checks being deposited are listed separately on the back of the deposit slip.

12. After a deposit has been made, the balance on the cashbook and the balance on the check register should be the same.

LESSON 1•3
MAKING BANK DEPOSITS

13. The bank will return your deposit slips and canceled checks when it sends you a bank statement.

14. The balance on a bank statement almost always differs from the balance on a check register.

LESSON 1•4
RECONCILING A BANK STATEMENT

Glossary

bank reconciliation	a statement showing how a checkbook balance and a bank statement balance are brought into agreement
bank statement	a report provided by a bank to the depositor showing the condition of the account
canceled check	a check that has been paid by a bank
cashbook	a bookkeeping record used to record all receipts and payments of company money
check	an order written by you, the depositor, directing the bank to pay out money
check register	a form on which a depositor keeps a record of deposits and checks
deposit slip	a form that accompanies a deposit and shows the items deposited—coins, paper money, and checks
drawee	the bank on which a check is drawn
drawer	the business or person who owns a checking account
outstanding check	a check given to the payee but not yet returned to the bank for payment
payee	the business or person who receives a check
restrictive endorsement	an endorsement that includes the words *For Deposit Only*, in addition to the signature on the back of a check, which transfers ownership of the check to another party
service charge	a fee charged by a bank for checking account services

INTERNET EXPLORATIONS

1. Visit the following online banking sites. What online banking services are offered?
   a. *www.bankofamerica.com*   b. *www.fleetbank.com*
   c. *www.citibank.com*   d. *www.chase.com*
   e. *www.bankofnewyork.com*   f. *www.bankofgeorgia.com*

2. Use your browser to find other similar online banking sites.

3. Some other financial institutions, such as credit unions, offer similar services. Visit the two sites listed below.
   a. *www.telhio.org*   b. *www.georgiatelco.org*

4. Can you find other similar sites?

UNIT 1 • BANKING AND BOOKKEEPING

ACTIVITY 1•1   WRITING CHECKS — pages 1 & 2

Directions: Assume you are the manager of 18 Wheeler Truck Lines. Using the forms provided, complete 6 checks and 2 deposit slips for 18 Wheeler. You will need a pencil to complete the check register and a pen to complete checks and deposit slips.

1. Prepare Check No. 816. Turn to *page 54 in this Student Reference Book*. Find the steps titled *Follow these steps when you prepare a check.* **Complete steps 2 and 3.** Write the check to Popular Designs for $282.45. Date the check July 15, 20‒‒. On the FOR line, write *Service Invoice No. 7043.*

Inc.

Check Register

Page _1_ of _1_

NUMBER	DATE	DESCRIPTION OF TRANSACTION	PAYMENT/DEBIT (–)		✓C	DEPOSIT/CREDIT (+)		BALANCE	
						BALANCE BROUGHT FORWARD →		8,000	00
816	7/15/07	Popular Designs	282	45				7,717	55
817	7/17/07	Deposit				8920	00	16,637	55
817	7/19/07	Passports-2-Go	2500	00					
818	7/20/07	Lee Community Center	100	00					
D	7/21/07	Deposit				10089	50		
819	7/23/07	Buckeye Equipment	63	18					
820	7/25/07	Hollywood & Vine Videos	106	00					
821	7/30/07	Pettisville Post Office	38	40					

D

?

18 WHEELER TRUCK LINES

18 Wheeler Truck Lines
1208 Oshkosh Blvd.
Pettisville, OH 43553-0177
Telephone: 419-555-0119

816

56-25
412

DATE 7/15/07

PAY TO THE ORDER OF   Popular Designs $ 282.45

Two Hundred Eighty-two and 45/100 _____ DOLLARS

FOR SIMULATION USE ONLY

P PETTISVILLE BANK
101 Greenback Drive • Pettisville, OH 43553-0178

FOR Service Invoice No. 7043   Devin Kuchynka

⑈000816⑈ ⑉041200257⑉ 734⑈7220⑈

2. Prepare a deposit. Turn to *page 66 in this Student Reference Book*. Find the steps titled *Follow these steps when making a deposit at the bank*. Prepare a deposit slip by **completing step 6.** NOTE: In step 6, <u>you will not have an incoming cash slip</u>. Date the deposit slip July 17, 20––. Your cash sales for the week are $8,920.00. Record that figure on the currency line of the deposit slip. Bring down the amount on the currency line to the total line. **Complete steps 14a through 14c** on *page 69 in this Student Reference Book*.

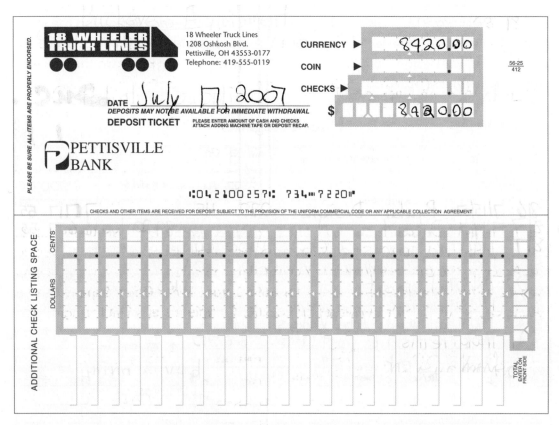

3. Prepare Check No. 817. First, record the check on your check register. Date the check July 19, 20––. Write the check to Passports-2-Go for $2,500.00. On the FOR line, write *Group Travel to Anaheim*.

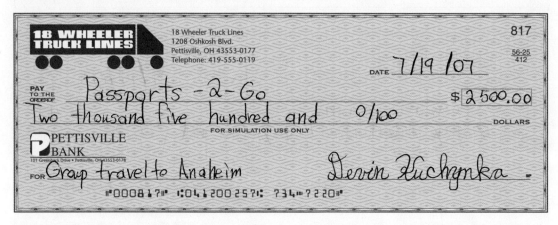

ACTIVITY 1•1 WRITING CHECKS pages 3 & 4

4. Prepare Check No. 818. Date the check July 20, 20--. Write the check to Lee Community Center for $100.00. On the FOR line, write *Donation*.

5. Prepare a deposit. Turn to *page 66 in this Student Reference Book*. **Complete step 6.** Date the deposit slip July 21, 20--. Your cash sales for the week are $9,895.00. Record that figure on the currency line of the deposit slip. You have also received two checks from customers: You received a check for $69.50 from Taylor Office Supplies and a second check from The Denim Maker for $125.00. **Complete steps 14a through 14c.**

UNIT 1 • BANKING AND BOOKKEEPING

6. Prepare Check No. 819. Date the check July 23, 20--. Write the check to Buckeye Equipment for $63.18. On the FOR line, write *Custodial Supplies*.

7. Prepare Check No. 820. Date the check July 25, 20--. Write the check to Hollywood & Vine Videos for $106.00. On the FOR line, write *Training Videos*.

8. Prepare Check No. 821. Date the check July 30, 20--. Write the check to Pettisville Post Office for $38.40. On the FOR line, write *Express Mail*.

ACTIVITY 1·2 POSTING TO A CASHBOOK

Directions: *To complete this activity, you will need a sharp pencil, a ruler, and a scratch sheet of paper. Assume you are the manager of Hollywood & Vine Videos. You post cash payments and receipts of company money to the cashbook. Use the form on the back of this sheet to record your entries.*

1. Turn to page *58 in this Student Reference Book*. Find the steps titled *Follow these steps when recording cash payments (by check) in the cashbook*. **Complete steps 2 through 7b** as you post the following checks:
   - On July 18, you write Check No. 716 for $422.00 to Creative Advertising Agency for 30-second radio spots.
   - On July 18, you write Check No. 717 for $763.20 to Taylor Office Supplies for an executive desk.
   - On July 19, you write Check No. 718 for $1,293.00 to Pettisville Bank for the monthly mortgage payment. When you come to step 5, be sure to record the payment under the MORTGAGE, OTHER column of the cashbook.

2. Several months ago you signed a promissory note at Creative Advertising Agency to borrow $3,000.00. The promissory note has now matured, and you owe the principal ($3,000.00) plus the interest ($90.00). On July 20, you write Check No. 719 for $3,090.00 to Creative Advertising Agency to pay for a promissory note plus the interest. Turn to *page 59 in this Student Reference Book*. Find the steps titled *Follow these steps when recording a check for a promissory note*. **Complete steps 2 through 7b**. *In step 3, remember to record the face value of the note ($3,000.00) on one line and the interest ($90.00) on a separate line in the EXPLANATION column of the cashbook*. (Refer to lines 4 and 5 of the illustration on *page 57 in this Student Reference Book*.)

3. On July 21, you count the money in your cash drawer. It totals $816.35. Turn to *page 60 in this Student Reference Book*. Find the steps titled *Follow these steps when recording cash sales (cash receipts) in the cashbook*. **Complete steps 2 through 6b**.

4. On July 22, you receive a check for $212.00 from Passports-2-Go in payment of your Item Invoice No. 2068. This check is a payment to you for training videos you sold. Turn to *page 61 in this Student Reference Book*. Find the steps titled *Follow these steps when recording incoming checks (cash receipts) in the cashbook*. **Complete steps 2 through 6b**.

5. On July 30, you balance and rule your cashbook for the month. Turn to *page 63 in this Student Reference Book*. Complete the steps titled *Follow these steps when balancing and ruling a manual cashbook*.

UNIT 1 • BANKING AND BOOKKEEPING

CASHBOOK

FIRM _Hollywood & Vine Videos_   Page _1_ of _1_

#	DATE	EXPLANATION	CHECK NO.	CASH IN	CASH OUT	CASH BALANCE	RECEIPTS — SALES, FEES, COMMISSION, etc.	RECEIPTS — OTHER	PAYMENTS — EXPENSES, PURCHASES	PAYMENTS — MORTGAGE, OTHER
1	July 2	Beginning Checkbook Balance				42220 00				
2	July 18	30 second Radio Spot	716		422.00	41798.00			422 00	
3	July 18	Executive Desk	717		763.80	41 334.80			763. 80	1293.00
4	July 19	Monthly Payment	718		1293.00	39741.80				1.293.00
5	July 20	Promissory Note	719		3000.00	36741.80				3000.00
6		+ Interest	909		90.00	36651.80			40.00	90.00
7	July 21	Cash sales		816.35		37468.15	816.35			
8	July 22	Training Videos		212.00		37680.15	212.00			
9	July 30	Totals		1028.35	5568.80		1028.35		1195.80	4383.00
10										
11										
12										
13										
14										
15										
16										
17										
18										
19										
20										
21										
22										
23										
24										
25										

ACTIVITY 1·3 WRITING CHECKS, POSTING TO A CASHBOOK, AND MAKING BANK DEPOSITS

Directions: *Assume you are the manager of Mean Jeans Manufacturing Co. Using the forms provided, complete two checks, one deposit slip, and a cashbook for Mean Jeans Manufacturing Co.*

1. Turn to *page 54 in this Student Reference Book*. Find the steps titled *Follow these steps when you prepare a check*. Write Check No. 801 by **completing steps 2 and 3**. Date the check July 12, 20--. Write the check to Taylor Office Supplies for $87.25. On the FOR line, write *Invoice # 1999—Office Supplies*.

2. **Complete step 5** on *page 55 in this Student Reference Book*.

3. Turn to *page 60 in this Student Reference Book*. Find the steps titled *Follow these steps when recording cash sales (cash receipts) in the cashbook*. **Complete steps 2 through 6b**. Date the cashbook July 13, 20--. Write *Cash Sales* in the EXPLANATION column, and record $10,500.00 in the CASH IN column.

MEAN JEANS MANUFACTURING CO.

45 Maple Street
Pettisville, Ohio 43553-0175
Telephone 419-555-0100

801

56-25
412

DATE 7/12/07

PAY TO THE ORDER OF _Taylor Office Supplies_ $ 87.25

Eighty-seven and 25/100 DOLLARS

FOR SIMULATION USE ONLY

PETTISVILLE BANK
101 Greenback Drive • Pettisville, OH 43553-0178

FOR _Invoice # 1999—Office Supplies_ _Devin Kuchynka_
MANAGER

⑈000801⑈ ⑆041200257⑆ 771⑈6000⑈

Check Register

Page ___ of ___

NUMBER	DATE	DESCRIPTION OF TRANSACTION	PAYMENT/DEBIT (−)	✓C	DEPOSIT/CREDIT (+)	BALANCE	
	7/12/07	Office Supplies	BALANCE BROUGHT FORWARD →			87,220	00
801	7/12/07	Cash Sales	87	25		87/32	75
D	7/13/07	Deposit			10,500 00	97532	75
802	7/14/07	postage	100	00		97532	75

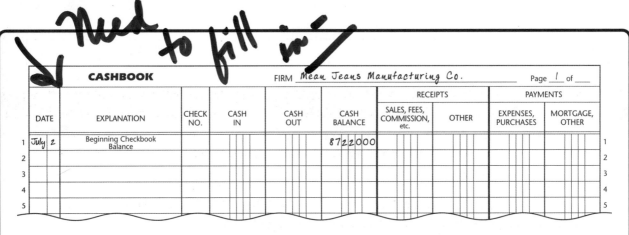

Need to fill in!

	DATE	EXPLANATION	CHECK NO.	CASH IN	CASH OUT	CASH BALANCE	RECEIPTS		PAYMENTS		
							SALES, FEES, COMMISSION, etc.	OTHER	EXPENSES, PURCHASES	MORTGAGE, OTHER	
1	July 2	Beginning Checkbook Balance				8722000					1
2											2
3											3
4											4
5											5

CASHBOOK   FIRM *Mean Jeans Manufacturing Co.*   Page *1* of ___

4. Turn to *page 66 in this Student Reference Book*. Find the steps titled *Follow these steps when making a deposit at the bank.* Prepare the deposit slip by **completing step 6** on *page 66 in this Student Reference Book*. Date the deposit slip July 13, 20--. Your cash sales for the week are $10,500.00. Record that figure on the currency line of the deposit slip. **Complete steps 14a through 14c.**

5. Prepare Check No. 802. Complete the record of the check on the check register. Make the check payable to Pettisville Post Office for $100.00. Date the check July 14, 20--. On the FOR line, write *Postage.* Record the payment for the check in the cashbook.

6. Make sure the balance on the check register equals the balance on the cashbook.

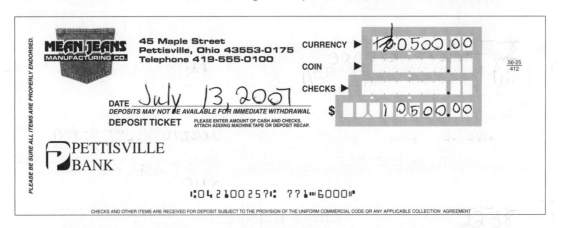

ACTIVITY 1·4 RECONCILING A BANK STATEMENT

Directions: Assume you are the manager of Popular Designs. You receive from Pettisville Bank the bank statement shown below. Reconcile the statement using the check register and bank reconciliation forms shown on the back of this sheet.

1. Turn to *page 75 in this Student Reference Book*. Find the steps titled *Follow these steps when you reconcile a bank statement*. **Complete step 4.**

2. Compare the checks and deposits on the bank statement to the checks and deposits on the check register. Place a checkmark under the ✔/C column on the check register that agrees with an amount on the statement.

3. **Complete steps 5e, 5i, and 5j** on *pages 76-77 in this Student Reference Book*.

4. **Complete steps 6 through 8f.**

5. Check to make sure you have three balances that match: the two balances shown on the bottom of the bank reconciliation and the new balance on your check register.

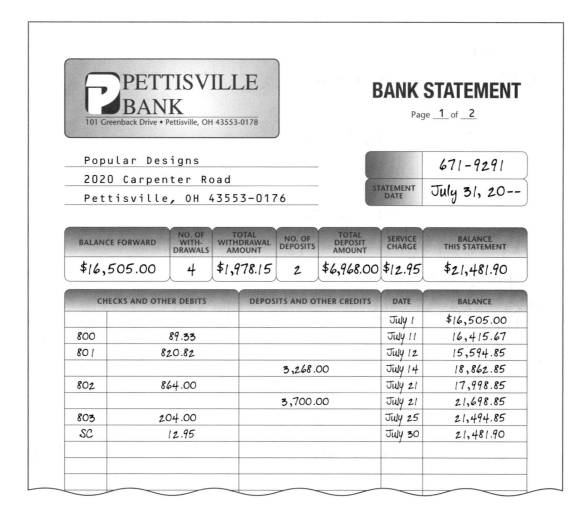

PETTISVILLE BANK
101 Greenback Drive • Pettisville, OH 43553-0178

BANK STATEMENT
Page 1 of 2

Popular Designs
2020 Carpenter Road
Pettisville, OH 43553-0176

671-9291

STATEMENT DATE July 31, 20--

BALANCE FORWARD	NO. OF WITHDRAWALS	TOTAL WITHDRAWAL AMOUNT	NO. OF DEPOSITS	TOTAL DEPOSIT AMOUNT	SERVICE CHARGE	BALANCE THIS STATEMENT
$16,505.00	4	$1,978.15	2	$6,968.00	$12.95	$21,481.90

CHECKS AND OTHER DEBITS		DEPOSITS AND OTHER CREDITS	DATE	BALANCE
			July 1	$16,505.00
800	89.33		July 11	16,415.67
801	820.82		July 12	15,594.85
		3,268.00	July 14	18,862.85
802	864.00		July 21	17,998.85
		3,700.00	July 21	21,698.85
803	204.00		July 25	21,494.85
SC	12.95		July 30	21,481.90

Check Register

NUMBER	DATE	DESCRIPTION OF TRANSACTION	PAYMENT/DEBIT (–)	✓C	DEPOSIT/CREDIT (+)	BALANCE	
		BALANCE BROUGHT FORWARD →				16,505	00
800	July 7	Buckeye Equipment	89 33			16,415	67
801	July 8	Pettisville Bank	820 82			15,594	85
	July 14	Deposit			3,268 00	18,862	85
802	July 15	Creative Advertising Agency	864 00			17,998	85
803	July 18	United Communications	204 00			17,794	85
	July 21	Deposit			3,700 00	21,494	85
804	July 25	Cash (Payroll)	2,588 00			18,906	85
805	July 26	Pettisville Post Office	33 00			18,873	85
	July 30	Deposit			3,514 00	22,387	85

RECONCILIATION

YOU CAN EASILY BALANCE YOUR CHECKBOOK BY FOLLOWING THIS PROCEDURE

FILL IN BELOW THE AMOUNTS FROM YOUR BANK STATEMENT AND CHECKBOOK   22387.85

BALANCE SHOWN ON BANK STATEMENT	$ 21,481.90	BALANCE SHOWN IN CHECKBOOK	$ ~~22374.90~~ 87
ADD DEPOSITS NOT ON STATEMENT	$ 3,514.00	ADD DEPOSITS NOT ALREADY ENTERED IN CHECKBOOK	$ _____
TOTAL	$ 24,995.90	TOTAL	$ ~~22374.90~~ 22,387.85
SUBTRACT CHECKS ISSUED BUT NOT ON STATEMENT 804 $ 2,588.00 805 33.00		SUBTRACT SERVICE CHARGES AND OTHER BANK CHARGES NOT IN CHECKBOOK $ 12.95	
TOTAL	$ 2,621.00	TOTAL	$ 12.95
CORRECTED BANK STATEMENT BALANCE	$ 22,374.90	CORRECTED CHECKBOOK BALANCE	$ 22,374.90 ✓

UNIT 1 • BANKING AND BOOKKEEPING

BUSINESS COMMUNICATIONS

Much of a manager's time is spent communicating—speaking, listening, reading, and writing. In fact, managers spend approximately two-thirds of their time communicating. During one day as manager of a business in the model community, you may find yourself communicating in a variety of ways, such as writing a letter to another business, listening to an explanation from a coworker, reading directions in your Student Reference Book, sending an e-mail, and persuading a customer to buy your product. How you present yourself will make a positive or negative impression on your employees and your customers.

Unit Lessons

Lesson 2•1	**Writing Business Letters**
Lesson 2•2	**Using Telephone and E-Mail**
Lesson 2•3	**Speaking in Public**

Unit Activities

Activity 2•1	**Writing Business Letters**
Activity 2•2	**Using the Telephone**
Activity 2•3	**Using E-mail**
Activity 2•4	**Speaking in Public**

I MAKE It RAIN Yie!

LESSON 2·1

WRITING BUSINESS LETTERS

All business letters are written on company **letterhead** (business stationery with the company name and address printed at the top). You will make a copy of each letter you write, which will be kept in the Office File for future reference. The body of a business letter usually includes at least three paragraphs: (1) the introduction, which explains the purpose of the letter; (2) the body, which gives the reader detailed information; and (3) the conclusion, which provides a statement of goodwill and/or summarizes the main points.

Business letters may be composed using either the modified block letter style or the block letter style. When using the **modified block letter style**, begin the date and the closing lines at the horizontal center of the letterhead. The rest of the lines (except the first line of each paragraph) begin at the left margin. When using the **block letter style**, begin all lines at the left margin. You may use either mixed or open punctuation. When using **mixed punctuation**, a colon follows the salutation and a comma follows the complimentary close. When using **open punctuation**, there is no punctuation following the salutation and complimentary close.

©GETTY IMAGES/PHOTODISC

CHECKPOINT

Business Letter Styles

Answer the following questions.

1. When using mixed punctuation, a _____ follows the salutation and a _____ follows the complimentary close. You should omit punctuation after the salutation and complimentary close when using _____ punctuation.

2. The body of a business letter should include at least _____ paragraphs.

◆ BUSINESS LETTERS

Look at the two illustrations on _pages 96-97 in this Student Reference Book_. Notice that the letters a through h in the illustrations correspond to the letters in the steps below.

a. Both letters are composed on Mean Jeans _letterhead_.

b. The _date_ appears as the first part of the letter.

c. The **letter address** is the part of a business letter that contains the name and address of the recipient of the letter. In the modified block letter style illustrated, the recipient is a company (Taylor Office Supplies). In the block letter style illustrated, the letter address also includes a person's name and title (Mr. Leon V. Weeks, Manager).

d. The **salutation** is the part of a business letter that contains a formal greeting. In the modified block letter style illustrated, the salutation "Ladies and Gentlemen" is used because the letter is addressed to a company. In the block letter style illustrated, the salutation "Dear Mr. Weeks" is used because the letter is addressed to a person. Notice also that the letter addressed to Taylor Office Supplies uses _mixed punctuation_ while the letter addressed to Mr. Leon V. Weeks uses _open punctuation_.

e. Paragraphs in the _body_ of a modified block letter may be indented from the left margin. Paragraphs in the _body_ of a block letter always appear flush with the left margin.

f. The **complimentary close** is the part of a business letter that contains a formal closing. Only the first word in the complimentary close "Sincerely yours" is capitalized.

g. All business letters include a _signature_. When a letter is keyed, however, the writer's name is keyed underneath the signature. A signature may also be followed by the _writer's title_.

h. The **enclosure notation** (illustrated in the modified block letter) is the part of a business letter that serves as a reminder that there is something in the envelope in addition to the letter itself. For example, a check or other business paper may be enclosed.

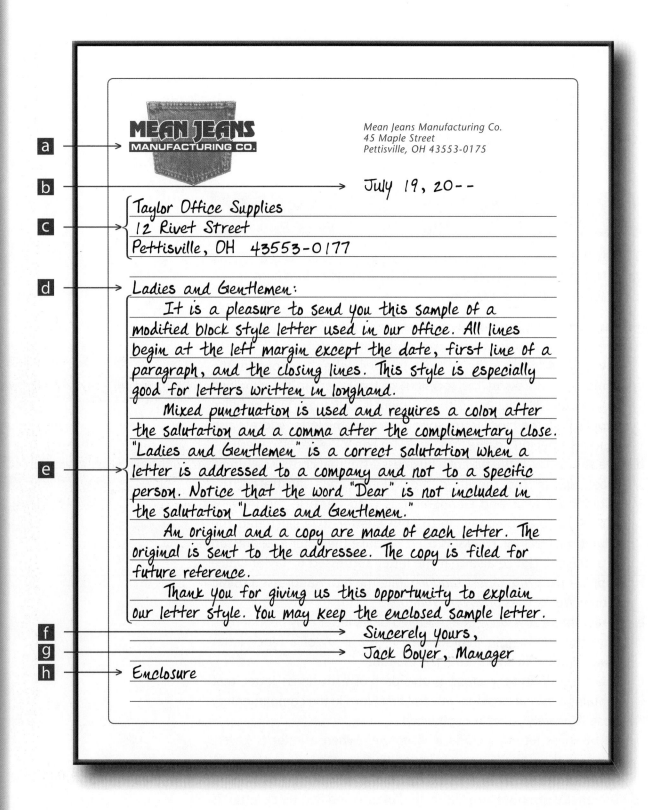

a — Mean Jeans Manufacturing Co.
45 Maple Street
Pettisville, OH 43553-0175

b — July 19, 20--

c — Taylor Office Supplies
12 Rivet Street
Pettisville, OH 43553-0177

d — Ladies and Gentlemen:

e — It is a pleasure to send you this sample of a modified block style letter used in our office. All lines begin at the left margin except the date, first line of a paragraph, and the closing lines. This style is especially good for letters written in longhand.

Mixed punctuation is used and requires a colon after the salutation and a comma after the complimentary close. "Ladies and Gentlemen" is a correct salutation when a letter is addressed to a company and not to a specific person. Notice that the word "Dear" is not included in the salutation "Ladies and Gentlemen."

An original and a copy are made of each letter. The original is sent to the addressee. The copy is filed for future reference.

Thank you for giving us this opportunity to explain our letter style. You may keep the enclosed sample letter.

f — Sincerely yours,

g — Jack Boyer, Manager

h — Enclosure

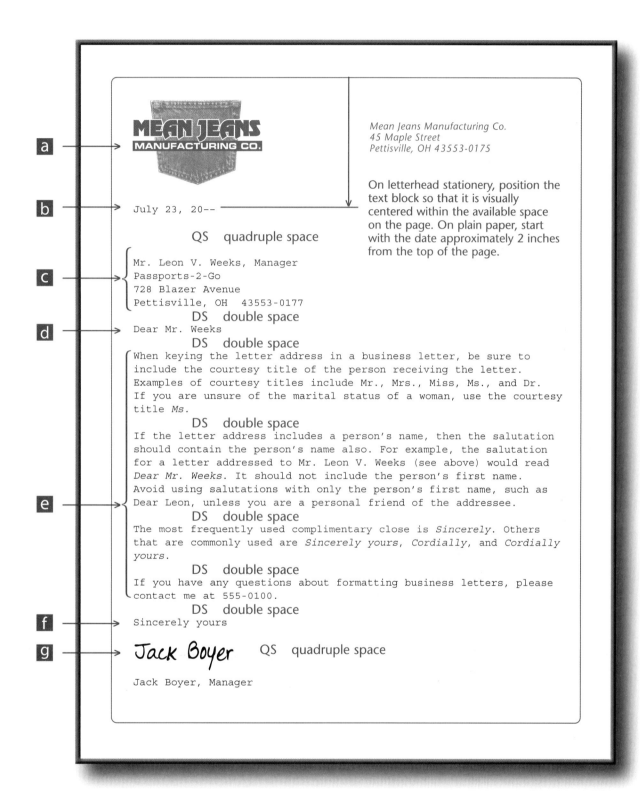

a

b

July 23, 20--

QS   quadruple space

Mean Jeans Manufacturing Co.
45 Maple Street
Pettisville, OH 43553-0175

On letterhead stationery, position the text block so that it is visually centered within the available space on the page. On plain paper, start with the date approximately 2 inches from the top of the page.

c

Mr. Leon V. Weeks, Manager
Passports-2-Go
728 Blazer Avenue
Pettisville, OH 43553-0177

DS   double space

d

Dear Mr. Weeks

DS   double space

e

When keying the letter address in a business letter, be sure to include the courtesy title of the person receiving the letter. Examples of courtesy titles include Mr., Mrs., Miss, Ms., and Dr. If you are unsure of the marital status of a woman, use the courtesy title *Ms*.

DS   double space

If the letter address includes a person's name, then the salutation should contain the person's name also. For example, the salutation for a letter addressed to Mr. Leon V. Weeks (see above) would read *Dear Mr. Weeks*. It should not include the person's first name. Avoid using salutations with only the person's first name, such as Dear Leon, unless you are a personal friend of the addressee.

DS   double space

The most frequently used complimentary close is *Sincerely*. Others that are commonly used are *Sincerely yours*, *Cordially*, and *Cordially yours*.

DS   double space

If you have any questions about formatting business letters, please contact me at 555-0100.

DS   double space

f

Sincerely yours

g

Jack Boyer   QS   quadruple space

Jack Boyer, Manager

CHECKPOINT

Business Letter Salutations

Write the correct salutation for the following names.

1. _____   A business letter addressed to John Marcinko.

2. _____   A business letter addressed to Pettisville Bank.

3. _____   A business letter addressed to Maria Alvarez.

Follow these steps when writing letters

1. Find your letterhead.

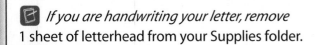 *If you are handwriting your letter, remove* 1 sheet of letterhead from your Supplies folder.

If you are keying your letter, open your company letterhead.

2. Remove 1 envelope from your Supplies folder.

3. Compose the letter. Include 3 paragraphs—the introduction, the body, and the conclusion. Write the letter as if you were personally talking with the person or persons to whom you are writing. Avoid starting sentences with "I" or "We." Make sure your letter is clear, correct, complete, courteous, and concise.

4. Read the letter. Make sure you have included all necessary information. Make sure there are no spelling or grammatical errors. Make sure the letter is neat and attractive.

5. Include an enclosure notation if you are sending a check or other business paper along with the letter.

6. Make a copy of the letter.

If you are handwriting your letter, ask your Instructor to make 1 photocopy of the letter. After your Instructor gives you the photocopy of the letter, sign your name to both copies of the letter.

If you are keying your letter, print 2 copies of the letter now. When you save business letters, include the recipient's name and the date in the file name. For example, a letter written on July 13 to Taylor Office Supplies would be named *Taylor 07-13*. After printing the letter, sign your name to both copies of the letter.

7. Address a business envelope. See the opposite page for instructions for preparing envelopes.

8. Fold the letter. (See the illustration below for instructions.)

FOLDING A LETTER FOR MAILING

STEP 1
With the letter face up, fold slightly less than ⅓ of sheet toward top.

STEP 2
Fold down top of sheet to within ½ inch of bottom fold.

STEP 3
Insert letter into envelope with last crease toward bottom of envelope.

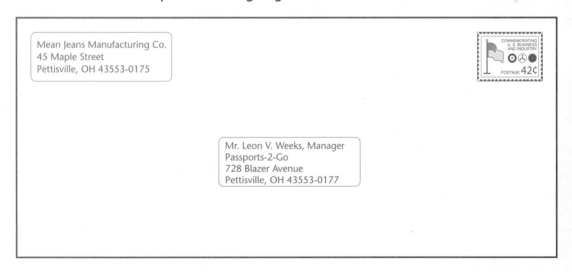

9. Place the letter (and any enclosures) in the envelope.

10. Place the proper amount of postage on the envelope. Mail the envelope.

11. File the copy of the letter in the Office File.

◆ ADDRESSING ENVELOPES

You will address envelopes for all outgoing mail.

Mean Jeans Manufacturing Co.
45 Maple Street
Pettisville, OH 43553-0175

COMMEMORATING
U. S. BUSINESS
AND INDUSTRY
POSTAGE 42¢

Mr. Leon V. Weeks, Manager
Passports-2-Go
728 Blazer Avenue
Pettisville, OH 43553-0177

■ Follow these steps when addressing envelopes

1. Remove 1 envelope from the Supplies folder.

2. Remove the sheet of address labels and the sheet of return address labels from the Office File.

3. Remove from the return address labels sheet a return address label with your company's name and address on it. Place the label in the upper left-hand corner of the envelope.

4. Remove from the address labels sheet a mailing address label for the person or business with whom you are corresponding. Place the label approximately one inch to the left of the horizontal center of the envelope.

5. Place the business paper(s) in the envelope. (Refer to the illustration on _page 99 in this Student Reference Book_.)

6. Place the proper postage on the envelope.

7. Mail the envelope.

©GETTY IMAGES/PHOTODISC

CHECKPOINT

Rules for Business Letters

Answer the following questions.

1. A/An _____ notation is used if you are sending a check or other business paper along with the letter.

2. Only the _____ word in a complimentary close is capitalized.

3. Use the salutation _____ for a letter addressed to a company.

4. When preparing an envelope for mailing, fold the letter in thirds so that the top of the sheet comes to within _____ inch(es) of the bottom fold.

USING TELEPHONE AND E-MAIL

 BASIC BUSINESS TELEPHONE TECHNIQUES

It is your responsibility as manager of a Pettisville business to use proper telephone techniques that save time and create goodwill for your business. Each time you are told in your *DAILY ACTIVITIES* to go in person to another place of business, call the manager and arrange the visit (if telephone equipment is available in your classroom).

■ Follow these steps when you place or receive a business call

1. Answer the telephone promptly, both as courtesy to the caller and to clear the line as quickly as possible for other calls.

2. Identify yourself immediately when placing or receiving calls so that the caller will know to whom he or she is speaking. For example, the manager of Lee Community Center might answer the phone in this way: "Lee Community Center. This is Kurt Oliva. May I help you?"

3. Give the caller your full attention. Don't continue to converse with someone in your presence after you pick up the receiver.

4. Speak distinctly, pleasantly, enthusiastically, and naturally—with your mouth close to the mouthpiece. Avoid distracting noises.

5. Be prepared when placing a call. Gather the data you need to give complete information to the person you are calling.

6. Keep a pad and pencil handy so you can record messages, take orders for products or services, or just jot down reminders for your own reference.

©CORBIS CORPORATION

7. When taking a message, include the time and date, name of caller, telephone number of caller in case the call must be returned, the message, and your initials or name as the person who took the message.

8. Give requested information clearly and tactfully. Make sure the caller understands fully the information you give. Ask the caller to repeat essential facts if there is any doubt about the information.

9. Don't leave the line for more than a brief period. Instead, get any necessary information and call back promptly. When you can't avoid leaving the line, explain what you're doing. Return as quickly as possible. Thank the caller for waiting.

10. Remember that you represent your business as you speak. Let your voice and selection of words reflect a sincere interest. Remember the value of words such as "please" and "thank you."

CHECKPOINT

Telephone Do's and Don'ts

Name 3 Do's and 3 Don'ts about using the telephone.

Do _____

Do _____

Do _____

Don't _____

Don't _____

Don't _____

◆ TAKING TELEPHONE MESSAGES

There may be times when you find it necessary to take a telephone message for the second manager of your business when he or she is away from the office. In that case, you will complete a telephone message on a "While You Were Out" form.

■ Follow these steps when you take a telephone message

1. Get a "While You Were Out" form from your Supplies folder, or print one from the forms document on your computer.

2. Complete the telephone message form.
   a. Print the employee's name on the *For* line.
   b. Record the date and time on the lines provided.

c. Complete the caller's courtesy title (Mr. or Ms.) on the *M* line followed by his or her name.

d. Write the caller's company name on the *Of* line.

e. Record the caller's complete telephone number, Fax number, and/or Mobile number on the appropriate line. Place a check in the checkbox to indicate the type of number the caller provided.

f. Check the appropriate boxes on the message form describing the telephone call.

g. Record any information the caller provides on the *Message* lines.

h. Sign your name on the line titled *Signed*.

3. Place the "While You Were Out" form in a convenient location so that the recipient will see it as soon as he or she returns to the office.

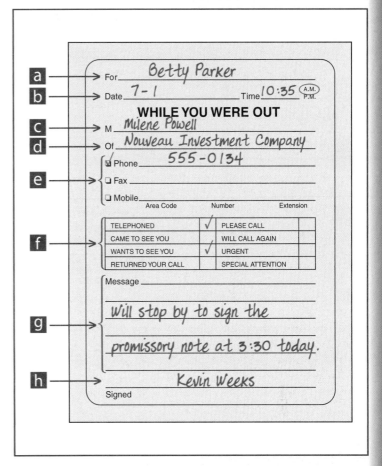

◆ ELECTRONIC MAIL (E-MAIL)

Electronic mail (e-mail) is the electronic transfer of messages among users of a computer network. It is a fast, inexpensive way to communicate with co-workers and employees of other businesses. Most e-mail software programs contain the parts described on the next page.

©GETTY IMAGES/PHOTODISC

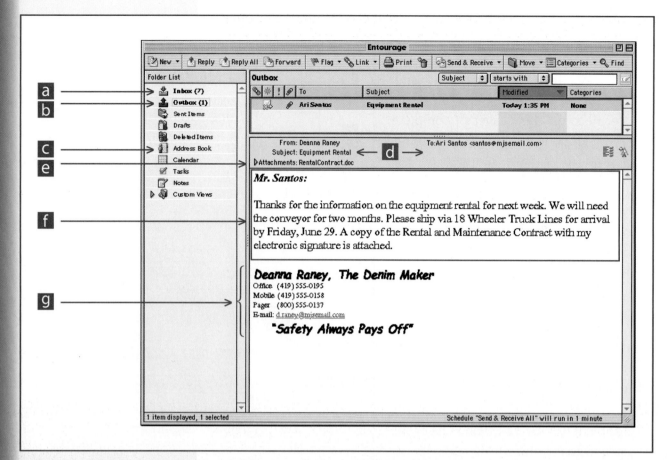

a. Inbox—a storage area for incoming messages

b. Outbox—a storage area that holds messages to be sent to others

c. Address book—a storage area for the user's most frequently used addresses

d. Heading—an area that includes the address of the recipient and a subject line

e. Attachments—a section for attaching files containing text and/or graphics

f. Body—the section where the text of the message is keyed

g. Signature footer—a place to record the writer's name, title, business name, and perhaps address and telephone number

Electronic mail is so popular today that businesses have found it necessary to develop guidelines for its use. The relaxed nature of e-mail can promote poor writing habits and lack of courtesy between users. **Netiquette** is a term that describes the generally accepted manners for electronic communications.

■ Follow these steps when you send or receive an e-mail

1. Make your messages courteous.

2. Remember the basic rules of grammar, punctuation, and spelling.

3. Keep your messages short and to the point.

4. Check the e-mail address before you send a message.

5. Honor others' right to privacy. The sender of the message you received may not want that message forwarded to others.

6. Check your mailbox frequently. Reply to messages promptly. File or delete your messages regularly.

7. Don't use all capital letters for words. This practice is considered "shouting."

8. Avoid using "smileys" and other pictures showing emotions. They are unprofessional when used in the workplace.

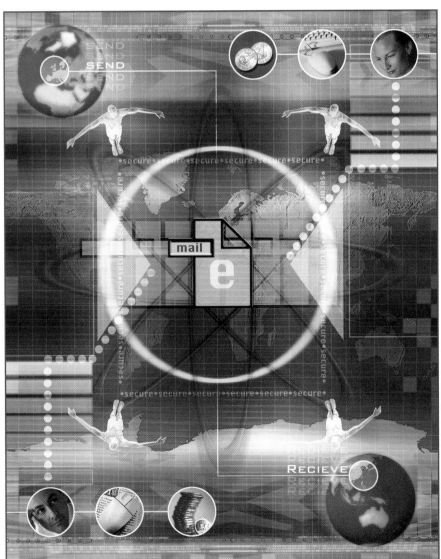

9. Use acronyms sparingly. Examples include FYI (for your information), and BTW (by the way). They may be confusing to the reader.

10. Don't send an e-mail that you would mind others reading. Others may have access to your messages, including your employer.

11. Never give your user ID or password to another person.

12. Avoid sending chain letters through the Internet.

13. Don't send or respond to "flames" (angry or abusive messages.)

14. Always include a subject line on your e-mails. This will help the recipients to organize and give priority to their e-mails.

CHECKPOINT

E-mail

1. Most e-mail software programs contain a _____, which is a place to record the writer's name, title, business name, and address or phone number.

2. The relaxed nature of e-mail can promote poor _____ habits and lack of _____ between users.

3. If you access your private e-mail account at work, it may be read by your _____.

4. Using all capital letters for words in an e-mail message is considered _____.

5. _____ is a term that describes the generally accepted manners for electronic communications.

Doing Business on the 'Net

Free E-mail

Free e-mail is available in a variety of languages through providers like MSN and Yahoo! Anyone with a computer who has a connection to the World Wide Web can access free e-mail services.

Service providers offer free e-mail because of the support of advertisers. When you sign up for an account, the information you provide is used to display ads that are likely to be of interest to you.

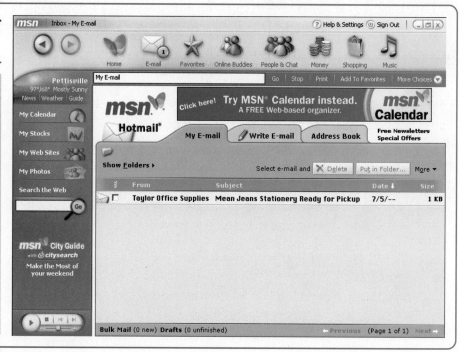

SPEAKING IN PUBLIC

An effective public speaker is able to get the attention of his or her audience by being emotionally involved in what is being spoken. This tells the audience how interested the speaker is in the topic of his or her speech and encourages the audience to listen intently. Once the speaker has gained the audience's attention, he or she must speak clearly, pronounce words correctly, and express ideas concisely. A good public speaker must also consider the interests and needs of the listeners and plan the speech with the audience in mind.

©GETTY IMAGES/PHOTODISC

Your Instructor may ask you to give a speech in front of the other managers in the model business community. The outline for your speech will come from a presimulation report about the business to which you have been assigned. Your Instructor will tell you when to give your speech. If you plan your speech well and follow the steps given below, you should have an effective speech. Unless you are told otherwise, your oral report should be three to five minutes in length. If there are two managers operating your business, both managers should give part of the speech.

After you have written a business plan, you may also be asked to give a speech from the written outline of your business plan. This speech should be three to five minutes in length.

■ Follow these steps when you are told to give a speech

1. **Define the purpose of your speech.** There are four goals of speaking: to entertain, inspire, instruct, and persuade. Decide which of these goals you want to accomplish.

2. **Plan the outline for your speech.** Use the outline you prepared for your report to give your speech. Unless you are told otherwise, your speech should be 3 to 5 minutes long. (See *page 243 in this Student Reference Book* for instructions for preparing the outline.)

3. **Think of a novel introduction.** Consider different ways to gain the attention and interest of your audience with a lively introduction related to the topic: an unusual event, a joke, a quotation, etc. Remember, the purpose of the introduction is to get the audience's attention. It should be brief.

4. **Practice your speech.** Don't try to memorize or read your speech. Practice in front of someone else or in front of a mirror. Be sure to time yourself. If possible, record your speech and play it back to yourself.

5. **Dress appropriately.** Improper dress or loud colors will detract from your speech. Also, be sure to watch your body language—posture, hand gestures, facial expressions, and eye contact. They have a big effect on an audience.

6. **Summarize the main points.** The end of your speech is just as important as the beginning. The audience should know you are concluding your speech. Summarize the main points, add humor, or give a concluding statement such as "To summarize briefly …"

©GETTY IMAGES/PHOTODISC

CHECKPOINT

Speaking in Public

1. A good public speaker must plan a speech with the _____ in mind.

2. The four goals of public speaking are _____, _____, _____, and _____.

3. The purpose of the introduction to a speech is to get the _____ of the audience.

4. A good public speaker should never try to _____ or read a speech.

5. By being emotionally involved in what is being spoken, an effective public speaker can encourage the audience to _____ intently.

UNIT SUMMARY

1. *Ladies and Gentlemen* is an appropriate salutation for a letter addressed to a company and not to a specific person.

2. The body of a business letter usually includes at least three paragraphs—the introduction, which explains the purpose of the letter; the body, which gives the reader detailed information; and the conclusion, which provides a statement of goodwill and/or summarizes the main points.

3. Paragraphs in modified block letters may be indented from the left margin, but paragraphs in block letters always appear flush with the left margin.

4. Only the first word in a complimentary close is capitalized.

5. An enclosure notation is used if you are sending a check or other business paper along with the letter.

LESSON 2•1 WRITING BUSINESS LETTERS

6. Identify yourself immediately when placing or receiving telephone calls.

7. Be prepared when placing a call. Before you place the call, gather the information you need to give to the person you are calling.

8. When taking a telephone message, include the time and date, name of caller, telephone number of caller, the message, and your initials or name as the person who took the message.

9. The relaxed nature of e-mail can promote poor writing habits and lack of courtesy between users.

10. E-mail is not private. Others may have access to your messages, including your employer.

LESSON 2•2 USING TELEPHONE AND E-MAIL

11. The first step in planning a speech is to define the purpose of the speech—to entertain, to inspire, to instruct, or to persuade.

12. An effective speaker is able to get the attention of his or her audience by being emotionally involved in what is being spoken.

13. A good speaker must consider the interests and needs of the listeners and plan the speech with the audience in mind.

LESSON 2•3 SPEAKING IN PUBLIC

Glossary

block letter style	a business letter format where all parts of the letter begin at the left margin
complimentary close	the part of a business letter that contains a formal closing
electronic mail (e-mail)	the electronic transfer of messages among users of a computer network
enclosure notation	the part of a business letter that serves as a reminder that there is something in the envelope in addition to the letter itself
letter address	the part of a business letter that contains the name and address of the recipient of the letter
letterhead	business stationery with the company name and address printed at the top
mixed punctuation	a special format for a business letter that places a colon after the salutation and a comma after the complimentary close
modified block letter style	a business letter format that places the date and closing lines at the horizontal center of the letterhead and the remaining lines (except the first line of each paragraph) beginning at the left margin
netiquette	the generally accepted manners for electronic communications
open punctuation	a special format for a business letter that omits any punctuation after the salutation and complimentary close
salutation	the part of a business letter that contains a formal greeting

INTERNET EXPLORATIONS

1. Visit the following online "search engine" sites. Do all of these sites offer free e-mail service?
   a. www.yahoo.com
   b. www.altavista.com
   c. www.lycos.com
   d. www.hotmail.com
   e. www.e-mailanywhere.com
   f. www.usa.net

2. How is instant messaging different from e-mail?

3. If you use an Internet Service Provider (ISP), e-mail service is part of the subscription package. Check out these sites.
   a. www.aol.com
   b. www.earthlink.com

4. Your phone company may also provide e-mail service in addition to your phone service. What forms of electronic communication do these companies offer?
   a. www.qwest.com
   b. www.excel3.com
   c. www.mciworldcom.com
   d. www.att.com

ACTIVITY 2-1: WRITING BUSINESS LETTERS

Directions: Turn to _pages 95-97 in this Student Reference Book_. Study the illustrations for business letters. Identify the parts of the business letter illustrated below.

LEE COMMUNITY CENTER
ONE VALE STREET • PETTISVILLE, OH 43553-0177

_____

_____ June 27, 20--

The Towne Crier
P.O. Box 276   } _____
Pettisville, OH 43553-0176

Ladies and Gentlemen _____

This letter is to confirm the arrangements for your annual awards banquet. The banquet is scheduled for Friday, July 20, at 12 noon in the Sullivan Room at Lee Community Center.

The Sullivan Room should easily accommodate your 40 guests. As requested, we are providing a speaker's podium. Henri, our caterer, will provide luncheon. The menu includes Carolina Chicken Salad, yeast rolls with butter, and Henri's specialty, Strawberry Fantasia. A service invoice for $380 for the luncheon is enclosed.

If I can be of further assistance to you, please call me at 555-0166. You may also contact me by e-mail at r.craven@mjsemail.com.

_____ Sincerely yours

_____ _Ruth Craven_

Ruth Craven, Manager

Enclosure _____

* _____

UNIT 2 • BUSINESS COMMUNICATIONS

Directions: Compose a letter to your school principal. You may either key the letter on your computer or use the sheet of Mean Jeans letterhead located on *page 379 in this Student Reference Book*. Your Instructor will provide an envelope and give you the school address. Use the lines below to write a first draft of your letter.

The letter to your principal should include the following information in three paragraphs: (1) an explanation of the model business community in your classroom, (2) a description of one business for which you would like to work, and (3) an invitation to the principal to visit your classroom to see the model business community.

1. Turn to PART 2: Orientation to the 15 Businesses on *pages 16-47 in this Student Reference Book*. PART 2 of the *Student Reference Book* provides information about each of the businesses in the model business community. You will want to use some of this information in your description of the business you have selected.

2. Turn to *page 98 in this Student Reference Book*. Find the steps titled Follow these steps when writing letters. **Complete steps 3 through 5.**

3. **Complete steps 7 through 9** on *pages 98-99 in this Student Reference Book*.

_____

_____

_____

_____

_____

_____

_____

_____

_____

_____

_____

_____

_____

_____

_____

_____

_____

_____

_____

_____

ACTIVITY 2-2: USING THE TELEPHONE

Directions: *Your Instructor will ask you to work with another student. You may complete this assignment with or without telephone equipment. Decide who will place phone calls and who will answer phone calls. After you have completed the assignment, switch places so that both you and your partner have placed and received phone calls.*

If you are placing phone calls, assume you are the caller in Telephone Situation 1 and Telephone Situation 2 below.

- **Telephone Situation 1**—Call Mean Jeans Manufacturing Co. stating that you are answering Mean Jeans' classified ad in *The Town Crier*. You want to apply for the job of forklift operator. Your phone number is 555-0129.

- **Telephone Situation 2**—You are the manager of The Clothes Closet. Call Mean Jeans Manufacturing Co. stating that you want to place an order for designer skirts and leather belts. Your phone number is 419-555-0198, Extension 62.

If you are answering phone calls, follow the directions given below.

- Assume that you are an employee of Mean Jeans Manufacturing Co. On July 1, you are instructed to take messages for the department managers while they are at a meeting in Toledo. Read the information about the managers and their responsibilities in the chart that follows. Choose the correct person to return each call in Telephone Situation 1 and Telephone Situation 2. Compose a telephone message for Situation 1 at 10:58 a.m. Compose a telephone message for Situation 2 at 11:10 a.m.

Employee Name	Department	Manager's Job Responsibilities
Rex Allen	Accounting	Pays employees and suppliers; invoices customers
LaShunda Cox	Sales	Handles customer accounts; sells goods to retailers
Felipe Logan	Human Resources	Interviews and hires job applicants, handles personnel problems, and negotiates with the labor union
Meghan Kern	Shipping	Ships merchandise by 18 Wheeler and the post office

- Turn to *page 102 in this Student Reference Book*. Find the steps titled *Follow these steps when you take a telephone message*. **Complete step 2.** Use the "While You Were Out" forms on the back of this sheet to complete the phone messages.

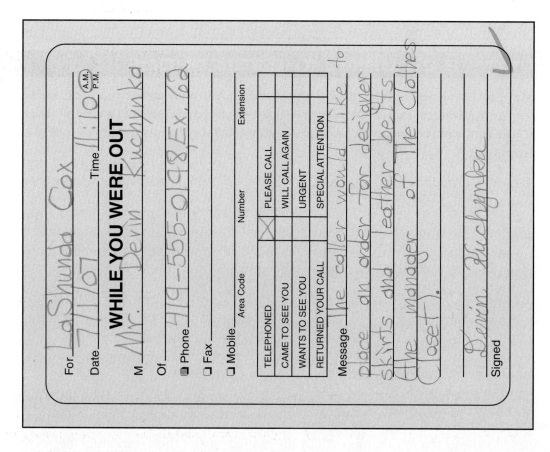

For LaShunda Cox

Date 7/1/07   Time 11:10 A.M. P.M.

WHILE YOU WERE OUT

M Mr. Devin Kuchynka

Of _____

☒ Phone 419-555-0198 Ex. 62

☐ Fax _____

☐ Mobile _____

  Area Code   Number   Extension

TELEPHONED	☒	PLEASE CALL	
CAME TO SEE YOU		WILL CALL AGAIN	
WANTS TO SEE YOU		URGENT	
RETURNED YOUR CALL		SPECIAL ATTENTION	

Message The caller would like to place an order for designer skirts and leather belts (he's the manager of The Clothes Closet).

Signed Devin Kuchynka

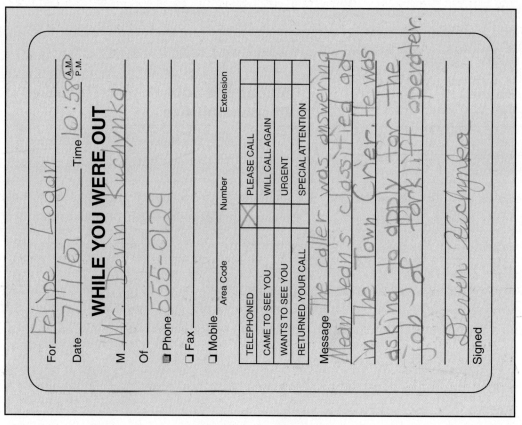

For Felipe Logan

Date 7/1/07   Time 10:58 A.M. P.M.

WHILE YOU WERE OUT

M Mr. Devin Kuchynka

Of _____

☒ Phone 555-0139

☐ Fax _____

☐ Mobile _____

  Area Code   Number   Extension

TELEPHONED	☒	PLEASE CALL	
CAME TO SEE YOU		WILL CALL AGAIN	
WANTS TO SEE YOU		URGENT	
RETURNED YOUR CALL		SPECIAL ATTENTION	

Message The caller was answering Mean Jean's classified ad in The Town Crier. He was asking to apply for the job of forklift operator.

Signed Devin Kuchynka

ACTIVITY 2-3: USING E-MAIL

Directions: During the "Presimulation: Group Activity," each student in your classroom will create a Mean Jeans e-mail account to use while working in the model business community. Your Instructor will then make an e-mail address list of all the managers in the model business community. You will compose and send 3 e-mail messages to your classmates.

1. Follow these steps to set up your account.

   a. Access the Internet and select an Internet search engine.

   b. Choose to open a new e-mail account.

   c. Give the name for your account as **MEANJEANS_YOUR LAST NAME**, substituting your last name after the underscore. For example, a manager whose last name is Carlson would use the e-mail name of MEANSJEANS_CARLSON. (If your name is already taken, you may have to use a slight variation of your name.)

   d. Give your e-mail address to your Instructor.

2. Assume you are the manager of Hollywood & Vine Videos. Use the lines on the bottom of this page to compose a draft of an e-mail to send to one of your classmates. Turn to page 105 in this Student Reference Book. Find the steps titled *Follow these steps when you send or receive an e-mail*. **Complete steps 1 through 14** as you write your draft of the e-mail to your classmate. Use the following information in writing your e-mail.

   • The subject of your e-mail is *Committee Meeting*.

   • Remind your classmate about the upcoming meeting you have scheduled for the members of the Western Roundup Days Committee.

   • The meeting will be held in the Sonesta Room of Lee Community Center.

   • You plan to meet at 7 p.m. on Thursday, July 5.

   • End the e-mail with your name followed by the name of your company, Hollywood & Vine Videos.

S- Committee Meeting

I would like to remind you about the upcoming meeting I have scheduled for the members of the Western Roundup Days Committee, at the Sonesta Room of Lee Community Center at 7 p.m. on Thursday July 5.   Devin Kuchynka, Hollywood&Vine Videos.

3. Use the lines below to compose a draft of an e-mail to send to another classmate. Include the following information in your message, but keep your e-mail brief.

- The subject of your e-mail is *New Release*.

- Thank the manager for stopping by your video store to ask about your training videos.

- You are sorry that the training video "Dress for Success" had not been released at the time it was requested.

- It is now available, and your rush order for the video should arrive within the next 12 days. You will let the manager know just as soon as the video arrives.

- End the e-mail with your name followed by the name of your company, Hollywood & Vine Videos. ✓

S- New Release

Thank you for stopping by Hollywood & Vine Videos to ask for training videos. We are sorry the "Dress for Success" training video was not released then. We now have it and your order should arrive in about 12 days, we will let you know as soon as it arrives.

Devin Kuchynka, Hollywood & Vine Videos.

4. Use the lines below to compose a draft of an e-mail to send to a third classmate. Include the following information in your message, but keep your e-mail brief.

- The subject of your e-mail is *Pettisville Charity Campaign*.

- You appreciate the opportunity to serve as campaign chairperson for this year's fundraising effort.

- You hope that the community will exceed this year's goal of $480,000.

- You would appreciate any suggestions for improving this year's fundraising efforts.

- End the e-mail with your name followed by the name of your company, Hollywood & Vine Videos.

S- Pettisville Charity Campaign

I appreciate the opportunity to serve as campaign chairperson for this year's fundraising effort. I hope the community will beat this year's goal of $480,000. I would appreciate any suggestions for improvement.

Devin Kuchynka, Hollywood & Vine Videos.

5. When your Instructor gives you the e-mail address list, select three of the e-mail addresses. Access your new e-mail account and send the messages to your classmates.

ACTIVITY 2-4: SPEAKING IN PUBLIC

Directions: *During the "Presimulation: Group Activity," you will be asked to prepare a presimulation report. This report describes the business you will manage. After preparing the report outline, you will then make an oral presentation to the managers within the model business community. Your Instructor will appoint a time for you to give your speech.*

©GETTY IMAGES/PHOTODISC

1. Turn to *page 107 in this Student Reference Book*. Complete the steps titled *Follow these steps when you are told to give a speech*.

2. Read each of the 10 evaluation methods listed on the Speech Evaluation Form on the back of this sheet.

3. Complete the top portion of the Speech Evaluation Form on the back of this sheet. Write your name, the topic of your speech, the date, and the purpose of your speech. Give the form to your Instructor. He or she will then assign you a time to give the speech.

4. Give your speech! Remember, everyone gets nervous when speaking in front of an audience. You will do a good job if you plan well and practice your speech.

UNIT 2 • BUSINESS COMMUNICATIONS

SPEECH EVALUATION FORM

Name_____ Date _____

Topic_____ Purpose _____
(entertain, inform, inspire, or persuade)

Did speaker:	Outstanding (10 pts.)	Very Good (8 pts.)	Satisfactory (6 pts.)
1. Arouse audience's attention in the introduction?	_____	_____	_____
2. Present ideas clearly in logical sequence?	_____	_____	_____
3. Maintain eye contact with audience?	_____	_____	_____
4. Speak in a conversational tone using notes well?	_____	_____	_____
5. Avoid lazy or sloppy enunciation of words and slang?	_____	_____	_____
6. Speak loud enough and vary the tone of voice?	_____	_____	_____
7. Maintain good posture using natural gestures?	_____	_____	_____
8. Pace the speech (not too fast or too slow)?	_____	_____	_____
9. Summarize main points?	_____	_____	_____
10. Maintain interest throughout the speech?	_____	_____	_____
TOTAL POINTS	_____	_____	_____

PAYROLL

Businesses use several methods to prepare payroll. A large company may have its central accounting office complete the payroll electronically. Many small businesses prepare their payroll manually (by hand). Some companies have arrangements with their banks to have employees' pay automatically deposited into employees' bank accounts. Your Instructor will tell you whether to prepare payroll electronically, complete the payroll manually, or ask Pettisville Bank to deposit your employees' pay directly into their bank accounts.

One of your responsibilities as a manager is to prepare payroll records. Your employees will be paid biweekly (every two weeks). For this simulation, employees will be paid on July 13 and July 27. It is very important that you prepare the payroll carefully and your records be error-free. Employees will not tolerate mistakes on their paychecks! After you have prepared your biweekly payroll, ask your Instructor to check your payroll records for accuracy.

Unit Lessons

Lesson 3•1	**Preparing Time Cards**
Lesson 3•2	**Completing a Payroll Register**
Lesson 3•3	**Paying Federal Withholding and FICA Taxes**

Unit Activities

Activity 3•1	**Preparing Time Cards**
Activity 3•2	**Completing a Payroll Register**
Activity 3•3	**Paying Federal Withholding and FICA Taxes**

LESSON 3·1

PREPARING TIME CARDS

Many businesses use time clocks and time cards to keep accurate records of the hours each employee works. A **time card** records an employee's time spent on the job. The information recorded on the time card will be different from business to business. Basically, employees are asked to "punch in" (record the time) when they arrive at the beginning of the workday and "punch out" at the end of the workday. Time cards are inserted into a machine with a clock on it. The time is automatically printed on the card.

An employee's overtime is also recorded on the time card. **Overtime** is time worked past the regular 8-hour workday or 40-hour workweek. Overtime for employees is computed at one and one-half times the regular rate of pay and is commonly referred to as "time and a half."

You will receive time cards for yourself and the employees of your business that identify each employee by number but have omitted the names. You will write each employee's name on a time card. You will also receive a blank time card. During the month of July, you will advertise for and hire a new employee. The blank time card will be used to record your new employee's time spent on the job.

In the illustration on the left, Gwen Belue worked a total of 80 regular hours and 4 overtime hours. She was paid at the rate of $9.00 per hour for regular hours and $13.50 per hour for overtime hours. Gwen's gross pay for the two-week period was $774.00.

At the end of the pay period, the total regular (TOTAL REG.) column is added to determine a total for the pay period. The total overtime (TOTAL OT) column is also added to determine a total. The bottom of the time card is used as a worksheet to determine the GROSS PAY.

TIME CARD
Mean Jeans Mfg. Co.

EMPLOYEE NO. _1_

PAY PERIOD ENDING _July 27, 20--_

NAME _Gwen Belue_

SOCIAL SECURITY NO. _280-56-1505_

MARITAL STATUS _✓_ S ___ M EXEMPTIONS _1_

Heath Insurance $ _49.00_   Other Deduction $ _—_

DATE	REGULAR HOURS		OVERTIME HOURS		TOTAL REG.	TOTAL OT
	IN	OUT	IN	OUT		
7–16	7:58	12:01			8	
	12:59	5:02				
7–17	7:59	12:00			8	
	12:59	5:02				
7–18	8:01	12:03			8	
	12:59	5:00				
7–19	7:59	12:02			8	
	12:58	5:01				
7–20	7:57	12:01			8	
	1:01	5:00				
7–23	7:58	12:00			8	
	12:59	5:01				
7–24	7:57	12:01			8	1
	1:00	5:00	5:00	6:00		
7–25	8:01	12:03			8	3
	12:59	5:01	5:30	8:30		
7–26	7:59	12:00			8	
	12:58	5:00				
7–27	7:59	12:01			8	
	1:00	5:03				
				TOTAL	80	4

	HOURS	RATE	AMOUNT
REGULAR	80	$9.00	$720.00
OVERTIME	4	13.50	54.00
TOTAL HOURS	84	GROSS PAY	$774.00

The overtime rate is computed by adding one-half of the regular rate to the total of the regular rate. It may also be computed by multiplying the regular rate times 1.5. The illustration below shows how the overtime rate was determined for Gwen Belue.

Regular Rate	$ 9.00	Regular Rate	$ 9.00
Plus $\frac{1}{2}$ of Regular Rate	4.50		× 1.5
Overtime Rate	$13.50	Overtime Rate	$13.50

■ Follow these steps when preparing time cards

1. Find the time cards.

📋 *If you are using Instructor-provided forms,* remove the time cards for the *current pay period* (either July 13 or July 27) from the Supplies folder.

🖨 *If you are printing your forms,* open the forms document. Find Unit 3 Payroll. Print the time cards *for the current pay period* (either July 13 or July 27).

---

2. Check to be sure you have the correct date for the current pay period. July 13 is the *first* pay period, and July 27 is the *second* pay period.

3. Find the 2 time cards listing gross pay as $1,352. These 2 time cards are for the managers of your business. Use a pencil to complete the time cards. Print your name and social security number on the first time card. If you have a second manager, print that manager's name and social security number on the second card. If there is only one manager for your business, write the following name and social security number on the time card for the second manager: Joe Marcinkowski, #256-87-3805.

©GETTY IMAGES/PHOTODISC

4. Assign names for the remaining time cards (unless a card is blank). *If you have a blank time card, do not write on this card yet.* You will use the blank card for the new employee you will hire. The social security numbers for these time cards have already been recorded on the cards.

5. Place the time cards in the Office File.

1. Find the notice of employment form for your business.

🖰 *If you are using Instructor-provided forms,* remove the notice of employment from the Supplies folder.

🖱 *If you are printing your forms,* open the forms document. Find Unit 3 Payroll. Print the notice of employment form.

2. Remove the time cards for the current pay period from the Office File. Find the blank time card. (This is your new employee's time card.)

NOTICE OF EMPLOYMENT

Mean Jeans Manufacturing Co.

This notice is to inform you that the position you had available has been filled. The most qualified applicant for the position has been notified of the appointment. The following information is for your records:

NAME OF EMPLOYEE ___ Horton, ___ Vivian ___
   Last   First   Middle Initial

ADDRESS ___ 202 Benmac Road ___ Napoleon, ___ OH ___ 43545-0162 ___
   Street   City   State   ZIP Code

TELEPHONE NO. ___ 555-0169 ___   SOCIAL SECURITY NO. ___ 371-24-1485 ___

MARITAL STATUS ___ single ___   EXEMPTIONS ___ zero ___

POSITION ASSIGNED ___ Receptionist ___

DAILY WORK SCHEDULE ___ 8:00-12:00 ___ a.m. ___ 1:00-5:00 ___ p.m.

SALARY INFORMATION:

   Date Scheduled to Report for Work ___ July 25, 20-- ___

   Hourly Rate ___ $8.30 ___ Overtime Rate ___ Time and one-half ___

   Health Insurance ___ none ___

- - - - - - - - Cut here and give Form W-4 to your employer. Keep the top part for your records. - - - - - - - -

Form **W-4**	**Employee's Withholding Allowance Certificate**	OMB No. 1545-0010

Department of the Treasury Internal Revenue Service ▶ Whether you are entitled to claim a certain number of allowances or exemptions from withholding is subject to review by the IRS. Your employer may be required to send a copy of this form to the IRS.

20 --

1 Type or print your first name and middle initial | Last name | 2 Your social security number
Vivian | **Horton** | **371 24 1485**

Home address (number and street or rural route)
202 Benmac Road

3 ☒ Single ☐ Married ☐ Married, but withhold at higher Single rate.
Note: *If married, but legally separated, or spouse is a nonresident alien, check the Single box.*

City or town, state, and ZIP code
Napoleon, OH 43545-0162

4 If your last name differs from that on your social security card, check here. You must call 1-800-772-1213 for a new card ▶ ☐

5 Total number of allowances you are claiming (from line H above OR from the worksheet on page 2) | 5 | **0**
6 Additional amount, if any, you want withheld from each paycheck | 6 | $
7 I claim exemption from withholding for 20--, and I certify that I meet **BOTH** of the following conditions for exemption:
   • Last year I had a right to a refund of **ALL** Federal income tax withheld because I had **NO** tax liability **AND**
   • This year I expect a refund of **ALL** Federal income tax withheld because I expect to have **NO** tax liability.
   If you meet both conditions, enter "EXEMPT" here ▶ | 7 |

Under penalties of perjury, I declare that I have examined this certificate and to the best of my knowledge and belief, it is true, correct, and complete.

Employee's signature
(Form is not valid unless you sign it) ▶ *Vivian Horton*   Date ▶ *July 25, 20--*

8 Employer's name and address (Employer: Complete 8 and 10 only if sending to the IRS.) | 9 Office code (optional) | 10 Employer identification number

For Privacy Act and Paperwork Reduction Act Notice, see page 2.   Cat. No. 102200   Form **W-4** (2005)

TIME CARD
Mean Jeans Mfg. Co.   EMPLOYEE NO. **6**

PAY PERIOD ENDING ___ July 27, 20-- ___

NAME ___ Vivian Horton ___

SOCIAL SECURITY NO. ___ 371-24-1485 ___

MARITAL STATUS ✓ S ___ M ___ EXEMPTIONS **0**

Heath Insurance $ — ___ Other Deduction $ —

DATE	REGULAR HOURS		OVERTIME HOURS		TOTAL REG.	TOTAL OT
	IN	OUT	IN	OUT		
7-16						
7-17						
7-18						
7-19						
7-20						
7-23						
7-24						
7-25	7:56	12:02			8	
	12:59	5:01				
7-26						
7-27						
				TOTAL		

	HOURS	RATE	AMOUNT
REGULAR		$8.30	
OVERTIME		12.45	
TOTAL HOURS		GROSS PAY	

---

3. Look at the time card illustrated. Complete the time card for your new employee. The information you'll need to complete the time card can be found on the notice of employment sheet and the Employee's Withholding Allowance Certificate.

UNIT 3 • PAYROLL

a. Complete the top portion of the time card.
   - Record the new employee's name, social security number, marital status, and number of exemptions.
   - List any other deductions, such as the amount of health insurance.
b. Complete the middle portion of the time card. Find today's simulation date in the DATE column.
   - Record the regular hours in and out today (Your new employee clocked in at 7:56 a.m. and out at 12:02 p.m. and then clocked in again at 12:59 p.m. and out again at 5:01 p.m.)
   - Leave the OVERTIME HOURS column blank. (No overtime was worked today.)
   - Record the total regular hours worked (8).
c. Complete the bottom portion of the time card.
   - Record the regular hourly RATE.
   - Record the OVERTIME RATE. Employees are paid time and a half for overtime. Vivian Horton's overtime rate would be computed as follows.

Regular Rate	$ 8.30	Regular Rate	$ 8.30
Plus $\frac{1}{2}$ of Regular Rate	4.15		× 1.5
Overtime Rate	$12.45	Overtime Rate	$12.45

4. Place the time cards and the notice of employment form in the Office File.

CHECKPOINT

Preparing Time Cards

Answer the following questions.

1. Employees are paid time and a half for _____.

2. A business form that records one employee's time on the job is called a _____.

3. If an employee's regular rate is $8.50 per hour, the employee's overtime rate is $_____ per hour.

4. If an employee's regular rate is $12.25 per hour, the employee's overtime rate is $_____ per hour.

5. If an employee's regular rate is $9.75 per hour, the employee's overtime rate is $_____ per hour.

LESSON 3·2

COMPLETING A PAYROLL REGISTER

A **payroll register** is a business form listing gross pay, deductions, and net pay for each employee in a business. The information for completing the payroll register is taken from employee time cards. As a manager, you may prepare payroll either electronically or manually. If you are preparing the payroll manually, use a pencil to make the entries so that you can easily correct errors. If you are preparing your payroll electronically, much of the information will be automatically recorded for you. After you complete an electronic payroll register, print a hard copy to give to your Instructor.

Manual Payroll Register ▼

PAYROLL REGISTER

MEAN JEANS MANUFACTURING CO.

Pay Period Ending _____ July 27, 20-- _____

Manager's Name _____ Melissa Yale _____

Instructor's Approval: M♀W

EMPLOYEE		EARNINGS			DEDUCTIONS								
								FICA					
No.	Name	Regular Hours	Overtime Hours	Gross Pay	Federal Withholding Tax	State Withholding Tax 6%	City Withholding Tax 2%	Medicare 1.45%	Soc. Sec. 6.2%	Health Insurance	Other	Total Deductions	NET PAY
1	Gwen Belue	80	4	$ 774.00	$68.00	$ 46.44	$15.48	$11.22	$47.99	$ 49.00		$238.13	$535.87
2	Melissa Yale	80	2	996.00	101.00	59.76	19.92	14.44	61.75			256.87	739.13
3	Lance Cooper	76		722.00	80.00	43.32	14.44	10.47	44.76	49.00	20.00	261.99	460.01
4	Katy Morgan	80		1,056.00	110.00	63.36	21.12	15.31	65.47	49.00		324.26	731.74
5	Britt Powell	80	3	1,330.88	182.00	79.85	26.62	19.30	82.51	49.00		439.28	891.60
6	Vivian Horton	24		199.20	10.00	11.95	3.98	2.89	12.35			41.17	158.03
	TOTALS	420	9	$5,078.08	$551.00	$304.68	$101.56	$73.63	$314.83	$196.00	$20.00	$1,561.70	$3,516.38

Some businesses use electronic funds transfer at Pettisville Bank to pay their employees. **Electronic Funds Transfer (EFT)** is a way in which money is moved electronically from one account or bank to another. When payroll is transferred electronically, the bank adds the amount earned to each employee's account at the bank and subtracts that amount from the company's account at the bank.

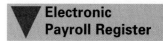

▼ **Electronic Payroll Register**

MEAN JEANS MANUFACTURING CO.
45 Maple Street
Pettisville, Ohio
43553-0175

Pay Period Ending   **July 27,20—**

Manager's Name   **Melissa Yale**

Instructor's Approval

| | EMPLOYEE DATA | | | EARNINGS | | | DEDUCTIONS | | | | | | | NET PAY |
| | | | | | | | Withholding Taxes | | | FICA | | | | | |
No.	Name	No. of Exemptions	Rate	Regular Hours	Overtime Hours	Gross Pay	Federal Tax	State Tax 6%	City Tax 2%	Medicare 1.45%	Soc. Sec. 6.2%	Health Insurance	Other	Total Deductions	NET PAY
1	Gwen Belue	1	$9.00	80.00 / $720.00	4.00 / $54.00	$774.00	$68.00	$46.44	$15.48	$11.22	$47.99	☑ $49.00		$238.13	$535.87
2	Melissa Yale	1	$12.00	80.00 / $960.00	2.00 / $36.00	$996.00	$101.00	$59.76	$19.92	$14.44	$61.75	☐		$256.87	$739.13
3	Lance Cooper		$9.50	76.00 / $722.00		$722.00	$80.00	$43.32	$14.44	$10.47	$44.76	☑ $49.00	$20.00	$261.99	$460.01
4	Katy Morgan	1	$13.20	80.00 / $1,056.00		$1,056.00	$110.00	$63.36	$21.12	$15.31	$65.47	☑ $49.00		$324.26	$731.74
5	Britt Powell		$15.75	80.00 / $1,260.00	3.00 / $70.88	$1,330.88	$182.00	$79.85	$26.62	$19.30	$82.51	☑ $49.00		$439.28	$891.60
6	Vivian Horton		$8.30	24.00 / $199.20		$199.20	$10.00	$11.95	$3.98	$2.89	$12.35	☐		$41.17	$158.03
7												☐			
8												☐			
9												☐			
10												☐			
11												☐			
12												☐			
	TOTALS			420.00 / $4,917.20	9.00 / $160.88	$5,078.08	$551.00	$304.68	$101.56	$73.63	$314.83	$196.00	$20.00	$1,561.70	$3,516.38

Look closely at the illustrations. The payroll registers are divided into four sections: EMPLOYEE DATA, EARNINGS, DEDUCTIONS, and NET PAY. **Gross pay** is the amount a person receives *before* taxes and other deductions are withheld from the paycheck. **Net pay** (also known as net earnings or "take-home pay") is the amount a person receives *after* taxes and other deductions are withheld from the paycheck.

In the manual payroll register, the EMPLOYEE section is divided into two columns—No. and Name. This information is recorded from the employee time cards. In the electronic payroll register, two additional columns are provided to record the pay rate and the number of exemptions chosen by each employee.

The EARNINGS section is divided into three columns showing Regular Hours, Overtime Hours, and Gross Pay. Information for the EARNINGS section is taken from the employee time cards.

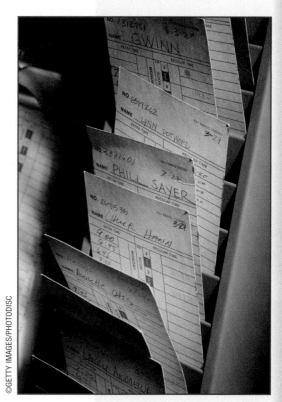

©GETTY IMAGES/PHOTODISC

The DEDUCTIONS section is divided into eight columns—Federal Withholding Tax, State Withholding Tax, City Withholding Tax, Medicare tax, Social Security tax, Health Insurance, Other, and Total Deductions.

- Federal withholding tax is based on each employee's number of exemptions. An employee whose time card lists marital status as "Single" may claim either no (0) exemptions or 1 exemption.
- For this simulation, 6% of gross pay will be withheld for state withholding tax.
- For this simulation, 2% of gross pay will be withheld for city withholding tax.
- For this simulation, 1.45% of gross pay will be withheld for Medicare tax.
- For this simulation, 6.2% of gross pay will be withheld for Social Security tax.
- For this simulation, $49.00 will be deducted from the gross pay for each employee who requests a deduction for health insurance.
- The Other column lists any additional amounts, such as savings, that employees wish to have withheld from their paychecks.
- The Total Deductions column is calculated by adding all of the amounts in the previous columns of the DEDUCTIONS section.

The NET PAY section has only one column. Net pay is determined by subtracting the total of the deductions from the Gross Pay.

Look at the payroll register illustrated on _page 125 in this Student Reference Book_. Notice that all columns containing figures are totaled at the bottom of the payroll register. Six Mean Jeans Manufacturing Co. employees totaled $5,078.08 in gross pay for the pay period ending July 27. Deductions totaling $1,561.70 were subtracted from gross pay. A total of $3,516.38 in net pay was paid to the six employees.

computationalresources

ROUNDING NUMBERS

Rule To round calculations to the nearest cent
- round UP when the third digit after the decimal point is 5 or higher.
- round DOWN when the third digit after the decimal point is 4 or lower.

Example Round $58.0954 to the nearest cent.

Solution Because the third digit after the decimal point is 5, the number is rounded UP. The answer is $58.10.

Example Round $58.0934 to the nearest cent.

Solution Because the third digit after the decimal point is 4 or lower, the number is rounded DOWN. The answer is $58.09.

■ Follow these steps when preparing a payroll register

1. Remove the employee time cards for the current pay period from the Office File. Use the time cards to make the entries for each employee on the payroll register.

2. Find your payroll register.

📓 *If you are preparing your payroll manually,* remove 1 payroll register from the Supplies folder. Use a pencil to make your entries.

🖱 *If you are preparing your payroll register electronically,* open the payroll register. Enter data only in the white cells. The totals will be automatically calculated in the yellow cells. Use the tab key to move from cell to cell.

---

3. Record the date (either July 13, 20-- or July 27, 20--) after the words *Pay Period Ending*. Record your name after the words *Manager's Name*.

4. Complete the EMPLOYEE and EARNINGS sections of the payroll register.

📓 *If you are preparing your payroll register manually,* refer to the illustration on *page 124 in this Student Reference Book*.

  a. Record the number and name for each employee.

  b. Record the Regular Hours, Overtime Hours, and Gross Pay for each employee.

🖱 *If you are preparing your payroll register electronically,* refer to the illustration on *page 125 in this Student Reference Book*.

  a. Record the name, number of exemptions, and rate for each employee.

  b. Record the Regular Hours and Overtime Hours. The Gross Pay will be calculated automatically.

USING A TAX TABLE

SINGLE Persons—**BIWEEKLY** Payroll Period
(For Wages Paid in 20 —)

If the wages are—		And the number of withholding allowances claimed is—										
At least	But less than	0	1	2	3	4	5	6	7	8	9	10
		The amount of income tax to be withheld is—										
$0	$105	0	0	0	0	0	0	0	0	0	0	0
105	110	1	0	0	0	0	0	0	0	0	0	0
110	115	1	0	0	0	0	0	0	0	0	0	0
115	120	2	0	0	0	0	0	0	0	0	0	0
120	125	2	0	0	0	0	0	0	0	0	0	0
700	720	77	59	41	24	12	0	0	0	0	0	0
720	740	80	62	44	26	14	1	0	0	0	0	0
740	760	83	65	47	28	16	3	0	0	0	0	0
760	780	86	68	50	31	18	5	0	0	0	0	0
780	800	89	71	53	34	20	7	0	0	0	0	0

NOTE: The shaded bars show how a deduction of $68.00 would be determined for an employee who earned $774.00 during the pay period. The time card illustrated on *page 120 in this Student Reference Book* shows that Employee No. 1 (Gwen Belue) earned $774.00 and claimed 1 exemption. The horizontal bar highlights wages that fall within the range of *At least $760.00 But less than $780.00*. The vertical bar highlights the *1-exemption* column. The amount at this point of intersection is $68.00, the total that should be withheld from this employee's paycheck.

5. Complete the DEDUCTIONS section of the payroll register.

If you are preparing your payroll register manually

a. Use the Federal Income Tax Withholding Table on *pages 131 and 132 in this Student Reference Book* to find the Federal Withholding Tax for each employee. (The illustration on *page 127 in this Student Reference Book* explains how to use the Federal Income Tax Withholding Table.) Record the amount to be withheld in the Federal Withholding Tax column.

b. Find the State Withholding Tax for each employee. Multiply the gross pay times 6% (0.06) and record the amount in the State Withholding Tax column.

c. Find the City Withholding Tax for each employee. Multiply the gross pay times 2% (0.02) and record the amount in the City Withholding Tax column.

d. Find the Medicare Tax for each employee. Multiply the gross pay times 1.45% (0.0145) and record the amount in the Medicare Tax column.

e. Find the Social Security Tax for each employee. Multiply the gross pay times 6.2% (0.062) and record the amount in the Social Security Tax column.

f. Look at each employee's time card to determine if an employee has Health Insurance and record the amount in the Health Insurance column.

g. Look at each employee's time card to determine if an employee has claimed an additional deduction under Other Deduction and record the amount in the Other Deduction column.

h. Find the total deductions for each employee. Add all amounts recorded in the previous columns of the DEDUCTIONS section. Record the total deductions in the Total Deductions column.

If you are preparing your payroll register electronically

a. Look at the Federal Withholding, State Withholding, City Withholding, Medicare, and Social Security tax columns. These totals are calculated automatically.

b. Look at the Health Insurance entry on each time card. For each time card that lists Health Insurance, check the Health Insurance box on the payroll register.

c. Look again at the time cards. Check to see if any employee claimed an additional deduction under Other Deduction. Record additional amounts for other deductions on the payroll register.

d. Look at the Total Deductions column. This total is calculated automatically.

6. Complete the NET PAY and TOTALS sections of the payroll register.

 If you are preparing your payroll manually
   a. Find the net pay for each employee. Subtract the Total Deductions from the Gross Pay. Record that amount in the NET PAY column of the payroll register.
   b. Total all payroll register columns containing figures. Add each column at least twice to make sure the total is correct before you record it on the TOTALS line at the bottom of each column.

 If you are preparing your payroll electronically
   a. Look at the NET PAY column. Net pay is calculated automatically.
   b. Look at the TOTALS columns. All totals columns are calculated automatically.

7. Check the accuracy of your work.

 If you are preparing your payroll manually, ask yourself
   a. Does the Total Deductions column equal the sum of the totals of all columns in the DEDUCTIONS section?
   b. When the totals of the NET PAY and Total Deductions columns are added together, does that new total equal the total of the Gross Pay column?

 If you are preparing your payroll electronically
   a. Compare the information on the time cards to the entries made on the payroll register. Be sure all information has been correctly transferred from the time cards to the payroll register.
   b. Print 1 copy of your payroll register. Save your work.

Ask your Instructor to check your payroll register for accuracy. Do not continue in your *DAILY ACTIVITIES* until your Instructor has checked your payroll register.

8. Ask your Instructor to initial your payroll register to show that the payroll register is completely accurate.

9. Remove the checkbook from the Cash File.
   a. Write a check for the total of the NET PAY column. On the line marked PAY TO THE ORDER OF, write the word *Cash*. Record the word *Payroll* on the line marked FOR on the check *and* under the DESCRIPTION column of the check register.
   b. Return the checkbook to the Cash File.
   c. Write *Paid by Check No.* ___ across the front of the payroll register.
   d. Place the payroll register and the time cards in the Office File.

10. Record the payment by check in the cashbook. If necessary, turn to *page 58 in this Student Reference Book*. Complete the steps there for recording cash payments by check. Record *Payroll* in the EXPLANATION column of the cashbook.

11. Take the check for the payroll to Pettisville Bank. No cash will actually be given to you. For this simulation, you must assume that you received the cash and that you paid your employees in cash.

CHECKPOINT

Understanding Payroll

Answer the following questions.

1. Federal withholding tax, state withholding tax, city withholding tax, Medicare tax, and Social Security tax, are examples of payroll _____.

2. Many people choose to pay their _____ through their employer.

3. Payroll may be transferred electronically through the banking system with the use of _____.

4. An employee may earn wages based on _____ hours or _____ hours worked.

5. The amount a person receives after taxes and other deductions are withheld is called _____.

Doing Business on the 'Net

Online Payroll

Because preparing payroll is a time-consuming task, some companies use an outside payroll service available over the Internet. The employer signs up for the service and provides all the necessary information about its employees. To process payroll, the employer accesses a secure web site and provides the employees' regular and overtime hours and any special deductions. Typical services include

❏ direct deposit of employee earnings

❏ filing of state and federal tax returns

❏ preparation of earnings statements and pay stubs

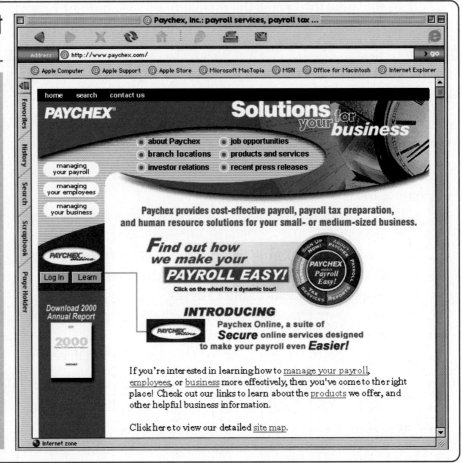

SINGLE Persons—BIWEEKLY Payroll Period
(For Wages Paid in 20 —)

If the wages are—		And the number of withholding allowances claimed is—										
At least	But less than	0	1	2	3	4	5	6	7	8	9	10
		The amount of income tax to be withheld is—										
$0	$105	$0	$0	$0	$0	$0	$0	$0	$0	$0	$0	$0
105	110	1	0	0	0	0	0	0	0	0	0	0
110	115	1	0	0	0	0	0	0	0	0	0	0
115	120	2	0	0	0	0	0	0	0	0	0	0
120	125	2	0	0	0	0	0	0	0	0	0	0
125	130	3	0	0	0	0	0	0	0	0	0	0
130	135	3	0	0	0	0	0	0	0	0	0	0
135	140	4	0	0	0	0	0	0	0	0	0	0
140	145	4	0	0	0	0	0	0	0	0	0	0
145	150	5	0	0	0	0	0	0	0	0	0	0
150	155	5	0	0	0	0	0	0	0	0	0	0
155	160	6	0	0	0	0	0	0	0	0	0	0
160	165	6	0	0	0	0	0	0	0	0	0	0
165	170	7	0	0	0	0	0	0	0	0	0	0
170	175	7	0	0	0	0	0	0	0	0	0	0
175	180	8	0	0	0	0	0	0	0	0	0	0
180	185	8	0	0	0	0	0	0	0	0	0	0
185	190	9	0	0	0	0	0	0	0	0	0	0
190	195	9	0	0	0	0	0	0	0	0	0	0
195	200	10	0	0	0	0	0	0	0	0	0	0
200	205	10	0	0	0	0	0	0	0	0	0	0
205	210	11	0	0	0	0	0	0	0	0	0	0
210	215	11	0	0	0	0	0	0	0	0	0	0
215	220	12	0	0	0	0	0	0	0	0	0	0
220	225	12	0	0	0	0	0	0	0	0	0	0
225	230	13	0	0	0	0	0	0	0	0	0	0
230	235	13	1	0	0	0	0	0	0	0	0	0
235	240	14	1	0	0	0	0	0	0	0	0	0
240	245	14	2	0	0	0	0	0	0	0	0	0
245	250	15	2	0	0	0	0	0	0	0	0	0
250	260	15	3	0	0	0	0	0	0	0	0	0
260	270	16	4	0	0	0	0	0	0	0	0	0
270	280	17	5	0	0	0	0	0	0	0	0	0
280	290	18	6	0	0	0	0	0	0	0	0	0
290	300	19	7	0	0	0	0	0	0	0	0	0
300	310	20	8	0	0	0	0	0	0	0	0	0
310	320	21	9	0	0	0	0	0	0	0	0	0
320	330	22	10	0	0	0	0	0	0	0	0	0
330	340	23	11	0	0	0	0	0	0	0	0	0
340	350	24	12	0	0	0	0	0	0	0	0	0
350	360	25	13	1	0	0	0	0	0	0	0	0
360	370	26	14	2	0	0	0	0	0	0	0	0
370	380	27	15	3	0	0	0	0	0	0	0	0
380	390	29	16	4	0	0	0	0	0	0	0	0
390	400	30	17	5	0	0	0	0	0	0	0	0
400	410	32	18	6	0	0	0	0	0	0	0	0
410	420	33	19	7	0	0	0	0	0	0	0	0
420	430	35	20	8	0	0	0	0	0	0	0	0
430	440	36	21	9	0	0	0	0	0	0	0	0
440	450	38	22	10	0	0	0	0	0	0	0	0
450	460	39	23	11	0	0	0	0	0	0	0	0
460	470	41	24	12	0	0	0	0	0	0	0	0
470	480	42	25	13	0	0	0	0	0	0	0	0
480	490	44	26	14	1	0	0	0	0	0	0	0
490	500	45	27	15	2	0	0	0	0	0	0	0
500	520	47	29	16	4	0	0	0	0	0	0	0
520	540	50	32	18	6	0	0	0	0	0	0	0
540	560	53	35	20	8	0	0	0	0	0	0	0
560	580	56	38	22	10	0	0	0	0	0	0	0
580	600	59	41	24	12	0	0	0	0	0	0	0
600	620	62	44	26	14	2	0	0	0	0	0	0
620	640	65	47	29	16	4	0	0	0	0	0	0
640	660	68	50	32	18	6	0	0	0	0	0	0
660	680	71	53	35	20	8	0	0	0	0	0	0
680	700	74	56	38	22	10	0	0	0	0	0	0
700	720	77	59	41	24	12	0	0	0	0	0	0
720	740	80	62	44	26	14	1	0	0	0	0	0
740	760	83	65	47	28	16	3	0	0	0	0	0
760	780	86	68	50	31	18	5	0	0	0	0	0
780	800	89	71	53	34	20	7	0	0	0	0	0

SINGLE Persons—BIWEEKLY Payroll Period
(For Wages Paid in 20 —)

If the wages are—		And the number of withholding allowances claimed is—										
At least	But less than	0	1	2	3	4	5	6	7	8	9	10
		The amount of income tax to be withheld is—										
$800	$820	$92	$74	$56	$37	$22	$9	$0	$0	$0	$0	$0
820	840	95	77	59	40	24	11	0	0	0	0	0
840	860	98	80	62	43	26	13	1	0	0	0	0
860	880	101	83	65	46	28	15	3	0	0	0	0
880	900	104	86	68	49	31	17	5	0	0	0	0
900	920	107	89	71	52	34	19	7	0	0	0	0
920	940	110	92	74	55	37	21	9	0	0	0	0
940	960	113	95	77	58	40	23	11	0	0	0	0
960	980	116	98	80	61	43	25	13	1	0	0	0
980	1,000	119	101	83	64	46	27	15	3	0	0	0
1,000	1,020	122	104	86	67	49	30	17	5	0	0	0
1,020	1,040	125	107	89	70	52	33	19	7	0	0	0
1,040	1,060	128	110	92	73	55	36	21	9	0	0	0
1,060	1,080	131	113	95	76	58	39	23	11	0	0	0
1,080	1,100	134	116	98	79	61	42	25	13	0	0	0
1,100	1,120	137	119	101	82	64	45	27	15	2	0	0
1,120	1,140	140	122	104	85	67	48	30	17	4	0	0
1,140	1,160	143	125	107	88	70	51	33	19	6	0	0
1,160	1,180	146	128	110	91	73	54	36	21	8	0	0
1,180	1,200	149	131	113	94	76	57	39	23	10	0	0
1,200	1,220	152	134	116	97	79	60	42	25	12	0	0
1,220	1,240	157	137	119	100	82	63	45	27	14	2	0
1,240	1,260	162	140	122	103	85	66	48	29	16	4	0
1,260	1,280	167	143	125	106	88	69	51	32	18	6	0
1,280	1,300	172	146	128	109	91	72	54	35	20	8	0
1,300	1,320	177	149	131	112	94	75	57	38	22	10	0
1,320	1,340	182	152	134	115	97	78	60	41	24	12	0
1,340	1,360	187	157	137	118	100	81	63	44	26	14	2
1,360	1,380	192	162	140	121	103	84	66	47	29	16	4
1,380	1,400	197	167	143	124	106	87	69	50	32	18	6
1,400	1,420	202	172	146	127	109	90	72	53	35	20	8
1,420	1,440	207	177	149	130	112	93	75	56	38	22	10
1,440	1,460	212	182	152	133	115	96	78	59	41	24	12
1,460	1,480	217	187	156	136	118	99	81	62	44	26	14
1,480	1,500	222	192	161	139	121	102	84	65	47	28	16
1,500	1,520	227	197	166	142	124	105	87	68	50	31	18
1,520	1,540	232	202	171	145	127	108	90	71	53	34	20
1,540	1,560	237	207	176	148	130	111	93	74	56	37	22
1,560	1,580	242	212	181	151	133	114	96	77	59	40	24
1,580	1,600	247	217	186	155	136	117	99	80	62	43	26
1,600	1,620	252	222	191	160	139	120	102	83	65	46	28
1,620	1,640	257	227	196	165	142	123	105	86	68	49	31
1,640	1,660	262	232	201	170	145	126	108	89	71	52	34
1,660	1,680	267	237	206	175	148	129	111	92	74	55	37
1,680	1,700	272	242	211	180	151	132	114	95	77	58	40
1,700	1,720	277	247	216	185	154	135	117	98	80	61	43
1,720	1,740	282	252	221	190	159	138	120	101	83	64	46
1,740	1,760	287	257	226	195	164	141	123	104	86	67	49
1,760	1,780	292	262	231	200	169	144	126	107	89	70	52
1,780	1,800	297	267	236	205	174	147	129	110	92	73	55
1,800	1,820	302	272	241	210	179	150	132	113	95	76	58
1,820	1,840	307	277	246	215	184	153	135	116	98	79	61
1,840	1,860	312	282	251	220	189	158	138	119	101	82	64
1,860	1,880	317	287	256	225	194	163	141	122	104	85	67
1,880	1,900	322	292	261	230	199	168	144	125	107	88	70
1,900	1,920	327	297	266	235	204	173	147	128	110	91	73
1,920	1,940	332	302	271	240	209	178	150	131	113	94	76
1,940	1,960	337	307	276	245	214	183	153	134	116	97	79
1,960	1,980	342	312	281	250	219	188	158	137	119	100	82
1,980	2,000	347	317	286	255	224	193	163	140	122	103	85
2,000	2,020	352	322	291	260	229	198	168	143	125	106	88
2,020	2,040	357	327	296	265	234	203	173	146	128	109	91
2,040	2,060	362	332	301	270	239	208	178	149	131	112	94
2,060	2,080	367	337	306	275	244	213	183	152	134	115	97
2,080	2,100	372	342	311	280	249	218	188	157	137	118	100

2,100 and over   Biweekly wages over 2,100 are not used in the Mean Jeans Business Simulation.

UNIT 3 • PAYROLL

PAYING FEDERAL WITHHOLDING AND FICA TAXES

©GETTY IMAGES/PHOTODISC

Employers are responsible for collecting federal income and FICA taxes from each employee. The federal income tax is based upon (1) the total amount of earnings and (2) the number of exemptions claimed on the Employee's Withholding Allowance Certificate (W-4).

Exemptions are the number of allowances an employee claims for himself or herself plus his or her dependents. The **Employee's Withholding Allowance Certificate (W-4)** is a form used by employers to determine the amount of income tax to withhold for the Internal Revenue Service (IRS). The employee completes it when he or she is first hired.

FICA (Federal Insurance Contributions Act) is the law that requires workers to contribute to Social Security and Medicare. *Social Security* tax provides assistance to persons who are faced with old age, disability, or unemployment. *Medicare* tax reimburses hospitals and physicians for medical care to qualified people over 65 years old.

©GETTY IMAGES/PHOTODISC

Only one-half of the premium for the employee's FICA tax is withheld from the wages of the employee. The employer must pay the other one-half of the premium. To find the total of the FICA tax to be paid to the Internal Revenue Service, multiply by 2 the total of the Medicare and Social Security tax columns on the payroll register.

Many businesses pay their federal withholding and FICA taxes electronically through a program called *EFTPS*, the Electronic Federal Tax Payment System. Your business will use a Federal Tax Deposit Coupon when paying federal income and FICA withholding taxes. A **Federal Tax Deposit Coupon** is a form used to transfer taxes withheld through a local bank to the Internal Revenue Service. Rather than send payments directly to the IRS, you will take your payment to Pettisville Bank. The bank serves as a depository for the Internal Revenue Service by collecting tax payments and then forwarding them to the IRS.

©GETTY IMAGES/PHOTODISC

©GETTY IMAGES/PHOTODISC

The amount of the federal income and FICA withholding taxes to be deposited is based on the totals from the payroll register. It is calculated as follows.

Total Federal Withholding	+	Total Medicare × 2	+	Total Social Security × 2
$551.00	+	$ 73.63 × 2	+	$314.83 × 2
$551.00	+	$147.26	+	$629.66
$551.00	+	$776.92		

The total deposit to the IRS is $1,327.92.

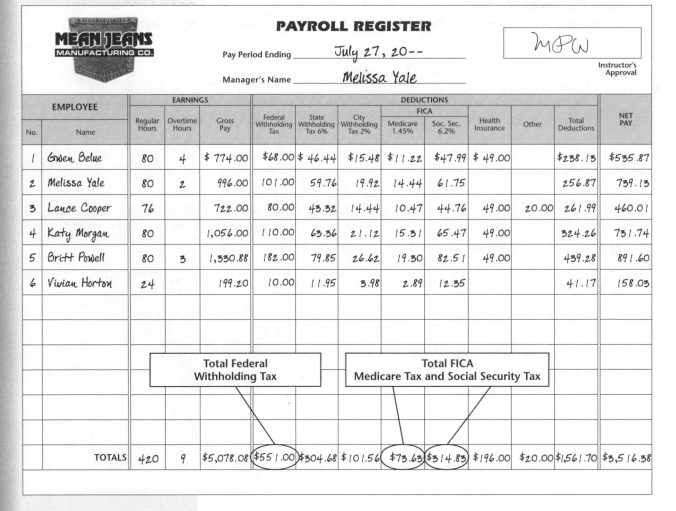

PAYROLL REGISTER

Pay Period Ending _____ July 27, 20-- _____

Manager's Name _____ Melissa Yale _____

Instructor's Approval

No.	Name	Regular Hours	Overtime Hours	Gross Pay	Federal Withholding Tax	State Withholding Tax 6%	City Withholding Tax 2%	Medicare 1.45%	Soc. Sec. 6.2%	Health Insurance	Other	Total Deductions	NET PAY
1	Gwen Belue	80	4	$ 774.00	$68.00	$ 46.44	$15.48	$11.22	$47.99	$ 49.00		$238.13	$535.87
2	Melissa Yale	80	2	996.00	101.00	59.76	19.92	14.44	61.75			256.87	739.13
3	Lance Cooper	76		722.00	80.00	43.32	14.44	10.47	44.76	49.00	20.00	261.99	460.01
4	Katy Morgan	80		1,056.00	110.00	63.36	21.12	15.31	65.47	49.00		324.26	731.74
5	Britt Powell	80	3	1,330.88	182.00	79.85	26.62	19.30	82.51	49.00		439.28	891.60
6	Vivian Horton	24		199.20	10.00	11.95	3.98	2.89	12.35			41.17	158.03
	TOTALS	420	9	$5,078.08	$551.00	$304.68	$101.56	$73.63	$314.83	$196.00	$20.00	$1,561.70	$3,516.38

Total Federal Withholding Tax

Total FICA Medicare Tax and Social Security Tax

Follow these steps when paying federal income and FICA withholding taxes

1. Remove the payroll register from the Office File.

2. Find the column titled FICA on the payroll register. Multiply the total of the Medicare tax times 2. Then multiply the total of the Social Security tax times 2. Next, find the total of the federal withholding tax on your payroll register. Add these three amounts to find the total tax owed to the IRS.

   • Record the total tax owed for the payroll ending July 13: $_____

   • Record the total tax owed for the payroll ending July 27: $_____

3. Find the Federal Tax Deposit Coupon. (If this is the second time you have prepared the tax deposit, use the Federal Tax Deposit Coupon you placed in the Supplies folder.)

Caution!

Don't let the word *deposit* on the Federal Tax Deposit Coupon confuse you. You are placing the money on deposit for the Internal Revenue Service. The IRS is receiving the deposit, and you are making the payment!

 *If you are using Instructor-provided forms,* remove the sheet of 2 Federal Tax Deposit Coupons from your Supplies folder.

If you are printing your forms, open the forms document. Find Unit 3 Payroll. Print the sheet of 2 Federal Tax Deposit Coupons.

---

4. Use scissors to remove one of the forms from the sheet. Place the extra form in your Supplies folder.

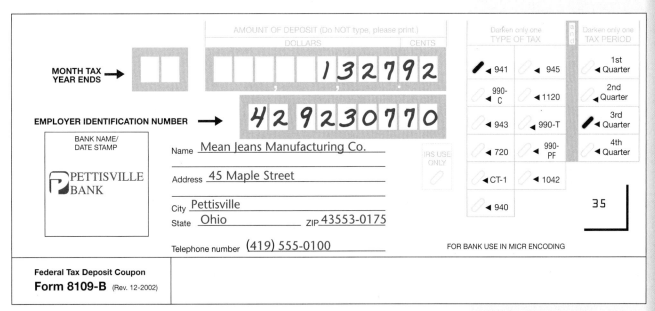

5. Use a #2 pencil to complete the Federal Tax Deposit Coupon so that optical scanning equipment will be able to read the AMOUNT OF DEPOSIT, TYPE OF TAX, and TAX PERIOD on the coupon.

 a. Under AMOUNT OF DEPOSIT, write in pencil the amount of your payment. (This is the total you added in step 2.)

 b. Under TYPE OF TAX, use your pencil to darken *941*.

 c. Under TAX PERIOD, use your pencil to darken the quarter of your payment. If you are making a payment for payroll taxes withheld during June, you will darken *2nd Quarter*. If you are making a payment for payroll taxes withheld during July, you will darken *3rd Quarter*.

 d. Write the telephone number for your business at the bottom of the coupon.

6. Prepare a check for the amount of the payment. Make the check payable to the *Internal Revenue Service*. On the FOR line of the check, record *Fed. Inc. & FICA Taxes*.

7. Record the payment in your cashbook. Turn to *page 58 in this Student Reference Book*. Complete the steps titled *Follow these steps when recording cash payments (by check) in the cashbook*. When you come to step 3, record *Fed. Inc. & FICA Taxes* in the EXPLANATION column of the cashbook.

8. Paper clip the check to the completed Federal Tax Deposit Coupon.

9. Walk to the bank to pay the withholding taxes. Do not use the drive-in window. You must deal directly with the bank manager.

10. Return to your place of business. File the bank receipt for the withholding tax deposit in the Office File.

CHECKPOINT

Paying Payroll Taxes

Answer the following questions.

1. What is commonly called FICA is the deduction that includes both _Social Security_ taxes and _Medicare_ taxes.

2. A married man with two children may claim a total of _____ exemptions.

3. The _____ completes the Employee's Withholding Allowance Certificate (W-4).

4. If a company's total employee tax for federal withholding is $806, the total employee tax for Medicare is $110, and the employee tax for Social Security is $460, then the total amount owed by the company to the IRS is $_____.

5. In the model business community, _____ is a depository for the Internal Revenue Service.

UNIT SUMMARY

1. Businesses use time clocks and time cards to keep accurate records of employee time spent on the job.

2. Employee overtime is computed at one and one-half the regular rate of pay.

3. A regular workday is 8 hours, and a regular workweek is 40 hours.

LESSON 3•1 PREPARING TIME CARDS

4. The information for completing a payroll register is taken from the employee time cards.

5. When a business uses electronic funds transfer for payroll, the bank adds the amount earned to each employee's account at the bank and subtracts that amount from the company's account at the bank.

6. Examples of payroll deductions are federal withholding tax, state withholding tax, city withholding tax, FICA (Social Security tax and Medicare tax), and health insurance.

7. Many employees pay for their health insurance through payroll deductions.

8. An employee's federal income tax withheld is based on the gross pay earned and the number of exemptions claimed by the employee.

9. An employee's net pay is determined by subtracting the total of the deductions from the gross pay.

LESSON 3•2 COMPLETING A PAYROLL REGISTER

10. An employee may claim one exemption for self plus one exemption for each of his or her dependents.

11. The Internal Revenue Service is the U.S. government agency that collects federal income and FICA taxes.

12. Employers must pay one-half of the employee's FICA tax.

13. When a new employee is hired, he or she must complete an Employee's Withholding Allowance Certificate (W-4).

LESSON 3•3 PAYING FEDERAL WITHHOLDING AND FICA TAXES

electronic funds transfer (EFT)	a way in which money is moved electronically from one account or bank to another
Employee's Withholding Allowance Certificate (W-4)	a form used by employers to determine the amount of income tax to withhold for the Internal Revenue Service
exemptions	the number of allowances an employee claims for self plus dependents that determines the amount of income tax withheld from the paycheck
Federal Tax Deposit Coupon	a form used to transfer taxes withheld through a local bank to the Internal Revenue Service
FICA (Federal Insurance Contributions Act)	the law that requires workers to contribute to Social Security and Medicare
gross pay	the amount a person receives before taxes and other deductions are withheld from the paycheck
net pay	the amount a person receives after taxes and other deductions are withheld from the paycheck
overtime	time worked past the regular 8-hour workday or 40-hour workweek
payroll register	a business form listing gross pay, deductions, and net pay for each employee in a business
time card	a record of one employee's time spent on the job

INTERNET EXPLORATIONS

1. There are some excellent software programs available that enable small businesses to manage their payroll. Check these out.
   a. *www.myob.com*
   b. *www.quickbooks.com*
   c. *www.quicken.com*
   d. *www.peachtree.com*

2. Many companies use outside companies to manage their payroll for them. Go to the following sites. What services are offered?
   a. *www.adp.com*
   b. *www.paychex.com*
   c. *www.surepayroll.com*
   d. *www.virtualpayroll.com*
   e. *www.prioritypay.com*
   f. *www.telepayroll.com*

3. Don't forget books as a valuable source of information. Go the the following sites and search for titles on the subject of payroll.
   a. *www.bn.com*
   b. *www.borders.com*

UNIT 3 • PAYROLL

ACTIVITY 3•1 PREPARING TIME CARDS

Directions: Assume you are the manager of Mean Jeans Manufacturing Co. You will complete 9 time cards in preparation for the pay period ending July 27, 20––. Look at the 3 time cards below and the 6 time cards on the back of this sheet. Notice that the top portion of each card is complete. Now look at the middle portion of each card. The time and hours for each day have already been recorded. You will total the regular and overtime hours on the 9 cards. You will then complete the bottom portion of each of the 9 cards.

1. Turn to *page 122 in this Student Reference Book*. Find the steps titled *Follow these steps when you add a new employee to the payroll.* **Complete step 3c only.** List the following regular hourly rates on the time cards.

   Time Card No. 1 – $8.00   Time Card No. 2 – $ 7.00   Time Card No. 3 – $10.60
   Time Card No. 4 – $9.40   Time Card No. 5 – $ 7.20   Time Card No. 6 – $ 8.50
   Time Card No. 7 – $9.70   Time Card No. 8 – $10.30   Time Card No. 9 – $12.78

2. Add the figures in the TOTAL REG. column of each time card. Record the TOTAL. Write the same figure under HOURS (REGULAR) at the bottom of each card, then multiply by the RATE to find the AMOUNT.

3. Add the figures in the TOTAL OT column of each time card. Record the TOTAL. Write the same figure under HOURS (OVERTIME) at the bottom of each card, then multiply by the RATE to find the AMOUNT. Record the TOTAL HOURS and GROSS PAY.

UNIT 3 • PAYROLL

regular rate × 1.5 = overtime rate

TIME CARD
Mean Jeans Mfg. Co. EMPLOYEE NO. 4

PAY PERIOD ENDING July 27, 20--
NAME Domenic Esposito
SOCIAL SECURITY NO. 268-87-4472
MARITAL STATUS ✓ S ___ M EXEMPTIONS 1
Heath Insurance $49.00   Other Deduction $ ___

DATE	REGULAR HOURS		OVERTIME HOURS		TOTAL REG.	TOTAL OT
	IN	OUT	IN	OUT		
7-16	7:58	12:01			8	
	12:58	5:00				
7-17	7:57	12:00			8	4
	12:59	5:05	6:00	10:01		
7-18	7:59	12:03			8	
	12:58	5:00				
7-19	8:00	11:57			8	
	1:00	5:04				
7-20	7:56	12:01			8	
	12:58	5:00				
7-23	7:58	11:58			8	1
	12:59	5:00	5:00	6:00		
7-24	8:00	12:00			8	
	12:56	5:02				
7-25	7:59	12:00			8	
	12:56	5:02				
7-26	7:59	12:00			8	
	12:57	5:01				
7-27	7:56	11:57			8	
	12:58	5:01				
				TOTAL	80	5

	HOURS	RATE	AMOUNT
REGULAR	80	$9.40	$752.00
OVERTIME	5	$14.10	$70.50
TOTAL HOURS	85	GROSS PAY	$822.50

TIME CARD
Mean Jeans Mfg. Co. EMPLOYEE NO. 5

PAY PERIOD ENDING July 27, 20--
NAME Melissa Yale
SOCIAL SECURITY NO. 487-83-9255
MARITAL STATUS ✓ S ___ M EXEMPTIONS 1
Heath Insurance $49.00   Other Deduction $ ___

DATE	REGULAR HOURS		OVERTIME HOURS		TOTAL REG.	TOTAL OT
	IN	OUT	IN	OUT		
7-16	8:00	12:01			8	3
	12:59	5:00	6:00	9:00		
7-17	7:58	12:05			8	3
	1:01	5:02	5:59	9:02		
7-18	7:59	12:00			8	2
	12:58	5:00	5:58	8:03		
7-19	8:01	12:02			8	3
	1:01	5:04	6:00	9:02		
7-20	8:00	11:59			8	3
	1:00	5:02	6:01	9:03		
7-23	7:59	12:00			8	2
	12:58	5:00	5:59	7:59		
7-24	7:57	12:01			8	2.5
	1:00	5:01	6:02	8:35		
7-25	8:01	12:00			8	2
	12:57	5:01	6:30	8:32		
7-26	8:00	11:59			8	3
	12:59	5:01	5:59	9:01		
7-27	7:58	12:04			8	3
	12:56	5:00	5:58	8:59		
				TOTAL	80	26.5

	HOURS	RATE	AMOUNT
REGULAR	80	$7.20	$576.00
OVERTIME	26.5	$10.80	$286.20
TOTAL HOURS	106.5	GROSS PAY	$862.20

TIME CARD
Mean Jeans Mfg. Co. EMPLOYEE NO. 6

PAY PERIOD ENDING July 27, 20--
NAME Stan Tullos
SOCIAL SECURITY NO. 268-43-3963
MARITAL STATUS ✓ S ___ M EXEMPTIONS 0
Heath Insurance $49.00   Other Deduction $ ___

DATE	REGULAR HOURS		OVERTIME HOURS		TOTAL REG.	TOTAL OT
	IN	OUT	IN	OUT		
7-16	7:58	12:01			8	3
	12:58	5:05	6:05	9:08		
7-17	8:00	12:00			8	1
	1:00	5:00	6:00	7:00		
7-18	7:59	12:05			8	2
	12:55	5:00	5:00	7:02		
7-19	7:55	12:00			8	
	12:58	5:00				
7-20	8:00	12:03			8	
	12:59	5:04				
7-23	7:58	12:04			8	
	1:00	5:04				
7-24	7:56	12:00			8	
	12:58	5:02				
7-25	7:59	12:05			8	
	12:57	5:00				
7-26	8:00	12:02			8	
	12:59	5:02				
7-27	Sick Leave				8	
				TOTAL	80	6

	HOURS	RATE	AMOUNT
REGULAR	80	$8.50	$680.00
OVERTIME	6	$12.75	$76.50
TOTAL HOURS	86	GROSS PAY	$756.50

TIME CARD
Mean Jeans Mfg. Co EMPLOYEE NO. 7

PAY PERIOD ENDING July 27, 20--
NAME Anton Schepp
SOCIAL SECURITY NO. 165-83-8350
MARITAL STATUS ✓ S ___ M EXEMPTIONS 1
Heath Insurance $ ___   Other Deduction $25.00

DATE	REGULAR HOURS		OVERTIME HOURS		TOTAL REG.	TOTAL OT
	IN	OUT	IN	OUT		
7-16	8:00	11:58			8	
	12:55	5:02				
7-17	7:58	12:04			7	
	1:00	4:00				
7-18	8:00	12:00			8	
	12:59	5:00				
7-19	7:57	12:00			7	
	1:00	4:05				
7-20	7:55	12:05			8	
	12:57	5:02				
7-23	7:59	12:02			8	
	12:56	5:00				
7-24	8:00	11:59			7	
	12:59	4:00				
7-25	7:55	12:04			8	
	1:00	5:02				
7-26	7:58	12:02			7	
	1:00	4:04				
7-27	8:01	12:00			8	
	12:55	5:00				
				TOTAL	76	0

	HOURS	RATE	AMOUNT
REGULAR	76	$9.70	$737.20
OVERTIME	0	$0.00	$0.00
TOTAL HOURS	76	GROSS PAY	$737.20

TIME CARD
Mean Jeans Mfg. Co EMPLOYEE NO. 8

PAY PERIOD ENDING July 27, 20--
NAME Lakisha Anderson
SOCIAL SECURITY NO. 298-97-7124
MARITAL STATUS ✓ S ___ M EXEMPTIONS 0
Heath Insurance $49.00   Other Deduction $ ___

DATE	REGULAR HOURS		OVERTIME HOURS		TOTAL REG.	TOTAL OT
	IN	OUT	IN	OUT		
7-16	8:00	12:01			8	
	12:59	5:00				
7-17	7:58	12:05			8	3
	1:01	5:02	5:59	9:02		
7-18	7:59	12:00			8	2
	12:58	5:00	5:58	8:03		
7-19	8:01	12:02			8	
	1:01	5:04				
7-20	8:00	11:59			8	3
	1:00	5:02	6:01	9:03		
7-23	7:59	12:00			8	2
	12:58	5:00	5:59	7:59		
7-24	7:57	12:01			8	
	1:00	5:01				
7-25	8:01	12:00			8	
	12:57	5:01				
7-26	8:00	11:59			8	3
	12:59	5:01	5:59	9:01		
7-27	7:58	12:04			8	
	12:56	5:00				
				TOTAL	80	13

	HOURS	RATE	AMOUNT
REGULAR	80	$10.30	$824.00
OVERTIME	13	$15.45	$200.85
TOTAL HOURS	43	GROSS PAY	$1024.85

TIME CARD
Mean Jeans Mfg. Co EMPLOYEE NO. 9

PAY PERIOD ENDING July 27, 20--
NAME Trent Taylor
SOCIAL SECURITY NO. 347-75-9182
MARITAL STATUS ✓ S ___ M EXEMPTIONS 0
Heath Insurance $ ___   Other Deduction $ ___

DATE	REGULAR HOURS		OVERTIME HOURS		TOTAL REG.	TOTAL OT
	IN	OUT	IN	OUT		
7-16	8:00	11:58			6	
	1:00	3:02				
7-17	7:58	12:00			6	
	1:01	3:05				
7-18	7:55	11:59			6	
	12:58	3:00				
7-19	8:01	12:02			6	
	12:58	3:01				
7-20	8:00	12:00			6	
	1:01	3:03				
7-23	7:56	12:00			6	
	1:01	3:00				
7-24	8:00	12:01			6	
	12:59	3:00				
7-25	7:58	12:01			6	
	12:59	2:59				
7-26	7:59	12:01			6	
	1:00	3:04				
7-27	8:00	12:00			6	
	1:00	3:03				
				TOTAL	60	0

	HOURS	RATE	AMOUNT
REGULAR	60	$12.78	$766.80
OVERTIME	0	$0.00	$0.00
TOTAL HOURS	60	GROSS PAY	$766.80

ACTIVITY 3·2 COMPLETING A PAYROLL REGISTER

Directions: Assume you are the manager of Mean Jeans Manufacturing Co. You have just hired a new employee and must add the new employee to the payroll. You will use the 9 time cards in Activity 3.1 and the time card for the new employee (below) to prepare a payroll register for the pay period ending July 27, 20––.

1. Use the time card at right to add a new employee to your payroll. On July 27 you hired Carol Ann Logan as a sewing machine operator. Record on the date line of 7-27 the regular hours worked (8:00 a.m. to 12:01 p.m. and 1:00 p.m. to 5:02 p.m.). Record the TOTAL REG. hours worked (8). Bring down the total hours for 7-27 to the TOTAL line. No overtime was worked.

2. Complete the bottom portion of the time card. Record the number of REGULAR HOURS. Multiply the regular hours times the rate to find the amount. Record the TOTAL HOURS and GROSS PAY.

3. Prepare a payroll register for your 10 employees. Use the time cards you prepared in Activity 3.1 and Time Card No. 10 at the right. Turn to *page 127 in this Student Reference Book*. Find the steps titled *Follow these steps when preparing a payroll register*. **Complete steps 3 through 7.**

TIME CARD
Mean Jeans Mfg. Co.   EMPLOYEE NO. 10

PAY PERIOD ENDING ___July 27, 20--___
NAME ___Carol Ann Logan___
SOCIAL SECURITY NO. ___465-02-2314___
MARITAL STATUS ✓ S ___ M EXEMPTIONS 0
Heath Insurance $___—___   Other Deduction $___—___

DATE	REGULAR HOURS		OVERTIME HOURS		TOTAL REG.	TOTAL OT
	IN	OUT	IN	OUT		
7-16						
7-17						
7-18						
7-19						
7-20						
7-23						
7-24						
7-25						
7-26						
7-27	8:00 1:00	12:01 5:02			8	
TOTAL					8	0

	HOURS	RATE	AMOUNT
REGULAR	8	$13.30	$106.40
OVERTIME	0	$19.95	$000.00
TOTAL HOURS	8	GROSS PAY	$106.40

UNIT 3 · PAYROLL

MEAN JEANS MANUFACTURING CO.

PAYROLL REGISTER

Pay Period Ending: July 27, 2007

Manager's Name: Devin Kuchynka

Instructor's Approval: CW

use chart

EMPLOYEE		EARNINGS			DEDUCTIONS			FICA		Health Insurance	Other	Total Deductions	NET PAY
No.	Name	Regular Hours	Overtime Hours	Gross Pay	Federal Withholding Tax	State Withholding Tax 6%	City Withholding Tax 2%	Medicare 1.45%	Soc. Sec. 6.2%				
1	Ouida Lampert	80	5	$700.00	$7.00	$42.00	$14.00	$10.15	$43.40	$44.00	$0.00	$285.55	$464.45
2	Gwen Jamie	76	0	$532.00	$50.00	$31.92	$10.64	$7.71	$32.98	$0.00	$0.00	$153.25	$378.75
3	Bikram Moriarity	80	20	$1166.00	$128.00	$69.96	$23.32	$16.91	$72.29	$49.00	$0.00	$359.48	$806.52
4	Domenic Esposito	80	5	$822.50	$77.00	$49.35	$16.45	$11.93	$50.99	$44.00	$0.00	$254.71	$567.79
5	Melissa Yale	80	26.5	$862.20	$83.00	$51.73	$17.24	$12.50	$53.45	$19.00	$0.00	$236.92	$625.28
6	Stan Tullos	80	6	$756.50	$83.00	$45.39	$15.13	$10.96	$46.90	$49.00	$0.00	$250.38	$506.12
7	Anton Schepp	76	0	$737.30	$62.00	$44.24	$14.74	$10.69	$45.71	$0.00	$0.00	$208.35	$534.85
8	LaKisha Anderson	80	13	$1004.85	$125.00	$60.49	$20.49	$14.82	$63.54	$44.00	$0.00	$331.38	$1090.47
9	Trent Taylor	60	0	$766.80	$86.00	$46.01	$15.34	$11.12	$47.54	$0.00	$0.00	$206.01	$520.79
10	Carol Ann Loggi	8	0	$106.40	$1.00	$6.38	$2.13	$1.54	$6.59	$0.00	$0.00	$17.64	$88.76
	TOTALS	700	75.5	$7474.45	$772.5	$448.48	$149.48	$108.35	$463.29	$294	$45	$2280.00	$5193.78

Name	Evaluation

ACTIVITY 3·3 PAYING FEDERAL WITHHOLDING AND FICA TAXES

Directions: Assume that today is July 27. As manager of Nouveau Invesment Company, you completed the payroll register at the bottom of this page. You must now pay the federal income and FICA taxes owed to the Internal Revenue Service.

1. Turn to *page 135 in this Student Reference Book*. Find the steps titled *Follow these steps when paying federal income and FICA withholding taxes*. **Complete step 2.**

   • Record the total tax owed for this pay period. $ _216.20_

2. Use the Federal Tax Deposit Coupon on the back of this sheet to **complete step 5** on *page 136 in this Student Reference Book*. When you come to step 5d, write the telephone number of Nouveau as (419) 555-0134.

3. Use the check and cashbook on the back of this sheet to **complete steps 6 and 7** on *page 136 in this Student Reference Book*.

PAYROLL REGISTER

NOUVEAU INVESTMENT COMPANY

Pay Period Ending July 27, 20--
Manager's Name Gabe Sirmans

Instructor's Approval: MPW

No.	Name	Regular Hours	Overtime Hours	Gross Pay	Federal Withholding Tax	State Withholding Tax 6%	City Withholding Tax 2%	Medicare 1.45%	Soc. Sec. 6.2%	Health Insurance	Other	Total Deductions	NET PAY
1	Gabe Sirmans	80	4	$729.00	$62.00	$43.74	$14.58	$10.57	$45.19	$49.00		$225.08	$503.92
2	Brandi Watkins	56		492.00	27.00	29.52	9.84	7.13	30.50	49.00		152.99	339.01
3	Tinicia Redmon	80		1,270.00	143.00	76.20	25.40	18.42	78.74	49.00		390.76	879.24
4	Amber Raney	80	1	960.00	98.00	57.60	19.20	13.92	59.52		50.00	298.24	661.76
5	Cathy Malone	72		561.00	56.00	33.66	11.22	8.13	34.78	49.00		192.79	368.21
6	Newman Sanchez	80	2	872.00	83.00	52.32	17.44	12.64	54.06			219.46	652.54
	TOTALS	448	7	$4,884.00	$469.00	$293.04	$97.68	$70.81	$302.79	$196.00	$50.00	$1,479.32	$3,404.68

UNIT 3 Payroll

UNIT 3 • PAYROLL

143

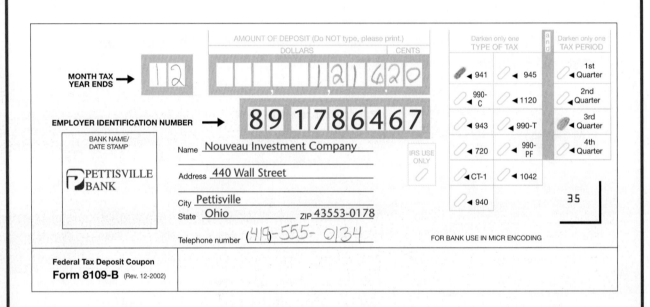

Check

NOUVEAU INVESTMENT COMPANY
440 Wall Street
Pettisville, Ohio
43553-0178

819

56-25/412

DATE 7/27/07

PAY TO THE ORDER OF _Internal Revenue Service_ $ 1216.20

One-Thousand, two-hundred sixteen and 20/100 DOLLARS

FOR SIMULATION USE ONLY

PETTISVILLE BANK
101 Greenback Drive • Pettisville, OH 43553-0178

FOR _Fed. Inc. & FICA Taxes_ _Devin Kuchynka_ MP

⑈000819⑈ ⑆041200257⑆ 404⑈4151⑈

Federal Tax Deposit Coupon

AMOUNT OF DEPOSIT (Do NOT type, please print.)

DOLLARS — CENTS — 121620

MONTH TAX YEAR ENDS → 12

EMPLOYER IDENTIFICATION NUMBER → 89 1786467

Darken only one TYPE OF TAX

◄ 941	◄ 945
◄ 990-C	◄ 1120
◄ 943	◄ 990-T
◄ 720	◄ 990-PF
◄ CT-1	◄ 1042
◄ 940	

Darken only one TAX PERIOD

1st Quarter
2nd Quarter
3rd Quarter
4th Quarter

35

BANK NAME/ DATE STAMP

PETTISVILLE BANK

Name _Nouveau Investment Company_

Address _440 Wall Street_

City _Pettisville_

State _Ohio_ ZIP _43553-0178_

Telephone number _(419-555-0134)_

IRS USE ONLY

FOR BANK USE IN MICR ENCODING

Federal Tax Deposit Coupon
Form 8109-B (Rev. 12-2002)

Cashbook

	CASHBOOK		FIRM _Nouveau Investment Company_					Page ____ of ____	
							RECEIPTS		PAYMENTS
DATE	EXPLANATION	CHECK NO.	CASH IN	CASH OUT	CASH BALANCE	SALES, FEES, COMMISSION, etc.	OTHER	EXPENSES, PURCHASES	MORTGAGE, OTHER
15	July 25 Office Supplies	818		8400	321820 0			8400	15
16	July 26 Cash Sales		432900		365110 0	432900			16
17	July 27 Fed. Inc. & FICA Taxes	819		121620	352448 0			121620	17
18									18
19									19
20									20
21									21
22									22

ACCOUNTS PAYABLE AND RECEIVABLE

Successful managers are involved in all five functions of management—planning, leading, organizing, staffing, and controlling. Many businesses fail because the manager does not take an active role in the area of control. Financial control is a necessary function of management, and no business will be successful for long without it. Cash flow—the money coming into and going out of the company—is the lifeblood of the business.

During the model business community simulation, you will be responsible for preparing purchase orders to buy merchandise from suppliers within the community. You will use the suppliers' published price lists located at the back of this book. When a business that sells merchandise receives a purchase order, that business will ship the goods requested and prepare an item invoice for the customer. However, some businesses sell services rather than merchandise. Those businesses will prepare service invoices to bill their customers. Purchase orders, item invoices, and service invoices may be prepared either manually (by hand) or electronically.

Unit Lessons

Lesson 4•1	**Preparing Purchase Orders**
Lesson 4•2	**Using Item Invoices**
Lesson 4•3	**Using Service Invoices**

Unit Activities

Activity 4•1	**Preparing a Purchase Order**
Activity 4•2	**Ordering Office Supplies**
Activity 4•3	**Invoicing and Shipping**
Activity 4•4	**Preparing a Service Invoice**

PREPARING PURCHASE ORDERS

When a business makes a purchase, it is usually recorded on a purchase order. A **purchase order** is a form used to order merchandise, supplies, or equipment from a supplier. Businesses use purchase orders for two reasons. First, the purchase order grants approval to the person making the purchase. Employees usually must have permission from management before making purchases. Second, it provides a written record of what goods are being purchased, how much they will cost, how the items will be shipped, and what terms have been agreed upon.

The **terms** on a purchase order are the method of payment agreed upon between the buyer and the seller. A purchase made on credit by a business is known as an account payable. **Accounts payable** are amounts of money owed by a business to its suppliers for purchases made but not yet paid for.

Purchase orders are sent to retailers and wholesalers. A **retailer** is a business that

THE DENIM MAKER

752 Gold Mine Lane • Pettisville, OH 43553-0176

PURCHASE ORDER

☑ ORIGINAL ☐ COPY

SUPPLIER
Buckeye Equipment
1313 Olentangy Road
Pettisville, OH 43553-0175

DATE
July 11, 20--

PURCHASE ORDER NO.
5004

SHIP VIA
18 Wheeler Truck Lines

TERMS
Cash upon receipt of invoice

QTY.	CAT. NO.	DESCRIPTION	UNIT PRICE	AMOUNT	
1	16-442	Carpet cleaner, traffic lane pretreatment spray	$53.35	$53	35
3	13-681	Hand soap, liquid	37.60	112	80
		TOTAL ▶		$166.15	

Approved by _____ Jack Parker _____ , Manager

Heading

Body

sells merchandise in small quantities to consumers or the general public. A **wholesaler** is a business that sells merchandise in large quantities to retailers or to other wholesalers. Retailers and wholesalers are also called suppliers because they supply other businesses with their goods.

Notice that the purchase order is divided into two parts. The top part is called the heading, and the main part is called the body. The heading describes the buyer who prepared the purchase order (The Denim Maker) and the supplier who will receive the purchase order (Buckeye Equipment). The heading also shows the DATE, PURCHASE ORDER NO., method of shipment (SHIP VIA), and method of payment (TERMS).

The main part (or body) of the purchase order is made up of five columns: quantity (QTY.), catalog number (CAT. NO.), DESCRIPTION, UNIT PRICE, and AMOUNT. The **unit price** is the price for one item. Look closely at the body of the purchase order in the illustration on the opposite page. Note that two types of items are being ordered. The first item ordered by The Denim Maker is 1 case of carpet cleaner (Catalog No. 16-442). Since only 1 case of carpet cleaner is being ordered, the unit price ($53.35) and the amount ($53.35) are the same. The second item is 3 cases of liquid hand soap (Catalog No. 13-681). The unit price for 1 case of liquid soap is $37.60. The amount for 3 cases of liquid soap is determined by multiplying the quantity times the unit price (3 × $37.60 = $112.80).

After each item has been listed, figures in the amount column are added together to find the total of the purchase order ($166.15). Jack Parker, manager of The Denim Maker, signed the purchase order.

©GETTY IMAGES/PHOTODISC

All businesses in the model community will prepare purchase orders for merchandise ordered from these Pettisville suppliers—Buckeye Equipment, The Clothes Closet, The Denim Maker, Hollywood & Vine Videos, Mean Jeans Manufacturing Co., and Taylor Office Supplies. You will mail your purchase order to the supplier (unless the order is for office supplies), and your supplier will ship the goods to you.

Communities usually have a variety of carriers to transport shipments, such as Roadway Express, United Parcel Service (UPS), FedEx, and the U.S. Postal Service. In the Pettisville business community, orders are shipped via 18 Wheeler Truck Lines or the U.S. Postal Service depending on the weight of the shipment. Your DAILY ACTIVITIES will tell you which shipping method to use.

The procedure for ordering from suppliers is the same except for orders of office supplies. If you are ordering office supplies from Taylor Office Supplies, turn to *page 152 in this Student Reference Book* and follow the steps there for ordering office supplies. For all other orders, follow the steps below.

▨ Follow these steps when preparing a purchase order

1. Find your purchase order.

📋 *If you are preparing your purchase order manually,* remove 1 purchase order from your Supplies folder.

🖱 *If you are preparing your purchase order electronically,* open the purchase order. Use the tab key to move from line to line. You may access information to complete the form by clicking the drop-down menus that appear on the purchase order.

---

2. Complete the top part (the heading) of the purchase order. If necessary, refer to the purchase order illustrated on the next page.
   a. Record the name and mailing address for the supplier in the SUPPLIER box. If necessary, refer to the mailing address list on *page 4 in this Student Reference Book*.
   b. Record the July date (given in your *DAILY ACTIVITIES*).
   c. Record the Purchase Order No. Purchase orders should be numbered consecutively beginning with No. 5000. Use the first number that is not crossed off the Purchase Order Number List on the next page. Cross off the number you used so that it cannot be used again.

PURCHASE ORDER NUMBER LIST

~~4999~~	5000	5001	5002	5003	5004
5005	5006	5007	5008	5009	5010

d. Record Cash upon receipt of invoice in the box labeled TERMS.

e. Record the method of shipping in the box labeled SHIP VIA. Your DAILY ACTIVITIES will tell you which method to use.

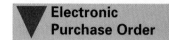

3. Complete the body of the purchase order.

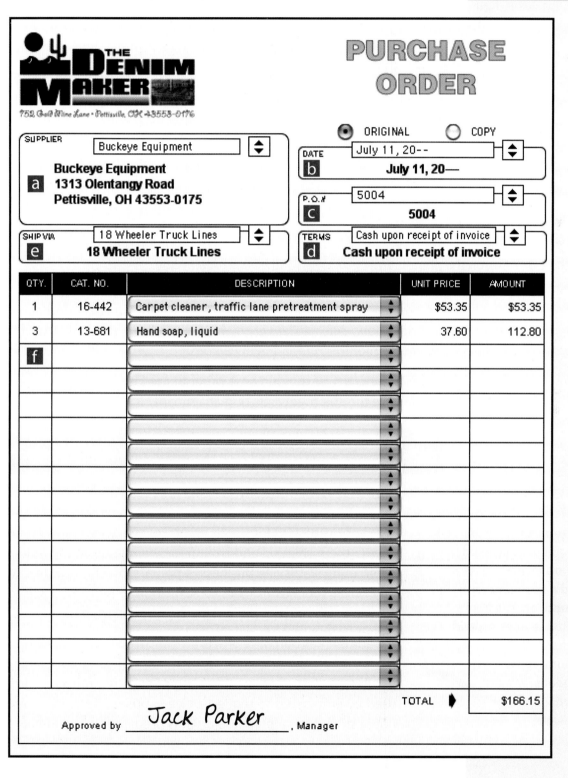

If you are preparing the purchase order manually

f. Record the quantity (QTY.), catalog number (CAT. NO.), DESCRIPTION, UNIT PRICE, and AMOUNT for each item ordered. (This information is located within the price lists on *pages 351-366 in this Student Reference Book*.) Add the figures in the AMOUNT column and record the TOTAL.

g. Check your work to be sure that all information is accurate and that all mathematical calculations are correct. Sign your name on the *Approved by* line.

h. Ask your Instructor to make 1 photocopy of the purchase order. Be sure to come back to these steps when you receive the photocopy.

i. Identify the original and the copy of the purchase order. Place a ✔ in the ORIGINAL box on the original purchase order and a ✔ in the COPY box on the photocopy.

If you are preparing the purchase order electronically, use the tab key to move from column to column. If you make a mistake on an entry, delete the entry and replace it. The balance will adjust itself.

f. Record the quantity (QTY.) and DESCRIPTION for each item ordered. You may access supplier descriptions by clicking on the drop-down menu under the DESCRIPTION column. The CAT. NO., UNIT PRICE, AMOUNT, and TOTAL are automatically recorded.

g. Check your work to be sure that all information is accurate.

h. Select ORIGINAL before you print the purchase order. Print 1 ORIGINAL purchase order. Now select COPY. Print 1 COPY of the purchase order. Save your work.

i. Sign both copies of the purchase order on the *Approved by* line.

4. Prepare an envelope to mail the ORIGINAL purchase order. If necessary, refer to *page 99 in this Student Reference Book* for instructions for preparing envelopes.

5. File the COPY of the purchase order in the Pending File until you receive the shipment form and an item invoice.

ORDERING OFFICE SUPPLIES

Caution!

Do not write a check for the amount of the purchase order. Wait until you receive an item invoice and a shipment form from the supplier. The item invoice includes sales tax and shipping charges. The shipment form represents the goods you ordered.

Businesses sell to customers either on a cash-and-carry basis or on credit. When a Pettisville business sells **cash and carry**, the customer pays cash for goods and takes the goods rather than having them shipped and paying for them later. In the model community, Pettisville businesses prepare purchase orders to buy office supplies from Taylor Office Supplies. Taylor Office Supplies sells office supplies on a cash-and-carry basis.

Sometimes purchase orders are prepared from requisitions. For example, an employee who needs office supplies may requisition them on an **office supplies requisition**, a form used by employees to request office supplies. If the items are not in stock, then a purchase order is prepared to buy them.

OFFICE SUPPLIES REQUISITION

CLOTHES CLOSET
61 Dungaree Drive • Pettisville, OH 43553-0178

Supplier	Requisition No.
Taylor Office Supplies 12 Rivet Street Pettisville, OH 43553-0177	6
	Date
	July 3, 20--

Quantity	Description
3 boxes	garment tags
1 jar	rubber cement

Requisitioned by _Roper_   Dept. _Sales_
Authorized by _John Walker_

OFFICE SUPPLIES REQUISITION

CLOTHES CLOSET
61 Dungaree Drive • Pettisville, OH 43553-0178

Supplier	Requisition No.
Taylor Office Supplies 12 Rivet Street Pettisville, OH 43553-0177	8
	Date
	July 3, 20--

Quantity	Description
3	jars of rubber cement
1	receipt book

Requisitioned by _Karen Peters_   Dept. _Sales_
Authorized by _John Walker_

Look at the requisitions illustrated above. Requisition No. 6 and Requisition No. 8 were prepared by two different employees. Notice that 4 items have been requisitioned but that one item, jars of rubber cement, appears on both requisitions. The total number of jars of rubber cement being requisitioned is 4. When the manager of The Clothes Closet prepared the purchase order to buy these office supplies, only 3 types of office supplies were listed on the purchase order—rubber cement, a receipt book, and garment tags.

Look at the body of the purchase order to the right. The first item is for 4 jars of rubber cement (Catalog No. YH-0845). The unit price of $1.45 is multiplied by the quantity (4) to find the amount ($5.80). The second item is for 1 receipt book (Catalog No. NQ-6590). One receipt book costs $13.99. Since only one book is being ordered, $13.99 is also recorded in the amount column. The third item is for 3 boxes of garment tags (Catalog No. SQ-4473). The unit price of $20.00 is multiplied by the quantity (3) to find the amount ($60.00).

PURCHASE ORDER

CLOTHES CLOSET
61 Dungaree Drive • Pettisville, OH 43553-0178

⦿ ORIGINAL   ◯ COPY

SUPPLIER Taylor Office Supplies
Taylor Office Supplies
12 Rivet Street
Pettisville, OH 43553-0177

DATE July 5, 20-- / July 5, 20—
P.O.# 5002 / 5002

SHIP VIA --Choose to Print Blank P.O.
TERMS Cash and carry / Cash and carry

QTY.	CAT. NO.	DESCRIPTION	UNIT PRICE	AMOUNT
4	YH-0845	Rubber cement, 4-oz. jar with brush	$1.45	$5.80
1	NQ-6590	Receipts for money, NCR paper	13.99	13.99
3	SQ-4473	Garment tags, black ink on white stock	20.00	60.00
			TOTAL	$79.79

Approved by _Bimil Alimchandani_, Manager

After each item has been listed, figures in the amount column are added together to find the total of the purchase order ($79.79). In the illustration, Bimil Alimchandani, manager of The Clothes Closet, signed the purchase order.

Follow these steps when ordering office supplies

1. Find your office supplies requisitions. The forms list in your *DAILY ACTIVITIES* will tell you which 2 office supplies requisitions you need.

If you are using Instructor-supplied forms, remove the 2 office supplies requisitions from your Supplies folder.

If you are printing your forms, open the forms document. Find Unit 4 Accounts Payable and Receivable. Print the 2 office supplies requisitions.

2. Compare the items listed on the requisitions. When an item appears on both requisitions, add the number of that item listed on the 2 requisitions. The total is the number of that item you need to order. For example, in Requisitions No. 6 and No. 8 illustrated on *page 151 in this Student Reference Book*, the total number of jars of rubber cement that appear on both requisitions is 4. If an item appears only on 1 requisition, then no addition is necessary to determine the quantity to order.

3. Find your purchase order.

If you are preparing your purchase order manually, remove 1 purchase order from your Supplies folder.

If you are preparing your purchase order electronically, open the purchase order. Use the tab key to move from line to line. You may access information to complete the form by clicking the drop-down menus that appear on the purchase order.

4. Complete the top part (the heading) of the purchase order. Refer to the purchase order illustrated on *page 151 in this Student Reference Book*.
   a. Record the name and mailing address for Taylor Office Supplies in the SUPPLIER box. If necessary, refer to the mailing address list on *page 4 in this Student Reference Book* to find Taylor's mailing address.
   b. Record the July date (given in your *DAILY ACTIVITIES*).
   c. Record the Purchase Order No. Refer to the Purchase Order Number List on *page 149 in this Student Reference Book*. Purchase orders should be numbered consecutively beginning with No. 5000. Use the first number that is not crossed off the Purchase Order Number List. Cross off the number you used so that it cannot be used again.

d. Record Cash and carry in the TERMS box.

e. Leave the SHIP VIA box blank.

5. Complete the body of the purchase order. Refer to the purchase order illustrated on *page 151 in this Student Reference Book*.

If you are preparing the purchase order manually

f. Record the quantity (QTY.), catalog number (CAT. NO.), DESCRIPTION, UNIT PRICE, and AMOUNT for each item ordered. Refer to Taylor's price list on *page 363 in this Student Reference Book*. Add the figures in the AMOUNT column and record the TOTAL.

g. Check your work to be sure that all information is accurate and that all mathematical calculations are correct. Sign your name on the Approved by line.

h. Ask your Instructor to make 1 photocopy of the purchase order. Be sure to come back to these steps when you receive the photocopy.

i. Identify the original and the copy of the purchase order. Place a ✔ in the ORIGINAL box on the original purchase order and a ✔ in the COPY box on the photocopy.

If you are preparing the purchase order electronically, use the tab key to move from column to column. If you make a mistake on an entry, delete the entry and replace it. The balance will adjust itself.

f. Record the quantity (QTY.) and DESCRIPTION for each item ordered. You may access supplier descriptions by clicking on the drop-down menu under the DESCRIPTION column. The CAT. NO., UNIT PRICE, AMOUNT, and TOTAL are automatically recorded.

g. Check your work to be sure that all information is accurate.

h. Select ORIGINAL before you print the purchase order. Print 1 ORIGINAL purchase order. Now select COPY. Print 1 COPY of the purchase order. Save your work.

i. Sign both copies of the purchase order on the *Approved by* line.

NOTE: Do *not* write a check for the amount on the purchase order. Wait until you receive an item invoice from Taylor; the invoice will include sales tax.

---

6. Take the ORIGINAL purchase order and your checkbook and go to Taylor Office Supplies. Give the purchase order to the manager. Wait while the manager verifies your order with the price list and completes an item invoice.

7. Write a check for the full amount of the invoice. Return to your place of business.

8. Record the payment for supplies in the cashbook. Complete the steps titled *Follow these steps when recording cash payments (by check) in the cashbook* on *page 58 in this Student Reference Book*. Record *Office Supplies* in the EXPLANATION column of the cashbook.

9. Staple or paper clip the 2 requisitions and the purchase order to the back of the invoice. Write PAID BY CHECK No. _____ across the invoice. Place these papers in the Office File.

CHECKPOINT

Purchase Orders

Answer the following questions.

1. Who prepares a purchase order—the buyer or the seller? _____

2. The total cost of 5 items ordered at the unit price of $15.00 each is $_____.

3. The method of payment agreed upon between the buyer and the seller is referred to as _____ on a purchase order.

4. The purchase order grants _____ to the person making the purchase.

5. A business that sells merchandise in small quantities to consumers or the general public is called a _____.

Doing Business on the 'Net

Ordering Online

Efficient business managers should be as careful with the company's dollars as they would be with their own money. Every dollar saved equals another dollar in company profits. That is why it is important to shop carefully when you buy for your business. Comparison shopping for office supplies and equipment has never been easier. It is made simple through a host of online shopping services. Can you name at least ten types of office supplies that you could purchase for your office?

UNIT 4 • ACCOUNTS PAYABLE AND RECEIVABLE

USING ITEM INVOICES

An **item invoice** is a form for billing a customer for merchandise purchased. Whenever a business receives a purchase order from a customer, an item invoice is prepared in duplicate (the original to be sent to the customer and the copy for your files). For this simulation, you will assume that all items ordered are in stock and are ready to be shipped to your customer.

Customers frequently buy on credit. When a business sells goods or services on credit, the sale is known as an account receivable. **Accounts receivable** are amounts of money owed to a business by the company's customers. In the model business community, payments for invoices are due when they are received by the customer.

▼ **Manual Item Invoice**

There are three steps that must be completed when you receive a purchase order.

- First, you must verify the accuracy of the purchase order.
- Second, you must arrange the shipment. You must find the weight of the item(s) ordered, prepare a shipment form, and take the shipment form to either the post office or 18 Wheeler Truck Lines.
- Third, you must send an item invoice to the customer.

Information needed to complete the item invoice is taken from the customer's purchase order. Look at the item invoice on the right. Notice that it is divided into two parts. You will prepare the top portion of the invoice either manually (by hand) or electronically. The bottom portion is the remittance slip. A **remittance slip** is the part of an invoice that is completed by the customer and returned with the customer's payment.

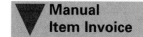

BUCKEYE EQUIPMENT
1313 Olentangy Road
Pettisville, OH 43553-0175

ITEM INVOICE

INVOICE NO. _2008_

BILL DATE	AMOUNT DUE
July 13, 20--	$201.17

NAME AND ADDRESS
The Denim Maker
752 Gold Mine Lane
Pettisville, OH 43553-0176

CUSTOMER ORDER NO. 5004

SOLD BY C. G.

SHIPPED VIA 18 Wheeler Truck Lines

QTY.	CAT. NO.	DESCRIPTION	UNIT PRICE	AMOUNT	
1	16-442	case of carpet cleaner	53.35	$ 53	35
3	13-681	cases of liquid hand soap	37.60	112	80

SUBTOTAL	$166	15
6% SALES TAX (IF APPLICABLE)	9	97
SHIPPING CHARGES	25	05
☑ ORIGINAL ☐ COPY TOTAL ▶	$201	17

PLEASE DETACH ALONG DASHED LINE AND RETURN THE BOTTOM PORTION WITH YOUR REMITTANCE.

FROM:

INVOICE NO. _____

BILL DATE	AMOUNT DUE

REMITTANCE ADVICE
Please write your invoice number on your check to ensure proper credit and mail it with this remittance slip.

PLEASE MAKE CHECKS PAYABLE TO:

BUCKEYE EQUIPMENT
1313 Olentangy Road
Pettisville, OH 43553-0175

AMOUNT ENCLOSED	

TERMS: DUE UPON RECEIPT

Follow these steps when preparing an item invoice

1. Verify the purchase order. Do not assume that it is correct.

   a. Remove your business's price list from the Office File (or refer to *pages 351-366 in this Student Reference Book*).   Compare the description and unit price of each item ordered with the price list.

   b. Verify the extensions of each line by multiplying the quantity times the unit price.

      • If the numbers in the AMOUNT column are correct, place a tiny check mark beside each amount.

      • If the numbers in the AMOUNT column are not correct, make the necessary correction by drawing a single line through the wrong amount and writing the corrected amount above the wrong one in the AMOUNT column.

   c. Add the AMOUNT column.

      • If the TOTAL is correct, write your initials beside the TOTAL.

      • If the TOTAL is not correct, make the correction the same way just previously described in the step above. Then initial the change.

   d. If the purchase order is correct, go to step 2 that follows.

   e. If the purchase order is not correct, telephone, e-mail, or go in person to the business that issued the purchase order and call the error to the attention of the manager. Then return to your business and proceed to step 2.

2. Record the weight of the items on the available white space on the purchase order. Refer to your company's price list in the Office File for shipping weights (or see *pages 351-366 in this Student Reference Book*).

   a. If the quantity ordered is more than 1, multiply the quantity times the weight to find the total weight for those items, as shown on the illustration below.

QTY.	CAT. NO.	DESCRIPTION		UNIT PRICE	AMOUNT	
1	16-442	case of carpet cleaner	34 lbs NC	53.35	$ 53	35 √
3	13-681	cases of liquid hand soap		37.60	112	80 √
		3 × 17 = 51 lbs NC				
		Total Weight 81 lbs NC				

   b. *If you are shipping via 18 Wheeler Truck Lines,* write **C** beside the weight if the goods are crated; write **NC** beside the weight if the goods are not crated. Check the NOTE on the price list for information about crating. Some goods may be shipped on a crate or a pallet, but other items cannot be crated. Shipping rates are higher for goods that cannot be crated.

3. Arrange for shipping. After completing the shipping arrangements, be sure to return to these steps.

> ▪ *If you are shipping via priority mail,* turn to *page 183 in this Student Reference Book.* Complete the steps titled *Follow these steps when preparing a shipment form for the post office.*

> ▪ *If you are shipping via 18 Wheeler Truck Lines,* turn to *page 190 in this Student Reference Book.* Complete the steps titled *Follow these steps when shipping via 18 Wheeler Truck Lines.*

4. Find your item invoice.

> ▣ *If you are preparing your invoice manually,* remove 1 item invoice from your Supplies folder.

> 🖱 *If you are preparing your invoice electronically,* open the item invoice.

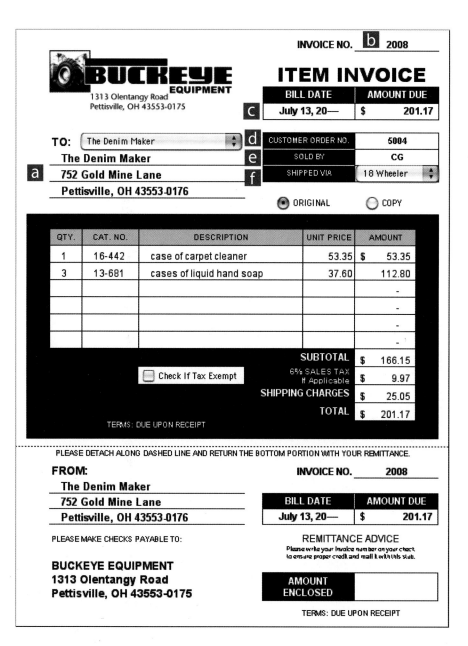

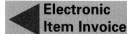
Electronic Item Invoice

5. Complete the top part (the heading) of the invoice. Refer to the invoice illustrated on _page 157 in this Student Reference Book_.

   a. Record the name and mailing address of your customer from the incoming purchase order. _If you are preparing your invoice electronically_, click on the drop-down menu to select customer names and mailing addresses.

   b. Number the invoice. Invoices should be numbered consecutively beginning with No. 2000. Use the first number that is not crossed off the Item Invoice Number List below. Cross off the number you used so that it cannot be used again.

©GETTY IMAGES/PHOTODISC

ITEM INVOICE NUMBER LIST

~~1999~~	~~2000~~	2001	2002	2003	2004	2005	2006
2007	2008	2009	2010	2011	2012	2013	2014
2015	2016	2017	2018	2019	2020	2021	2022
2023	2024	2025	2026	2027	2028	2029	2030

   c. Record the July date (given in your _DAILY ACTIVITIES_) in the BILL DATE box.

   d. Record the CUSTOMER ORDER NO. from the incoming purchase order (PURCHASE ORDER NO.).

   e. Record your initials in the SOLD BY box.

   f. Record the method of shipping from the purchase order into the SHIPPED VIA box.

6. Complete the main part (the body) of the invoice. (Refer to the invoice illustrated on _page 157 in this Student Reference Book_.)

   g. Record the quantity (QTY.), catalog number (CAT. NO.), DESCRIPTION, UNIT PRICE, and AMOUNT for each item ordered. (Catalog numbers and descriptions may be found within the price lists on _pages 351-366 in this Student Reference Book_.)

   h. Add the figures in the AMOUNT column and record the SUBTOTAL. If you are preparing your invoice electronically, the SUBTOTAL column will be calculated automatically.

   i. Record the sales tax, if applicable. (If your customer is exempt from paying sales tax, check the exempt box on the invoice.)

computational resources

CALCULATING SALES TAX

Example Calculate a 6% sales tax on a purchase of $459.95.

Solution Sales Tax = Purchase Price × Tax Rate
            =   459.95   ×   0.06
            = 27.5970, which rounds to $27.60

Example What is the total price including tax?

Solution $459.95 + $27.60 = $487.55

> *If you are preparing your invoice manually,* multiply the SUBTOTAL by 6% (0.06).

> *If you are preparing your invoice electronically,* sales tax will be computed automatically.

j. Record the amount of the shipping charges you calculated when you arranged to ship the goods. (You wrote this information on the customer's purchase order when you calculated the shipping charges.)

k. Total the invoice. Add the amounts in the SUBTOTAL, SALES TAX, and SHIPPING CHARGES columns and record the TOTAL and AMOUNT DUE. *If you are preparing your invoice electronically,* the TOTAL will be calculated automatically. **NOTE:** Do not make any entries on the lower portion (remittance slip) of the invoice.

l. Check your work to be sure that all information is accurate and that all mathematical calculations are correct.

m. Make a copy of the invoice.

Sales Tax Exemptions

Wholesale businesses, such as Mean Jeans Manufacturing Co. and The Denim Maker, do not charge sales tax on goods for resale. Non-profit businesses, such as Lee Community Center, do not pay sales tax provided that a sales tax certificate of exemption is attached to the first purchase order sent to a business.

> *If you are preparing your invoice manually,* ask your Instructor to make 1 photocopy of the invoice. (Be sure to come back to these steps when you receive the photocopy.) Identify the original and the copy of the invoice. Place a ✔ in the ORIGINAL box on the original invoice and a ✔ in the COPY box on the photocopy.

> *If you are preparing your invoice electronically,* select ORIGINAL before you print the invoice. Then print 1 ORIGINAL invoice. Now select COPY. Print 1 COPY of the invoice. Save your work.

7. Prepare an envelope to mail the ORIGINAL invoice. If necessary, follow the steps for addressing envelopes on *page 99 in this Student Reference Book*.

8. Staple or paper clip the purchase order to the back of the copy the invoice. Place these papers in the Pending File until you receive payment from the customer.

Follow these steps when you receive a check in payment of an item invoice

1. Remove the copy of the invoice and the purchase order from the Pending File.

2. Check to make sure that the customer has written the check in the proper amount and that the check is signed.

©GETTY IMAGES/PHOTODISC

3. Write *PAID* in large letters across the copy of the invoice. If the customer sent a remittance slip, staple or paper clip the slip to the back of the invoice.

4. Place the invoice (with its attachments) in the Office File.

5. Record the check in your cashbook. If necessary, turn to *page 61 in this Student Reference Book*. Complete the steps titled *Follow these steps when recording incoming checks (cash receipts) in the cashbook*.

6. Endorse the check for deposit. If necessary, refer to the illustration on *page 62 in this Student Reference Book*.

7. Place the check in the cash receipts envelope in the Cash File. Your *DAILY ACTIVITIES* will instruct you to deposit the check later.

Follow these steps when you receive an item invoice

1. Find the shipment form for the goods you ordered.

2. Remove your copy of the purchase order from the Pending File.

3. Make sure that the supplier shipped to you the exact items you ordered. Compare the information on the purchase order with the information on the invoice.
   a. Make sure that all calculations on the invoice are correct. If there is an error in the items shipped or in the calculations, telephone, e-mail, or go in person to the supplier and correct the error.
   b. Staple or paper clip the purchase order and the shipment form to the back of the invoice.

4. Remove your checkbook from the Cash File. Write a check for the total amount of the invoice. If necessary, turn to *page 54 in this Student Reference Book* and follow the steps there for writing checks. *Write Invoice No. 0000* on the line marked *FOR* on the check, substituting the invoice number for *0000*.

5. Record the payment in your cashbook. If necessary, turn to *page 58 in this Student Reference Book*. Complete the steps titled *Follow these steps when recording cash payments (by check) in the cashbook*.

6. Use scissors to separate the invoice from the remittance slip along the dashed lines. Return the remittance slip (lower portion) of the invoice with your check. The upper portion of the invoice is for your records.

Remember!

Wait until you have a shipment form in hand before paying an item invoice. If you do not receive a shipment form, check with the supplier or your Instructor. You will receive the goods (represented by the shipment form) from 18 Wheeler Truck Lines or Pettisville Post Office.

7. Complete the remittance slip.

📋 *If you have a handwritten invoice,*
  a. Use a return address label, or write your company name and address on the FROM lines.
  b. Copy the invoice number, date, and total from the top of the invoice onto the remittance slip.
  c. Write the amount of your check in the AMOUNT ENCLOSED box.

🖱 *If you have an electronic invoice,* write the amount of your check in the AMOUNT ENCLOSED box.

---

8. Prepare an envelope. Be sure to include the remittance slip in the envelope with the check. If necessary, follow the steps for addressing envelopes on *page 99 in this Student Reference Book*.

9. Write *PAID BY CHECK NO. ___* across the invoice. File the invoice (with the attachments) in the Office File.

CHECKPOINT

Using Item Invoices

Answer the following questions.

1. Amounts of money owed to a business by the company's customers are called _____.

2. A form for billing a customer for merchandise purchased is called a/an _____.

3. The first step you should take when you receive a purchase order is to verify the _____ of the purchase order.

4. When you arrange the shipment, you must find the _____ of the item(s) ordered, prepare a _____ form, and take the shipment form to either the post office or _____.

5. The payment for an item invoice is due when the item invoice is _____ by the customer.

LESSON 4•3

USING SERVICE INVOICES

Some businesses sell services rather than merchandise. For example, Passports-2-Go makes travel arrangements for customers, and Popular Designs creates fashion designs for a number of clients. Pettisville businesses providing services will prepare bills called service invoices. A **service invoice** is a bill for a service or services performed.

Manual Service Invoice ▼

CREATIVE ADVERTISING AGENCY
816 Corduroy Drive • Pettisville, OH 43553-0177

INVOICE NO. _7016_

SERVICE INVOICE

TO:
Security Insurance Company
643 Leonard Street
Maumee, OH 43537-2388

BILL DATE
July 9, 20--

☑ ORIGINAL   ☐ COPY

DESCRIPTION	AMOUNT
WADD-FM radio commercials, 3 one-minute spots @ $110 each	$330.00
Cassette preparation	152.00
Commission 15%	72.30

Cathy Raney
Manager's Signature

SUBTOTAL	$554.30
6% SALES TAX	33.26
TOTAL DUE	$587.56

Terms—Due upon receipt of invoice.

- -
PLEASE DETACH ALONG DASHED LINE AND RETURN THE BOTTOM PORTION WITH YOUR REMITTANCE.

FROM:
_____
_____
_____

INVOICE NO. _____

BILL DATE	AMOUNT DUE

PLEASE MAKE CHECKS PAYABLE TO:

CREATIVE ADVERTISING AGENCY
816 Corduroy Drive
Pettisville, OH 43553-0177

REMITTANCE ADVICE
Please write your invoice number on your check to ensure proper credit and mail it with this stub.

AMOUNT ENCLOSED	

TERMS: DUE UPON RECEIPT

Look at the service invoice on the left. Notice that it is divided into two parts. The top portion of the invoice may be prepared either manually (by hand) or electronically. The bottom portion is the remittance slip. The remittance slip is completed by the customer and returned with the customer's payment.

Service invoices may include commissions. A **commission** is a fee earned on a percentage of the sale. For example, Creative Advertising Agency charges 15% commission for its services, and Nouveau Investment Company charges a commission rate of 1/2% for purchases of stock.

Service invoices are prepared in duplicate. The original is sent to the customer. The seller keeps a copy in the Pending File until payment is received. Payments for service invoices are due when they are received by the customer.

INVOICE NO. **b** 7016

CREATIVE
ADVERTISING AGENCY
816 Corduroy Drive • Pettisville, OH 43553-0177

SERVICE
INVOICE

a

TO: Security Insurance Company

Security Insurance Company
643 Leonard Street
Maumee, OH 43537-2388

BILL DATE
c July 9, 20--

⦿ ORIGINAL ◯ COPY

	DESCRIPTION	AMOUNT
d	WADD-FM radio commercials, 3 one-minute spots @ $110 each	$ 330.00
	Cassette preparation	152.00
e	Commission 15%	72.30

Cathy Raney

Manager's Signature

SUBTOTAL	$ 554.30	**f**
6% SALES TAX If Applicable	$ 33.26	**g**
TOTAL DUE	$ 587.56	**h**

TERMS: DUE UPON RECEIPT

☐ Check If Tax Exempt

- -

PLEASE DETACH ALONG DASHED LINE AND RETURN THE BOTTOM PORTION WITH YOUR REMITTANCE.

FROM:

Security Insurance Company
643 Leonard Street
Maumee, OH 43537-2388

INVOICE NO. 7016

BILL DATE	AMOUNT DUE
July 9, 20--	$ 587.56

PLEASE MAKE CHECKS PAYABLE TO:

CREATIVE ADVERTISING AGENCY
816 Corduroy Drive
Pettisville, OH 43553-0177

REMITTANCE ADVICE
Please write your invoice number on your check
to ensure proper credit and mail it with this stub.

AMOUNT ENCLOSED	

TERMS: DUE UPON RECEIPT

← Remittance Slip

Follow these steps when preparing a service invoice

1. Find your service invoice.

If you are preparing your invoice manually, remove 1 service invoice from your Supplies folder.

If you are preparing your invoice electronically, open the service invoice. Use the tab key to move from line to line. If you make a mistake on an entry, delete the entry and replace it. The balance will adjust itself.

2. Complete the top part (the heading) of the invoice.
   a. Record the customer's name and mailing address in the TO box. If necessary, refer to the mailing address list on *page 3 in your Operations Manual* or on *page 4 in this Student Reference Book*.

b. Number the invoice. Service invoices are numbered consecutively beginning with No. 7000. Use the first number that is not crossed off the Service Invoice Number List below. Cross off the number you used so that it cannot be used again.

SERVICE INVOICE NUMBER LIST

~~6999~~	⌒7000⌒	7001	7002	7003	7004	7005	7006
7007	7008	7009	7010	7011	7012	7013	7014
7015	7016	7017	7018	7019	7020	7021	7022
7023	7024	7025	7026	7027	7028	7029	7030
7031	7032	7033	7034	7035	7036	7037	7038

c. Record the July date (given in your *DAILY ACTIVITIES*) in the BILL DATE box.

3. Complete the main part of the invoice. If you are preparing your invoice electronically, totals will be calculated automatically.
   d. Complete the DESCRIPTION and AMOUNT columns for each service performed.
   e. Record the commission (if applicable) under the DESCRIPTION and AMOUNT columns.
   f. Add the figures under the AMOUNT column and record the SUBTOTAL.
   g. Record the sales tax, if applicable. (If your customer is exempt from paying sales tax, check the exempt box on the invoice.)

If you are preparing your invoice manually, multiply the SUBTOTAL by 6% (0.06).

If you are preparing your invoice electronically, sales tax will be computed automatically.

About Sales Taxes

For this simulation, most services will be subject to a 6% sales tax. Some travel services at Passports-2-Go, such as airline tickets, already include sales tax. Lee Community Center does not charge sales tax on renewal of annual membership dues. Services provided to Lee Community Center are not taxed if a sales tax exemption certificate has been received from Lee Community Center.

h. Add the SUBTOTAL and SALES TAX columns and record the TOTAL DUE. Do not make any entries on the lower portion (remittance slip) of the invoice.
i. Check your work. Be sure that all information and all mathematical calculations are correct.

©GETTY IMAGES/PHOTODISC

4. Make a copy of the invoice.

📋 *If you are preparing your invoice manually,* ask your Instructor to make 1 photocopy of the invoice. (Be sure to come back to these steps when you receive the photocopy.) Identify the original and the copy of the invoice. Place a ✔ in the ORIGINAL box on the original invoice and a ✔ in the COPY box on the photocopy.

🖱 *If you are preparing your invoice electronically,* select ORIGINAL before you print the invoice. Then print 1 ORIGINAL invoice. Now select COPY. Print 1 COPY of the invoice. Save your work.

---

5. Sign your name as manager on both copies.

6. Prepare an envelope to mail the ORIGINAL invoice. If necessary, follow the steps for addressing envelopes on *page 99 in this Student Reference Book*.

7. Place the COPY of the invoice in the Pending File until you receive payment from the customer.

Follow these steps when you receive a check in payment of a service invoice

1. Remove the copy of the service invoice from the Pending File.

2. Check to make sure that the customer has written the check in the proper amount and that the check is signed.

3. Write *PAID* in large letters across the copy of the invoice. If the customer sent a remittance slip, staple or paper clip the slip to the back of the invoice.

4. Place your copy of the invoice in the Office File.

5. Record the check in your cashbook. If necessary, turn to *page 61 in this Student Reference Book* and complete the steps titled *Follow these steps when recording incoming checks (cash receipts) in the cashbook.*

6. Endorse the check for deposit. If necessary, refer to the illustration on *page 62 in this Student Reference Book*.

7. Place the check in the cash receipts envelope in the Cash File. Your *DAILY ACTIVITIES* will instruct you to deposit the check later.

Follow these steps when you receive a service invoice

1. Make sure that all calculations on the invoice are correct. If there is an error, telephone, e-mail, or go in person to the business and correct the error.

2. Remove your checkbook from the Cash File. Write a check for the total amount of the invoice. If necessary, turn to *page 54 in this Student Reference Book* and follow the steps there for writing checks.

Write *Invoice No. 0000* on the line marked *FOR* on the check. Substitute the invoice number for *0000*.

3. Record the payment in your cashbook. If necessary, turn to *page 58 in this Student Reference Book* and complete the steps titled *Follow these steps when recording cash payments (by check) in the cashbook.*

4. Use scissors to separate the invoice from the remittance slip along the dashed lines. Return the remittance slip (lower portion) of the invoice with your check. The upper portion of the invoice is for your records.

5. Complete the remittance slip.

If you have a handwritten invoice,
a. Use a return address label, or write your company name and address on the FROM lines.
b. Copy the invoice number, date, and total from the top of the invoice onto the remittance slip.
c. Write the amount of your check in the AMOUNT ENCLOSED box.

If you have an electronic invoice, write the amount of your check in the AMOUNT ENCLOSED box.

6. Prepare an envelope. Include the remittance slip in the envelope with the check. If necessary, turn to *page 99 in this Student Reference Book* and complete the steps there for addressing envelopes.

7. Write *PAID BY CHECK NO.____* across the invoice.

8. File the invoice in the Office File.

CHECKPOINT

Using Service Invoices

Answer the following questions.

1. A bill for a service performed is called a _____.

2. The bottom portion of a service invoice is called the remittance slip and is completed by the _____ when payment is made.

3. The seller keeps a copy of the service invoice in the _____ File until payment is received.

4. Some businesses sell services rather than _____.

5. Some service invoices include a/an _____, which is a fee earned based on a percentage of the sale.

UNIT SUMMARY

LESSON 4•1 PREPARING PURCHASE ORDERS

1. Cash flow—the money coming into and going out of the company—is the lifeblood of the business.

2. A purchase order grants approval to the person making the purchase and provides a written record of the order.

3. Purchase orders are prepared by a buyer to order goods from a supplier.

4. Retailers and wholesalers are also called suppliers because they supply other businesses with their goods.

5. The total on the amount column of a purchase order is determined by multiplying the quantity times the unit price.

6. Sometimes purchase orders are prepared from requisitions when the items being requisitioned are not in stock.

7. Businesses sell to customers either on a cash-and-carry basis or on credit.

LESSON 4•2 USING ITEM INVOICES

8. Before an order can be filled, the customer's purchase order must be verified for accuracy.

9. After a customer's order has been shipped, the supplier prepares an item invoice.

10. Wholesale businesses do not charge sales tax on goods for resale, and nonprofit businesses may be exempt from paying sales tax.

11. When a customer asks for an order to be shipped, the shipping charges are added to the item invoice.

LESSON 4•3 USING SERVICE INVOICES

12. Some businesses sell services rather than merchandise.

13. When paying an invoice, the customer should return the remittance slip with the payment.

14. Service invoices may include commissions earned for the service or services provided.

Glossary

accounts payable	amounts of money owed by a business to its suppliers for purchases made but not yet paid for
accounts receivable	amounts of money owed to a business by the company's customers
cash and carry	paying cash for goods and taking the goods rather than having them shipped and paying for them later
commission	a fee earned based on a percentage of the sale
item invoice	a form for billing a customer for merchandise purchased
office supplies requisition	a form used by employees to request office supplies
purchase order	a form used to order merchandise, supplies, or equipment from a supplier
remittance slip	the part of an invoice that is completed by the customer and returned with the customer's payment
retailer	a business that sells merchandise in small quantities to consumers or the general public
service invoice	a bill for a service or services performed
terms	the method of payment agreed upon between the buyer and the seller
unit price	the price for one item
wholesaler	a business that sells merchandise in large quantities to retailers or to other wholesalers

INTERNET EXPLORATIONS

1. Many office supply companies encourage customers to order online with discounts and free delivery. Check out these sites.
   - a. *www.officedepot.com*
   - b. *www.officemax.com*
   - c. *www.staples.com*
   - d. *www.officesupplies.com*
   - e. *www.reliable.com*
   - f. *www.vikingop.com*
2. Many banks provide online billpaying services. Explore these services at the following web sites.
   - a. *www.bankofamerica.com*
   - b. *www.fifththird.com*
   - c. *www.wingspanbank.com*
   - d. *www.compubank.com*
   - e. *www.everbank.com*
   - f. *www.sfnb.com*

Name		Evaluation

ACTIVITY 4•1: PREPARING A PURCHASE ORDER

Directions: *Assume you are the manager of The Clothes Closet. After reviewing your inventory list, you find that your inventory on some items is low. You decide to replenish by placing an order with Mean Jeans Manufacturing Co. After determining the quantity to order, you will prepare a purchase order to send to Mean Jeans.*

1. Look closely at the inventory list at the bottom of this page. Note the title of each column. Read the totals for each item in the *Maximum* column. Then read the totals for each item in the *Minimum* column. Now look at the *July 1 Balance* for each item. Notice that 2 items have fallen below the minimum balance.

   You want to order enough of these 2 items to bring the quantity on hand up to the *Maximum* number. To find the total to order, subtract the number on hand (July 1 Balance) from the maximum number. In the example below, the July 1 balance (30) was subtracted from the maximum number (100) to determine the number to order (70).

Item	Maximum	Minimum	July 1 Balance	No. to Order
Belts	100	50	30	70

2. Turn to Mean Jeans' price list on *page 357 in this Student Reference Book*. Find the catalog numbers, descriptions, and wholesale price for the 2 items to order.

3. Use the purchase order on the back of this sheet to order from Mean Jeans Manufacturing Co. the two items that have fallen below the minimum balance. Turn to *page 148 in this Student Reference Book*. Find the steps titled *Follow these steps when preparing a purchase order*. **Complete steps 2, 3f and 3g**. Include the following:
   * In step 2b, date the purchase order July 23, 20--
   * In step 2c, use Purchase Order No. 5001.
   * In step 2e, record *18 Wheeler Truck Lines* as the method of shipping.

Item	Supplier	Maximum	Minimum	July 1 Balance	Quantity to Order
Bandanna Scarves	Mean Jeans	500	100	200	
Baby Tees	Mean Jeans	300	50	75	
Men's 5-Pocket Jeans	Mean Jeans	200	100	75	125
Denim Jumper Girls' sizes	Mean Jeans	400	75	250	
Denim Jumper Juniors' & Misses'	Mean Jeans	500	100	300	
Denim Shirts Boys' & Girls'	Mean Jeans	400	75	100	
Denim Shirts Juniors' sizes	Mean Jeans	500	100	220	
Denim Shirts Misses' & Men's	Mean Jeans	500	100	170	
Designer Jeans	Mean Jeans	200	110	68	132
Designer Skirts Trouser Style	Mean Jeans	200	50	90	

THE

CLOTHES CLOSET

61 Dungaree Drive • Pettisville, OH 43553-0178

PURCHASE ORDER

☑ ORIGINAL   ☐ COPY

SUPPLIER
Mean Jeans Manufacturing Co. 45 Maple Street Pettisville OH 43553-0175, 419-555-0100 (Corporation)

DATE 7/23/07

PURCHASE ORDER NO. 5001

SHIP VIA
18 Wheeler Truck Lines

TERMS
cash and carry

QTY.	CAT. NO.	DESCRIPTION	UNIT PRICE	AMOUNT
132	62-8274	Designer Jeans	$49.00	$6468.00
125	23-458	Men's 5-pocket Jeans	$34.00	$4250.00

TOTAL ▶ $10,718.00

Approved by _Devin Kuchynka_ , Manager

✓

ACTIVITY 4•2: ORDERING OFFICE SUPPLIES

Directions: *Assume you are the manager of United Communications. You received the office supplies requisitions shown below from two of your employees. Complete the purchase order on the back of this sheet to order from Taylor Office Supplies the supplies requested by your employees. Date your purchase order July 16, 20––. Number your purchase order* **Purchase Order No. 5002.**

1. Turn to *page 152 in this Student Reference Book*. Find the steps titled *Follow these steps when ordering office supplies*. **Complete step 2.**

2. **Complete steps 4 through 5g** on *pages 152 and 153 in this Student Reference Book*.

UNITED COMMUNICATIONS

Information Circle • Pettisville, OH 43553-0176

OFFICE SUPPLIES REQUISITION

Supplier	Requisition No.
Taylor Office Supplies 12 Rivet Street Pettisville, OH 43553-0177	11

Quantity	Description
6 boxes	rubber bands
10 boxes	staples
6 pkgs.	self-stick note pads

Requisitioned by _OLG_
Authorized by _Jennifer Hicks_

UNITED COMMUNICATIONS

Information Circle • Pettisville, OH 43553-0176

OFFICE SUPPLIES REQUISITION

Supplier	Requisition No.
Taylor Office Supplies 12 Rivet Street Pettisville, OH 43553-0177	12
	Date
	June 27, 20––

Quantity	Description
3 boxes	staples
2 boxes	#10 envelopes
6 pkgs.	paper clips
12 rolls	package sealing tape

Requisitioned by _JEP_   Dept. _Accounting_
Authorized by _April Harrell_

UNITED COMMUNICATIONS

INFORMATION CIRCLE • PETTISVILLE, OH 43553-0176

PURCHASE ORDER

☑ ORIGINAL ☐ COPY

SUPPLIER Taylor Office Supplies
~~7002~~ River Street
~~Pettisville~~ Pettisville, OH 43553-0176

DATE 7/6/07

PURCHASE ORDER NO. 5002

SHIP VIA 18 Wheeler Truck Lines

TERMS cash and carry

QTY.	CAT. NO.	DESCRIPTION	UNIT PRICE	AMOUNT
6	IN-3575	Rubber bands	$3.99	$23.94
13	XP-5332	Staples	$1.25	$16.25
6	RH-3899	self-stick note pads	$10.95	$65.70
2	SS-9753	envelopes	$15.30	$30.60
6	HA-4120	paper clips	$2.99	$17.94
12	PN-2244	tape	$1.51	$18.12

Approved by _Devin Kuchynka_ , Manager

TOTAL ▶ $172.55

ACTIVITY 4•3: INVOICING AND SHIPPING

Directions: Assume you are the manager of Buckeye Equipment. On **July 9**, you received a purchase order from 18 Wheeler Truck Lines (see below). Use the shipment form at the bottom of this page and the item invoice on the back of this sheet to ship the goods and bill the customer. **Put the items ordered in one package.**

1. Turn to *page 156 in this Student Reference Book*. Find the steps titled *Follow these steps when preparing an item invoice*. **Complete steps 1 through 2a.**

2. Turn to *page 183 in this Student Reference Book*. Find the steps titled *Follow these steps when preparing a shipment form for the post office*. **Complete steps 2 and 3.**

3. Turn to *page 158 in this Student Reference Book*. **Complete steps 5 through 6l.**

5 lbs.
8 lbs.

18 WHEELER TRUCK LINES

1208 Oshkosh Blvd. • Pettisville, OH 43553-0177

PURCHASE ORDER

● ORIGINAL   ○ COPY

SUPPLIER

Buckeye Equipment
1313 Olentangy Road
Pettisville, OH 43553-0175

DATE   July 6, 20—

P.O. #   5007

SHIP VIA   Priority Mail

TERMS   Cash upon receipt of invoice

QTY.	CAT. NO.	DESCRIPTION	UNIT PRICE	AMOUNT
1	13-471	Work gloves, 13" long 5 lbs. NC	$39.60 ✓	$39.60
2	24-701	Floor brush, 36-inch length	16.99 ✓	33.98
		2x4 = 8 lbs. NC		
		Total Weight 13 lbs NC		

$10.00
Approved by *Stephanie Hamlen*   , Manager
13 lbs.

TOLTAL ◆ DK $73.58

BUCKEYE EQUIPMENT

1313 Olentangy Road
Pettisville, OH 43553-0175

DATE   July 9, 2007

SHIPMENT FORM

TOTAL WEIGHT   13 lbs.

SHIP VIA PETTISVILLE POST OFFICE
☑ PRIORITY MAIL
☐ EXPRESS MAIL

SHIP VIA 18 WHEELER TRUCK LINES
☐ CRATED (C)
☐ NOT CRATED (NC)

THIS END UP

FRAGILE

THIS FORM *REPRESENTS* A PACKAGE THAT YOU WISH TO SHIP.

SHIP TO 18 Wheeler Truck Lines 1208 Oshkosh Blvd. Pettisville OH 43553-0177 414-555-0119 (Corporation)

BUCKEYE EQUIPMENT
1313 Olentangy Road
Pettisville, OH 43553-0175

INVOICE NO. 2000

ITEM INVOICE

BILL DATE	AMOUNT DUE
July 9, 2007	$87.99

NAME AND ADDRESS
18 Wheeler Truck Lines
1208 Oshkosh Blvd, Pettisville, OH
43553-0177, 419-555-0119 (Corp.)

CUSTOMER ORDER NO. 5007

SOLD BY DK

SHIPPED VIA Priority Mail

QTY.	CAT. NO.	DESCRIPTION	UNIT PRICE	AMOUNT
1	13-471	Work gloves	$39.60	$ 39.60
2	24-701	Floor brush	$16.99	$ 33.98

SUBTOTAL	$73.58
6% SALES TAX (IF APPLICABLE)	$4.41
SHIPPING CHARGES	$10.00
TOTAL	$87.99

☑ ORIGINAL ☐ COPY

PLEASE DETACH ALONG DASHED LINE AND RETURN THE BOTTOM PORTION WITH YOUR REMITTANCE.

FROM:
18 Wheeler Truck Lines
1208 Oshkosh Blvd, Pettisville, OH
43553-0177, 419-555-0119 (Corp.)

INVOICE NO. 2000

BILL DATE	AMOUNT DUE
July 9, 2007	$87.99

REMITTANCE ADVICE
Please write your invoice number on your check to ensure proper credit and mail it with this remittance slip.

PLEASE MAKE CHECKS PAYABLE TO:

BUCKEYE EQUIPMENT
1313 Olentangy Road
Pettisville, OH 43553-0175

AMOUNT ENCLOSED	

TERMS: DUE UPON RECEIPT

Name	Evaluation

ACTIVITY 4·4: PREPARING A SERVICE INVOICE

Directions: *Assume you are the manager of Creative Advertising Agency. On* **July 8,** *you produced advertising brochures and fliers for Pettisville Bank. Use the form on the back of this sheet to prepare a service invoice for the bank.*

1. Study Creative Advertising Agency's rate chart at the bottom of this page. You will use this rate chart to find the fees for the services listed on the invoice.

2. Turn to *page 163 in this Student Reference Book*. Find the steps titled *Follow these steps when preparing a service invoice*. **Complete steps 2 and 3.** List the following charges on the invoice.

   500 four-color brochures with 6-page folds .... $ *650.00*

   3,000 fliers on 8-1/2 by 11-inch paper *100.00*

   Commission @ 15% *112.50*

3. Sign your name on the signature line.

ADVERTISING RATES CHART

Printing Rates

Advertising Brochures (4-color)

Number of copies	500	1,000	—	—	—	—
$8\frac{1}{2}$" x 11" with 6-page folds	$650	$700	—	—	—	—

Single Sheets (fliers and poster paper signs)

Number of copies	500	1,000	2,000	3,000	5,000	10,000
$8\frac{1}{2}$" x 11" 20 lb. stock	$49	$56	$ 78	$100	$144	$254
14" x 18" poster paper 16 lb.***	$75	$93	$130	$167	$240	$420

* Rate is lowest from 7 a.m. to 12 noon on Sunday. Rate is highest from 8 p.m. to 11 p.m. Monday through Saturday.
** Usage discount: A full-page ad is $4.00 per column inch.
*** The printing rates do not cover the cost of $.22 per sheet of poster paper.

816 Corduroy Drive • Pettisville, OH 43553-0177

INVOICE NO. 7000

SERVICE INVOICE

BILL DATE

July 8, 2007

TO: Pettisville Bank
101 Greenback Drive
Pettisville OH 43553-0178
414-555-0101 (Corp.)

☑ ORIGINAL   ☐ COPY

DESCRIPTION	AMOUNT
500 4-color brochures with 6-page folds	$650.00
3,000 fliers on 8½ by 11 in paper	$100.00
Commission @15%	$112.50

Devin Kuchynka
Manager's Signature

SUBTOTAL	$862.50
6% SALES TAX	$51.75
TOTAL DUE	$914.25

Terms—Due upon receipt of invoice.

PLEASE DETACH ALONG DASHED LINE AND RETURN THE BOTTOM PORTION WITH YOUR REMITTANCE.

FROM:

INVOICE NO. _____

BILL DATE	AMOUNT DUE

_____

_____

_____

REMITTANCE ADVICE
Please write your invoice number on your check to ensure proper credit and mail it with this stub.

PLEASE MAKE CHECKS PAYABLE TO:

CREATIVE ADVERTISING AGENCY
816 Corduroy Drive
Pettisville, OH 43553-0177

AMOUNT ENCLOSED	

TERMS: DUE UPON RECEIPT

POSTAL AND SHIPPING SERVICES

Two businesses in Pettisville provide the postal and shipping services for the other businesses within the model community.

The Pettisville Post Office handles delivery of all mail and accepts packages weighing up to 70 pounds. Mail deliveries are made daily Monday through Friday. The manager of the post office will deliver all mail addressed to people or businesses within the model business community. Your Instructor will receive all mail addressed to people or businesses outside the business community.

In addition to postal services, most communities have a variety of shipping services provided by trucks, buses, airplanes, and trains. United Parcel Service (UPS) and FedEx are examples of businesses that offer fast, efficient delivery of small packages. Many trucking companies ship freight that is too heavy or bulky to meet postal standards. In the Pettisville business community, freight services for shipments over 70 pounds are handled by 18 Wheeler Truck Lines.

Unit Lessons

Lesson 5•1	**Using Postal Services**
Lesson 5•2	**Using Postage Meters**
Lesson 5•3	**Using Freight Services**

Unit Activities

Activity 5•1	**Using Postal Services**
Activity 5•2	**Using Postage Meters**
Activity 5•3	**Shipping Via 18 Wheeler Truck Lines**

USING POSTAL SERVICES

Pettisville Post Office offers a variety of postal services. Rates are set according to the weight of the mail and its zone of destination. Besides delivering letters, the post office delivers packages weighing up to 70 pounds. A special standard mail rate is available for large mailings. Other services include certified mail, insured mail, and international mail. Some postal customers use metered mail. Lesson 5.2 explains the use of postage meter machines.

Envelopes may be mailed either at the post office or dropped in the community mailbox. Only envelopes may be put in the mailbox. Packages must be mailed at the post office. When paying for postage and other postal services, managers should write checks payable to *Pettisville Post Office*.

USING POSTAGE STAMPS

Businesses without postage meter machines (except for Pettisville Post Office) will use postage stamps to mail envelopes. Mail delivered from Pettisville Post Office will have a special mailing notation in the top right-hand corner of each envelope that reads *Official Business*. Envelopes are sent by first-class mail and require one 42¢ stamp.

All businesses without postage meter machines will have six 42¢ stamps when they open for business on July 2. Additional postage stamps may then be purchased by check from Pettisville Post Office when all stamps have been used or when the *DAILY ACTIVITIES* direct it—whichever comes first.

CHOOSING CLASSES OF MAIL

Pettisville Post Office offers three classes of mail delivery—priority mail, express mail, and standard mail.

Priority mail is first-class mail rated by weight and distance carried. It includes first-class letters and packages weighing more than 12 ounces.

Express mail is the fastest delivery service offered by the U.S. Postal Service. Since postal rates for express mail are expensive, priority mail is normally used unless speed of delivery is important.

Standard mail is mail sent in bulk and addressed, sorted, and prepared according to postal standards. Mailings must be at least 200 pieces or 50 pounds. Sorting and bundling the mail reduces handling by the post office, so a reduced postage rate is charged. Lower nonprofit rates are available for standard mail but require special authorization. Businesses that use standard mail must have a permit and pay an annual fee of $150. Standard mail is frequently used by nonprofit organizations and by businesses that advertise using direct mail. Two Pettisville businesses use standard mail. Lee Community Center sends monthly newsletters to residents in the community, and Mean Jeans Manufacturing Co. sends direct mail advertising at standard mail rates.

 USING SPECIAL POSTAL SERVICES

Insured mail is mail that includes a small fee, in addition to the regular postage, to insure the value of the contents of a package against loss, damage, or rifling. Both domestic and international mail may be insured. If a loss occurs, the post office will pay for the depreciated value of the contents or the cost of repairs.

©GETTY IMAGES/PHOTODISC

International mail is mail sent to an address outside the borders of the United States. The general categories of international mail include Global Mail Express Guaranteed, Global Mail Express, Global Priority, Airmail, and Economy.

Certified mail is a postal service that provides a mailing receipt for the sender and proof of delivery. Certified mail should not be used for items of value. Use certified mail when proof of mailing and the delivery date are important on mail that has no value of its own, such as a contract or an important notice.

 USING EXPRESS MAIL

When speed of delivery is urgent, you should send envelopes or packages by express mail. Mail sent for express delivery will arrive on the next day or the second day. The rate for delivery from post office to post office is slightly less than delivery from the post office to the addressee.

Follow these steps when sending express mail

1. Ask your Instructor for a large manila envelope (approximately 9 inches by 12 inches).

2. Find your express mail label.

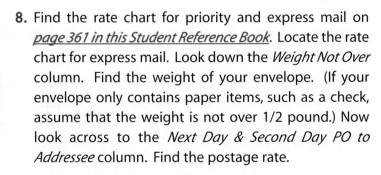
3. Notice there are 2 forms on the sheet. Use scissors and cut along the dashed lines and through the middle of the page to separate the 2 forms. Use one of the forms as a mailing label for the package. Discard the extra form.

4. Remove the address labels and return address labels from the Office File. Remove 1 address label for the addressee (the person or business receiving the mail). Remove 1 return address label for your business. Return the address labels sheets to the Office File.

5. Look at the express mail form. Notice the section of the form titled *CUSTOMER USE ONLY*. Affix the return address label for your business in the box titled *FROM* at the bottom left-hand side of the form. Write the telephone number for your business on the *PHONE* line.

6. Affix the address label for the addressee in the box titled *TO* at the bottom right-hand side of the form. Write the telephone number for your addressee on the *PHONE* line.

7. Use glue or strong tape to affix the label to the front of the manila envelope. Place the item(s) in the envelope and seal the envelope.

©GETTY IMAGES/PHOTODISC

8. Find the rate chart for priority and express mail on <u>page 361 in this Student Reference Book</u>. Locate the rate chart for express mail. Look down the *Weight Not Over* column. Find the weight of your envelope. (If your envelope only contains paper items, such as a check, assume that the weight is not over 1/2 pound.) Now look across to the *Next Day & Second Day PO to Addressee* column. Find the postage rate.

9. Take your checkbook and the express mail envelope to the post office. Tell the manager that you want to send this envelope by express mail. Pay the fee for the postage.

10. Return to your place of business. Record the payment for the postage in your cashbook. If necessary, turn to <u>page 58 in this Student Reference Book</u>. Complete the steps titled *Follow these steps when recording <u>cash payments</u> (by check) in the cashbook*. Record *Postage* in the EXPLANATION column of the cashbook.

UNIT 5 • POSTAL AND SHIPPING SERVICES

❖ MAILING PACKAGES OUTSIDE THE BUSINESS COMMUNITY

Packages mailed to destinations outside the business community must be within the limits of size and weight that are in effect at Pettisville Post Office. The *DAILY ACTIVITIES* describe the size and weight of packages you mail in your classroom. Your Instructor may provide you with pre-addressed shipping labels.

For this simulation, use priority (first-class) mail for packages weighing less than 70 pounds when time is not a major concern. Use express mail for packages weighing less than 70 pounds when time is a major concern.

Please Note

If you are shipping to an address OUTSIDE of Pettisville, you will get a cardboard box from your Instructor and wrap a package. If you are shipping to an address WITHIN Pettisville, you will prepare a shipment form rather than wrap a package. The shipment form represents the goods being shipped.

Follow these steps when preparing a package for mailing

1. Get a cardboard box from your Instructor—one that will hold the size of the item(s) you are sending.

2. Remove 1 sheet of plain paper from your Supplies folder. Write the name of the item(s) you are sending on the sheet of paper. Place the sheet of paper in the cardboard box. This sheet of paper represents the item(s) you will mail.

3. Cushion the contents with wadded newspaper, if available. Seal the box with strong tape. Make sure all edges of the box are tightly sealed.

4. Remove the large pre-addressed shipping label from the Supplies folder. (This is an optional form and may not be provided by your Instructor. If you do not have shipping labels, use the mailing address labels in your Office File.)

5. Affix the shipping label to the center of the box.

6. Calculate the postal charges. Your *DAILY ACTIVITIES* will tell you the weight of the package. Turn to *page 182 in this Student Reference Book*. Find the steps titled *Follow these steps when calculating postal charges*. **Complete steps 1, 2, and 3**. Then return to these steps.

   Write the amount of the postage fee
   $_____ (package #1) $_____ (package #2)

7. Take the wrapped package and your checkbook and go to Pettisville Post Office. Be prepared to tell the manager the weight of the package.

UNIT 5 • POSTAL AND SHIPPING SERVICES

8. Tell the manager if any special service (such as insurance or certified mail) is needed. Your *DAILY ACTIVITIES* will tell you if you are to request any special service.

9. Write a check for the amount of the postage.

10. Return to your place of business. Record the payment in your cashbook. If necessary, turn to *page 58 in this Student Reference Book*. Complete the steps titled *Follow these steps when recording cash payments (by check) in the cashbook*. Record *Postage Fees* in the EXPLANATION column of the cashbook.

◆ CALCULATING POSTAL CHARGES

By using the rate charts for Pettisville Post Office located on *pages 359-362 in this Student Reference Book*, you will be able to calculate postal charges before you carry your package to the post office.

Follow these steps when calculating postal charges

1. Check to be sure the package does not weigh more than 70 pounds.

2. Find the zone of destination.

■ *If you are shipping express mail,* go to step 3 below.

■ *If you are shipping priority mail within Pettisville,* go to step 3 below. Use the *Local 1, 2, & 3* column of the rate chart.

■ *If you are shipping priority mail outside of Pettisville,* find the zone of destination on the Zone Chart on *page 360 in this Student Reference Book*. Locate the first three digits of the ZIP Code to which the package is addressed. To the right of the first three digits of the ZIP Code is the postal zone. The number may fall within a range of numbers. For example, in the ZIP code 31702, the first 3 digits (317) fall within the range 312…329. ZIP code 31702 is in Zone 5.

3. Find the postal rate. Refer to the Chart of Priority and Express Mail Rates on *page 361 in this Student Reference Book*.

■ *If you are shipping priority mail,* use the chart on the left side of the rate chart. Find the weight of your package. Then move across to the column showing the zones.

■ *If you are shipping express mail,* use the chart on the right side of the rate chart. Find the weight of your package. Then move across to the *Next Day & Second Day PO to Addressee* column.

4. Write the amount of the charge for postage on a scratch sheet of paper, or, if you are processing a purchase order, on the available white space on the purchase order.

5. Return to your previous steps for shipping.

❖ PREPARING SHIPMENT FORMS FOR GOODS SHIPPED WITHIN THE BUSINESS COMMUNITY

Products sold by your business shipped to destinations within the business community must meet the limits of size and weight that are in effect at Pettisville Post Office. Your *DAILY ACTIVITIES* will describe the size and weight of the package(s).

▓ Follow these steps when preparing a shipment form for the post office

1. Find your shipment form. A shipment form represents the goods you are shipping and will be delivered by the post office.

📓 *If you are using Instructor-provided forms,* remove 1 set of shipment forms from your Supplies folder. If there are 2 shipment forms on the sheet, use scissors to remove 1 form from the sheet. Place the extra form in the Supplies folder.

🖱 *If you are printing your forms,* open the forms document. Find Unit 5 Postal and Shipping Services. Print 1 set of shipment forms. Use scissors to remove 1 shipment form from the sheet. Place the extra form in the Supplies folder.

---

2. Complete the shipment form.
    a. Write today's July DATE in the box provided.
    b. Write the TOTAL WEIGHT in the box provided. This information comes from the notations you made on the purchase order, the price lists within *pages 351-366 in this Student Reference Book,* or your *DAILY ACTIVITIES.*
    c. Place a ✔ in the PRIORITY MAIL or EXPRESS MAIL section provided for postal shipments. This information comes from the customer's purchase order or your *DAILY ACTIVITIES.*
    d. Use a mailing address label, or write the name and address of the business or person receiving the shipment in the SHIP TO box.

3. Calculate the postal charges. Look at the opposite page. Complete the steps titled *Follow these steps when calculating postal charges.* Then return to these steps.

4. Take the shipment form and your checkbook and go to the post office. Write a check for the amount of postage.

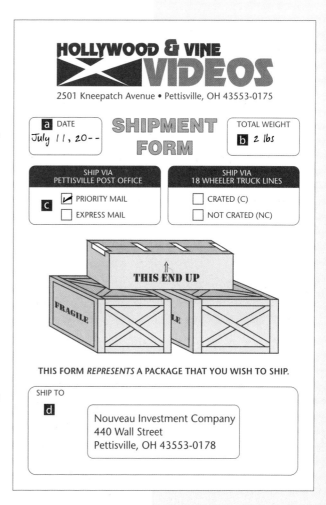

5. Return to your place of business. Record the payment in your cashbook. If necessary, turn to *page 58 in this Student Reference Book*. Complete the steps titled *Follow these steps when recording cash payments (by check) in the cashbook*. Record *Postage Fees* in the EXPLANATION column of the cashbook. **NOTE:** If you are preparing an item invoice, be sure to return to the steps for completing your invoice.

CHECKPOINT

Choosing the Correct Postal Service

Answer the following questions.

1. A $200 camera sent through the U.S. Postal Service should be __insured__ to protect the value of the contents.

2. An important contract should be sent __certified__ mail to make sure the addressee receives it.

3. A letter mailed to Germany should be sent by __international__ mail.

4. A first-class letter should be sent by __priority__ mail.

5. A church mailing 400 bulletins each week to its members should use __standard__ to get a reduced postage rate.

Doing Business on the 'Net

USPS Online

At the USPS web site, **www.usps.com**, you can

❏ look up ZIP codes
❏ calculate postage
❏ buy stamps
❏ purchase phone cards, stationery, and gifts
❏ send secure electronic documents
❏ locate post offices
❏ track and confirm shipments
❏ order shipping supplies

USING POSTAGE METERS

LESSON 5•2

A **postage meter** is a machine that prints the amount of postage on an envelope and seals the envelope. The postage may be printed either directly on an envelope or onto a pre-moistened label that is affixed to an envelope or package. Metered mail is already dated and postmarked. Therefore, it is processed much faster than stamped mail. The imprint of a fully automatic meter machine may also carry a slogan or a line of advertising.

Businesses today replenish the postage on the meter electronically either by phone or through the Internet. In the past, businesses removed the head of the meter and took it to the post office to replenish the postage. For this simulation, the postage meter sheet will represent a postage meter. If your business has a postage meter, then you will take this sheet to the post office to replenish your postage.

©PITNEY BOWES

The meter registers the amount of postage used on each piece of mail, the amount of postage remaining on the meter, and the number of pieces that have passed through the machine.

All envelopes are sent by first-class mail and require 42¢ postage. An imprint made by a postage meter machine follows.

City in which company is located ——→ PETTISVILLE

Date ——→ JUL 00 – –

State ——→ OHIO

P.B. METER 6 9 6 2 3 4

U.S. POSTAGE ≈ 0.42 ≈

Proper postage

Meter number

The following four Pettisville businesses use postage meter machines. All four have postage on their meters when they open for business on July 2.

- Creative Advertising Agency
- Pettisville Bank
- Taylor Office Supplies
- United Communications

Follow these steps when using a postage meter

POSTAGE METER SHEET

POSTAGE METER NUMBER: **216077**

NAME OF COMPANY TO WHOM POSTAGE METER IS ISSUED: *Pettisville Bank*

TO BE COMPLETED BY POSTAL OFFICIAL

DATE	AMOUNT OF POSTAGE	INITIALS OF POSTAL OFFICIAL
_____	_____	_____
_____	_____	_____

TO BE COMPLETED BY MANAGER

DATE	POSTAGE PURCHASED	POSTAGE USED	POSTAGE REMAINING ON METER*
July 1	_____	_____	$10.99
July 3	_____	.42	10.57
July 5	200.00	_____	210.57
	_____	_____	_____
	_____	_____	_____
	_____	_____	_____
	_____	_____	_____
	_____	_____	_____
	_____	_____	_____
	_____	_____	_____
	_____	_____	_____

*When the amount in this column drops below $10.00, you must purchase additional postage.

1. Remove 1 envelope from the Supplies folder. Remove a postage meter imprint from the postage envelope in your Cash File. Affix it to the top right-hand corner of the envelope.

PETTISVILLE
JUL 00 --
OHIO

U.S. POSTAGE
≈ 0.42 ≈
P.B. METER
256077

2. Remove the Postage Meter Sheet from the Cash File.

3. Make a record of the postage used. Notice that the upper portion of the sheet is to be completed by the post office. Complete the lower portion of the sheet each time you mail an envelope. Record the July date under the DATE column. Record the amount of postage used under the POSTAGE USED column. Subtract the postage used from the balance in the POSTAGE REMAINING ON METER column. Record the new balance.

4. Return the Postage Meter Sheet to the Cash File.

5. Address and mail the envelope. Turn to *page 99 in this Student Reference Book*. Find the steps titled *Follow these steps when addressing envelopes*. **Complete steps 2 through 5.**

Follow these steps when you replenish the postage on your postage meter

1. Read the information about postage meters on *pages 185-186 in this Student Reference Book*.

2. Remove your postage meter sheet and checkbook from the Cash File. Take both of these with you and go to the post office.

3. Write a check for $100.00 payable to *Pettisville Post Office*. Give the check and the postage meter sheet to the manager. When the

186

STUDENT REFERENCE BOOK • PART 3 Reference Guide

UNIT 5 • POSTAL AND SHIPPING SERVICES

manager hands the postage meter labels to you, return to your place of business.

4. Make a record of the postage purchased. Write today's July date and the amount of postage purchased. Add the amount purchased to the balance remaining on the meter and record the new balance.

5. Record the payment in your cashbook. Turn to *page 58 in this Student Reference Book*. Complete the steps titled *Follow these steps when recording cash payments (by check) in the cashbook*. Record *Postage* in the EXPLANATION column of the cashbook.

CHECKPOINT

Using a Postage Meter

Answer the following questions.

1. _____ labels are used to affix postage to a package using a postage meter.

2. A postage meter prints the amount of postage on an envelope and also _____ the envelope.

3. The imprint of a meter machine may carry a slogan or a line of _____ .

4. Many businesses today use _____ services that reset the meter right in their offices.

5. _____ is dated, postmarked mail that is processed much faster than stamped mail.

INTERNET EXPLORATIONS

1. Below are web addresses for several well-known companies that specialize in postage meters and other mail-handling equipment. Explore their sites.
   a. *www.pitneybowes.com*   b. *www.neopost.com*
   c. *www.francotyp.com*

2. You can print your own postage from your computer. Go to the following web site and play the demo to see how this is done.
   a. *www.stamps.com*

3. Today, the pace of business is so fast that many companies use "overnight services" to move their small packages for next-day delivery. Explore the following sites.
   a. *www.fedex.com*   b. *www.ups.com*
   c. *www.airborne.com*   d. *www.dhl.com*

USING FREIGHT SERVICES

Freight services are usually the most economical way to transport heavy items, bulky goods, large quantities, and unpackaged or uncrated freight. Goods that are transported are called **freight** or shipments. A local trucking company, 18 Wheeler Truck Lines, provides next-day delivery service within the community. Although this truck line offers coast-to-coast delivery service, you will arrange shipments only for local deliveries.

You will use 18 Wheeler Truck Lines whenever you have a shipment that weighs over 70 pounds. Local shipments (deliveries made in the Pettisville area) are rated according to the total weight and whether the shipment is crated/palletized or not crated/not palletized. **Crated** freight is transported in wooden boxes called crates while **palletized** freight is transported on portable wooden platforms called pallets. Freight placed in crates or on pallets can be lifted by forklift operators, but loose freight must be lifted by warehouse employees. The rate chart shown on *page 351 in this Student Reference Book* shows the rates charged for shipping goods.

When you ship via 18 Wheeler Truck Lines, you will prepare a bill of lading. A **bill of lading** is a form listing goods received for shipment by a trucking company promising delivery. The bill of lading shows what goods have been turned over to 18 Wheeler to ship and the weight of the goods.

STRAIGHT BILL OF LADING

SHORT FORM – Original – Not Negotiable
RECEIVED, subject to the classifications and tariffs in effect on the date of the issue of this Bill of Lading.

SHIPPER'S NO. _751_

AGENT'S NO. _279_

Carrier _18 Wheeler Truck Lines_

SHIPPER _The Denim Maker_   Date _July 9,_ 20 _– –_

Consigned to _Mean Jeans Manufacturing Co._

Street _45 Maple Street_   City _Pettisville_   State _OH_

Routing _____

Delivering Carrier _18 Wheeler Truck Lines_   Vehicle or Car Initial _____ No. _____

The property described below, in apparent good order, except as noted (contents and condition of contents of packages unknown) marked consigned and destined as indicated below, which said carrier (the word carrier being understood throughout this contract as meaning any person or corporation in possession of the property under the contract) agrees to carry to its usual place of delivery at said destination, if on its route, otherwise to deliver to another carrier on the route to said destination. It is mutually agreed, as to each carrier of all or any of said property over all or any portion of said route to destination, and as to each party at any time interested in all or any of said property that every service to be performed hereunder shall be subject to all the terms and conditions of the Uniform Domestic Straight Bill of Lading set forth (1) in Official Southern Western and Illinois Freight Classifications in effect on the date hereof, if this is a rail or rail-water shipment or (2) in the applicable motor carrier classification or tariff if this is a motor carrier shipment.
    Shipper hereby certifies that he is familiar with all the terms and conditions of the said bill of lading, including those on the back thereof, set forth in the classification or tariff which governs the transportation of this shipment, and the said terms and conditions are hereby agreed to by the shipper and accepted for himself and his assigns.

NO. PACKAGES	DESCRIPTION OF ARTICLES	WEIGHT
1	bolt brown duck denim	320#

If the shipment moves between two ports by a carrier by water, the law requires that the bill of lading shall state whether it is "carrier's or shipper's weight."
NOTE—Where the rate is dependent on value, shippers are reqired to state specifically in writing the agreed or declared value of the property.
The agreed or declared value of the property is hereby specifically stated by the shipper to be not exceeding _____ per _____

SHIPPER _The Denim Maker_   Per _JGB_

SHIPPER'S ADDRESS _752 Gold Mine Lane, Pettisville, OH 43553-0176_

Agent _18 Wheeler Truck Lines_   Per _DLM_   _July 10,_ 20 _– –_

Subject to Section 7 of conditions of applicable bill of lading, if this shipment is to be delivered to the consignee without recourse on the consignor, the consignor shall sign the following statement.
    The carrier shall not make delivery of this shipment without payment of freight and all other lawful charges.

_____
(Signature of Consignor)

Received $ _____
to apply in prepayment of the charges on the property described hereon.

_____
Agent or Cashier

Per _____
(The signature here acknowledges only the amount prepaid.)

If charges are to be prepaid, write or stamp here, "To be Prepaid."

To Be Prepaid

Charges Advanced $ _____

†Shipper's imprint in lieu of stamp not a part of Bill of Lading approved by the Interstate Commerce Commission.

†"The fibre boxes used for this shipment conform to the specifications set forth in the box maker's certificate thereon, and all other requirements of Uniform Freight Classification."

☑ ORIGINAL   ☐ SHIPPING ORDER   ☐ MEMORANDUM

Look at the bill of lading illustrated on the previous page. Three names appear on the bill of lading—the carrier (or agent), the shipper, and the consignee. The **carrier** (18 Wheeler Truck Lines) is the agent transporting goods from the shipper to the consignee. The **consignee** (Mean Jeans) is the business receiving the goods. The *shipper* (The Denim Maker) is the business shipping the freight.

©GETTY IMAGES/PHOTODISC

Each bill of lading lists a shipper number and an agent number. Shipper numbers are provided for each business shipping by 18 Wheeler. The agent's number for 18 Wheeler is No. 279. Look at the body of the bill of lading. One bolt of brown duck denim is being shipped. The shipment weighs 320 pounds. The # symbol is frequently used as an abbreviation for pounds.

A shipment form is also prepared to hand to the 18 Wheeler driver. For this simulation, the shipment form represents the actual goods being shipped. After goods have been delivered, 18 Wheeler Truck Lines will send a freight bill to the shipper. A **freight bill** is a bill for a shipment of merchandise prepared by a common carrier, such as a trucking company.

Bills of lading are completed in triplicate by the shipper. The ORIGINAL copy is mailed to the consignee (the business receiving the goods), the SHIPPING ORDER copy is given to the carrier (18 Wheeler Truck Lines) when the shipment is picked up, and the MEMORANDUM copy is retained for the shipper's files. Bills of lading may be prepared either manually (by hand) or electronically.

Look at the diagram below. It shows the steps completed from the time the buyer places an order until the shipment actually arrives at the buyer's place of business. Carefully follow the steps outlined below for completing a bill of lading and arranging a shipment.

Day 1	**Day 2**	**Day 2**	**Day 3**	**Day 3**
Buyer (consignee) prepares the purchase order and mails it to the supplier.	Supplier (shipper) receives the purchase order in the mail and prepares the 1. shipment form 2. bill of lading 3. item invoice	1. Shipper takes the bill of lading to 18 Wheeler to arrange the shipment. 2. 18 Wheeler (carrier) uses bill of lading to prepare a freight bill that will be sent to the shipper later. 3. Shipper leaves with the bill of lading in hand.	1. 18 Wheeler drives to shipper's address. 2. The 18 Wheeler driver fills in the agent number and the bottom portion of the bill of lading. 3. Driver drives away with the goods (shipment form) and the SHIPPING ORDER copy of the bill of lading.	1. 18 Wheeler delivers goods (shipment form) to consignee. 2. Consignee signs the delivery log.

1. Find your shipment form.

If you are using Instructor-provided forms, remove 1 set of shipment forms from your Supplies folder. If there are 2 shipment forms on the sheet, use scissors to remove 1 form from the sheet. Place the extra form in the Supplies folder.

If you are printing your forms, open the forms document. Find Unit 5 Postal and Shipping Services. Print 1 set of shipment forms. Use scissors to remove 1 shipment form from the sheet. Place the extra form in the Supplies folder.

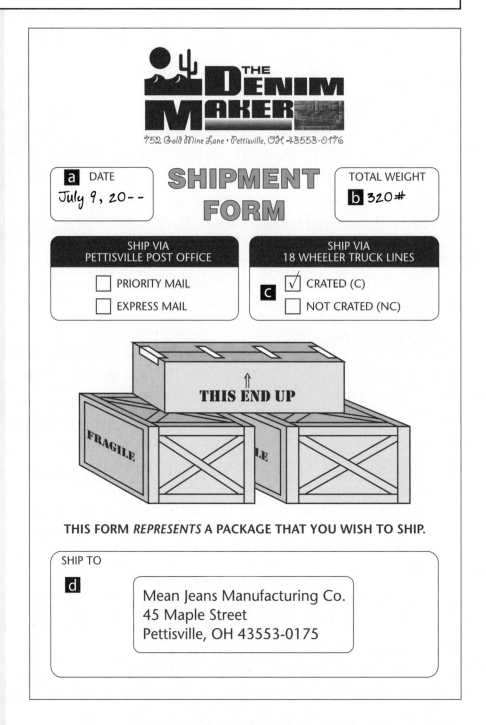

THE DENIM MAKER

752 Gold Mine Lane • Pettisville, OH 43553-0176

a DATE
July 9, 20--

SHIPMENT FORM

TOTAL WEIGHT
b 320#

SHIP VIA
PETTISVILLE POST OFFICE

☐ PRIORITY MAIL
☐ EXPRESS MAIL

SHIP VIA
18 WHEELER TRUCK LINES

c ☑ CRATED (C)
☐ NOT CRATED (NC)

THIS END UP

FRAGILE

THIS FORM *REPRESENTS* A PACKAGE THAT YOU WISH TO SHIP.

SHIP TO

d
Mean Jeans Manufacturing Co.
45 Maple Street
Pettisville, OH 43553-0175

2. Complete the shipment form. This form represents the goods you are shipping and will be delivered by 18 Wheeler.

   a. Write today's July DATE in the box provided.

   b. Write the TOTAL WEIGHT in the box provided. (This information comes from the notations you made on the purchase order, the price lists within *pages 351-366 in this Student Reference Book*, or your *DAILY ACTIVITIES*.)

   c. Place a ✔ in the CRATED or NOT CRATED section provided for 18 Wheeler shipments. (This information comes from the notations you made on the purchase order, the footnotes at the bottom of the price lists within *pages 351-366 in this Student Reference Book*, or your *DAILY ACTIVITIES*.)

   d. Use a mailing address label, or write the name and address of the business receiving the shipment in the SHIP TO box.

3. Calculate the rate. Turn to 18 Wheeler's Local Cartage Rates chart on *page 351 in this Student Reference Book*. Look down the WEIGHT/POUNDS column and find the total weight of the shipment. Then look across the rate chart to the CRATED/PALLETIZED or NOT CRATED/NOT PALLETIZED columns. Find the rate for your shipment. Write the total of the rate on the available white space on the purchase order. (If you are preparing a rental and maintenance contract, you will not have a purchase order.)

4. Place the shipment form in your Pending File.

5. Find your bill of lading.

> **Please Note**
>
> The letter designations in the illustration on *page 192 in this Student Reference Book* correspond to the letters "a" through "k" that follow. The portions of the bill of lading that do not have these letters will be completed by the 18 Wheeler driver, not by the shipper, or will be left blank.

📄 *If you are preparing your bill of lading manually,* remove 1 bill of lading from your Supplies folder.	🖱 *If you are preparing your bill of lading electronically,* open the bill of lading. Use the tab key to move from line to line.

---

6. Complete the top part (the heading) of the bill of lading. Keep in mind that you are the shipper.

   a. Record the SHIPPER'S NO. Use the first number that is not crossed off the Shipper's Number List below. Cross off the number you used so that it cannot be used again.

SHIPPER'S NUMBER LIST

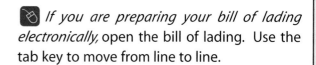

~~751~~ ~~752~~ 753 754 755 756 757 758 759 760 761
762 763 764 765 766 767 768 769 770 771 772

   b. Record *18 Wheeler Truck Lines* as the carrier.

   c. Record your company name as the SHIPPER.

d. Record today's July date.

e. Record the name and address of the consignee (the business receiving the shipment) on the *Consigned to* lines. Leave the next line (the Routing line) blank.

f. Record *18 Wheeler Truck Lines* on the *Delivering Carrier* line. Leave the *Vehicle or Car Initial* and the *No.* lines blank.

STRAIGHT BILL OF LADING

a SHIPPER'S NO. _____ **751** _____

SHORT FORM – Original – Not Negotiable

RECEIVED, subject to the classifications and tariffs in effect on the date of the issue of this Bill of Lading.

AGENT'S NO. _____

b → Carrier   **18 Wheeler Truck Lines** _____

c → SHIPPER   **The Denim Maker** _____ Date **d** **July 9** 20 **--**

e → Consigned to **Mean Jeans Manufacturing Co.** _____

Street   **45 Maple Street** _____ City **Pettisville** State **OH**

Routing _____

f → Delivering
Carrier   **18 Wheeler Truck Lines** _____ Vehicle or Car Initial _____ No. _____

The property described below, in apparent good order, except as noted (contents and condition of contents of packages unknown) marked consigned and destined as indicated below, which said carrier (the word carrier being understood throughout this contract as meaning any person or corporation in possession of the property under the contract) agrees to carry to its usual place of delivery at said destination, if on its route, otherwise to deliver to another carrier on the route to said destination. It is mutually agreed, as to each carrier of all or any of said property over all or any portion of said route to destination, and as to each party at any time interested in all or any of said property, that every service to be performed hereunder shall be subject to all the terms and conditions of the Uniform Domestic Straight Bill of Lading set forth (1) in Official Southern Western and Illinois Freight Classifications in effect on the date hereof, if this is a rail or rail-water shipment or (2) in the applicable motor carrier classification or tariff if this is a motor carrier shipment.

Shipper hereby certifies that he is familiar with all the terms and conditions of the said bill of lading, including those on the back thereof, set forth in the classification or tariff which governs the transportation of his shipment, and the said terms and conditions are hereby agreed to by the shipper and accepted for himself and his assigns.

NO. PACKAGES	DESCRIPTION OF ARTICLES	WEIGHT
g → 1	bolt of brown duck denim	320#

If the shipment moves between two ports by a carrier by water, the law requires that the bill of lading shall state whether it is "carrier's or shipper's weight." **NOTE**—Where the rate is dependent on value, shippers are required to state specifically in writing the agreed or declared value of the property. The agreed or declared value of the property is hereby specifically stated by the shipper to be not exceeding _____ per _____

h → SHIPPER   **The Denim Maker** _____ Per **JGB** **i**

j → SHIPPER'S ADDRESS   **752 Gold Mine Lane, Pettisville, Ohio 43553-0176** _____

AGENT _____ Per _____ _____ 20 ____

Subject to Section 7 of conditions of applicable bill of lading if this shipment is to be delivered to the consignee without recourse on the consignor, the consignor shall sign the following statement.

The carrier shall not make delivery of this shipment without payment of freight and all other lawful charges.

_____
(Signature of Consignor)

Received $ _____
to apply in prepayment of the charges on the property described hereon.

_____
Agent or Cashier

Per _____
(The signature here acknowledges only the amount prepaid.)

If charges are to be prepaid, write or stamp here, "To be Prepaid."

k → **To Be Prepaid**

Charges Advanced $ _____

†Shipper's imprint in lieu of stamp not a part of Bill of Lading approved by the Interstate Commerce Commission.

†"The fibre boxes used for this shipment conform to the specifications set forth in the box maker's certificate thereon, and all other requirements of Uniform Freight Classification."

⦿ ORIGINAL   ◯ SHIPPING ORDER   ◯ MEMORANDUM

7. Complete the main part (body) of the bill of lading.

    g. Record the NO. PACKAGES, DESCRIPTION OF ARTICLES, and the WEIGHT of each package shipped. Leave the next line blank—the line below the 3 columns.

    h. Record your business's name on the SHIPPER line.

    i. Record your initials on the *Per* line beside your business's name. Doing so indicates that you agree with all information on the form.

    j. Record your business's address on the SHIPPER'S ADDRESS line. Leave the *Agent*, *Per*, and date lines blank.

8. Complete the bottom part of the bill of lading. Notice there are 4 boxes at the bottom of the bill of lading. Leave 3 of these boxes blank.

    k. Record the words *To Be Prepaid* in the bottom left-hand box.

9. Make copies of the bill of lading.

If you are preparing your bill of lading *manually*, ask your Instructor to make 2 photocopies of the bill of lading. Be sure to come back to these steps when you receive the photocopies. Identify the 3 copies of the bill of lading. Place a ✔ in the ORIGINAL box on one form, another ✔ in the SHIPPING ORDER box on a second form, and a ✔ in the MEMORANDUM box on a third form.

If you are preparing your bill of lading *electronically*, be sure ORIGINAL has been selected before you print the bill of lading. Print 1 ORIGINAL. Then select SHIPPING ORDER. Print 1 SHIPPING ORDER. Now select MEMORANDUM. Print 1 MEMORANDUM. Save your work.

---

10. Take 1 copy of the bill of lading and go in person to the carrier (18 Wheeler Truck Lines) to arrange to have the shipment picked up. The carrier will need the information from the bill of lading to prepare a freight bill. Determine a specific date and time of day when the shipment will be picked up.

11. Take the bill of lading with you and return to your place of business. Record on your July calendar the exact date and time the goods will be picked up by the carrier.

JULY APPOINTMENT CALENDAR			Name:			
SUNDAY	MONDAY	TUESDAY	WEDNESDAY	THURSDAY	FRIDAY	SATURDAY
1	2	3	4 Independence Day	5	6	7
8	9	10 9 a.m. goods to be picked up by 18 Wheeler	11	12	13	14
15	16	17	18	19	20	21
22	23	24	25	26	27	28
29	30	31	Notes:			

©GETTY IMAGES/PHOTODISC

12. Paper clip the 3 copies of the bill of lading to the shipment form. Place all 4 papers in the Pending File. These forms will remain in the Pending File until the carrier comes to pick up the shipment.

13. Return to the steps for completing your invoice or rental and maintenance contract. When the 18 Wheeler driver arrives to pick up the shipment, you will complete steps 14 through 18 below.

When the Carrier Arrives to Pick Up the Shipment

14. Remove the 3 copies of the bill of lading and the shipment form from your Pending File.

STRAIGHT BILL OF LADING

SHORT FORM – Original – Not Negotiable

RECEIVED, subject to the classifications and tariffs in effect on the date of the issue of this Bill of Lading.

SHIPPER'S NO. **751**

AGENT'S NO. **279** **a**

Carrier **18 Wheeler Truck Lines**

SHIPPER **The Denim Maker** Date **July 9** 20 —

Consigned to **Mean Jeans Manufacturing Co.**

Street **45 Maple Street** City **Pettisville** State **OH**

Routing

Delivering Carrier **18 Wheeler Truck Lines** Vehicle or Car Initial ___ No. ___

The property described below, in apparent good order, except as noted (contents and condition of contents of packages unknown) marked consigned and destined as indicated below, which said carrier (the word carrier being understood throughout this contract as meaning any person or corporation in possession of the property under the contract) agrees to carry to its usual place of delivery at said destination, if on its route, otherwise to deliver to another carrier on the route to said destination. It is mutually agreed, as to each carrier of all or any of said property over all or any portion of said route to destination, and as to each party at any time interested in all or any of said property, that every service to be performed hereunder shall be subject to all the terms and conditions of the Uniform Domestic Straight Bill of Lading set forth (1) in Official, Southern, Western and Illinois Freight Classifications in effect on the date hereof, if this is a rail or rail-water shipment or (2) in the applicable motor carrier classification or tariff if this is a motor carrier shipment.

Shipper hereby certifies that he is familiar with all the terms and conditions of the said bill of lading, including those on the back thereof, set forth in the classification or tariff which governs the transportation of this shipment, and the said terms and conditions are hereby agreed to by the shipper and accepted for himself and his assigns.

NO. PACKAGES	DESCRIPTION OF ARTICLES	WEIGHT
1	bolt of brown duck denim	320#

If the shipment moves between two ports by a carrier by water, the law requires that the bill of lading shall state whether it is "carrier's or shipper's weight." NOTE—Where the rate is dependent on value, shippers are required to state specifically in writing the agreed or declared value of the property. The agreed or declared value of the property is hereby specifically stated by the shipper to be not exceeding _____ per _____

SHIPPER **The Denim Maker** Per **JGB**

SHIPPER'S ADDRESS **752 Gold Mine Lane, Pettisville, Ohio 43553-0176** **c** **d**

b →

AGENT *18 Wheeler Truck Lines* Per *DLM* *July 10,* 20 - -

Subject to Section 7 of conditions of applicable bill of lading if this shipment is to be delivered to the consignee without recourse on the consignor, the consignor shall sign the following statement.

The carrier shall not make delivery of this shipment without payment of freight and all other lawful charges.

_____
(Signature of Consignor)

Received $ _____ to apply in prepayment of the charges on the property described hereon.

Agent or Cashier

Per _____
(The signature here acknowledges only the amount prepaid.)

If charges are to be prepaid, write or stamp here, "To be Prepaid."

To Be Prepaid

Charges Advanced $ _____

†Shipper's imprint in lieu of stamp not a part of Bill of Lading approved by the Interstate Commerce Commission.

†"The fibre boxes used for this shipment conform to the specifications set forth in the box maker's certificate thereon, and all other requirements of Uniform Freight Classification."

● ORIGINAL ○ SHIPPING ORDER ○ MEMORANDUM

194

15. Ask the driver from 18 Wheeler Truck Lines to complete the bill of lading. Use the illustration on the previous page as a guide. *Notations must be made on all 3 copies of the bill of lading.* The driver should
    a. Write the Agent's No. at the top of all 3 copies of the form.
    b. Write *18 Wheeler Truck Lines* on the line marked *Agent* at the bottom of all 3 copies of the form.
    c. Write his or her initials after the word *Per* at the bottom of all 3 copies of the form.
    d. Write the July date at the bottom of all 3 copies of the form.

16. Give the shipment form and the SHIPPING ORDER copy of the bill of lading to the driver. You should now assume that your shipment has been loaded on the truck.

When the Carrier Drives Away with the Shipment

17. Mail the ORIGINAL bill of lading to the company who ordered the goods. If necessary, refer to *page 99 in this Student Reference Book* for steps for preparing envelopes.

18. File the MEMORANDUM copy of the bill of lading in your Pending File until you receive a freight bill for the shipment.

Follow these steps when you receive a freight bill from 18 Wheeler Truck Lines

1. Remove all MEMORANDUM copies of bills of lading from the Pending File.

2. Verify the accuracy of the freight bills. Compare the information on each bill of lading with the information on each freight bill. If you prepared an item invoice for this shipment, find the matching copy of the invoice in your Pending File or your Office File. Compare the shipping charges on the invoice with the amount of the matching freight bill.

3. Add the total of the freight bills (if you have more than one).

4. Write a check for the total amount shown on the freight bill(s). Record *Freight Charges* on the FOR line of the check.

5. Record the payment in your cashbook. If necessary, refer to *page 58 in this Student Reference Book* for the steps for recording payments in the cashbook. Record *Freight Charges* in the EXPLANATION column of the cashbook.

©GETTY IMAGES/PHOTODISC

6. Use scissors to separate the freight bill(s) from the remittance slip(s) along the dashed lines. The remittance slip is the lower portion of the freight bill. The upper portion of the freight bill is for your records.

7. Complete the remittance slip.

If you have a handwritten freight bill,

a. Use a return address label, or write your company name and address on the FROM lines.

b. Copy the FREIGHT BILL NO., BILL DATE, and AMOUNT DUE from the top of the freight bill onto the slip.

c. Write the amount of your check in the AMOUNT ENCLOSED box.

If you have an electronic freight bill, write the amount of your check in the AMOUNT ENCLOSED box.

---

8. Address an envelope and mail the check and the remittance slip.

9. Write *PAID BY CHECK NO._____* on the front of the freight bill.

10. Gather the related forms.

If you prepared an invoice for this shipment, staple or paper clip 3 matching forms together—the invoice, freight bill, and bill of lading. Place these papers in the Office File. (If the invoice has not been paid, place the papers in the Pending File.)

If you prepared a rental and maintenance contract for this shipment, staple or paper clip 3 matching forms together—the rental and maintenance contract, freight bill, and bill of lading. Place these papers in the Office File.

CHECKPOINT

Shipping Freight

Answer the following questions.

1. Assume that Mean Jeans Manufacturing Co. ordered a tractor/front loader weighing 5,075 pounds from Buckeye Equipment. Since a tractor can't be shipped in your classroom, a _____ will represent the tractor.

2. If you prepared a bill of lading to ship the tractor, the bill of lading would list Mean Jeans as the _____, Buckeye Equipment as the _____, and 18 Wheeler Truck Lines as the _____.

3. The cost of sending freight by 18 Wheeler Truck Lines to other Pettisville businesses is determined by the total _____ of the shipment and whether or not the shipment is _____ or _____.

UNIT SUMMARY

LESSON 5•1 USING POSTAL SERVICES

1. Postal rates are set according to the weight of the mail and its zone of destination.

2. The post office delivers packages weighing up to 70 pounds.

3. Standard mail (bulk mail) is frequently used by nonprofit businesses and businesses that use direct (advertising) mail.

4. If insured mail is lost or damaged, the post office will pay for the depreciated value of the contents or the cost of repairs.

5. Certified mail should be used when proof of mailing and the delivery date is important on mail that has no value of its own, such as a contract or important notice.

6. Express mail is delivered on the next day or the second day.

LESSON 5•2 USING POSTAGE METERS

7. A postage meter registers the amount of postage used on each piece of mail, the amount of postage remaining on the meter, and the number of pieces that have passed through the machine.

8. Many businesses today use computerized services that reset the meter right in their offices.

LESSON 5•3 USING FREIGHT SERVICES

9. Freight services are usually the most economical way to transport heavy items, bulky goods, large quantities, and unpackaged or uncrated freight.

10. Freight placed in crates or on pallets can be lifted by forklift operators, but loose freight must be lifted by warehouse employees.

11. The original copy of a bill of lading is mailed to the consignee, the shipping order copy is given to the carrier when the shipment is picked up, and the memorandum copy is retained for the shipper's files.

12. A shipper prepares goods for shipment and completes a bill of lading and an item invoice.

13. The consignee signs a delivery log when a shipment is delivered.

Glossary

bill of lading	a form listing goods received for shipment by a trucking company promising delivery
carrier	the agent transporting goods from the shipper to the consignee
certified mail	a postal service that provides a mailing receipt for the sender and proof of delivery
consignee	the business or person who receives a shipment
crated	transported by wooden boxes called crates
express mail	the fastest delivery service offered by the U.S. Postal Service
freight	goods that are transported (same as shipment)
freight bill	a bill for a shipment of merchandise prepared by a common carrier, such as a trucking company
insured mail	mail that includes a small fee, in addition to the regular postage, to insure the value of the contents of a package against loss, damage, or rifling
international mail	mail sent to an address outside the borders of the United States
palletized	transported by portable wooden platforms called pallets
postage meter	a machine that prints the amount of postage on an envelope and seals the envelope
priority mail	first-class mail rated by weight and distance carried
standard mail	mail sent in bulk and addressed, sorted, and prepared according to postal standards

INTERNET EXPLORATIONS

The web site for the U.S. Postal Service, *www.usps.com*, has numerous online solutions to help its customers. You can look up a ZIP code for an address, calculate a postal rate, or complete a change of address form online.

1. Look up ZIP codes for the following addresses.
   a. Coca Cola, 1 Coca Cola Plaza, Atlanta, GA
   b. Oshkosh B'Gosh Inc., 11211 120th Avenue, Kenosha, WI

2. Use the domestic rate calculator to find the postage rate for a package weighing 3 lbs. 6 oz. sent by priority mail from ZIP code 30066 to ZIP code 80906.

3. Use the international rate calculator to find the postage rate for a package sent global express mail to Mozambique weighing 8 lb. 3 oz.

Name	Evaluation

ACTIVITY 5•1 USING POSTAL SERVICES

Directions: Use the zone chart and rate charts for the Pettisville Post Office to calculate the rates on letters, packages, and special services.

1. Turn to *page 179 in this Student Reference Book*. Find the steps titled *Follow these steps when sending express mail.* **Complete step 8** to find the express mail rates for the following.

   $ _13.65_ a letter weighing 4 ounces

   $ _39.20_ a package weighing 11 pounds

2. Turn to *page 182 in this Student Reference Book*. Find the steps titled *Follow these steps when calculating postal charges.* **Complete steps 2 and 3** to find the priority mail rates for the following packages.

   $ _19.75_ a 15-lb. package addressed to ZIP code 33950

   $ _20.65_ a 33-lb. package addressed to Taylor Office Supplies in Pettisville, Ohio

   $ _39.80_ a 22-lb. package addressed to ZIP code 92677

3. Use the Postage, Fees, and Services chart on *page 359 in this Student Reference Book* to find the following.

   $ _5.20_ the fee for insuring a package for $350

   $ _2.30_ the fee to send an envelope by certified mail

   $ _0.23_ the fee to mail a single postal card

4. Use the Chart of Priority and Express Mail Rates on *page 361 in this Student Reference Book* and the Postage, Fees, and Services chart on *page 359 in this Student Reference Book* to calculate the following.

   $ _26.60_ the fee to ship a 45-lb. package by priority mail within Pettisville

   $ _6.20_ the fee to insure the package for $500.00

   $ _32.80_ the total charges (shipping plus insurance)

5. Use the international rate chart on *page 362 in this Student Reference Book* to find the rate for a 4-lb. package addressed to Denmark.

   a. Find Denmark in the COUNTRY LISTING table at the bottom of the international rate chart. Look across the table to the Airmail Parcel Post Rate Group column and find the number code for Denmark. _6_

   b. Go to the rate table for Parcel Post—Air (All Countries) at the top of the international rate chart. Look down the weight column and find the weight of the package. Now look across the table to find the number code for Denmark.

   $ _20.25_

ACTIVITY 5•2 USING POSTAGE METERS

Directions: Assume you are the manager of Taylor Office Supplies. Use the postage meter sheet below to record postage used and postage purchased.

1. On July 5, you mailed a 42¢ letter to Mean Jeans Manufacturing Co. Turn to *page 186 in this Student Reference Book*. Find the steps titled *Follow these steps when using a postage meter*. **Complete step 3.**

2. On July 6, you wrote a check to the post office for $100.00 to replenish the postage on your postage meter. Turn to *page 186 in this Student Reference Book*. Find the steps titled *Follow these steps when you replenish the postage on your postage meter*. **Complete step 4.**

POSTAGE METER SHEET

POSTAGE METER NUMBER:	098341

NAME OF COMPANY TO WHOM POSTAGE METER IS ISSUED:	*Taylor Office Supplies*

TO BE COMPLETED BY POSTAL OFFICIAL

DATE	AMOUNT OF POSTAGE	INITIALS OF POSTAL OFFICIAL
_____	_____	_____
_____	_____	_____

TO BE COMPLETED BY MANAGER

DATE	POSTAGE PURCHASED	POSTAGE USED	POSTAGE REMAINING ON METER*
July 1			$10.94
July 2		.42	10.52
July 5		.42	10.10
July 6	100		110.10

*When the amount in this column drops below $10.00, you must purchase additional postage.

UNIT 5 • POSTAL AND SHIPPING SERVICES

ACTIVITY 5•3 SHIPPING VIA 18 WHEELER TRUCK LINES

Directions: *Assume you are the manager of Buckeye Equipment. You received a purchase order from Mean Jeans Manufacturing Co. for 1 garden tractor to be shipped via 18 Wheeler Truck Lines. Complete the shipment form at the bottom of this page and the bill of lading on the back of this sheet to ship the tractor. Use the date July 12, 20––.*

1. Turn to Buckeye's price list on *page 352 in this Student Reference Book*. Find the weight of the garden tractor. Look at the note at the bottom of the price list. Determine if the tractor is crated or not crated.

2. Turn to *page 190 in this Student Reference Book*. Find the steps titled *Follow these steps when shipping via 18 Wheeler Truck Lines*. **Complete step 2.**

3. **Complete step 3** on *page 191 in this Student Reference Book*.

   What is the local cartage rate for this shipment? $ <u>102.40</u>

4. **Complete steps 6 through 8** on *pages 191-193 in this Student Reference Book*.

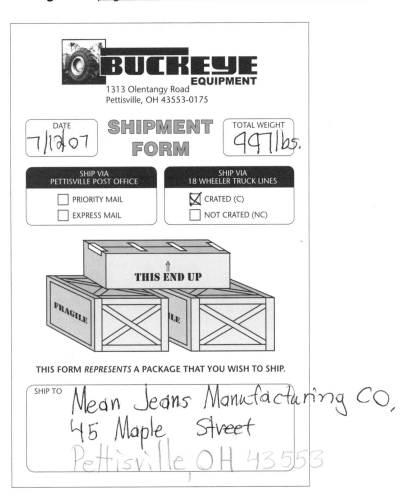

BUCKEYE EQUIPMENT
1313 Olentangy Road
Pettisville, OH 43553-0175

DATE 7/12/07

SHIPMENT FORM

TOTAL WEIGHT 497 lbs.

SHIP VIA PETTISVILLE POST OFFICE
☐ PRIORITY MAIL
☐ EXPRESS MAIL

SHIP VIA 18 WHEELER TRUCK LINES
☒ CRATED (C)
☐ NOT CRATED (NC)

THIS END UP

FRAGILE

THIS FORM *REPRESENTS* A PACKAGE THAT YOU WISH TO SHIP.

SHIP TO Mean Jeans Manufacturing Co,
45 Maple Street
Pettisville, OH 43553

STRAIGHT BILL OF LADING

SHORT FORM – Original – Not Negotiable

RECEIVED, subject to the classifications and tariffs in effect on the date of the issue of this Bill of Lading.

SHIPPER'S NO. _752_

AGENT'S NO. _____

Carrier _18 Wheeler Truck Lines_

SHIPPER _Buckeye Equipment_   Date _July 12_, 20 _07_

Consigned to _Mean Jeans Manufacturing_

Street _45 Maple Street_ City _Pettisville_ State _OH_

Routing _____

Delivering Carrier _18 Wheeler Truck Lines_ Vehicle or Car Initial _____ No. _____

The property described below, in apparent good order, except as noted (contents and condition of contents of packages unknown) marked consigned and destined as indicated above, which said carrier (the word carrier being understood throughout this contract as meaning any person or corporation in possession of the property under the contract) agrees to carry to its usual place of delivery at said destination, if on its route, otherwise to deliver to another carrier on the route to said destination. It is mutually agreed, as to each carrier of all or any of said property over all or any portion of said route to destination, and as to each party at any time interested in all or any of said property that every service to be performed hereunder shall be subject to all the terms and conditions of the Uniform Domestic Straight Bill of Lading set forth (1) in Official Southern Western and Illinois Freight Classifications in effect on the date hereof, if this is a rail or rail-water shipment or (2) in the applicable motor carrier classification or tariff if this is a motor carrier shipment.

Shipper hereby certifies that he is familiar with all the terms and conditions of the said bill of lading, including those on the back thereof, set forth in the classification or tariff which governs the transportation of this shipment, and the said terms and conditions are hereby agreed to by the shipper and accepted for himself and his assigns.

NO. PACKAGES	DESCRIPTION OF ARTICLES	WEIGHT
1	Garden Tractor	997 lbs.

If the shipment moves between two ports by a carrier by water, the law requires that the bill of lading shall state whether it is "carrier's or shipper's weight."

NOTE:–Where the rate is dependent on value, shippers are reqired to state specifically in writing the agreed or declared value of the property.

The agreed or declared value of the property is hereby specifically stated by the shipper to be not exceeding _____ per _____

SHIPPER _Buckeye Equipment_   Per _DK_

SHIPPER'S ADDRESS _313 Olentangy Road, Pettisville, Ohio 43553-0175_

Agent _____   Per _____ _____ 20 ___

Subject to Section 7 of conditions of applicable bill of lading, if this shipment is to be delivered to the consignee without recourse on the consignor, the consignor shall sign the following statement.

The carrier shall not make delivery of this shipment without payment of freight and all other lawful charges.

_____
(Signature of Consignor)

Received $ _____
to apply in prepayment of the charges on the property described hereon.

_____
Agent or Cashier

Per _____
(The signature here acknowledges only the amount prepaid.)

If charges are to be prepaid, write or stamp here, "To be Prepaid."

"To be Prepaid"

Charges Advanced $ _____

†Shipper's imprint in lieu of stamp not a part of Bill of Lading approved by the Interstate Commerce Commission.

†"The fibre boxes used for this shipment conform to the specifications set forth in the box maker's certificate thereon, and all other requirements of Uniform Freight Classification."

☑ ORIGINAL   ☐ SHIPPING ORDER   ☐ MEMORANDUM

BORROWING MONEY

UNIT
6

Regardless of their size, businesses often borrow money. Loans made to businesses may be short-term notes that must be repaid within a year or capital borrowed for longer than a year. Many short-term loans are repaid in 30, 60, or 90 days. Long-term loans are usually repaid in monthly installments over a period of years.

As a manager in the model business community, your responsibilities include offering loans to other businesses and/or repaying loans for your business. Be sure you repay your loans on time. Your reputation for being dependable will be an asset to you as you carry out the duties of managing a business within the model community.

Unit Lessons

Lesson 6•1   **Using Promissory Notes**
Lesson 6•2   **Paying Mortgage and Installment Loans**

Unit Activities

Activity 6•1   **Completing Promissory Notes**
Activity 6•2   **Calculating Interest and Finding Maturity Dates**
Activity 6•3   **Making Mortgage Loan Payments**

LESSON 6·1

USING PROMISSORY NOTES

Businesses borrow money for many reasons. A store might take out a loan to purchase a building, buy a van to make deliveries, or restock the store's inventory. **Inventory** is the stock of goods a business has for sale. Banks frequently grant loans, but businesses also offer loans to each other.

UNIT 6 • BORROWING MONEY

PRINCIPAL—the amount that is promised to be paid; the face value of the note

TIME—the days or months from the date of the note until it should be paid

PAYEE—the one to whom the note is payable

Promissory Note

May 16, , 20 --

$ 2,000.00
(Principal Amount Borrowed)

Pettisville, Ohio
(City and State)

sixty days
(Number of days after date of note)
after date   we   promise to pay to
(I/We)

the order of   Farmers & Merchants State Bank
(Name of Lender)

Two thousand and 001/100
(Amount)
dollars

Payable at   Farmers & Merchants State Bank
(Location where payment is to be made)

VALUE RECEIVED WITH INTEREST AT   12 %

NO.   13   DUE   July 15, 20--

Popular Designs
(Name of Borrower)

Felicia Hernandez
(Authorized Signature)

DATE OF MATURITY—the date on which the note is due

INTEREST RATE—the interest paid for the use of the money

MAKER—the one who promises to make the payment

When a person borrows money from another person or a business, a promissory note may be signed. A **promissory note** is a written promise to repay the amount borrowed on a specific date, at a designated place, and at a stated rate of interest. The total of a loan includes the **principal** (the amount borrowed) and the **interest** (the amount paid for the use of the money for a period of time). The maker signs over the promissory note to the payee on the date the money is borrowed. The payee keeps the promissory note in a safe place until payment is received.

Study the illustration of a promissory note on the previous page. On May 16, Popular Designs (the maker) borrowed $2,000 (the principal) from Farmers & Merchants State Bank (the payee). The principal of $2,000 plus 12% interest must be paid to the Farmers & Merchants State Bank on July 15 (the date of maturity).

 CALCULATING INTEREST

The formula for calculating interest is

$$\text{Principal} \times \text{Rate} \times \text{Time}$$

Remember that (1) the rate of interest must be expressed as a fraction or percentage; (2) the interest is charged for each dollar, or part of a dollar, borrowed; and (3) the interest rate is based on one year.

Interest is expressed as a fraction of a dollar. This part of a dollar, or percent, is called the rate of interest. For example, an interest rate of 12 percent means that 12 cents must be paid for every dollar borrowed. The amount of the interest charged is found by multiplying the *principal* by the *rate of interest*. The amount of interest is computed this way.

$$\$2,000.00 \times 0.12 = \$240.00$$

If you borrow $2,000 at 12 percent for 1 year, you must pay back the $2,000 plus $240 interest. If you borrow the same amount of money at the same rate of interest for 2 years, you pay twice as much interest, or $480. If the money is borrowed for 3 years, you pay back $720, and so forth. The amount of interest at 12 percent for 2 years is computed this way.

$$\$2,000.00 \times 0.12 \qquad = \$240.00$$
$$\$2,000.00 \times 0.12 \times 2 = \$480.00$$

When a loan is made for a number of months (such as 1, 3, or 6 months) rather than a year, the number of months is shown as a fraction of a year. A 3-month promissory note is computed this way.

$$\$2,000.00 \times 0.12 \times \tfrac{3}{12} = \$60.00$$

©GETTY IMAGES/PHOTODISC

UNIT 6 • BORROWING MONEY

When a loan is made for a certain number of days (such as 30, 60, or 90 days) rather than a year, the interest is determined by days. To make the calculation easy, it is customary to use 360 days as a year. The interest for the promissory note shown on the following page is computed this way.

Principal   Rate   Time
$2,000.00 × 0.12 × $\frac{60}{360}$ (60 days) = $40.00

The total amount to be paid to the lender is $2,040.00.

Principal		Interest		Amount Paid at Maturity
$2,000.00	+	$40.00	=	$2,040.00

FINDING THE MATURITY DATE

How Many Days Are In Each Month?

This well-known rhyme will help you remember. *Thirty days has September, April, June, and November. All the rest have 31 except the second month alone to which we 28 assign til Leap Year gives it 29.*

The **maturity date** refers to the date on which a promissory note becomes due. To find the maturity date, look to see if the length of the loan is stated in months or days. If the loan is stated in months, the date of maturity is the same day of the month as the date on which the loan was made. For example, if a loan is made on April 15 and is to run one month, it will be due on May 15. If it is to run two months, it will be due on June 15, and so forth.

When the time of the loan is stated in days, the exact number of days must be counted to find the date of maturity. To do this, (1) find the number of days remaining in the month when the loan was made and then (2) add days in the following months until the total equals the required number of days. The date of maturity of the 60-day promissory note shown on the following page is figured as follows.

May 16 through May 31 = 15 days
June 1 through June 30 = 30 days
July 1 through July 15 = <u>15 days</u>
                                        60 days

When a promissory note is completed, two dates are recorded on the note. The first date is the day the maker signs the note. The second date is the maturity date, the day on which the note becomes due. After the note is signed, the payee (lender) keeps the original promissory note. When the loan is repaid, the original promissory note is given to the maker (borrower).

▐ **Follow these steps when completing a promissory note**

1. Find your promissory note.

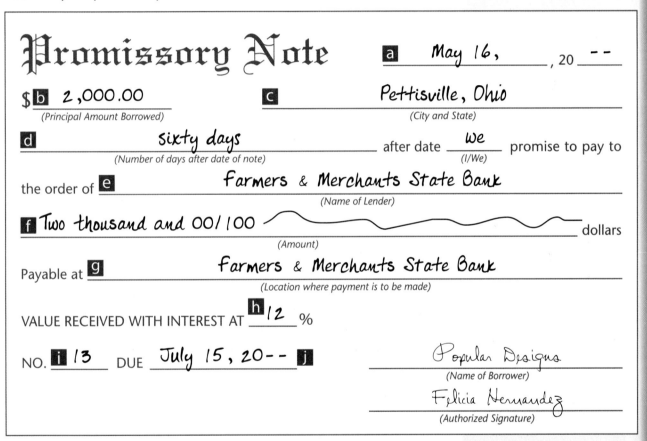

> 📋 *If you are using Instructor-provided forms,* remove 1 promissory note from your Supplies folder.

> 🖨 *If you are printing your forms,* open the forms document. Find Unit 6 Borrowing Money. Print 1 promissory note.

2. Use scissors to separate the COPY from the original promissory note. Set aside the COPY.

3. Use the illustration above as a guide as you complete the promissory note.

UNIT 6 • BORROWING MONEY

©GETTY IMAGES/PHOTODISC

UNIT 6 • BORROWING MONEY

a. Record today's July date in the top right-hand corner of the note.

b. Write the amount of money being loaned (the principal) beside the dollar sign in the upper left-hand corner of the note.

c. Write *Pettisville, Ohio* as the city and state.

d. Record the number of days or months of the loan and the word *we* on the next line.

e. Write the name of the lender on the line beginning with the words the *order of.*

f. Write the principal amount borrowed on the *Amount* line. (Record the dollar amount in words and the cents in figures.)

g. Write the payee's name (the name of the business loaning the money) on the *Payable at* line.

h. Write the interest rate on the *VALUE RECEIVED WITH INTEREST AT* line.

i. Record the number of the note. Your *DAILY ACTIVITIES* will tell you the number.

4. Find the maturity date. Read the information given on

page 206 in this Student Reference Book titled **Finding the Maturity Date.** If you have any difficulties determining the correct date, ask your Instructor for help.

j. Write the date of maturity on the *DUE* line.

5. Find the blank form marked COPY that you cut from the original promissory note. Make a copy of the promissory note. Your *DAILY ACTIVITIES* will tell you if you are to hold the note at your business or mail the promissory note.

Follow these steps when filing a promissory note

1. Remove the promissory note and check from the Pending File.

2. Ask the customer to sign both copies of the note. Hand the COPY of the note and the check to the customer.

3. Make a notation on your appointment calendar.

If you are using a paper calendar, remove the calendar from the Office File.
a. Write the following notation on the "Notes" at the bottom of the calendar. *Promissory note from (name of business) matures on (date).*
b. Return the appointment calendar to the Office File.

If you are using an electronic calendar, open the calendar.
a. Make the following notation on the "Notes" at the bottom of the calendar. *Promissory note from (name of business) matures on (date).*
b. Save your work. Close the calendar.

4. Place the original promissory note in the Office File.

Promissory Note

May 16, _, 20 _ _ _

$ _2,000.00_
(Principal Amount Borrowed)

Pettisville, Ohio
(City and State)

sixty days ___ after date ___ _I/We_ promise to pay to
(Number of days after date of note)   (I/We)

the order of _Farmers & Merchant's State Bank_
(Name of Lender)

Two thousand and 00/100 ___ dollars
(Amount)

Payable at _Farmers & Merchants State Bank_
(Location where payment to be made)

VALUE RECEIVED WITH INTEREST AT _12_ %

NO. _13_ DUE _July_ ___

Paid
July 15, 20- -
Maria Mendez

Popular Designs
(Name of Borrower)

Felicia Hernandez
(Authorized Signature)

■ Follow these steps when a promissory note you are holding reaches the maturity date

1. Remove the promissory note from the Cash File.

2. If a telephone system is available, call the maker (borrower) to tell him or her when you will present the promissory note for payment. If a telephone system is not available, e-mail or go to the maker's place of business and tell the maker in person.

3. When payment is received, write _PAID_, the date, and your name across the face of the note as shown in the illustration above.

4. Return the note to the maker.

5. Record the amount of the check in the OTHER column of the RECEIPTS section of the cashbook. If necessary, follow the steps on _page 61 in this Student Reference Book_ for recording incoming checks.

6. Endorse the check for deposit. Follow the instructions given in the box at the bottom of _page 62 in this Student Reference Book_. Use the illustration as a guide.

©GETTY IMAGES/PHOTODISC

7. Place the check in the cash receipts envelope in the Cash File. Include this check in your next bank deposit.

When your business borrows money, you will sign a promissory note. Be sure to read the entire note before you sign it.

NO. ___13___ DUE __July 15, 20--__   *Popular Designs*
                                             (Name of Borrower)
                                             Felicia Hernandez
                                             (Authorized Signature)

Follow these steps when you borrow money and sign a promissory note

1. Go in person to the place of business that has agreed to lend money to you.

2. Carefully read the promissory note that has been prepared for your signature by the lender.

3. If you agree with the conditions as stated on the note, sign both copies of the promissory note. Write the name of your business and sign your name as manager. Refer to the illustration above.

4. Take your copy of the promissory note and the check and return to your place of business.

5. Record the check in the OTHER column of the RECEIPTS section of the cashbook. Turn to *page 61 in this Student Reference Book*. Complete the steps titled *Follow these steps when recording incoming checks (cash receipts) in the cashbook*.

6. Place the check you endorsed in the cash receipts envelope in the Cash File. Do not deposit the check yet. You will deposit it when you make your regular weekly deposit.

7. Make a notation on your appointment calendar.

If you are using a paper calendar, remove the calendar from the Office File.
  a. Make the following notation on the "Notes" at the bottom of the calendar. *Promissory note from (name of business) matures on (date).*
  b. Return the appointment calendar to the Office File.

If you are using an electronic calendar, open the calendar.
  a. Make the following notation on the "Notes" at the bottom of the calendar. *Promissory note from (name of business) matures on (date).*
  b. Save your work. Close the calendar.

8. File the copy of the promissory note in the Office File.

CHECKPOINT

Promissory Notes

Answer the following questions.

1. A written _____promise_____ to repay the amount borrowed on a specific date is called a promissory note.

2. The formula for computing interest is _____principal_____ times _____rate_____ times _____time_____.

3. The _____maturity_____ date is the day on which a promissory note becomes due.

4. When a loan is stated in number of days, the number of days in a year is considered _____360_____ instead of 365.

5. The amount paid for the use of money is called _____interest_____.

Doing Business on the 'Net
Borrowing Money Online

Most people are careful shoppers. They take their time, examine products, and try to get the most for their dollar. You should shop for a loan in just the same way. By going on-line, you can easily compare interest rates and terms offered by lenders.

Remember, though, a lengthy loan at a high interest rate can add thousands of dollars to the cost of your new car. The following are some tips for shopping for your loan.

❏ Get the lowest interest rate possible.

❏ Ask if there are loan fees.

❏ Make a large down payment.

❏ Pay off the loan quickly.

PAYING MORTGAGE AND INSTALLMENT LOANS

Pettisville Bank holds mortgage and installment loan contracts on several Pettisville businesses. These are long-term notes that are repaid in monthly installments over a period of years. They include the amount borrowed plus the interest on the loan.

◆ PAYING MORTGAGE LOANS

Some businesses pay rent for their buildings. Other businesses choose to purchase their facilities. Pettisville Bank holds notes on Pettisville businesses that signed **mortgage** loans when they bought their buildings. A mortgage is a legal paper giving a lender a claim against real estate if the loan is not repaid. Mortgages are long-term loans, and payments are usually made over a period of from 10 to 30 years.

Mortgage payments include the principal (the amount borrowed) and the interest on the loan. The monthly payment may also include taxes and insurance. In the early years of a mortgage payoff, most of the payment is applied toward the interest on the loan. When the borrower makes a monthly payment, only part of the payment is applied to the balance on the principal.

In the illustration on the next page, Pettisville Bank holds the mortgage on Hollywood & Vine Videos' store for $120,000. The last completed line of the contract shows a monthly payment of $1,079.67. A total of $193.61 of the payment is applied toward the balance on the principal. The remainder ($886.06) is applied toward the interest on the loan.

Follow these steps when making a mortgage loan payment at Pettisville Bank

1. Remove the mortgage loan contract from the Office File.

2. Read the contract. Pay special attention to the 5 headings on the chart at the bottom of the contract.

MORTGAGE LOAN

NO. __340__   __Pettisville__ , Ohio

$ __120,000__   Date __July 10,__ 20 __--__

I, We, or either of us, promise to pay to the order of __Pettisville Bank, Pettisville__ , *OHIO*
__One hundred twenty thousand and no/100__ -------------------------- *DOLLARS*
with interest at _____nine_____ (_9_) *percent per annum in minimum* ____monthly____ *payments*
of __One thousand seventy-nine and 67/100__ --------- *Dollars* (__$1,079.67__) *including*
interest, commencing ____August 10, 20--____ *and on the same date each* ___month___ *thereafter at*
its banking house, for value received, interest to be computed on unpaid balance on the ___fifth___ *day of each*
___month___ *and payments to be applied first to interest and then to principal, provided, however, that*
all upaid principal and interest shall be due and payable ____twenty____ *years from date hereof.*

If any installment is not paid when due or within thirty days thereafter; or if the maker or makers of this note or the owner or owners of the real estate mortgaged to secure the payment of this note with said interest, or any one of them, fail to keep all taxes, assessments or other charges levied on said real estate paid as they become due and payable; or fail to keep the buildings on said real estate in good and proper repair; or fail to keep the premises so mortgaged insured against fire and wind as provided in said mortgage, all policies delivered promptly to said mortgagee, each containing a clause providing that the loss, if any, shall be payable to said mortgagee according to its mortgage interest; or if the buildings on said real estate are altered, remodeled, destroyed or removed without written consent of said mortgagee, then and on such default in whole or in part, all of the indebtedness so secured by such mortgage and owing on this note shall thereupon become due and payable at the option of said mortgagee, or the legal owner of this note, and said mortgagee or owner may enforce the repayment of all said indebtedness, including all accrued interest and money expended for taxes, insurance, assessments or other charges as provided for in said mortgage according to law.

This note shall, at the option of the legal owner hereof, become due and payable in full and said mortgage enforceable should a change occur in the ownership of said real estate or any part thereof without the express written consent of the holder hereof.

All of the principal of this note not paid when due and any installment of interest not paid when due shall draw interest at a rate which is ten percentage points above the interest rate first above stated but no higher than the highest rate permitted by law.

We jointly and severally hereby authorize any attorney-at-law to appear in any court of record in the State of Ohio or elsewhere in the United States, after the above money becomes due, and waive the issuing and serving of process, and confess judgment against us or any of us in favor of the holder of this note, for the amount appearing due and cost of suit and thereupon release all errors and waive all right to appeal and stay of execution in our behalf.

PREPAYMENTS SHALL BE APPLIED TO INSTALLMENTS NEXT DUE AND PAYABLE.

> *WARNING— BY SIGNING THIS PAPER, YOU GIVE UP YOUR RIGHT TO NOTICE AND COURT TRIAL. IF YOU DO NOT PAY ON TIME, A COURT JUDGMENT MAY BE TAKEN AGAINST YOU WITHOUT YOUR PRIOR KNOWLEDGE AND THE POWERS OF A COURT CAN BE USED TO COLLECT FROM YOU REGARDLESS OF ANY CLAIMS YOU MAY HAVE AGAINST THE CREDITOR WHETHER FOR RETURNED GOODS, FAULTY GOODS, FAILURE ON HIS PART TO COMPLY WITH THE AGREEMENT, OR ANY OTHER CAUSE.*

Pettisville Bank   Hollywood & Vine Videos
Avon Seiler   Kathy Ripley
Loan Officer

NOTE: *The lending institution usually provides a payment book for the borrower to submit with each payment. In this simulation, the following record will be used for payment data.*

Date	Applied to Principal	Interest	Monthly Payment	Balance of Principal
AUG 10	$179.67	$900.00	$1,079.67	$119,820.33
SPT 10	181.02	898.65	1,079.67	119,639.31
OCT 10	182.38	897.29	1,079.67	119,456.93
NOV 10	183.74	895.93	1,079.67	119,273.19
DEC 10	185.12	894.55	1,079.67	119,088.07
JAN 10	186.51	893.16	1,079.67	118,901.56
FEB 10	187.91	891.76	1,079.67	118,713.65
MAR 10	189.32	890.35	1,079.67	118,524.33
APR 10	190.74	888.93	1,079.67	118,333.59
MAY 10	192.17	887.50	1,079.67	118,141.42
JUN 10	193.61	886.06	1,079.67	117,947.81

3. Follow the steps below to find the interest for the month of July and the balance on the principal as of July 10. Look at the last column on the chart, Balance of Principal. List that amount on the line below. Then multiply the June 10 Balance of Principal times the interest rate. Record your answer. *Round off all answers to the nearest cent.*

   a. Find the interest for 1 year.

$$\$ \underline{\hspace{2cm}} \quad \times \quad 0.09\ (9\%) \quad = \quad \$ \underline{\hspace{2cm}}$$

        Balance of   Interest   Interest
       Principal June 10   Rate   for 1 Year

   b. Find the interest for 1 month (the month of July).

$$\$ \underline{\hspace{2cm}} \quad \div \quad 12 \quad = \quad \$ \underline{\hspace{2cm}}$$

        Interest for   Months   Interest
        1 Year   in a Year   for 1 Month

   c. Find the amount to be Applied to the Principal. Note that monthly payments are the same each month.

$$\$ \underline{\hspace{2cm}} \quad - \quad \$ \underline{\hspace{2cm}} \quad = \quad \$ \underline{\hspace{2cm}}$$

        Monthly   Interest for   Applied to
        Payment   1 Month   Principal

   d. Look at the Balance of Principal for June 10 on the contract. Record that amount on the line below. Then find the Balance of Principal for July 10.

$$\$ \underline{\hspace{2cm}} \quad - \quad \$ \underline{\hspace{2cm}} \quad = \quad \$ \underline{\hspace{2cm}}$$

        Balance of   Applied to   Balance of
      Principal June 10   Principal   Principal July 10

4. Complete the last line of the contract.
   a. Write *JUL 10* under the Date column.
   b. Write the amount that is Applied to the Principal for July 10 (step 3c above).
   c. Write the interest for 1 month in the Interest column (step 3b above).
   d. Write the amount of the monthly payment in the Monthly Payment column.
   e. Write the Balance of Principal for July 10 (step 3d above).

5. Write a check payable to Pettisville Bank for the amount of the monthly payment. If necessary, refer to the instructions for writing checks on *page 54 in this Student Reference Book*.

6. Record the payment in the MORTGAGE, OTHER column of the cashbook. Turn to *page 58 in this Student Reference Book*. Follow the steps titled *Follow these steps when recording cash payments (by check) in the cashbook*. Record *Mortgage Payment* in the EXPLANATION column of the cashbook.

7. Take the check and contract to Pettisville Bank. You cannot use the drive-in window for this transaction. The manager of the bank will take your check and verify the accuracy of your calculations.

8. Return to your place of business. Place the contract in the Office File.

◆ PAYING INSTALLMENT LOANS

An **installment loan** is a loan where regular payments are made in specific amounts over a period of time. Several Pettisville businesses signed installment loan contracts with Pettisville Bank when they purchased company vehicles.

©GETTY IMAGES/PHOTODISC

Installment credit is frequently used to finance expensive items that have a long life, such as automobiles, furniture, and equipment. If the payments are not made in a timely manner, the seller has the right to *repossess* (take back) the merchandise in partial or full settlement of the debt. With an installment loan, the title to the merchandise does not pass to the buyer until all payments have been made.

In the contract illustrated on *page 216 in this Student Reference Book*, the officers of Nouveau Investment Company signed an installment loan on June 18. The payoff on the loan ($63,201) includes the principal ($50,000) and the interest on the loan ($13,201). Sonja and Pierre Nouveau pay $1,317 per month on two company vehicles.

Follow these steps when making an installment loan payment at Pettisville Bank

1. Remove the installment loan contract from the Office File. Read the contract and find the amount of the monthly payment.

2. Write a check payable to *Pettisville Bank* for the amount of the monthly payment. If necessary, refer to the instructions for writing checks on *page 54 in this Student Reference Book*.

3. Record the payment in the MORTGAGE, OTHER column of the cashbook. Turn to *page 58 in this Student Reference Book*. Follow the steps titled *Follow these steps when recording cash payments (by check) in the cashbook*. Record *Installment Loan Payment* in the EXPLANATION column of the cashbook.

4. Take the check and the contract and go to Pettisville Bank. You cannot use the drive-in window for this transaction. The manager of the bank will take your check and record the payment on your installment loan contract.

5. Return to your place of business. Place the contract in the Office File.

Loan Number ___817___ Due __June 18, 20--__ Amount of Note _____$63,201.00_____

INSTALLMENT LOAN

Borrower __Nouveau Investment Company__   Lender __PETTISVILLE BANK__
__440 Wall Street__   __101 Greenback Drive__
__Pettisville, OH 43553-0178__   __Pettisville, OH 43553-0178__

In this agreement, the words I, me, and mine mean each and all those who signed it. The words you, your, and bank mean the Bank named above.

I promise to pay to the order of the Bank the amount shown below as the Time Balance, Amount of Note, and Total of Payments (line 5) in accordance with the payment schedule below.

INSURANCE

Credit Life for term of _____ months   _____

Disability for term of _____ months   _____

Credit Insurance is not required, but I desire the above coverages which show a premium figure. I empower the bank to obtain it for me.

_____   _____
Date   Customer's Signature

_____   _____
Date   Customer's Signature

The term of any such insurance shall be equal to the original term of the obligation unless terminated earlier.

PAYMENT SCHEDULE

Amount of each regular payment	$1,317.00
Number of regular payments	41
First regular payment due date	July 18, 20--
Amount of final payment	$1,302.00

HERE IS A BREAKDOWN OF MY LOAN:
1. Amount of credit — $50,000.00
2. Other charges
   a. Title Fees _____
   b. Taxes _____
   c. Recording and Filing Fees _____
   d. License Fees _____
   e. Credit Life Insurance _____
   f. Property Insurance _____
   g. Disability Insurance _____
   h. Memorandum Title _____
3. Amount financed (1 + 2) — $50,000.00
4. FINANCE CHARGE:
   Interest $13,201.00
   Other _____
   Total — 13,201.00
5. Time Balance, Amount of Note, and Total of Payments (3 + 4) — $63,201.00
6. ANNUAL PERCENTAGE RATE — 12 %

The Finance Charge will begin on the date of this Note or the date of disbursement, whichever is later.

This credit is secured by the goods described below:

Motor Vehicles	Year Model	Make	Model	Number Cylinders	Other Description	Manufacturer's Serial Number
1	(New)	Jeep	Cherokee	6	maroon	IM88882767885
2	(New)	Cadillac	Catera	6	silver	IM77AA8542362

OTHER COLLATERAL _____
I will keep the goods insured at all times against loss.

I hereby agree to be bound by the terms and conditions of this note and acknowledge receipt of a completely filled-in copy of it.

Pierre Nouveau June 18, 20--
Borrower's Signature   Date

Sonja Nouveau June 18, 20--
Borrower's Signature   Date

440 Wall St., Pettisville, Ohio
Borrower's Address

Hilda Mehring, Loan Dept.
Bank's Signature

PAYMENT RECORD		
DATE	AMOUNT PAID	BALANCE TO BE PAID
July 1		$63,201.00

CHECKPOINT

Mortgage and Installment Loans

Answer the following questions.

1. A legal paper giving a lender a claim against real estate if the loan is not repaid is called a/an _____ loan.

2. A loan where regular payments are made in specific amounts over a period of time is called a/an _____ loan.

3. Mortgage payments may also include _____ and _____ in addition to the interest paid and the amount borrowed.

4. With an installment loan, the _____ does not pass to the buyer until all payments have been made.

UNIT SUMMARY

1. The maker of a promissory note signs over the note to the payee on the day the money is borrowed.

2. The formula for calculating interest is *principal x rate x time*.

3. If you borrow the same amount of money at the same rate of interest for two years, you pay twice as much interest as you would for one year.

4. When the time of the loan is stated in days, the exact number of days must be counted to find the date of maturity.

5. Many short-term loans are repaid in 30, 60, or 90 days.

6. In calculating interest on loans, it is customary to use 360 days as a year.

7. The amount paid at maturity includes both the principal and the interest on the loan.

8. Mortgage and installment loans are long-term notes that are repaid in monthly installments over a period of years.

9. Mortgage payments may also include taxes and insurance in addition to principal and interest and are usually made over a period of from 10 to 30 years.

10. In the early years of a mortgage payoff, most of the payment is applied toward the interest on the loan.

11. Installment credit is frequently used to finance expensive items that have a long life, such as automobiles, furniture, and equipment.

12. With an installment loan, the title does not pass to the buyer until all payments have been made.

13. If the payments on an installment loan are not made in a timely manner, the seller has the right to repossess (take back) the merchandise in partial or full settlement of the debt.

Glossary

installment loan	a loan where regular payments are made in specific amounts over a period of time
interest	money paid for the use of someone else's money for a period of time
inventory	the stock of goods a business has for sale
maturity date	the date on which a promissory note becomes due
mortgage	a legal paper giving a lender a claim against real estate if the loan is not repaid
principal	the amount borrowed on a loan
promissory note	a written promise to repay the amount borrowed on a specific date, at a designated place, and at a stated rate of interest

INTERNET EXPLORATIONS

Monthly payments on a mortgage loan vary depending on the amount of interest paid and the number of years on the loan. By paying a few dollars more each month on the principal, a borrower can save thousands of dollars in interest. For example, the monthly payment on a mortgage loan for $120,000 at 7% interest for 30 years is $798, but the same mortgage can be paid off in just 25 years for only $50 a month more. And the borrower saves a whopping $33,000 in interest!

Use a mortgage calculator online to find the monthly payments and total interest on the mortgage loan shown below. Then change the interest rate and the length of the loan. Note the difference in the monthly payments and the total interest paid.

A $100,000 mortgage loan
- a. @ 7% interest for 30 years
- b. @ 7% interest for 25 years
- c. @ 7% interest for 15 years
- d. @ 8% interest for 30 years
- e. @ 8.125% interest for 30 years

Mortgage loan calculators can be found on the following web sites.
- a. *www.interest.com*
- b. *www.loanlane.com*
- c. *www.mortgage-calc.com*

ACTIVITY 6•1 COMPLETING PROMISSORY NOTES

Directions: *Assume you are the manager of Pettisville Bank. Today you extended a loan to Mouse-n-Louse Exterminator Service. The manager of Mouse-n-Louse will stop by today (**July 20, —**) to sign the note. Calculate the interest on the loan and find the maturity date. Then prepare* **Promissory Note No. 82** *for $20,000 at 12% interest for 60 days.*

1. Turn to *page 205 in this Student Reference Book*. Read the information under the heading **Calculating Interest**. Calculate the interest on the loan to Mouse-n-Louse.

$\underset{\text{principal}}{\$\,\underline{20,000}} \times \underset{\text{rate}}{\underline{0.12}\%} \times \underset{\text{time}}{\underline{60\ days}} = \underset{\text{interest}}{\$\,\underline{144000}}$

2. Complete a promissory note for Mouse-n-Louse. Turn to *page 207 in this Student Reference Book*. Find the steps titled *Follow these steps when completing a promissory note*. **Complete steps 3 and 4.**

Promissory Note   <u>July 20</u>, 20 <u>07</u>

$ <u>20,000</u>   <u>Pettisville, OH</u>
(Principal Amount Borrowed)   (City and State)

<u>60 days</u> after date <u>I</u> promise to pay to
(Number of **days after date of note**)   (I/We)

the order of <u>Pettisville Bank</u>
(Name of **Lender**)

<u>$164,000</u> dollars
(Amount)

Payable at <u>Pettisville Bank</u>
(Location **where payment is to be made**)

VALUE RECEIVED WITH INTEREST AT <u>12</u> %

NO. <u>82</u> DUE <u>September 18, 07</u>   <u>Devin Kuchynka</u>
(Name of **Borrower**)

<u>Devin Kuchynka</u>
(Authorized Signature)

UNIT 6 • BORROWING MONEY

ACTIVITY 6•2 CALCULATING INTEREST AND FINDING MATURITY DATES

Directions: *Assume you are the manager of Pettisville Bank. One of your responsibilities as manager is to make loans to businesses. Calculate the interest and find the total loan for the five promissory notes below. Then determine the maturity dates on the notes.*

1. Read the information under the heading **Calculating Interest** on *page 205 in this Student Reference Book*. Calculate the interest for the following promissory notes.

Principal × Rate × Time = Interest

Note #1 $2,000 at 14% for 3 months   2000 × 0.14 × 90/360 = $ 70

Note #2 $2,000 at 13.5% for 6 months   2000 × 0.135 × 180/360 = $ 135

Note #3 $15,000 at 12% for 30 days   15,000 × 0.12 × 30/360 = $ 150

Note #4 $15,000 at 12% for 60 days   15,000 × 0.12 × 60/360 = $ 300

Note #5 $16,000 at 13% for 90 days   16,000 × 0.13 × 90/360 = $ 520

2. Find the amount paid at maturity for the promissory notes above by adding the principal plus the interest.

Principal + Interest = Amount Paid at Maturity

Note #1 $ 2,000   + $ 70   = $ 2070

Note #2 $ 2,000   + $ 135   = $ 2,135

Note #3 $ 15,000   + $ 150   = $ 15,150

Note #4 $ 15,000   + $ 300   = $ 15,300

Note #5 $ 16,000   + $ 520   = $ 16,520

3. Find the maturity dates for the promissory notes above. Turn to *page 206 in this Student Reference Book*. Read the information under the heading **Finding the Maturity Date**.

Note #1 for 3 months dated May 16 matures on ___August 16___ .

Note #2 for 6 months dated June 1 matures on ___December 1___ .

Note #3 for 30 days dated April 21 matures on ___May 21___ .

Note #4 for 60 days dated May 12 matures on ~~July 12~~ July 11 .

Note #5 for 90 days dated March 2 matures on ~~June 2~~ May 30 .

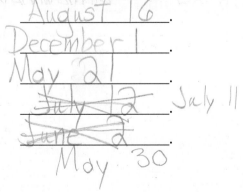

UNIT 6 • BORROWING MONEY

Name	Evaluation

ACTIVITY 6·3 MAKING MORTGAGE LOAN PAYMENTS

Directions: Assume you are the manager of The Clothes Closet. Pettisville Bank holds the mortgage on your building. Use the mortgage loan contract on the back of this sheet to record the balance on the principal after the July 10 mortgage payment is made. Use the forms at the bottom of this page to write a check for the mortgage payment and make an entry in the cashbook. Use the date *July 10, 20--.*

- Turn to *page 212 in this Student Reference Book*. Find the steps titled *Follow these steps when making a mortgage loan payment at Pettisville Bank.* **Complete steps 2 through 6.** Record your answers on the lines below.

a. $ 288,770.12 × 0.09 (9%) = $ 25,989.31
   Balance of Principal / Interest Rate / Interest for 1 Year
   June 10

b. $ 25,989.31 ÷ 12 = $ 2,105.47
   Interest for 1 Year / Months in a Year / Interest for 1 Month

c. $ 2,699.18 − $ 2165.77 = $ 533.41
   Monthly Payment / Interest for 1 month / Applied to Principal

d. $ 288,770.12 − $ 533.41 = $ 288,236.71
   Balance of Principal June 10 / Applied to Principal / Balance of Principal July 10

THE CLOTHES CLOSET — check no. 801 — Pay to Pettisville bank $2,699.18 — Two-thousand, six-hundred, ninety-nine and 18/100 DOLLARS — FOR mortgage payment — Devin Kuchynka

	DATE	EXPLANATION	CHECK NO.	CASH IN	CASH OUT	CASH BALANCE	SALES, FEES, COMMISSION, etc.	OTHER	EXPENSES, PURCHASES	MORTGAGE, OTHER	
1	July 2	Beginning Checkbook Balance				17230 00					1
2	July 3	Postage	800		35 00	17195 00			35 00		2
3	July 6	Cash Sales		9320 00		26515 00	9320 00				3
4	July 10	Mortgage payment	80		2699.18	23815.82				2699.18	4

CASHBOOK — FIRM The Clothes Closet — Page 1 of

MORTGAGE LOAN

NO. __310__   __Pettisville__ , Ohio

$ __300,000__   Date __July 10,__ 20 __--__

I, We, or either of us, promise to pay to the order of __Pettisville Bank, Pettisville__ , OHIO

__Three hundred thousand and no/100__ -------------------------------- *DOLLARS*

with interest at ___nine___ (_9_) *percent per annum in minimum* __monthly__ *payments*

of __Twenty-six hundred ninety-nine and 18/100__ ---- *Dollars (* __$2,699.18__ *) including*

interest, commencing __August 10, 20--__ *and on the same date each* __month__ *thereafter at*

its banking house, for value received, interest to be computed on unpaid balance on the __fifth__ *day of each*

__month__ *and payments to be applied first to interest and then to principal, provided, however, that*

all upaid principal and interest shall be due and payable ___twenty___ *years from date hereof.*

If any installment is not paid when due or within thirty days thereafter; or if the maker or makers of this note or the owner or owners of the real estate mortgaged to secure the payment of this note with said interest, or any one of them, fail to keep all taxes, assessments or other charges levied on said real estate paid as they become due and payable; or fail to keep the buildings on said real estate in good and proper repair; or fail to keep the premises so mortgaged insured against fire and wind as provided in said mortgage, all policies delivered promptly to said mortgagee, each containing a clause providing that the loss, if any, shall be payable to said mortgagee according to its mortgage interest; or if the buildings on said real estate are altered, remodeled, destroyed or removed without written consent of said mortgagee, then and on such default in whole or in part, all of the indebtedness so secured by such mortgage and owing on this note shall thereupon become due and payable at the option of said mortgagee, or the legal owner of this note, and said mortgagee or owner may enforce the repayment of all said indebtedness, including all accrued interest and money expended for taxes, insurance, assessments or other charges as provided for in said mortgage according to law.

This note shall, at the option of the legal owner hereof, become due and payable in full and said mortgage enforceable should a change occur in the ownership of said real estate or any part thereof without the express written consent of the holder hereof.

All of the principal of this note not paid when due and any installment of interest not paid when due shall draw interest at a rate which is ten percentage points above the interest rate first above stated but no higher than the highest rate permitted by law.

We jointly and severally hereby authorize any attorney-at-law to appear in any court of record in the State of Ohio or elsewhere in the Unted States, after the above money becomes due, and waive the issuing and serving of process, and confess judgment against us or any of us in favor of the holder of this note, for the amount appearing due and cost of suit and thereupon release all errors and waive all right to appeal and stay of execution in our behalf.

PREPAYMENTS SHALL BE APPLIED TO INSTALLMENTS NEXT DUE AND PAYABLE.

WARNING— BY SIGNING THIS PAPER, YOU GIVE UP YOUR RIGHT TO NOTICE AND COURT TRIAL. IF YOU DO NOT PAY ON TIME, A COURT JUDGMENT MAY BE TAKEN AGAINST YOU WITHOUT YOUR PRIOR KNOWLEDGE AND THE POWERS OF A COURT CAN BE USED TO COLLECT FROM YOU REGARDLESS OF ANY CLAIMS YOU MAY HAVE AGAINST THE CREDITOR WHETHER FOR RETURNED GOODS, FAULTY GOODS, FAILURE ON HIS PART TO COMPLY WITH THE AGREEMENT, OR ANY OTHER CAUSE.

Pettisville Bank   *The Clothes Closet*

Eileen Sweebe   *Kimo Yonekura*

Loan Officer

NOTE: *The lending institution usually provides a payment book for the borrower to submit with each payment. In this simulation, the following record will be used for payment data.*

Date	Applied to Principal	Interest	Monthly Payment	Balance of Principal
AUG 10	$491.31	$2,207.86	$2,699.18	$293,890.56
SPT 10	495.00	2,204.18	2,699.18	293,395.56
OCT 10	498.71	2,200.47	2,699.18	292,896.85
NOV 10	502.45	2,196.73	2,699.18	292,394.39
DEC 10	506.22	2,192.96	2,699.18	291,888.17
JAN 10	510.02	2,189.16	2,699.18	291,378.16
FEB 10	513.84	2,185.34	2,699.18	290,864.32
MAR 10	517.70	2,181.48	2,699.18	290,346.62
APR 10	521.58	2,177.60	2,699.18	289,825.04
MAY 10	525.49	2,173.69	2,699.18	289,299.55
JUN 10	529.43	2,169.75	2,699.18	288,770.12
Jul. 10	553.41	2165.77	2699.18	288076.71

ADVERTISING

Advertising is a method of communicating used to promote the sale of goods and services. Print media include newspapers, direct mail (such as fliers and letters), magazines, billboards, telephone directory advertising, signs, and posters. Electronic media include radio, television, scoreboards, web pages, and other Internet advertising.

One of your duties as a manager in the model business community is to arrange for advertising. You may seek the services of Creative Advertising Agency, which offers planning and creative assistance to clients, or you may design and create your own ads and arrange for publication. Your DAILY ACTIVITIES will tell you which type of advertising to use—billboard, radio, television, newspaper, etc.

Unit Lessons

Lesson 7·1	**Writing Classified Advertising**
Lesson 7·2	**Preparing Display Advertising**
Lesson 7·3	**Creating Electronic Advertising**

Unit Activities

Activity 7·1	**Writing Want Ads**
Activity 7·2	**Calculating the Cost of Want Ads**
Activity 7·3	**Preparing a Display Ad**
Activity 7·4	**Creating Electronic Advertising**

LESSON 7•1

WRITING CLASSIFIED ADVERTISING

©GETTY IMAGES/PHOTODISC

Classified advertising is advertising in the want ad section of a newspaper or other medium. Most businesses in the model community use classified advertising to solicit applicants for vacant or newly created positions in their firms. Your *DAILY ACTIVITIES* will tell you when to hire a new employee. You will write the draft of a want ad to be placed in the classified section of *The Towne Crier*, Pettisville's leading newspaper.

The cost of a want ad is calculated according to the number of issues the ad will run and the number of words used in the ad. Eliminating all unnecessary words can reduce the cost of the want ad. Use the following guidelines as you count the words in your want ad.

GUIDELINES FOR COUNTING WORDS IN A WANT AD

Count as 1 Word
- each word in the title, such as "MECHANIC"
- abbreviations, such as "St." or "min."
- short words, such as "a" or "of"
- telephone numbers, street numbers, zip codes, etc.
- hyphenated words, such as "86-A" or "rivet-setting"
- a symbol with a word or number, such as "& Company"
- a number with an abbreviation, such as "8 a.m."

Count as 2 Words
- words separated by a diagonal (/), such as "Male/Female"

SHOP MACHINIST

Local manufacturer seeks person skilled in set-up, operation, and maintenance of industrial sewing machines, commercial electronic shears, and rivet-setting equipment. High school graduation and two years experience required. We offer a competitive wage and benefit package. Send resume and salary requirements to 45 Maple Street, Pettisville, OH 43553-0175, or apply in person at Mean Jeans Manufacturing Co.

OFFICE MANAGER

Security Insurance Co. is seeking the right individual for the new position of office manager. Requires five years experience OR two years experience with college degree. Computer skills a must. Fax (419-555-0165) or e-mail your resume to Robin McGee at r.mcgee@security.mjs

PAINT STORE

Sales position open for dependable, mature person in our suburban store. Will train. High school diploma. Includes evening/weekend hours. Send resume to Color Dimensions & Wallpaper, 479 Airport Hwy., Wauseon, OH 43567-0979, or call 419-555-0153 between 9 a.m. and 6 p.m.

Follow these steps when you place a want ad

1. Determine the qualifications for the position. Use the following sources to find want ads. Note the type of information included in the ads.
   - The want ads illustrated on *pages 224-225 in this Student Reference Book*.
   - The want ads illustrated in Part 2, *pages 16-47 in this Student Reference Book*.
   - The classified section of your local newspaper.
   - The classifieds on the Internet.

2. Prepare the want ad.

If you are handwriting your want ad, remove 1 sheet of notebook paper from your Supplies folder.

If you are keying your want ad, open your word processor.

---

3. Compose the want ad. Ask yourself WHO, WHAT, WHEN, WHERE, and HOW about the subject. Begin by printing (or keying) the title of the job in capital letters. Make sure you include the following information.
   - TITLE OF JOB
   - Name of business placing the ad
   - Education required
   - Job duties
   - Experience needed
   - How and where to apply

4. Read your want ad. Have you included all necessary information? Have you removed all unnecessary words? Remember that the cost of the ad will be calculated according to the number of issues your ad will run and the number of words used in the ad.

5. Make a copy of the ad.

📋 *If you are handwriting your ad,* ask your Instructor to make 1 photocopy of the ad.

🖱️ *If you are keying your ad,* print 2 copies of the want ad. Save your work.

---

6. Calculate the cost of your want ad. Count the number of words in the ad. (Use the Guidelines for Counting Words in a Want Ad on *page 224 in this Student Reference Book*.) Turn to The Towne Crier's rate chart on *page 364 in this Student Reference Book*. Use the classified (want ad) rates at the bottom of the rate chart to find the cost of your want ad. Record below the number of words in your ad and the fee for the ad.

_____87_____ number of words in the ad

$_____ charge for placing the want ad in _____ issues of *The Towne Crier*

7. Take the want ad and your checkbook and go in person to The Towne Crier. The manager of The Towne Crier will want to know whether you wish to run your ad for 1, 2, 3, or 4 issues.

8. Write a check to The Towne Crier for the amount of the want ad. If necessary, refer to *page 54 in this Student Reference Book* and follow the steps there for writing checks.

9. Return to your place of business. Record the payment in your cashbook. Turn to *page 58 in this Student Reference Book*. Complete the steps titled *Follow these steps when recording cash payments (by check) in the cashbook*. Record *Want Ad* in the EXPLANATION column of the cashbook.

10. Staple or paper clip the want ad receipt to your copy of the ad. Place these papers in the Office File.

CHECKPOINT

Classified Advertising

Answer the following questions.

1. Advertising in the want ad section of a newspaper is called _____ advertising.

2. The cost of a want ad is calculated according to the number words in the ad and the number of _____ the ad will run.

3. You can reduce the cost of a want ad by eliminating all _____ words.

4. The words *evening/weekend* appearing in a want ad should be counted as _____ word(s).

5. The words *Color Dimensions & Wallpaper* appearing in a want ad should be counted as _____ words.

PREPARING DISPLAY ADVERTISING

©GETTY IMAGES/PHOTODISC

Display advertising is advertising that uses both art and words to promote the sale of products or services. A sign in a store window is an example of a display ad. Other types of display advertising include ads in magazines, newspapers, billboards, and telephone directories. **Directory advertising** is advertising displayed within the Yellow Pages of a telephone book.

Some businesses in the model community use the services of Creative Advertising Agency. An **advertising agency** is a company that handles all types of advertising for its clients. Advertising agencies produce advertising by writing copy, creating artwork, and producing ads or commercials. They charge their customers for the cost of each ad plus a commission for their services.

Most newspapers have advertising departments that design ads for their customers. Many businesses create their own display ads. For example, a business may design an ad and submit it to The Towne Crier for publication in the newspaper. Another business might create a sign to display on the counter or in the aisle of its store.

©NOVA DEVELOPMENT CORPORATION

THE GOLDEN PHEASANT

R E S T A U R A N T

Located in the
Maumee River Mall, Toledo

STEAK, SEAFOOD
DUCK, PHEASANT,
AND QUAIL
CATERING
BANQUET FACILITIES
FOR 300
THE TIMBERS LOUNGE
ENTERTAINMENT

555-0149

In the model business community, display ads may be designed either manually or electronically. Clip art may be cut and glued onto a page or retrieved from the clip art folder on your computer and then copied onto your word processing document.

Follow these steps when creating a display ad manually

1. Remove 1 whole sheet of plain paper from your Supplies folder.

2. Remove the sheet(s) of clip art from your Office File. (Some businesses may store clip art in other files, such as the Newspaper File or Supplies folder.)

3. Obtain scissors, felt-tip markers, and rubber cement or glue from your "mini filing cabinet" or your Instructor. Make sure you have these items before you begin.

4. Cut all of the items from the clip art sheet(s) that you will need for the ad. (You may have more clip art than you need.)

5. Turn the sheet of paper so that the short edge $\left(8\frac{1}{2}"\right)$ is at the top. On a flat surface, LAY OUT BUT DO NOT GLUE the clip art in an attractive arrangement on the page. An attractive arrangement is one that makes the best use of the space available without looking cluttered.

6. Print any other information given in your *DAILY ACTIVITIES* to be included on the page.

7. Glue the cutouts onto the page.

8. Ask your Instructor to make 1 photocopy of the layout.

9. File the photocopy in the Office File. Your *DAILY ACTIVITIES* will tell you if you are to mail the original of the ad, use it in your business, or take it to another business.

Follow these steps when creating a display ad electronically

1. Open your word processor.

2. Open the clip art folder. Find the clip art for your ad and copy it onto your word processing document. *If you are using Microsoft Word,* use the Insert command on your toolbar to insert a picture "From File." To resize clip art, refer to the instructions on the template.

3. Arrange the pieces of clip art attractively on the page. An attractive arrangement is one that makes the best use of the space available without looking cluttered. Use plenty of white space (blank areas) around the text and clip art, and limit the use of different fonts and colors to avoid a confusing appearance.

4. Key any other information given in your *DAILY ACTIVITIES* to be included on the page.

5. Print 2 copies of the ad now. Save your work.

6. Place 1 copy of the ad in your Office File. Your *DAILY ACTIVITIES* will tell you if you are to mail the ad, use it in your business, or take it to another business.

CHECKPOINT

Display Advertising

Answer the following questions.

1. Directory advertising is found within the _____ of a telephone book.

2. Advertising agencies charge their customers for the cost of each ad plus a _____ for their services.

3. Display advertising is advertising that uses both _____ and _____ to promote the sale of products or services.

4. Most newspapers have advertising _____ that design ads for their customers.

5. Examples of ads that a business might design for itself are _____

   _____.

Doing Business on the 'Net

Sample Ads Online

Westlake Advertising is one of many advertising agencies that solicit business over the Internet. This ad agency creates

❏ logos

❏ print ads

❏ product catalogs

❏ package designs

❏ web designs

❏ computer illustrations

Explore their site at
www.westlakeadvertising.com

CREATING ELECTRONIC ADVERTISING

©GETTY IMAGES/PHOTODISC

The main purpose of any ad is to get the audience's attention. Sometimes advertising gives little information that will help the consumer make an informed decision. For example, when a television ad appeared showing animated characters dancing to the tune of "I Heard It Through the Grapevine," the sale of California raisins skyrocketed. After that ad campaign, the total sale of raisins—plus all the clothing, dolls, and other merchandise that promoted the commercial—exploded, increasing from $60 million to $300 million per year.

Consumers were captivated by the California raisins ad campaign, but they were never informed about the health benefits of eating raisins! Remember that the main goal of advertising is to grab the audience's attention. But you should also strive to inform consumers about the benefits of the product or service you are promoting.

The cost of a television ad may range from several thousand dollars to $2.4 million for a 30-second spot during the Super Bowl. Television and radio ads are usually sold in 30- and 60-second spots. Radio advertising is much less expensive and can usually target local markets better than television. For example, a commercial designed to attract the teenage market might appear on a rock station whose audience is mostly teenagers. While television advertising concentrates on both sight and sound, radio advertising is solely audio.

The Internet has introduced new forms of advertising. Companies purchase ads, called *banners* and *pop-ups*, to promote the sale of their products and services. Most companies today have their own web pages. A **web page** is an Internet site that greets visitors using a variety of text, animation, audio, and video. The web address begins with a home page, which serves as an introduction to the other pages. In addition to businesses, many individuals have their own personal web addresses. Surfing the Internet has become so popular that there are thousands of new web pages added every hour.

Some of the businesses in the model community will write advertising for electronic media—television, radio, or scoreboards. If your *DAILY ACTIVITIES* instruct you to create an electronic ad, strive to make your advertising appeal to the eyes, ears, and tastes of your target market.

30-SECOND RADIO COMMERCIAL TO SPONSOR PETTISVILLE HIGH SCHOOL PANTHER FOOTBALL TEAM

Nobody makes jeans like Mean Jeans! Be bold and be bad this summer in Mean Jeans for juniors and men. Slide into a pair of 5-pocket jeans with relaxed fit and cargo pockets, or slip your boots into Mean Jeans cowboy denims with stretch bootlegs.

Visit The Clothes Closet on Dungaree Drive today to see a complete line of Mean Jeans products including denim accessories. While you're there, check out our bib overalls and baby tees. We are open 9 to 5 Monday through Friday.

Simply sensational! That's the authentic styling of Mean Jeans! They are made for guys and gals who want to be bold and be bad this summer.

Follow these steps when creating a television or radio commercial

1. Prepare the commercial.

If you are handwriting the script for the commercial, remove 1 sheet of notebook paper from your Supplies folder.

If you are keying the script for the commercial, open your word processor. Double space the body of the commercial.

2. Print (or key) a heading—in CAPITAL LETTERS—on the first line of the page. Include the following information in the heading.
   - The length of the commercial (30- or 60-second spot)
   - The name of the organization being sponsored

3. Compose the script for the commercial. Use your own words to make the wording conversational and cheery. Use catchy phrases to get the audience's attention.

4. List the store hours for the business. Include the days of the week and the actual hours the business is open.

5. Make a copy of the commercial.

If you are handwriting your commercial, ask your Instructor to make 1 photocopy of the commercial.

If you are keying your commercial, print 2 copies of the commercial. Save your work.

Record Your Commercial

Check with your Instructor to see if equipment is available to record your commercial. Arrange a date and time to air your television or radio spot in the Pettisville community.

6. Place 1 copy of the commercial in the Pending File until your *DAILY ACTIVITIES* tell you if you are to mail the commercial or take it to another business.

7. File 1 copy of the commercial in the Office File.

CHECKPOINT

Electronic Advertising

Answer the following questions.

1. Advertising should _____ consumers about products and services for sale.

2. Banners and pop-ups are new types of advertising appearing on the _____.

3. The main purpose of an ad is to get the audience's _____.

4. Radio advertising is better at targeting _____ markets than television advertising.

5. An Internet site that greets visitors using a variety of text, animation, audio, and video is called a/an _____ page.

UNIT SUMMARY

LESSON 7·1 WRITING CLASSIFIED ADVERTISING

1. Businesses use classified advertising to solicit applicants for vacant or newly created positions in their firms.

2. The cost of a want ad is calculated according to the number of issues the ad will run and the number of words used in the ad.

3. Eliminating unnecessary words will reduce the cost of a want ad.

LESSON 7·2 PREPARING DISPLAY ADVERTISING

4. Types of display advertising include advertising in magazines, newspapers, billboards, and telephone directories.

5. Advertising agencies produce advertising by writing copy, creating artwork, and producing ads or commercials.

6. Many businesses create their own ads, such as a sign in a store window.

7. Most newspapers have advertising departments that design ads for their customers.

8. Advertising agencies charge for the cost of advertising plus commissions for their services.

LESSON 7·3 CREATING ELECTRONIC ADVERTISING

9. The main purpose of any ad is to get the audience's attention.

10. Advertising should strive to inform consumers about the benefits of the products and services being promoted.

11. The cost of a television commercial may range from several thousand dollars to several million dollars.

12. Radio advertising can usually target local markets better than television advertising.

13. The Internet has introduced new forms of advertising, such as ads called banners and pop-ups and company web pages.

14. A web address begins with a home page, which serves as an introduction to the other pages.

Glossary

advertising agency	a company that handles all types of advertising for its clients
classified advertising	advertising in the want ad section of a newspaper or other medium
directory advertising	advertising displayed within the Yellow Pages of a telephone book
display advertising	advertising that uses both art and words to promote the sale of products or services
web page	an Internet site that greets visitors using a variety of text, animation, audio, and video

INTERNET EXPLORATIONS

Most of America's major corporations have their own web sites today. It is one form of electronic advertising. Rate each site listed below with respect to how well it manages to advance the corporation's advertising and promotional objectives.

Site	Poor	Fair	Good	Excellent		Site	Poor	Fair	Good	Excellent
www.americangreetings.com	☐	☐	☐	☐		www.gillette.com	☐	☐	☐	☐
www.atlantabraves.com	☐	☐	☐	☐		www.hersheys.com	☐	☐	☐	☐
www.bankofamerica.com	☐	☐	☐	☐		www.homedepot.com	☐	☐	☐	☐
www.basspro.com	☐	☐	☐	☐		www.kfc.com	☐	☐	☐	☐
www.baylinerboats.com	☐	☐	☐	☐		www.kodak.com	☐	☐	☐	☐
www.benjerry.com	☐	☐	☐	☐		www.lodging.com	☐	☐	☐	☐
www.booksamillion.com	☐	☐	☐	☐		www.marriott.com	☐	☐	☐	☐
www.cabelas.com	☐	☐	☐	☐		www.marykay.com	☐	☐	☐	☐
www.campbellsoup.com	☐	☐	☐	☐		www.mcdonalds.com	☐	☐	☐	☐
www.chick-fil-a.com	☐	☐	☐	☐		www.microsoft.com	☐	☐	☐	☐
www.clairestores.com	☐	☐	☐	☐		www.mrsfields.com	☐	☐	☐	☐
www.coca-cola.com	☐	☐	☐	☐		www.nike.com	☐	☐	☐	☐
www.delta.com	☐	☐	☐	☐		www.nissan-usa.com	☐	☐	☐	☐
www.flowers.com	☐	☐	☐	☐		www.oldnavy.com	☐	☐	☐	☐
www.footlocker.com	☐	☐	☐	☐		www.ringling.com	☐	☐	☐	☐
www.ford.com	☐	☐	☐	☐		www.seventeen.com	☐	☐	☐	☐
www.fossil.com	☐	☐	☐	☐		www.tommy.com	☐	☐	☐	☐
www.fritolay.com	☐	☐	☐	☐		www.toysrus.com	☐	☐	☐	☐

ACTIVITY 7•1 WRITING WANT ADS

Apply to:

Human Resources Department
Mean Jeans Manufacturing Co.
45 Maple Street
Pettisville, OH 43553-0175

Directions: *Assume you are the manager of Mean Jeans Manufacturing Co. Your job responsibilities have become so hectic that you decide to hire an administrative assistant to handle many of the tasks you perform. Use the lines below to write a want ad to place in The Town Crier, Pettisville's leading newspaper. Ask applicants to apply to the Human Resources Department at Mean Jeans.*

Turn to *page 225 in this Student Reference Book*. Find the steps titled *Follow these steps when you place a want ad*. **Complete steps 3 and 4.** Include the following information in your want ad.

- You want the applicant applying for this position to be able to write reports, plan meetings, and perform numerous tasks on the computer.

- You want the applicant to have at least two years of experience and have a working knowledge of word processing, spreadsheets, and a database.

- You want someone who has a business degree.

- You want job applicants to mail their resumes to Mean Jeans (see the address shown at the top of this page), or fax them to Mean Jeans' Human Resources Department at Fax No. 419-555-0110.

_____

_____

_____

_____

_____

_____

_____

_____

_____

_____

_____

UNIT 7 • ADVERTISING

ACTIVITY 7•2 CALCULATING THE COST OF WANT ADS

Directions: Use the Guidelines for Counting Words in a Want Ad and the rate chart for The Towne Crier to calculate the cost of 3 want ads.

1. Calculate the cost of the want ad you wrote in Activity 7.1. Turn to *page 226 in this Student Reference Book*. **Complete step 6**. List your answers on the lines below.

   _____ number of words in the ad

   $_____ charge for placing the ad in 1 issue of the newspaper

2. Calculate the cost of the want ad for the storeroom assistant illustrated on the right.

   _____ number of words in the ad

   $_____ charge for placing the ad in 2 issues of the newspaper

STOREROOM ASSISTANT

Local manufacturer seeking individual experienced in shipping and receiving, inventory control, and issuing parts & tools. General hand tool and computer knowledge preferred. HS diploma or GED required. Excellent benefit package. Call 419-555-0193 for application/appointment.

FRONT DESK CLERK

Lamplighter Inn has PT and FT positions available for front desk clerks. Several evening shifts available. Apply in person at 2508 Kneepatch Ave., Pettisville. Drug-free workplace. EOE.

3. Calculate the cost of the want ad for the front desk clerk illustrated above.

   _____ number of words in the ad

   $_____ charge for placing the ad in 3 issues of the newspaper

ACTIVITY 7•3 PREPARING A DISPLAY AD

Directions: Assume you are the assistant to the president of Pettisville Chamber of Commerce. Each year, the Chamber sponsors Western Roundup Days. This is a community-wide event that creates excitement in the whole town! You will use either electronic clip art or the clip art on the back of this sheet to design an ad that can be displayed in store windows in the business community. **NOTE: Read all of the instructions below BEFORE you begin cutting the clip art from the back of this sheet.**

1. Look at the sample display ad below. Note the arrangement of the ad. An attractive ad uses both art and words in an arrangement that is pleasing to the eye. Your Western Roundup Days ad should include a selection of a few pieces of electronic clip art or clip art from the back of this sheet.

2. *If you are prepeparing your display ad manually,* your Instructor will provide you with a sheet of plain paper for your design and the other materials you will need. Turn to *page 228 in this Student Reference Book.* Find the steps titled *Follow these steps when creating a display ad manually.* **Complete steps 3, 4, 5 and 7.** (You do not need felt-tip markers.)

   If you are prepeparing your display ad electronically, access the Mean Jeans folder on your computer. Open the clip art folder for any of the 15 businesses. Then select the folder titled *Western Roundup Days.* Turn to *page 228 in this Student Reference Book.* Find the steps titled *Follow these steps when creating a display ad electronically.* **Complete steps 1, 2, and 3.** Print one copy of your ad. Save your work.

Picture Yourself in Jeans... From Mean Jeans...

AVAILABLE AT FINE STORES EVERYWHERE
Ivey's The Man's Shop, Napoleon
The Clothes Closet, Pettisville
Maumee River Mall, Toledo
Michael's, Toledo

©NOVA DEVELOPMENT CORPORATION

UNIT 7 • ADVERTISING

Pettisville Chamber of Commerce Presents...

Western Roundup Days

PROGRAM OF EVENTS

Friday, July 27

9:00 a.m. – 5:00 p.m.	Special Store Events
12:00 noon	Parade
6:00 p.m. – 11 p.m.	Ox Roast
8:00 p.m.	Square Dance
10:00 p.m.	Fireworks

Saturday, July 28

9:00 a.m. – 12:00 noon	Special Store Events
9:00 a.m. – 12:00 noon	Fishing Contest
12:00 noon	Auction
1:00 p.m. – 5:00 p.m.	Electronic Games
2:00 p.m. – 4:00 p.m.	Rodeo

ACTIVITY 7•4 CREATING ELECTRONIC ADVERTISING

Directions: Assume you are the manager of Creative Advertising Agency. One of your clients, United Communications, asks you to write a 30-second commercial to be aired on WADD-FM Radio Station. United Communications also wants a message to be flashed on the scoreboard at Pettisville High School football games. Write a radio commercial, create an electronic scoreboard ad, and calculate the cost of the advertising. Before you begin, first study the telephone equipment available for sale at United Communications.

1. Turn to United Communications' telephone equipment chart on *page 365 in this Student Reference Book*. Study the types of telephone equipment available for sale. Notice that the phone company sells mobile phones, cellular phones, and DSL lines. (DSL lines are available for people who want a faster connection to the Internet.) Decide on one or two types of telephone equipment to include in your radio spot.

2. Use the lines at the bottom of this page to write your radio commercial. Turn to *page 231 in this Student Reference Book*. Find the steps titled *Follow these steps when creating a television or radio commercial*. **Complete steps 2 through 4.** Include the following information in your commercial.

   - The length of the radio commercial (30 seconds)
   - The name of the organization sponsored by United Communications (Pettisville High School Panther Football)
   - United Communications' store hours (9 to 5, Monday through Friday)

UNIT 7 • ADVERTISING

3. Use the box below to write a message that can be flashed on the scoreboard at Pettisville High School's football games. From the following list, choose 2 or 3 types of information to include in your scoreboard message for United Communications.

- wireless services
- convenient locations
- one-stop shopping
- Internet services
- 24-hour customer service
- rate plans right for you
- long distance services
- paging services

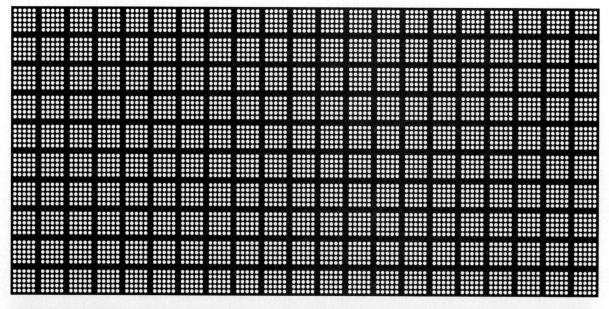

4. Calculate the cost of the advertising. Turn to Creative's advertising rates chart on *page 354 in this Student Reference Book*. Find the fee for scoreboard ads at Wildcat Stadium. (The charge at Panther Stadium is the same.) Record the fee on the line below.

5. Compute the 15% commission. Add the charge for the radio commercial to the charge for the scoreboard ad. Then multiply the total times 0.15. Compute the 6% sales tax by multiplying the Subtotal times 0.06. Find the TOTAL DUE.

$ 100.00   30-second radio commercial

_____   30-second ad flashed on screen 2 times per game for whole season

_____   15% Commission

_____   Subtotal

_____   6% Sales Tax

$_____   TOTAL DUE

REPORTS AND BUSINESS PLANS

Businesses rely on reports to communicate all types of information so that managers can make important decisions. During the model business simulation, you will prepare several types of reports. When you are assigned as manager of a business, you will give an oral presimulation report to the other managers describing your business. About mid-way through the month of July, you will prepare an audit summary. This report will help your Instructor identify problems you may be having in carrying out the duties as manager of your business. At the end of July, you will compile a final audit. The final audit will provide your Instructor with samples of your work as a manager in the model business community.

Your Instructor may also ask you to come up with an idea for a new business. If so, you will write a formal report called a business plan. Since this report will take a lot of planning and preparation, your Instructor will give you a due date well in advance.

Unit Lessons

Lesson 8•1   **Preparing a Presimulation Report**
Lesson 8•2   **Compiling Audit Reports**
Lesson 8•3   **Writing a Business Plan**
Lesson 8•4   **Preparing Financial Statements**

Unit Activities

Activity 8•1   **Preparing a Presimulation Report**
Activity 8•2   **Completing an Audit Summary**
Activity 8•3   **Writing a Business Plan**
Activity 8•4   **Preparing Financial Statements**

PREPARING A PRESIMULATION REPORT

About nine out of ten companies with more than 100 employees have formal orientation programs for new employees. **Orientation** is a program that introduces a new employee to the history, goals, and policies of the company. The purpose of an orientation program is to help the new employee to quickly "feel at home" and to understand the overall objectives of the company. A business that provides orientation for a new employee will be more likely to have a satisfied employee who strives to achieve the goals of the company.

During this job orientation, you will learn about your company by researching the business. Your research will also help you prepare your presimulation report. The purpose of this report is to share important information with the other managers about the operation of your business. During the "Presimulation: Group Activity," your Instructor will assign managers specific times to present reports. If your business has two managers, both managers should work together to prepare this report.

Look at the outline shown on the left. Notice the types of information the managers of Lopez Associates wrote about their business. You should strive to present information about your company that will be helpful as you conduct business with other managers during the model simulation. Remember, those listening to your report are potential customers!

Lopez Associates
Caleb Hutchinson and Alan Crim, Managers

Introduction	
Industry	Commercial real estate
History	Katrina Lopez grew up in Pettisville. Majored in real estate management at OSU. Lost her job in Toledo after company downsized. Moved back to Pettisville in 1975. Started Lopez Associates in 1976. Lopez sold the business to Caleb Hutchinson and Alan Crim in 1985.
Products/Services	Providing rental properties to area businesses.
Type of Ownership	Partnership
Location	Oshkosh Boulevard
Hours	9 a.m. to 5 p.m. daily 9 a.m. to 12 noon Saturday, July 28
Customers	Passports-2-Go Security Insurance Co. United Communications
Policies	1. Rents are due on the 15th of each month. 2. Rental rates include a weekly cleaning service. 3. A fee of 5% of the rental rate is charged for payments made after the 20th of the month.
Conclusion	

---

1. Refer to your outline notes in Activity 8.1, *page 275 in this Student Reference Book*. Write the name of your business on the first line of your outline notes. Write your name as manager.

2. Choose the type of industry associated with your business from the following list. Write your company's industry on your outline notes.

trucking	entertainment	government service
industrial sales	community service	fashions
clothing	financial	retail sales
advertising	travel	publishing
textiles	banking	communications

3. Describe the history of your business. Your company history should answer the following questions.

   - Who started the business?
   - When did the business begin?
   - How did the business begin?
   - How has the business changed through the years?

   Turn to PART 2, Orientation to the 15 Businesses, on *pages 16-47 in this Student Reference Book*. Find the 2-page orientation for your business. Use this information to write a company history on your outline notes.

4. Describe the products and/or services sold by your company. Turn again to PART 2, *pages 16-47 in this Student Reference Book*. Read the information there about the products and/or services you sell. The price lists located on *pages 351-366 in this Student Reference Book* also describe products and services in the model business community.

5. Name the type of ownership for your business. Turn to PART 4, Presimulation: Group Activity, on *page 336 in this Student Reference Book*. Read the information beginning on that page. Choose the type of business ownership from the following list.

corporation	federal agency	nonprofit corporation
partnership	sole proprietorship	limited liability company

6. Describe the location of your business. Turn to PART 1, Orientation to a Business Community Simulation. Find the location of your business on the map on *page 7 in this Student Reference Book*.

7. List the hours your company is open for business. Turn to INFORMATION YOU'LL NEED TO KNOW ABOUT YOUR BUSINESS, *page 2 in the Operations Manual* for your business. Find your store hours.

8. Describe the type of customers the business serves. This information is also located on *page 2 in the Operations Manual* for your business.

9. Describe specific policies and procedures the company follows in conducting business. (For example, the manager of Taylor Office Supplies will explain that orders for office supplies are sold *cash and carry*, which means that orders are placed and paid for *in person* at the store. Orders for equipment and/or furniture will be *mailed* to the store.) You will find information about your company's policies and procedures in the following sources.

- RESPONSIBILITIES OF THE MANAGER(S) beginning on *page 15 in the Operations Manual* for your business (except for Pettisville Bank and Pettisville Post Office). Managers of the bank should turn to *page 17 in their Operations Manuals*, and managers of the post office should turn to *page 13 in their Operations Manuals*.
- INFORMATION YOU'LL NEED TO KNOW ABOUT YOUR BUSINESS, *page 2 in the Operations Manual* for your business.
- PART 3, Reference Guide, *pages 48-325 in this Student Reference Book*.
- Company price lists, *pages 351-366 in this Student Reference Book*.

10. Ask your Instructor if you will prepare your presimulation report using Microsoft *PowerPoint*. If the answer is "yes," you will have electronic clip art available for your use. It is located on your computer in the clip art folder for your business.

11. *If you are handwriting your final outline*, use *page 276 in this Student Reference Book* (the back of the sheet for Activity 8.1).

If you are keying your final outline to prepare a PowerPoint presentation, insert clip art into your PowerPoint slides by using the Insert command on your toolbar to insert a picture "From File."

CHECKPOINT

Preparing Reports

Answer the following questions.

1. Businesses rely on reports to communicate all types of information so that managers can make important _____.

2. The purpose of the _____ report is to share important information with the other managers about the operation of your business.

3. A program that introduces a new employee to the history, goals, and policies of the company is called _____.

4. A business that provides orientation for a new employee will be more likely to have a satisfied employee who strives to achieve the _____ of the company.

5. One of the purposes of an orientation program is to help the new employee to quickly _____.

COMPILING AUDIT REPORTS

An **audit** is a formal periodic check of records. Audits are used to check to see that work has been completed and to evaluate the quality of the work. During the month of July, you will prepare two reports for your Instructor called the audit summary and the final audit. It is important that you complete these reports accurately and turn them in on time. All managers should participate in the preparation of these reports.

◆ THE AUDIT SUMMARY

Your *DAILY ACTIVITIES* will ask you to complete the audit summary between July 11 and July 13. You will be asked questions about the work that you have completed and about the procedures for carrying out assignments. Make sure all managers of your business are in agreement before you answer each question.

■ Follow these steps when you complete the audit summary

1. Find your audit summary.

🖃 *If you are using Instructor-provided forms,* remove the audit summary from your Supplies folder.

🖱 *If you are printing your forms,* open the forms document. Find Unit 8 Reports and Business Plans. Print the audit summary.

---

2. Read all the questions on the summary. Carefully answer each question.

3. Write your name(s) at the top of the audit summary. Hand your completed audit summary to your Instructor.

©GETTY IMAGES/PHOTODISC

The final audit will be prepared on July 31, the last day your business will be in operation. It will be the very last activity that you complete during the model business simulation. You will give your Instructor a sampling of the work you have completed during the model business simulation. *Do not attempt to complete this activity until you have finished all other activities through July 31.*

AUDIT SUMMARY
18 Wheeler Truck Lines

Manager 1

Manager 2

1. Assume you are to pick up a crated shipment ___ pounds; how much would you charge the sh___

2. What were the total charges billed to Buck___ shelter shipped to Creative Advertising Age___

3. What is another word for "crated"?

4. What was the total on the purchase order yo___ on July 6?

5. The _____ collects utility payments ___ Light Company.

6. When the symbol # follows a number (suc___ _____.

7. A freight bill is prepared from the informatio___ _____ of _____.

8. When delivering a shipment, the 18 Wheel___ to initial the _____ _____.

9. Name the file where incomplete work is pl___ period.

10. Name the file where all completed work is ___

11. Is 18 Wheeler Truck Lines a sole proprietors___ liability company, a corporation, or a feder___

12. What business sponsors the Western Round___

13. A confidential financial statement listing th___ worth of a business is called the _____

14. The best way to remember an upcoming ev___ your _____.

15. Who is the agent on a bill of lading?

16. An important bookkeeping record used to rec___ of company money is called the _____

17. How many deposits have been recorded o___

18. After making a deposit, the last amount in ___ the cashbook and the amount written under _____ should be the same.

19. A shipment arranged on July 2 should be p___ _____.

20. An appropriate salutation for a letter addre___ _____.

FINAL AUDIT

Manager 1

Manager 2

Instructions: The final audit is the last evaluation you will have as a manager in the model business community. Your Instructor will check to see that you have completed your daily activities for the month of July. Carefully review all of the documents listed. Then ✔ the left-hand column next to each item requested as you place the form in your Pending File. NOTE: Items with an asterisk (*) are available in an electronic version. If you are using the electronic version, you will need to print a copy.

✔	No.	Description	Date	Recipient	Grade
	1	Check Register*	July		
	2	Cashbook*	July		
	3	Appointment Calendar*	July		
	4	Payroll Register (ending July 13)	7/16		
	5	Payroll Register (ending July 27)	7/30		
	6	Bank Statement	7/30		
	7	Want Ad Receipt	7/11		
	8	Delivery Log	July		
	9	Letter	7/03	Truckers' Local 109	
	10	Letter	7/18	Creative Advertising	
	11	Letter	7/23	Popular Designs	
	12	Letter	7/24	Tandem Truck Sales	
	13	Purchase Order #5000	7/06	Buckeye Equipment	
	14	Purchase Order #5001	7/24	Taylor Office Supplies	
	15	Freight Bills (18 total)	July	Buckeye–10, Denim–2, and Taylor–6	
	16	2 Bank Receipts for Withholding Tax Deposits	7/17 7/30	Bank is depository for the Internal Revenue Service	
	17	Mortgage Loan Contract #360 Installment Loan Contract #818	7/10 7/18	Pettisville Bank Pettisville Bank	
	18	Audit Summary	7/13	Instructor	
	19	Western Roundup Questionnaire Priority Seating Reservation	7/02 7/20	Instructor	
	20	New York Stock Exchange Guide	7/24	Instructor	
				FINAL AUDIT GRADE ▶	

Follow these steps when completing the final audit

1. Find the final audit.

If you are using Instructor-provided forms, remove the final audit from your Supplies folder. Set the audit aside for now.

If you are printing your forms, open the forms document. Find Unit 8 Reports and Business Plans. Print the final audit. Set the audit aside for now.

---

2. Remove the Pending File from your "Mini Filing Cabinet." Make sure that all work in this folder has been completed. Complete any remaining work. You may have work that is incomplete because the manager of another business has not sent it to you or has not contacted you. In that case, leave the incomplete papers in the Pending File. Discard any used, postmarked envelopes.

3. Remove 1 sheet of notebook paper from your Supplies folder. Make a list of any work that remains undone because you were not able to complete the work. For example, you may have a copy of an unpaid invoice, an unanswered letter, or goods that were never shipped to you. Write the name of the business that was supposed to contact you and the assignment that is incomplete. Staple or paper clip the incomplete work to the back of this list. Place the papers in the Pending File. Return the Pending File to your "Mini Filing Cabinet."

> ### One Final Reminder
>
> **Have you recorded the service charge on both the check register and the cashbook, paid all outstanding invoices and bills, and balanced your bank statement?**
>
> **Are your cashbook balance and your checkbook balance in agreement?**
>
> **Have you balanced and ruled the cashbook?**

4. Remove the Supplies folder from your "Mini Filing Cabinet." Sort through the remaining items. Place unused items in one stack and used items in another stack. The used items should either be refiled in their proper place or discarded if they are unusable. Your stack of unused items should contain envelopes, plain paper, notebook paper, and forms. Take the stack of unused items to your Instructor. Return the empty Supplies folder to your "Mini Filing Cabinet."

5. Remove the Office File from your "Mini Filing Cabinet." Sort through the remaining items. Discard any used, postmarked envelopes. Staple or paper clip related items together. For example, an invoice may have a matching purchase order, shipment form, and bill of lading. Check to make sure that all paid invoices and bills are marked *PAID* across the front of the form. Complete any work that has not been finished. Return the Office File to your "Mini Filing Cabinet."

6. Repeat step 5 for any remaining folders in your "Mini Filing Cabinet." **NOTE:** When you remove the Cash File, leave the bank

statement with the canceled checks and deposit slips in the envelope sent by Pettisville Bank.

7. Remove all file folders from your "Mini Filing Cabinet." You will now begin placing items listed on the final audit in your Pending File.

8. Look at the list of items on the final audit.
   a. Notice that Item No. 1 is the check register. If you are using electronic forms, such as a check register, cashbook, or appointment calendar, you must print hard copies of these forms. Go to the Page Setup menu and select the size and number of pages you need to print.
   b. Record a ✔ on your final audit next to check register. Continue in this manner until all items on the final audit have been placed in the Pending File.

9. Place the list of incomplete items you wrote in step 2 above on the top of the stack in the Pending File.

10. Staple or paper clip the final audit to the front of the Pending File. Make sure all managers sign the final audit. Give the Pending File folder with your final audit to your Instructor. Place the remaining file folders in your "Mini Filing Cabinet."

11. Return equipment and miscellaneous supply items to your Instructor. Items to be returned include staplers, calculators, scissors, felt tip markers, paper clips, rulers, etc.

12. Remove your company sign and any posters or other signs from your place of business.

CHECKPOINT

Completing Audit Reports

Answer the following questions.

1. An audit is a formal periodic check of _____.

2. Your Instructor will use audits to check to see that your work has been completed and to evaluate the _____ of your work.

3. The audit summary asks questions about the work that has been completed and about the _____ for carrying out assignments.

4. The final audit contains a _____ of the work completed during the model business simulation.

5. If there are two managers in your business, _____ should complete the audit reports.

WRITING A BUSINESS PLAN

LESSON 8·3

It can be exciting—and also scary—to start a new business. Many people want to share in the American dream of becoming an **entrepreneur** (a person who starts a new business). The advantages of owning a business include being your own boss, earning profits, and enjoying the challenge of working for yourself.

The best way to ensure that your new business doesn't fail is to write a business plan. A **business plan** is a written guide describing the entrepreneur's plan to open and operate a successful business. Writing this report forces the entrepreneur to think about all the details of starting and operating a business. Most entrepreneurs must borrow at least part of the money needed to start a new business. Loan officers will ask to see their business plan before considering giving them a loan. A business plan should describe what product or service will be sold, how it will be produced, and who will buy it. Your business plan should include the following essential parts.

ESSENTIAL PARTS OF A BUSINESS PLAN

Introduction	This section is the first part of a business plan, but it is the last part written. Instructions for writing the introduction begin on *page 261 in this Student Reference Book*. It includes a cover letter, table of contents, and executive summary.
Description of the Business	This section identifies the short- and long-term goals for the business and provides a mission statement.
Marketing Plan	This section describes market research conducted to identify the target market.
Management Plan	This section includes an organization chart and job description for each employee of the business.
Financial Plan	This section estimates the income and expenses for the business.
Appendix	This section contains any documents not already in the body of the business plan.

Before you decide on the type of business you want to own, consider your interests, strengths, and weaknesses. Remember, too, that your business plan will be easier to write if you choose a small business. Your Instructor may ask you to work individually or with a group.

A business plan is a formal report that provides a complete description of the business. Since it is a long report, it should be divided into sections. Six sections have already been described—Introduction, Description of the Business, Marketing Plan, Management Plan, Financial Plan, and Appendix.

To make your report easier to follow, you may want to further subdivide the six sections. For example, after the introductory paragraph in the Description of the Business, consider including the following sub-sections—Goals of the Business, Products and Services, Business Organization, and Location of the Business.

Your business plan will also be easier to read if you include illustrations (charts, graphs, and pictures) along with the paragraphs. Always include a title for each illustration, and mention the illustration *before* you show it.

As you write your business plan, avoid using the words *I*, *me*, and *my*. For example, Areli Noriega should describe herself as a business owner in the following way: "The business will be organized as a sole proprietorship and owned by Areli Noriega" rather than "I will organize my business as a sole proprietorship."

Starting a business is exciting! There's nothing like the feeling of business ownership. Good luck with your business plan.

©GETTY IMAGES/PHOTODISC

The description of your business should include a **mission statement**, which explains the main purpose for the business. The mission statement shown here describes how Lite Fare, Inc. plans to meet the special dietary needs of its customers. The description of your business should also include short- and long-term goals for the business.

Lite Fare, Inc.
MISSION STATEMENT

Lite Fare's mission is to offer a unique dining experience that meets the special food needs of every customer. We serve low fat, low cal, low sodium, sugar free, and vegetarian dishes that are sure to please the most discriminating palate.

Jan Hamlen, Proprietor

©GETTY IMAGES/PHOTODISC

You should explain how you got the idea for the business, tell what you are selling, where your business will be located, and how it will be organized. The way a business is organized depends on the size and nature of the business.

Businesses may be organized as sole proprietorships, partnerships, corporations, or limited liability companies. A **sole proprietorship** is a business owned by one person. A **partnership** is a business owned by two or more people who share the profits or losses. A **corporation** is a business owned by stockholders and managed by a board of directors. And a **limited liability company** is a business owned and managed by members or selected managers. It operates much like a partnership but enjoys the corporate advantage of limited liability.

Although there is no written legal agreement for a sole proprietorship, other types of businesses do have legal agreements. Corporations must have a corporate charter called the *articles of incorporation*. Partners may have a *partnership agreement*. And limited liability companies have a legal agreement called the *articles of organization*. You will find examples of legal agreements in PART 4, Presimulation: Group Activity, beginning on *page 339 in this Student Reference Book*.

Follow these steps when you write the description of your business

1. Organize a notebook for your business plan. Find an appropriate report cover to keep all the materials you will gather as you write your business plan, such as a folder or 3-ring binder. If possible, obtain section dividers to better organize the materials for your notebook.

2. Design a mission statement for the business on a full sheet of paper. Arrange the page in landscape format by turning the page sideways (11 by 8-1/2 inches rather than 8-1/2 by 11 inches). *If you*

©GETTY IMAGES/PHOTODISC

are designing your mission statement using Microsoft Word, select File, Page Setup, Margins, and Landscape. The mission statement should

- include the words *MISSION STATEMENT* and the name of the business
- give a short statement of the purpose of the business
- create interest with appropriate art
- include a page border (*If you are preparing the page electronically using Microsoft Word*, select Format, Borders and Shading, then Page Borders.)

3. Compose an introductory paragraph. This section should
   - describe how you came up with the business idea and why you think it will work
   - provide a start-up date for the business
   - mention the mission statement and where to find it (such as on the following page).

4. Write a description of your goals for the business. Include one or two introductory sentences and then make a list of your goals. Remember that your goals must be *measurable*. For example, "to obtain a profit margin of at least 10 percent" is a measurable goal, but "to make a lot of profit" is not a measurable goal. This section should include

   a. Short-Term Goals (goals that can be attained within a year). Here are some examples.
      - to obtain a loan of $60,000 for the business
      - to have 2,000 regular customers by the end of the year
      - to design a web page on the Internet
      - to obtain a profit margin of at least 10 percent

   b. Long-Term Goals (goals that can be attained within 2-5 years). Here are some examples.
      - to pay off long-term loans within 5 years
      - to have 200 clients within 3 years
      - to generate 60% of sales from local customers and 40% of sales from out-of-town customers
      - to increase the profit margin to 25 percent

5. Compose a paragraph describing the products or services your business will offer. This section should

   - describe the strengths and weaknesses of your product or service
   - explain what makes your product or service more desirable than what is already on the market
   - tell what benefits your customers will receive from buying your product or service

©GETTY IMAGES/PHOTODISC

6. Write a legal document for your business (articles of incorporation, partnership agreement, or articles of organization). Refer to PART 4, Pre-simulation: Group Activity, on *pages 339-343 in this Student Reference Book* for a description of legal documents for partnerships, corporations, and limited liability companies. **NOTE:** If your business is a sole proprietorship, you will not have a legal document.

©GETTY IMAGES/PHOTODISC

7. Compose a paragraph describing your business organization. This section should
   - describe the main focus of the business—merchandising (selling) products, manufacturing products, or offering a service
   - tell how your business will be organized—as a sole proprietorship, a partnership, a corporation, or a limited liability company
   - explain if you will open a new business, take over an existing business, or start a franchise operation
   - mention the legal document for your business and where to find it

8. Design a floor plan for the business. Include the title *FLOOR PLAN FOR (YOUR BUSINESS)* at the top of the floor plan. If the Internet is available, you will find web sites to help you design a floor plan.

9. Compose a paragraph describing the location of your business. This section should
   - tell the location of the business (street address, city, and state)
   - give arguments for why this is a good location
   - explain how you will pay for the business's property (buy or lease)
   - mention the floor plan and where to find it

10. Find the evaluation form for the description of the business.

 If you are preparing your business plan manually, remove the evaluation form for the description of the business from your Supplies folder.

 If you are preparing your business plan electronically, open the forms document. Find Unit 8 Reports and Business Plans. Print Evaluation_Description of Business.

---

11. Staple the evaluation form to the front of the description of your business and give it to your Instructor.

12. When your Instructor returns the description of the business to you, place it in your business plan notebook in the order listed on the table of contents on *page 264 in this Student Reference Book*.

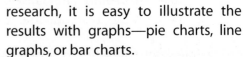

MARKETING PLAN

The marketing plan should identify your *target market*, the people who are interested in and have the money to buy your product or service. You must conduct market research to determine your target market, which includes *primary research* (conducted by the researcher) and *secondary research* (borrowed from other sources). For example, primary research may include interviews, observations, taste tests, or market research surveys; and secondary research may include books, periodicals, and Internet research.

A market research survey is one way you can identify your **customer profile**, the complete picture of the demographics of a company's prospective customers. *Demographics* include information such as a customer's age, income, and location. To get accurate results, the participants in your survey must be chosen randomly. For example, a business conducting telephone interviews might call every tenth person in the phone book. A sample market research survey and the customer profile derived from it are illustrated on *page 255 in this Student Reference Book*. After you have completed your market

research, it is easy to illustrate the results with graphs—pie charts, line graphs, or bar charts.

The marketing plan must also include information about your pricing and sales strategies, competition, and advertising. How you plan to sell your product or service and the price you charge will determine whether or not you will make a profit. You also must study your competition to find out what advantages you have over them and what advantages they have over you. Advertising is essential for a new business to become known in the community. When you write your financial plan, you will want to budget a generous amount of money for that purpose.

Follow these steps when you write the marketing plan

1. Compose a paragraph describing the marketing plan. It should
   - describe the target market
   - name the type of research conducted (a market research survey)
   - tell *when* the market research survey was conducted
   - explain *how* the market research survey was conducted

MARKET RESEARCH SURVEY

Directions: Thank you for participating in our Market Research Survey. Your answers will help Lite Fare, Inc. to best meet the needs of area consumers. Please check the box that best answers each question.

Age   ___ under 18   ___ 18-30   ___ 31-40   ___ 41-50   ___ 51-65   ___ over 65
Gender   ___ male   ___ female
Residence _____ State or _____ Country
Employment ___ full time   ___ part-time   ___ student   ___ retired
Family Income ___ under $25,000   ___ $25-50,000   ___ $50-100,000   ___ over $100,000

1. How often do you eat out? (check one)

    ___ daily   ___ once a month
    ___ several times a week   ___ several times a year
    ___ several times a month   ___ rarely

2. Do you have any special dietary needs?

    ___ yes   ___ no

    If you answered yes, describe your dietary restrictions. (check all that apply)

    ___ low fat   ___ low sodium   ___ low calorie
    ___ sugar free   ___ vegetarian

3. Would you be willing to eat in a restaurant that served mainly low fat, low sodium, low cal, sugar free, and vegetarian dishes?

    ___ yes   ___ no

    If you answered yes, how often would you visit a Lite Fare restaurant?

    ___ at least once a week
    ___ at least once a month
    ___ at least once a year

4. If you had to choose today between a Lite Fare restaurant and a regular restaurant, which one would you choose?

    ___ Lite Fare restaurant
    ___ regular restaurant

Customer Profile
Lite Fare, Inc.
Jan Hamlen, Proprietor

- 62% of customers are female, 38% are male

- 18% of customers are retired

- average family income of $51,000 per year

- 42% live in Georgia and Florida

- 58% live in mostly northern states and travel I-75

- few customers are teenagers

- age of customers: 18 to 75

- most frequent food request: low fat

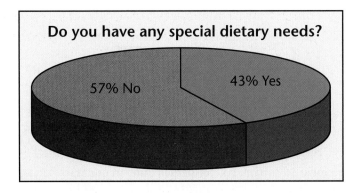

Do you have any special dietary needs?

57% No

43% Yes

2. Design a market research survey. Refer to the illustration on _page 255 in this Student Reference Book_. Include on the survey
   - the name of your business and the words _MARKET RESEARCH SURVEY_
   - directions explaining the purpose of the survey and how to complete it
   - demographic information (shown under the directions in the illustration)
   - 3-5 questions (Give several choices for answers.)

3. Conduct the survey. Get responses from a random sampling of age and income groups using one of the survey sheets to record a tally of the responses. For example, question #2 on the sample market research survey on _page 255 in this Student Reference Book_ asks, "Do you have any special dietary needs?" If 12 people answer "yes," record the number 12 in the _yes_ box. If 16 people answer "no," record the number 16 in the _no_ box. The total responses are 28 (12 yes + 16 no = 28). To find the percentage of "yes" responses, divide 12 by the total number of responses (12 ÷ 28 = 43%). To find the percentage of "no" responses, divide 16 by the total number of responses (16 ÷ 28 = 57%). A total of 43% "yes" responses plus 57% "no" responses equals a 100% response rate.

computational resources

HOW TO GRAPH YOUR SURVEY DATA

Example A market survey asked the question: "Do you have any special dietary needs?" Of the 28 people surveyed, 12 responded "yes" and 16 responded "no."

Problem Create a circle graph (pie chart) that shows the results of the survey.

Solution First, calculate the percentages for each response. Then, multiply each percentage by 360° (number of degrees in a circle) to find how many degrees are in each pie wedge.

"Yes" percent = 12 ÷ 28 ≈ 43%; 0.43 × 360° = 155°

"No" percent = 16 ÷ 28 ≈ 57%; 0.57 × 360° = 205°

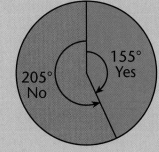

205°
No

155°
Yes

4. Create a graph to show the results of one of your survey questions. *If you are preparing your business plan electronically*, use the tools on your word processor to design a pie chart, line graph, or bar chart.

5. Compose a customer profile using the results of your market research survey. Refer to the illustration on *page 255 in this Student Reference Book*.

6. Write a short paragraph about the market research. This section should
   - describe the results of the market research
   - mention the survey and where to find it
   - mention the graph and where to find it
   - mention the customer profile and where to find it

7. Write a pricing and sales strategy. For example, a restaurant could design a menu. A pet store selling a variety of goods could explain the percentage of markup, such as 200% on pets, 100% on pet supplies, and 50% on pet food. This section should
   - explain how you will sell your product or service
   - list prices of your product or service
   - list your suppliers (the businesses you buy from regularly)

8. Write a paragraph describing your direct and indirect competition. For example, if you own a shoe store, another shoe store would be a direct competitor. But a department store that sells a variety of goods including shoes would be an indirect competitor. This section should
   - list the names and locations of your direct competitors
   - list the names and locations of your indirect competitors
   - explain the advantages you have over your competitors
   - explain the advantages your competitors have over you

9. Write or design an ad for your business. Choose from one of the following: display ad, TV or radio commercial, flier, or customer letter. (See Unit 7 on *pages 223-240 in this Student Reference Book*.)

10. Write a paragraph describing your advertising strategy. This section should
   - list and explain the ways you plan to promote your business— newspaper, fliers, television, radio, the Internet, direct mail, etc.
   - mention your ad and where to find it

11. Find the evaluation form for your marketing plan.

If you are preparing your business plan manually, remove the evaluation form for the marketing plan from your Supplies folder.

If you are preparing your business plan electronically, open the forms document. Find Unit 8 Reports and Business Plans. Print Evaluation_Marketing Plan.

---

12. Staple the evaluation form to the front of the marketing plan and give it to your Instructor.

13. When your Instructor returns the marketing plan to you, place it in your business plan notebook in the order listed on the table of contents on _page 264 in this Student Reference Book_.

MANAGEMENT PLAN

Your business plan should describe for its readers what qualifications you have to manage a business. Not only will you need to demonstrate your skills and abilities for running a business, but you must also show that you are capable of recruiting, hiring, and training a good staff of employees.

Your management plan should include a list of positions within your organization. These positions are frequently listed on an _organization chart_, a diagram that shows job titles in a company and the relationship between workers. Look at the organization chart below. The chart for Lite

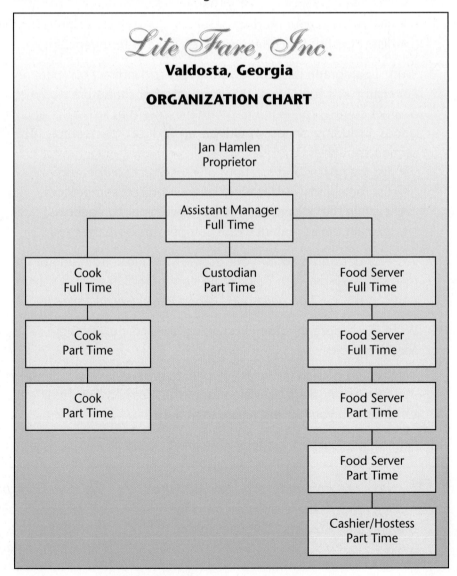

Lite Fare, Inc.
Valdosta, Georgia

ORGANIZATION CHART

- Jan Hamlen — Proprietor
  - Assistant Manager — Full Time
    - Cook — Full Time
      - Cook — Part Time
        - Cook — Part Time
    - Custodian — Part Time
    - Food Server — Full Time
      - Food Server — Full Time
        - Food Server — Part Time
          - Food Server — Part Time
            - Cashier/Hostess — Part Time

Fare shows the job titles and the chain of command within the organization. Nine employees will report to the assistant manager, who in turn will report directly to Ms. Hamlen.

You may also want to include a business card in your management plan. Managers make a habit of always carrying business cards with them. A *business card* provides important information to businesspersons with whom you come in contact.

Job descriptions for the positions within your company should be included in your management plan. A *job description* is a statement that lists the job title, qualifications, responsibilities, and salary or wages for a particular job.

Your plan may also include a work schedule

Lite Fare, Inc.

Jan Hamlen, Proprietor
2501 Sherwood Lane
Valdosta, GA 31602-0144
(229) 555-0143
www.litefare.mjs

Lite Fare, Inc.

Job Description

Job Title	Food Server
Responsibilities	Take customer food orders, serve meals, clean tables, assist the manager in opening/closing store.
Qualifications	High school diploma or GED. Experience preferred. Good communication skills. Well groomed.
Hourly Wage	$3.75 per hour plus tips

for your business. A *work schedule* is an illustration showing employees' work hours for a period of time. The illustration below shows the work schedule for Lite Fare, Inc. for the week ending July 13, 20—.

Lite Fare, Inc.

WORK SCHEDULE
For the week ending July 13, 20--

Sunday 7/8/20--	Monday 7/9/20--	Tuesday 7/10/20--	Wednesday 7/11/20--	Thursday 7/12/20--	Friday 7/13/20--	Saturday 7/14/20--
Jan	Jason	Jan	Jan	Jan	Jan	Jan
10am-8pm	10am-6pm	10am-8pm	10am-8pm	10am-6pm	10am-8pm	10am-8pm
Jason	Karen	Bipin	Bipin	Jason	Jason	Jason
11am-7pm	11am-8pm	11am-8pm	11am-8pm	11am-9pm	11am-9pm	11am-9pm
Karen	Randy	Randy	Randy	Karen	Karen	Karen
11am-7pm	11am-8pm	11am-8pm	11am-8pm	10am-2pm	2pm-10pm	2pm-10pm
Latasha	Latasha	Latasha	Latasha	Bipin	Bipin	Bipin
2pm-10pm	2pm-10pm	2pm-10pm	2pm-10pm	2pm-10pm	2pm-10pm	2pm-10pm
Felix	Felix	Felix	Felix	Kelvin	Kelvin	Kelvin
2pm-10pm	2pm-10pm	2pm-10pm	2pm-10pm	2pm-10pm	10am-6pm	10am-6pm

Follow these steps when you write the management plan

1. Compose a paragraph describing the qualifications of the owner(s) for running a successful business. This section should
   - list specific qualifications, such as education and work experience
   - describe human relations skills, such as ability to motivate employees, courtesy, and tactfulness
   - explain that the resume of the owner(s) is located in the appendix of this business plan

2. Design a personal business card. *If you are preparing the business card electronically*, there are web sites that will help you design a business card.

3. Design an organization chart for your business. *If you are designing the organization chart electronically*, use the tools available on your word processor.

4. Write a job description for one of your employees. Include the job title, duties, qualifications, and salary or hourly wage.

5. Create a work schedule for your employees. Include employee names and hours worked each day.

6. Write a paragraph explaining how you will staff the business. This section should
   - tell how many employees you will hire
   - describe employees' work hours (part-time, full-time, etc.)
   - mention the illustrations included in this section (business card, work schedule, organization chart, and job description) and where to find them

7. Find the evaluation form for the management plan.

If you are preparing your business plan manually, remove the evaluation form for the management plan from your Supplies folder.

If you are preparing your business plan electronically, open the forms document. Find Unit 8 Reports and Business Plans. Print Evaluation_Management Plan.

---

8. Staple the evaluation form to the front of the management plan and give it to your Instructor.

9. When your Instructor returns the management plan to you, place it in your business plan notebook in the order listed on the table of contents on *page 264 in this Student Reference Book*.

INTRODUCTION TO THE BUSINESS PLAN

The introduction includes a cover letter, a table of contents, and an executive summary. The purpose of the cover letter is to describe your business, tell why your business idea is a good one, and ask for a loan.

Jan Hamlen plans to open a new restaurant called Lite Fare, Inc. that will offer a menu to serve customers who have special dietary needs. The cover letter shown on *page 263 in this Student Reference Book* explains her business idea and requests a loan for $50,000.

The table of contents shown on *page 264 in this Student Reference Book* outlines for the reader the parts of the report. Although the table of contents appears at the front a business plan, you should wait until you have finished writing the entire report before you record the page numbers.

One of the most important parts of a business plan is the executive summary. (See the illustration on *page 265 in this Student Reference Book*.) The **executive summary** recounts the key points contained in a business plan. It should create excitement for your business concept and persuade the reader that your business will be successful. Although the executive summary appears in the introduction, it should be written after the business plan has been finalized.

Follow these steps when you write the introduction to your business plan

1. Create the letterhead for your business.

If you are handwriting your business plan, design a logo suitable for your business at the top of a plain sheet of paper. Print your company name, address, and telephone number close to the logo.

If you are preparing your business plan electronically, open your word processor. Find a logo suitable for your business. Use clip art available on your word processor, or find pictures from the Internet or other sources. Copy the clip art onto your document. Key the name, address, and telephone number for your business close to the logo. Save your work.

2. Compose the cover letter. Be sure to describe the product or service you will offer and explain the purpose for the loan. Refer to the sample cover letter on *page 263 in this Student Reference Book*. Address your letter to

    Ms. Maki Tsukada, Vice President
    Safe and Sure Bank, Inc.
    P. O. Box 555
    (Your City), (Your State) ZIP

3. Write a 4- to 6-paragraph executive summary. It should recount the key points in the body of your business plan. Include at least one paragraph about each of the following
   - description of the business
   - marketing plan
   - management plan
   - financial plan

4. Find the business plan table of contents.

If you are using Instructor-provided forms, remove the Business Plan Table of Contents from your Supplies folder.

If you are printing your forms, open the forms document. Find Unit 8 Reports and Business Plans. Print the Business Plan Table of Contents.

---

5. Insert page numbers on the table of contents. Write your company name and address at the top of the table of contents.

6. Find the evaluation form for the introduction.

If you are preparing your business plan manually, remove the evaluation form for the introduction from your Supplies folder.

If you are preparing your business plan electronically, open the forms document. Find Unit 8 Reports and Business Plans. Print Evaluation_Introduction.

---

7. Staple the evaluation form to the front of the introduction and give it to your Instructor.

8. When your Instructor returns the introduction to you, place it in your business plan notebook in the order listed on the table of contents on *page 264 in this Student Reference Book*.

©GETTY IMAGES/PHOTODISC

BUSINESS PLAN
COVER LETER

Lite Fare, Inc.

Lite Fare, Inc.
2501 Sherwood Lane
Valdosta, GA 31602-0144
(229) 555-0143

July 1, 20– –

Ms. Cheryle V. Bryan
Vice President
Safe and Sure Bank, Inc.
P. O. Box 555
Valdosta, GA 31601-0555

Dear Ms. Bryan

Enclosed is a copy of the business plan for Lite Fare, Inc. Lite Fare is a proposed new restaurant that will serve the special dietary needs of its customers. Currently, there is no restaurant in Georgia that offers diet foods as its main fare. During the past two years, I visited Salads Express in South Florida and Lite-n-Easy in San Diego, California. Both of these restaurants have enjoyed tremendous success. My research into these two operations has convinced me that there is a true market for this type of food service.

There are more than 30 restaurants located on Exit 18 off I-75. As you know, this area generates customers from all over South Georgia and North Florida in addition to the heavy volume of traffic from I-75. A prime one-acre location with a vacant restaurant is available on Exit 18 situated between a fast-food Italian restaurant and a gas station. The restaurant is well suited for my needs.

My plan is to sign a three-year lease with Bajalia and Associates to open a restaurant that will serve 60 patrons. I will personally invest $85,000 and need additional financing for $50,000. The financial plan enclosed will outline for you how I plan to repay this loan.

Should you need any additional information, please let me know. I am looking forward to hearing from you.

Sincerely

Janice M. Hamlen

Janice M. Hamlen

Enclosure

Lite Fare, Inc.

Lite Fare, Inc.
2501 Sherwood Lane
Valdosta, GA 31602-0144
(229) 555-0143

BUSINESS PLAN ▪ TABLE OF CONTENTS

PAGE NO.

I. INTRODUCTION

   A. Cover Letter

   B. Table of Contents

   C. Executive Summary

II. BODY

   A. Description of the Business
      1. Mission Statement
      2. Short- and Long-Term Goals of the Business
      3. Products or Services
      4. Organization of the Business
      5. Location of the Business
      6. Floor Plan

   B. Marketing Plan
      1. Market Research Survey
      2. Market Research Graph
      3. Customer Profile
      4. Pricing and Sales Strategy
      5. Competition
      6. Advertising

   C. Management Plan
      1. Staffing
      2. Business Card
      3. Organization Chart
      4. Job Descriptions
      5. Work Schedule

   D. Financial Plan
      1. Start-up Costs
      2. Pro Forma Cash Flow Statement
      3. Pro Forma Statement of Income
      4. Pro Forma Balance Sheet

III. APPENDIX

   A. Personal Resume(s)
   B. Bibliography
   C. Other Supporting Documents

BUSINESS PLAN
EXECUTIVE SUMMARY

Lite Fare, Inc.

Lite Fare, Inc.
2501 Sherwood Lane
Valdosta, GA 31602-0144
(229) 555-0143

EXECUTIVE SUMMARY

Lite Fare, Inc. will be established as a sole proprietorship in Valdosta, Georgia, and will be owned and operated by Jan Hamlen. Ms. Hamlen brings with her a long history of experience in the restaurant business. As a young girl, her parents owned and operated the Golden Oaks Restaurant where she worked during her middle school and high school years. Ms. Hamlen holds a degree in business administration from The University of Georgia with an emphasis in small business management. She has more than ten years of prior experience managing two other restaurants.

The mission of Lite Fare is to offer foods for customers who have special dietary needs. The main fare will be low fat, low cal, low sodium, sugar free dishes. Customers who are vegetarians will be able to choose from a wide variety of foods. There are no similar restaurants in Georgia and only one restaurant and one franchise chain in the United States that specialize in diet foods. These restaurants have captured a large market share of the food industry in their locations.

Lite Fare will take over the building of a previously owned restaurant on St. Augustine Road in Valdosta, Georgia. The building will be leased from Bajalia and Associates with only minor repairs and renovation required. A staff of ten will be hired—four full-time and six part-time employees. Ms. Hamlen will assume complete responsibility for keeping the business books and preparing payroll. An outside service will be hired for maintenance on an as-needed basis.

Lite Fare will be situated in a prime location where more than 30 restaurants already exist. Exit 18, located off I-75, is only 18 miles from the Florida line. It generates heavy traffic from out-of-state travelers and pulls customers from all over South Georgia and North Florida. Market research indicates that there is a target market of customers who desire a restaurant of this type and would frequent it if given the opportunity.

The business is being capitalized with a personal investment of $85,000 and bank financing of $50,000. Ms. Hamlen expects to repay the bank loan in four years.

The appendix of a business plan includes any supporting documents that are not included in the body of the business plan, such as your resume and a bibliography of your reference sources. Other examples of supporting documents for Lite Fare, Inc. would be tax returns, insurance policies, or a letter from the health department concerning food service regulations.

Follow these steps when you write the Appendix

1. Write a personal resume. Turn to _pages 284-287 in this Student Reference Book_. Complete the steps titled _Follow these steps when you prepare your resume._

2. Prepare a bibliography. The bibliography should include all sources used to prepare the business plan, such as web sites, books, periodicals, and interviews.

3. Write a short paragraph to introduce the appendix. This section should list the items contained in the appendix, such as

   - resume(s) of the owner(s)
   - bibliography
   - other supporting documents

4. Find the evaluation form for the appendix.

If you are preparing your business plan manually, remove the evaluation form for the appendix from your Supplies folder.

If you are preparing your business plan electronically, open the forms document. Find Unit 8 Reports and Business Plans. Print Evaluation_Appendix.

---

5. Staple the evaluation form to the front of the appendix and give it to your Instructor.

6. When your Instructor returns the appendix to you, place it in your business plan notebook in the order listed on the table of contents on _page 264 in this Student Reference Book_.

7. Prepare an oral presentation about your business plan if you Instructor directs you. Turn to _pages 107-108 in this Student Reference Book_. Complete the steps titled _Follow these steps when you are told to give a speech._

CHECKPOINT

The Business Plan

Answer the following questions.

1. Writing a business plan forces the entrepreneur to think about all the _____ of starting and operating a business.

2. The description of the business should include short- and long-term goals and a _____ _____ which explains the main purpose for the business.

3. An organization chart shows job titles and the chain of _____ within the organization.

4. The marketing plan should identify your _____, the people who are interested in and have the money to buy your product or service.

5. One of the most important parts of a business plan is the _____, which recounts the key points contained in the business plan.

Doing Business on the 'Net

Business Plans Online

A number of web sites offer books or services for sale to help you write a business plan. You can also get free assistance with sample business plans.

Access **www.bplans.com**. Key the word restaurant in its search feature to view examples of mission statements, executive summaries, and pro forma financial statements for restaurants.

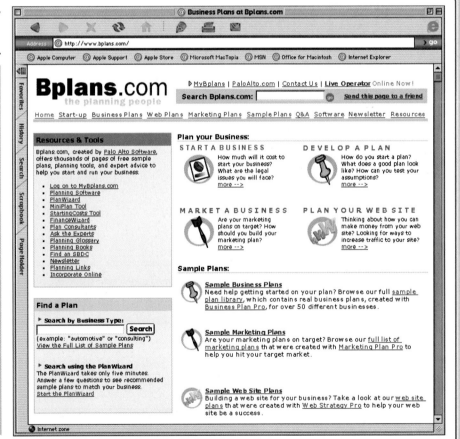

PREPARING FINANCIAL STATEMENTS

If your Instructor asks you to write a business plan, you will prepare a list of start-up costs for your business. You will then prepare pro forma financial statements. **Pro forma financial statements** are based on estimated income and expenses for a business.

Lite Fare, Inc.
START-UP COSTS
Jan Hamlen, Proprietor

Equipment		Restaurant Expenses	
Cash registers	$ 3,700	Food inventory	$ 4,200
Computer	1,950	Laminated menus	165
Ice machine	2,700		
Cooking utensils	2,600	**Supplies**	
Serving utensils	1,475	Restaurant supplies	$ 3,220
Walk-in freezer	5,010	Cleaning supplies	150
Commercial microwave	545	Office supplies	200
Griddle/steamer	1,250		
		Other Expenses	
Furniture and Fixtures		Store sign	$ 3,110
Tables and chairs	$ 1,900	Business license/permits	420
Serving bar	2,400	Utility and lease deposits	1,100
Front counter	600	Advertising/sales promotion	2,000
		TOTAL	$38,695

 START-UP COSTS
FOR A BUSINESS

The *start-up costs* for a new business include those expenses that are likely to occur only one time. The start-up costs for Lite Fare, Inc. listed above total $38,695.

Follow these steps when you prepare a list of start-up costs

1. Remove 1 sheet of notebook paper from your Supplies folder. Make a list of start-up costs. See the illustration above. Keep in mind start-up costs for your business will differ from those of other businesses.

2. Write (or key) your final list in an attractive format. If you are keying your list, print 1 copy. Save your work.

◆ FINANCIAL STATEMENTS

It is typical for a new business to lose money for several months or even several years. An entrepreneur must have enough cash on hand to cover these losses until the business turns a profit. An estimate of the flow of cash into and out of a business is called a *pro forma cash flow statement*. The pro forma cash flow statement illustrated on the right shows an estimated negative cash flow of $-4,435 for Lite Fare's first month of operation.

A **statement of income** shows the revenue (income), expenses, and profit or loss of a business. Ms. Hamlen expects to show a loss for the first year but believes she will turn a profit during Lite Fare's second year of operation. The pro forma statement of income illustrated on the following page shows an estimated profit for Year 2 of $14,280.

The **balance sheet** is a financial statement that reports the assets, liabilities, and owner's equity of a business on a specific date. **Assets** are items of value owned by a business, such as equipment. **Liabilities** are amounts of money owed by a business, such as loans. The net worth of a business is called owner's equity. **Owner's equity** is determined by subtracting the liabilities from the assets.

The reason this financial statement is called a balance sheet is because it is based on an equation that creates a "balance" between the assets, liabilities, and owner's equity of the business as shown below.

Assets = Liabilities + Owner's Equity

Whenever a start-up business estimates its assets, liabilities, and owner's equity, it is reported on a pro forma balance sheet. Ms. Hamlen prepared the *pro forma balance sheet* for Lite Fare illustrated on *page 271 of this Student Reference Book*.

For more information on financial statements, see PART 4, Presimulation: Group Activity, beginning on *page 345 in this Student Reference Book*.

Lite Fare, Inc.

PRO FORMA CASH FLOW STATEMENT

Jan Hamlen, Proprietor
September 20–– (first month)

Income	$17,500
Operating Expenses	
Advertising	$ 1,200
Food	6,250
Insurance	430
Maintenance	300
Other	150
Payroll taxes	825
Rent	2,500
Supplies	250
Telephone	50
Utilities	540
Wages and salaries	9,440
Total Expenses	$21,935
Cash Flow	–$4,435

■ Follow these steps when you prepare pro forma financial statements

1. Remove 3 sheets of notebook paper from your Supplies folder.

2. Refer to the list of possible business expenses on *page 272 in this Student Reference Book*. Place a ✔ next to each item listed that will be an expense for your business.

3. Write a draft of your pro forma cash flow statement for your *first month of operation*. Refer to the illustration on *page 269 in this Student Reference Book*.

4. Write a draft of your pro forma statement of income for *Year 2* of your business. Refer to the illustration below.

Lite Fare, Inc.

PRO FORMA STATEMENT OF INCOME

Jan Hamlen, Proprietor
September 20–– (Year 2)

Income	$315,000
Operating Expenses	
Advertising	$ 14,400
Food	112,500
Insurance	5,160
Maintenance	3,600
Other	1,800
Payroll taxes	9,900
Rent	30,000
Supplies	3,000
Telephone	600
Utilities	6,480
Wages and salaries	113,280
Total Expenses	$300,720
Profit	$ 14,280

5. Write a draft of your pro forma balance sheet for *Year 2* of your business. Refer to the illustration on the opposite page.

6. Write a paragraph describing your financial plan. It should
   - tell how much capital the owner(s) will invest
   - explain how long it will take the business to turn a profit

- describe how much you are asking for a loan and when it will be repaid
- mention the documents in the financial plan—start-up costs, pro forma cash flow statement, balance sheet, and income statement

---

Lite Fare, Inc.

PRO FORMA BALANCE SHEET

Jan Hamlen, Proprietor
September 1, 20–– (Year 2)

Current Assets		Current Liabilities	
Cash on hand	$ 6,400	Accounts payable	$ 2,010
Certificate of deposit	40,000		
Inventory	3,800	Long-term Liabilities	
Total current assets	$50,200	Loans payable	39,300
Fixed Assets		**TOTAL LIABILITIES**	$41,310
Equipment	$22,340		
Less depreciation	–4,465		
Furniture and fixtures	4,900	**OWNER'S EQUITY**	
Less depreciation	–490	Jan Hamlen, Proprietor	$50,775
Vehicle	24,500		
Less depreciation	–4,900		
Total fixed assets	$41,885		
		TOTAL LIABILITIES	
TOTAL ASSETS	$92,085	**AND OWNER'S EQUITY**	$92,085

---

7. Find the evaluation form for the financial plan.

If you are preparing your business plan manually, remove the evaluation form for the financial plan from your Supplies folder.

If you are preparing your business plan electronically, open the forms document. Find Unit 8 Reports and Business Plans. Print Evaluation_Financial Plan.

---

8. Staple the evaluation form to the front of the financial plan and give it to your Instructor.

9. When your Instructor returns the financial plan to you, place it in your business plan notebook in the order listed on the table of contents on *page 264 in this Student Reference Book*.

POSSIBLE BUSINESS EXPENSES CHECKLIST

Use the checklist below to determine which types of expenses your business may incur.

☐ advertising	☐ Internet service	☐ repairs
☐ bank charges	☐ legal & accounting fees	☐ supplies
☐ charitable contributions	☐ maintenance	☐ taxes
☐ custodial service	☐ miscellaneous	☐ telephone
☐ dues and subscriptions	☐ mortgage	☐ travel
☐ entertainment	☐ payroll taxes	☐ utilities
☐ gasoline	☐ remodeling	☐ vehicles
☐ insurance	☐ rent	☐ wages and salaries

CHECKPOINT

Preparing Financial Statements

Answer the following questions.

1. It is typical for a new business to _____ money for several months or even several years.

2. The equation that creates the "balance" on a balance sheet is

   _____ = _____ + _____ .

3. A statement of income shows the _____ or _____ for a business.

4. Before starting a new business, the owner should make a list of one-time expenses called _____ costs.

5. Pro forma financial statements are _____ of actual expenses and income for a new business.

UNIT SUMMARY

1. The purpose of an orientation program is to help the new employee to quickly "feel at home" and to understand the overall objectives of the company.

2. A business that provides orientation for a new employee will be more likely to have a satisfied employee who strives to achieve the goals of the company.

LESSON 8•1 PREPARING A PRESIMULATION REPORT

3. It is important that managers complete reports accurately and turn them in on time.

4. Audits are used to check to see that work has been completed and to evaluate the quality of the work.

LESSON 8•2 COMPILING AUDIT REPORTS

5. Advantages of owning a business include being your own boss, earning profits, and enjoying the challenge of working for yourself.

6. A business plan forces future business owners to think about all the details of starting and operating a business.

7. A business plan includes an introduction, a description of the business, a marketing plan, a management plan, a financial plan, and an appendix.

8. The introduction to a business plan includes a cover letter, a table of contents, and an executive summary.

9. The description of the business should explain the business idea, state the goals of the business, and tell what is being sold, where the business will be located, and how it will be organized.

10. A business plan should demonstrate the owner's skills and abilities for running a business.

LESSON 8•3 WRITING A BUSINESS PLAN

11. The start-up costs for a business include those expenses that are likely to occur only one time.

12. The balance sheet is based on the equation

$$\text{Assets} = \text{Liabilities} + \text{Owner's Equity.}$$

LESSON 8•4 PREPARING FINANCIAL STATEMENTS

assets	items of value owned by a business
audit	a formal periodic check of records
balance sheet	a financial statement that reports the assets, liabilities, and owner's equity of a business on a specific date
business plan	a written guide describing the entrepreneur's plan to open and operate a successful business
corporation	a business owned by stockholders and managed by a board of directors
customer profile	the complete picture of a company's prospective customers, such as age, income, and location
entrepreneur	a person who starts a new business
executive summary	a summary of the key points contained in a business plan
liabilities	amounts of money owed by a business
limited liability company	a business owned and managed by its members, which operates like a partnership but has the corporate advantage of limited liability
mission statement	a short description of the main purpose for a business
orientation	a program that introduces a new employee to the history, goals, and policies of the company
owner's equity	the net worth of a business determined by subtracting the liabilities from the assets
partnership	a business owned by two or more people who share the profits or losses
pro forma financial statements	financial statements based on estimated income and expenses for a business
sole proprietorship	a business owned by one person
statement of income	a financial statement showing the revenue, expenses, and profit or loss of a business

INTERNET EXPLORATIONS

Future business owners can find information online to assist them in finding a good business idea, writing a business plan, or designing business forms. Do you need ideas for a start-up business or help preparing a business plan? Explore the following web sites.

a. *www.entrepreneur.com*   b. *www.youngbiz.com*

c. *www.entreworld.org*   d. *www.youngentrepreneur.com*

e. *www.sba.gov*   f. *www.businessplans.org*

ACTIVITY 8•1 PREPARING A PRESIMULATION REPORT

Directions: During the "Presimulation: Group Activity," you will give a presimulation report to your class about your business. Use the lines below to take notes as you research your business. Then use the form on the back of this sheet to write the final outline for your presimulation report.

- Turn to *page 243 in this Student Reference Book*. Complete the steps titled *Follow these steps when preparing a presimulation report*.

Name of Business Being Researched _____

Name of Business Manager(s) _____

Type of Industry Associated with this Business _____

History of the Business _____

_____

_____

_____

_____

Products or Services _____

_____

_____

Type of Business Ownership _____

Location of Business _____

Hours the Company is Open for Business _____

Type of Customers Served _____

_____

Company's Policies and Procedures _____

_____

_____

_____

_____

_____

_____

_____

UNIT 8 • REPORTS AND BUSINESS PLANS

Name of Business _____

_____ , Manager(s)

Industry _____

History _____

_____

_____

_____

_____

_____

Products/Services _____

Type of Ownership _____

Location _____

Hours _____

Customers _____

_____

_____

_____

_____

Policies _____

_____

_____

_____

_____

_____

_____

_____

_____

_____

_____

Name	Evaluation

ACTIVITY 8•2 COMPLETING AN AUDIT SUMMARY

Directions: Your Instructor uses audit summaries to determine if you understand the procedures you are to follow in carrying out the duties of a business manager. This audit summary for Activity 8.2 is a review of Units 1 through 7.

- Turn to *page 245 in this Student Reference Book*. Find the steps titled *Follow these steps when you complete the audit summary*. **Complete steps 2 and 3**.

UNIT 1

_____ 1. A form on which a depositor keeps a record of deposits and checks is called a (a) bank statement, (b) cashbook, (c) check register, (d) deposit slip.

_____ 2. The total on a deposit slip should equal the total of the amounts recorded in which column of the cashbook? (a) Cash In, (b) Cash Out, (c) Cash Balance, (d) Payments.

_____ 3. The restrictive endorsement on the back of a check you deposit should include the name of your business and the word(s) (a) "Canceled," (b) "Deposit to the Account of," (c) "For Deposit Only," (d) "Pay to the Order Of."

_____ 4. Assume that Pettisville Bank sent you a bank statement on July 31 listing 15 canceled checks. You wrote 18 checks during July. What probably happened to the other 3 checks? (a) The checks are lost. (b) You are overdrawn. (c) The checks are hand canceled. (d) The checks are outstanding.

UNIT 2

_____ 5. Which of the following statements about e-mail is not correct? (a) E-mail is private. (b) E-mail is a fast, inexpensive way to communicate. (c) E-mail messages should be short and to the point. (d) E-mails contain signature footers.

_____ 6. Which of the following is an example of the best procedure for answering the telephone? (a) "Hello." (b) "How may I direct your call?" (c) "Buckeye Equipment." (d) "Buckeye Equipment. Ashlie Waites speaking. May I help you?"

_____ 7. The salutation on a business letter addressed to Steve Gee should read (a) Dear Steve, (b) Dear Mr. Gee, (c) Dear Mr. Steve Gee, (d) To Whom It May Concern.

_____ 8. A business letter format where all parts of the letter begin at the left margin is called the (a) block letter style, (b) modified block letter style, (c) simplified block letter style, (d) simplified letter style.

UNIT 3

_____ 9. If an employee's regular rate of pay is $8.00, the employee's overtime rate is (a) $4.00, (b) $11.45, (c) $12.00, (d) $16.00.

_____ 10. Health insurance is an example of a/an (a) deduction, (b) exemption, (c) federal tax, (d) Medicare tax.

_____ 11. An employer must pay one-half of the employee's (a) city tax, (b) federal withholding tax, (c) FICA tax, (d) health insurance.

_____ 12. Federal withholding tax is based on the employee's gross pay and (a) number of exemptions, (b) percentage of tax withheld, (c) Social Security number, (d) total deductions.

UNIT 4

_____ 13. Sometimes purchase orders are prepared from (a) bills of lading, (b) item invoices, (c) requisitions, (d) service invoices.

_____ 14. A nonprofit business may be exempt from paying the (a) retail price, (b) sales tax, (c) shipping charges, (d) unit price.

_____ 15. If an advertising agency bills a customer for producing a television commercial, the bill is called a/an (a) item invoice, (b) purchase order, (c) remittance slip, (d) service invoice.

_____ 16. Purchase orders do not include (a) catalog numbers, (b) quantity ordered, (c) sales tax and shipping charges, (d) unit prices.

UNIT 5

_____ 17. The cost of a package mailed outside the local area is determined by the weight of the package and the (a) contents of the package, (b) girth of the package, (c) postage meter number, (d) zone of destination.

_____ 18. A type of mail that is processed much faster than stamped mail is called (a) bulk mail, (b) certified mail, (c) insured mail, (d) metered mail.

_____ 19. On a bill of lading, the business or person receiving a shipment is called the (a) agent, (b) carrier, (c) consignee, (d) shipper.

UNIT 6

_____ 20. A 30-day promissory note signed on July 17 will mature on (a) August 16, (b) August 17, (c) August 18, (d) September 17.

_____ 21. In the early years of a mortgage payoff, most of the payment is applied to the (a) balance, (b) interest, (c) principal, (d) total loan.

_____ 22. If you borrow $1,000 at 10% interest for 1 year, the total interest will be $100; and if you borrow $1,000 at 10% for 2 years, the total interest will be (a) $10, (b) $100, (c) $150, (d) $200.

UNIT 7

_____ 23. A billboard is an example of a/an (a) classified ad, (b) display ad, (c) electronic ad, (d) want ad.

_____ 24. A classified ad is also called a (a) banner, (b) radio spot, (c) television spot, (d) want ad.

_____ 25. Advertising appearing in the Yellow Pages of a telephone book is called (a) banner advertising, (b) classified advertising, (c) direct mail, (d) directory advertising.

ACTIVITY 8·3 WRITING A BUSINESS PLAN

Directions: *Your Instructor will assign you to work with a group of students in your classroom. Members of your group will invest $20,000 each in the ownership of a new pet store in your hometown. Use the chart below (continued on the back of this sheet) to outline how your group will organize the business.*

1. Write the name of your business on the Business Plan Chart below.

2. Write a description of your business. Turn to *page 250 in this Student Reference Book*. Find the steps titled *Follow these steps when you write the description of your business.* **Complete steps 2, 5, 7, and 9.**

3. Write a marketing plan for your business. Turn to *page 254 in this Student Reference Book*. Find the steps titled *Follow these steps when you write the marketing plan.* **Complete steps 5, 7, 8, and 10.**

4. Describe how you will staff your business. Turn to *page 258 in this Student Reference Book*. Find the steps titled *Follow these steps when you write the management plan.* **Complete step 6.**

5. Make a list of start-up costs for your business. Turn to *page 268 in this Student Reference Book*. Find the steps titled *Follow these steps when you prepare a list of start-up costs.* **Complete step 1.**

BUSINESS PLAN CHART

Name of Business _____

Mission Statement _____

_____

_____

_____

Products/Services _____

_____

_____

Organization _____

_____

Location _____

_____

_____

UNIT 8 • REPORTS AND BUSINESS PLANS

BUSINESS PLAN CHART (continued)

Customer Profile _____
_____
_____
_____
_____
_____

Pricing/Sales _____
_____
_____
_____
_____

Competition _____
_____
_____
_____

Advertising _____
_____
_____
_____

Staffing _____
_____
_____

Start-up Costs _____
_____
_____
_____
_____
_____

ACTIVITY 8·4 PREPARING FINANCIAL STATEMENTS

Directions: *In Activity 8.3, you worked with a group of students in your classroom to prepare a business plan chart for a new pet store in your hometown. Your group will now prepare pro forma financial statements for this business. Use the chart below to prepare a pro forma cash flow statement for your pet store's **first month of operation**. Use the charts on the back of this sheet to prepare a pro forma statement of income and a pro forma balance sheet for **Year 2**.*

1. Prepare a pro forma cash flow statement. Turn to *page 269 in this Student Reference Book*.
   Complete step 3.

PRO FORMA CASH FLOW STATEMENT

_____
Name of Business
_____ (first month)

Income	$_____
Operating Expenses	
Advertising	_____
Company van	_____
Insurance	_____
Pets	_____
Pet food	_____
Pet supplies	_____
Rent	_____
Repairs	_____
Telephone	_____
Utilities	_____
Wages and salaries	_____
Total Expenses	$_____
Cash Flow	$_____

2. Prepare a pro forma statement of income. Turn to *page 270 in this Student Reference Book*. **Complete step 4.** Record your answers below.

PRO FORMA STATEMENT OF INCOME

_____
Name of Business
_____ **(Year _____)**

Income	$_____
Operating Expenses	
Advertising	_____
Company van	_____
Insurance	_____
Pets	_____
Pet food	_____
Pet supplies	_____
Rent	_____
Repairs	_____
Telephone	_____
Utilities	_____
Wages and salaries	_____
Total Expenses	$_____
Profit or Loss	$_____

3. Prepare a pro forma balance sheet. Turn to *page 270 in this Student Reference Book*. **Complete step 5.**

PRO FORMA BALANCE SHEET

_____
Name of Business
_____ **(Year _____)**

Current Assets		Current Liabilities	
Cash on hand	$_____	Accounts payable	$_____
Inventory	_____		
Total current assets	$_____	Long-term Liabilities	
		Loans payable	_____
Fixed Assets			
		TOTAL LIABILITIES	$_____
Equipment	$_____		
Furniture & fixtures	_____	**OWNERS' EQUITY**	
Company van	_____	_____, Owners	$_____
Total fixed assets	$_____		
		TOTAL LIABILITIES	
TOTAL ASSETS	$_____	**AND OWNERS' EQUITY**	$_____

HUMAN RESOURCES IN BUSINESS

Managing human resources involves recruiting, screening, and hiring employees. After employees are hired, managing human resources involves training and evaluating employees and resolving employee problems. Finding, hiring, and keeping good employees are responsibilities of all businesses. Large corporations have human resource managers who handle personnel duties. A small company usually depends on the general manager to assume the role of a human resource manager.

When you go to work, you join a team. People working for an organization, whether it is a large corporation or a small proprietorship, are part of a team. Workers are called human resources because they are a necessary part of producing goods and services. During the "Presimulation: Group Activity," you will apply for a position as a manager in the model business community. Once employed, you will want to demonstrate the human relations skills that will make you a successful employee, such as having good attendance, respecting your supervisor, and displaying a positive attitude.

Unit Lessons

Lesson 9•1	**Preparing for Work**
Lesson 9•2	**Evaluating Job Performance**

Unit Activities

Activity 9•1	**Writing a Resume and Letter of Application**
Activity 9•2	**Completing a Job Application**
Activity 9•3	**Completing the W-4**
Activity 9•4	**Evaluating Human Relations Skills**

PREPARING FOR WORK

Have you ever heard the expression, "You don't have a second chance to make a good first impression"? For prospective employees, the first impression is frequently a piece of paper—a job application, a cover letter, or a resume. The impression you make on paper could mean the difference between getting a job or remaining unemployed. The human resource manager who reads 50 resumes a day won't be impressed with yours if it contains misspelled words or grammatical errors. The small business owner who took your job application won't be interested in hiring you if it is sloppy or incomplete.

The first step in preparing for work involves researching a prospective employer. You will make a positive impression if you first familiarize yourself with a company's goals and objectives. Next, you should prepare an effective resume and letter of application. When you arrive for the interview, you will be given a job application to complete. After you have been hired, you will be asked to complete an Employee's Withholding Allowance Certificate (W-4).

◆ PREPARING A RESUME

A **resume** is a personal data sheet that summarizes the applicant's qualifications for a job. It is the "paper you"—an advertisement for yourself. Your ad must be better than another person's ad if you hope to land an interview.

In the resume illustrated on the opposite page, Lee Bradford has applied for a management position at Mean Jeans Manufacturing Co. Notice that the resume includes (a) personal information about the applicant (name, address, telephone number, and e-mail address), (b) an objective stating the applicant's career goal, (c) educational background, (d) extracurricular activities and honors, (e) work experience, and (f) a note about references.

RESUME FOR POSITION OF MANAGER

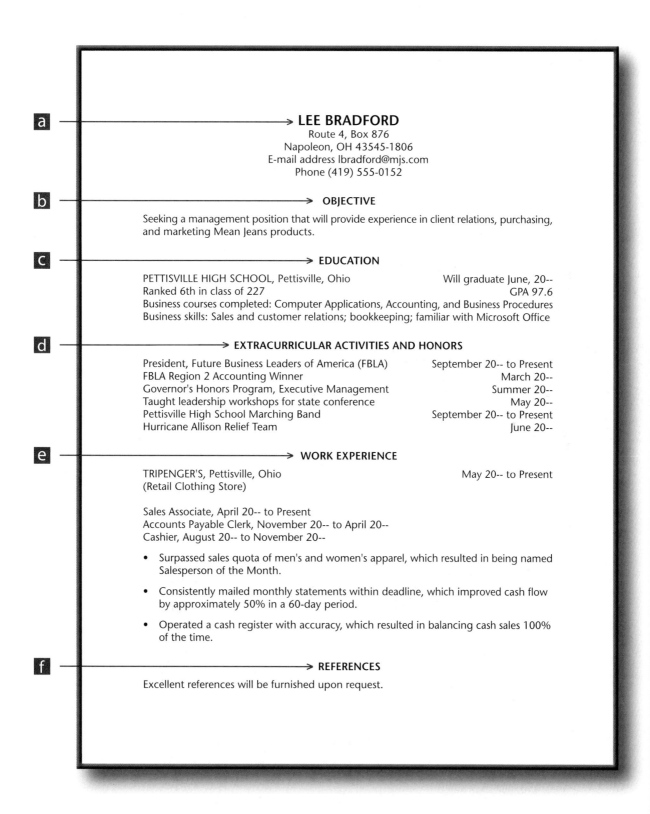

a → **LEE BRADFORD**
Route 4, Box 876
Napoleon, OH 43545-1806
E-mail address lbradford@mjs.com
Phone (419) 555-0152

b → **OBJECTIVE**

Seeking a management position that will provide experience in client relations, purchasing, and marketing Mean Jeans products.

c → **EDUCATION**

PETTISVILLE HIGH SCHOOL, Pettisville, Ohio   Will graduate June, 20--
Ranked 6th in class of 227   GPA 97.6
Business courses completed: Computer Applications, Accounting, and Business Procedures
Business skills: Sales and customer relations; bookkeeping; familiar with Microsoft Office

d → **EXTRACURRICULAR ACTIVITIES AND HONORS**

President, Future Business Leaders of America (FBLA)   September 20-- to Present
FBLA Region 2 Accounting Winner   March 20--
Governor's Honors Program, Executive Management   Summer 20--
Taught leadership workshops for state conference   May 20--
Pettisville High School Marching Band   September 20-- to Present
Hurricane Allison Relief Team   June 20--

e → **WORK EXPERIENCE**

TRIPENGER'S, Pettisville, Ohio   May 20-- to Present
(Retail Clothing Store)

Sales Associate, April 20-- to Present
Accounts Payable Clerk, November 20-- to April 20--
Cashier, August 20-- to November 20--

- Surpassed sales quota of men's and women's apparel, which resulted in being named Salesperson of the Month.

- Consistently mailed monthly statements within deadline, which improved cash flow by approximately 50% in a 60-day period.

- Operated a cash register with accuracy, which resulted in balancing cash sales 100% of the time.

f → **REFERENCES**

Excellent references will be furnished upon request.

The following guidelines will help you prepare your personal resume.

GUIDELINES FOR PREPARING A RESUME

- Make your resume brief, no more than one page.

- Provide enough details for an employer to judge your qualifications.

- Use short phrases that begin with action verbs.

- Do not use the word "I" on your resume.

- List your most recent job first and your most recent school first.

- State the month and year you began each job and the month and year you left each job. If you are still employed with the company, use the words *to Present*.

- Include the names, cities, and states of all present and prior employers.

- Include your job titles and job responsibilities.

- Avoid listing references on the resume. Instead, make them available upon request.

©GETTY IMAGES/PHOTODISC

Follow these steps when you prepare your resume

1. Use the outline on *page 301 in this Student Reference Book*. If you are keying your resume, write a draft of your resume first.

2. Complete the resume. See the illustration on *page 285 in this Student Reference Book*.
   a. Identify yourself at the top of the page. Include your name, address, telephone number, and e-mail address.
   b. Compose an objective that clearly states the position you are seeking and the reason why you want this job.
   c. List the last school you attended, the dates attended, and whether or not you have graduated. Include any other information about your education, such as grade point average, class rank, courses completed, type of degree, or other educational experiences.
   d. List extracurricular activities and honors received in their order of importance. Include community and church activities in addition to your school activities.
   e. *Beginning with your most recent job*, list each employer's name, city, and state. Tell the month and year you began the job and the month and year you left the position. Give a description of each position held, including the responsibilities of the job.
   f. Explain that references will be available upon request.

UNIT 9 • HUMAN RESOURCES IN BUSINESS

3. Read your resume. Ask yourself: Have I included all necessary information? Are there any spelling or grammatical errors? Is my resume neat and attractive? *If you are keying your resume*, print 1 copy now. Save your work.

◆ WRITING A LETTER OF APPLICATION

A letter of application should accompany a resume mailed to a prospective employer. The purpose of the letter is to attract the reader's attention and to introduce the resume. In your final paragraph, you should request an interview. Your letter will make a better impression if you take the initiative to contact the interviewer rather than asking the interviewer to contact you.

©GETTY IMAGES/PHOTODISC

Lee Bradford's letter of application illustrated on *page 288 in this Student Reference Book* includes the following information.

- A return address, telephone number, and e-mail address
- An explanation of the purpose of the letter
- A summary of qualifications for the desired position
- An explanation of the applicant's short- and long-range goals
- A reference to the enclosure (the resume)
- A request for an interview

■ Follow these steps when you prepare your letter of application

1. Use the outline on *page 302 in this Student Reference Book.* If you are keying your letter, write a draft of your letter first.

2. Include your return address above the date.

3. Date the letter June 15, 20––.

4. Use the company name and address for the business in the model community to which you are applying. Refer to the mailing list on *page 4 in this Student Reference Book* for correct mailing addresses. Address the letter as follows.

> Ms. Enid Nagel, Manager
> Human Resources Department
> (name of business in the model community)
> (address of business in the model community)

LETTER OF APPLICATION FOR POSITION OF MANAGER

LEE BRADFORD
Route 4, Box 876
Napoleon, OH 43545-1806
E-mail address lbradford@mjs.com
Phone (419) 555-0152

June 15, 20--

Ms. Enid Nagel, Manager
Human Resources Department
Mean Jeans Manufacturing Co.
45 Maple Street
Pettisville, OH 43553-0175

Dear Ms. Nagel

a → I am an upcoming senior at Pettisville High School with excellent communication skills and a strong interest in your company's management position.

b → During the past two years, I have performed various duties as a sales associate, accounts payable clerk, and cashier in a local retail clothing store. My duties consisted of selling men's and women's apparel, ordering and restocking inventory, and mailing monthly statements. I have decided to explore other opportunities to broaden my business and industry exposure.

c → My objective is to obtain a management position with a corporation such as yours that will provide opportunities for long-range career training and development.

d → Enclosed is my resume that contains my accomplishments in my school and work environments.

e → I will call you next week to set up a time when we can further discuss my qualifications and explore employment possibilities with Mean Jeans Manufacturing Co.

Sincerely

Lee Bradford

Lee Bradford

Enclosure

5. Compose the body of the letter using a minimum of 3 paragraphs. Be sure to include the following information.

   a. Describe the position you are applying for.

   b. Summarize your work and school experience.

   c. State the reason why you want this job.

   d. Mention that you are enclosing a resume.

   e. Request an interview.

6. Read the letter. Ask yourself: Have I included all necessary information? Are there any spelling or grammatical errors? Is the letter neat and attractive? Did I mention the enclosure?

7. Sign the letter. *If you are keying your letter*, print 1 copy now. Save your work.

Sample Interview Questions

1. **Tell me about yourself.**

2. **What do you know about our company?**

3. **Describe your most recent group effort.**

4. **What do you have to offer us?**

5. **Give me an example of a problem you faced at work or school and how you solved it.**

6. **What is your greatest weakness? (Turn a weakness into an asset: "I have poor handwriting, but I have learned to print so that others can read my writing.")**

COMPLETING THE JOB APPLICATION

Completing an employment application is an important step in getting a job. Your application will be judged based on its completeness, accuracy, and neatness. Remember that the interviewer will make important decisions about you based on how well you complete this application. Take your time. If possible, make a photocopy of the form and use the copy as a draft. Be sure you read the entire application before you start.

The job application contains personal information, education, employment history, and a list of references. **References** are adults who know you well and who can verify your job performance. Employers will not call your relatives or your young friends. Interviewers prefer to speak to individuals who can describe your work habits, such as a former supervisor or Instructor.

Follow these steps when you complete your job application

1. Get permission from your references to list them on the job application. Do not assume they will give you a reference.

2. Gather the necessary materials to complete the application. You will need a pen, your social security number, a copy of your resume, and a list of references.

3. Complete the job application on *page 303 in this Student Reference Book*. Refer to the application on the next two pages.

©GETTY IMAGES/PHOTODISC

JOB APPLICATION FOR POSITION OF MANAGER

JOB APPLICATION

Print your name ___Lee Bradford___   Home phone (_419_) _555-0152_

Current address ___Route 4, Box 876___   ___Napoleon___   _OH_ _43545-1806_
                  No.   Street   City   State   ZIP

Approximate time lost from school in past year ___2___ days   Reasons ___Ill___

_____

Are you employed at present? _yes___   If offered a position, how soon could you report for

work? _in two weeks_____

Give your top 3 management choices	Businesses with positions open for managers	
1st choice ___Mean Jeans Mfg. Co.___	18 Wheeler Truck Lines	Nouveau Investment Co.
	Buckeye Equipment	Passports-2-Go
2nd choice ___The Clothes Closet___	The Clothes Closet	Pettisville Bank
	Creative Advertising	Pettisville Post Office
3rd choice ___The Denim Maker___	The Denim Maker	Popular Designs
	Hollywood & Vine Videos	Taylor Office Supplies
	Lee Community Center	The Towne Crier
	Mean Jeans Mfg. Co. (Instructor)	United Communications

Have you had any experience working in this field?   Yes ✔   No ☐

If yes, describe your experience. ___I have a variety of responsibilities working at___
___a retail clothing store.___

Why would you like to be the manager of the business you chose? Be specific. _____
___I like the clothing industry and would like to be exposed to___
___international business.___

Would you prefer to have contact with many people during a workday or to work mainly alone?

Explain. ___I enjoy working with other employees and with customers.___

EDUCATION

Type of School	Name of School City and State	Months/Years From	To	Type of Diploma	GPA
Middle School	Pettisville M.S., Pettisville, OH	9/20--	6/20--		A
High School	Pettisville H.S., Pettisville, OH	9/20--	Present	College Prep	A
College	NA				
Other	NA				

(front)

JOB APPLICATION FOR POSITION OF MANAGER

EMPLOYMENT HISTORY				
Employer Name City and State	Time Employed Month Year	Month Year	Position Held	Supervisor
Tripenger's Pettisville, Ohio	April 20--	Present	Sales Associate	Mary Clark
Tripenger's Pettisville, Ohio	Nov. 20--	April 20--	A.P. Clerk	Mary Clark
Tripenger's Pettisville, Ohio	Aug. 20--	Nov. 20--	Cashier	James Bridges

PERSONAL DATA

Extracurricular activities FBLA, play saxophone in high school band, Hurricane Allison Relief Team   Offices held President of Future Business Leaders

In which subjects have you received your best grades in school? Business and Math

List the last two books you read (excluding textbooks). Rich Dad Poor Dad, The 7 Habits of Highly Effective Teens

Have you ever been terminated from a job? (If yes, please explain.) No

Have you ever been convicted of a crime? (Do not include misdemeanors and traffic tickets.)
No

List the business courses you have completed. Computer Applications, Accounting, Business Procedures

List software programs you are able to use. Word, Excel, FrontPage, and Dragon Naturally Speaking

REFERENCES			
Name	Complete Address	Phone Number	Occupation
Cheryl Tomlinson	2505 Lakewood Drive Pettisville, OH 43553	555-0114 (w) 555-0196 (h)	Sales Supervisor
Bipin Patel	369 Sandtown Road Napoleon, OH 43545	555-0127	Teacher
Parker Green	1909 Pineview Drive Pettisville, OH 43553	555-0125	Bank Officer

I certify that the above information is true and complete to the best of my knowledge. I understand that employment depends upon the accuracy and acceptability of the information.

Lee Bradford
Signature of Applicant

June 16, 20--
Date

(back)

Tips for Your Interview

Feet: Keep your feet flat on the floor.

Torso: Sit up straight.

Hands: Talk with your hands. It gives you power.

Smile: Smiling shows sparkle and enthusiasm.

Eyes: Maintain eye contact at all times.

Speech: Answer questions quickly; justify your answers.

4. Apply for the position of manager. Be sure that the information on the application matches the information on your resume.

   a. Print all information on the application except your signature.

   b. Answer every question. If a question does not apply to you, write *N/A* (not applicable).

   c. List the last school you attended under Education.

   d. List your *last job first* under Employment History.

   e. Give a complete mailing address for your references. If possible, provide both work and home telephone numbers.

   f. Sign and date the application June 16, 20––.

❖ COMPLETING THE EMPLOYEE'S WITHHOLDING ALLOWANCE CERTIFICATE (W-4)

As soon as you are hired, your employer will ask you to complete a W-4. **The Employee's Withholding Allowance Certificate (W-4)** is a form used by employers to determine the amount of income tax to withhold for the Internal Revenue Service. The amount of tax withheld is determined by your gross pay and number of exemptions. **Exemptions** are the number of allowances an employee claims for self plus dependents. A single person with no dependents may claim one exemption or no exemptions. A married person may claim one exemption for self, one exemption for a spouse, and one exemption for each dependent child.

Follow these steps when you complete the Employee's Withholding Allowance Certificate (W-4)

1. Read the letter from Jack Boyer (Activity 9.3, *page 305 in this Student Reference Book*).

2. Complete the notice of employment form on the back of the Activity 9.3 sheet. Complete the lines provided at the top of the page.

3. Complete the W-4 form. See the illustration on the next page.

   a. Print your name and home address on the lines under number 1.

   b. Write your social security number on line 2.

   c. Check the single box on line 3.

   d. Record 0 on line 5 for the number of allowances (exemptions).

   e. Sign your name on the employee signature line.

   f. Record the date as July 2, 20––.

4. Give the completed W-4 to your Instructor.

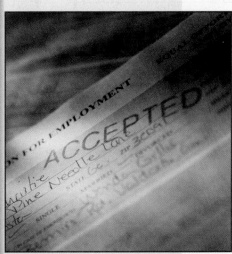
©GETTY IMAGES/PHOTODISC

ACCEPTANCE FORM FOR POSITION OF MANAGER

NOTICE OF EMPLOYMENT

This notice is to inform you that the position you had available has been filled. The most qualified applicant for the position has been notified of the appointment. The following information is for your records:

NAME OF EMPLOYEE ___Bradford,___ ___Lee___
Last   First   Middle Initial

ADDRESS ___Route 4, Box 876___ ___Napoleon,___ ___OH 43545-1806___
Street   City   State   ZIP Code

TELEPHONE NO. ___419-555-0152___ SOCIAL SECURITY NO. ___253-68-0486___

MARITAL STATUS ___Single___ EXEMPTIONS ___zero___

POSITION ASSIGNED ___Manager___

DAILY WORK SCHEDULE ___8:00-12:00___ a.m. ___1:00-5:00___ p.m.

SALARY INFORMATION:

Date Scheduled to Report for Work ___July 2, 20--___

Hourly Rate ___$16.90___ Overtime Rate ___Time and one-half___

Health Insurance ___$49.00 to be deducted from each paycheck___

------------------------------ **Cut here and give Form W-4 to your employer. Keep the top part for your records.** ------------------------------

Form **W-4** Department of the Treasury Internal Revenue Service	**Employee's Withholding Allowance Certificate** OMB No. 1545-0010 ▶ Whether you are entitled to claim a certain number of allowances or exemptions from withholding is subject to review by the IRS. Your employer may be required to send a copy of this form to the IRS. 20--

1 Type or print your first name and middle initial Lee	Last name Bradford	2 Your social security number 253 68 0486
Home address (number and street or rural route) Route 4, Box 876	3 ☒ Single ☐ Married ☐ Married, but withhold at higher Single rate. Note: *If married, but legally separated, or spouse is a nonresident alien, check the Single box.*	
City or town, state, and ZIP code Napoleon, OH 43545-1806	4 If your last name differs from that on your social security card, check here. **You must call 1-800-772-1213 for a new card** . . . ▶ ☐	

5   Total number of allowances you are claiming (from line H above **OR** from the worksheet on page 2) | 5 | *0*

6   Additional amount, if any, you want withheld from each paycheck . . . . | 6 | $

7   I claim exemption from withholding for 20--, and I certify that I meet **BOTH** of the following conditions for exemption:
- Last year I had a right to a refund of **ALL** Federal income tax withheld because I had **NO** tax liability **AND**
- This year I expect a refund of **ALL** Federal income tax withheld because I expect to have **NO** tax liability.

If you meet both conditions, enter "EXEMPT" here . . . . ▶ | 7 |

Under penalties of perjury, I declare that I have examined this certificate and to the best of my knowledge and belief, it is true, correct, and complete.

Employee's signature
(Form is not valid
unless you sign it) ▶   *Lee Bradford*   Date ▶   July 2, 20--

8 Employer's name and address (Employer: Complete 8 and 10 only if sending to the IRS.)	9 Office code (optional)	10 Employer identification number

For **Privacy Act and Paperwork Reduction Act Notice**, see page 2.   Cat. No. 10220Q   Form **W-4** (2005)

CHECKPOINT

Preparing for Work

Answer the following questions.

1. Large corporations have _____ managers who handle personnel duties.

2. Employers are listed on a resume beginning with the most _____.

3. A resume should be no more than _____ page(s).

4. Interviewers prefer to speak to references who can verify the applicant's job _____.

5. A married person with two children may claim up to _____ exemptions.

Doing Business on the 'Net

Finding a Job Online

Monster.com is one of many online job hunting services. Hundreds of thousands of jobs are posted at their web site. You may browse available jobs by company, by city, by state, or by country.

Access Monster First-Timers at **www.monster.com** to

❏ get career advice from experts

❏ search their database of jobs

❏ create up to 5 online resumes

❏ post your resume for employers

❏ get job listings delivered to your e-mail

❏ get help with job relocation

EVALUATING JOB PERFORMANCE

During the model business simulation, your Instructor will evaluate your job performance at regular intervals. Others will also evaluate your performance in an informal way. Your fellow employees and your customers will form opinions about your job performance based on how well you conduct business transactions and your attitude toward your work.

All businesses want to hire and keep the best employees they can find. You will probably not get hired for a job unless you are truly qualified to handle the work. However, it is not job knowledge that will help you keep the job. Your human relations skills—your attitude toward your work—is one of the most important ingredients of job success.

Another important part of your job success is your ethical behavior. **Business ethics** are rules of right and wrong about how employees and employers behave in the workplace. A business cannot be successful and achieve its profit motive if the employees or their supervisors do not behave ethically. That is why many businesses write codes of ethics for their employees to follow. A company's code of ethics may cover such topics as personal use of e-mail and telephone and theft of company property.

◆ JOB PERFORMANCE EVALUATION

At school, you are accustomed to receiving report cards at regular intervals. Did you know that you may also receive report cards at work? They are called job performance evaluations. A **job performance evaluation** is an appraisal conducted by an employer of how well an employee performs his or her job.

A job performance evaluation is designed to help you identify the strengths and weaknesses of your work performance. Such an evaluation will help you develop better work habits and stronger managerial skills. Your Instructor will use the manager's weekly job performance evaluation to appraise your performance as manager of a Pettisville business.

MANAGER'S PERFORMANCE EVALUATION FORM

MANAGER'S WEEKLY JOB PERFORMANCE EVALUATION

MANAGER ___Lee Bradford_____ , MEAN JEANS MANUFACTURING CO.

WORKWEEK ENDING: (July 6)   July 13   July 20   July 27   (CIRCLE ONE)

RATINGS	8 points – outstanding performance	4 points – average performance
	6 points – above average performance	2 points – needs improvement
	0 points – unacceptable performance	

ATTITUDE TOWARD WORK
Shows an enthusiastic interest in work; is highly motivated to learn .... 8 ___8___
Shows interest in work and has desire to learn .... 6 _____
Shows moderate interest in work .... 4 _____
Shows little interest or enthusiasm for work .... 2 _____
Shows no interest in work or desire to learn .... 0 _____
INSTRUCTOR COMMENT:

ATTENDANCE AND PUNCTUALITY
Never absent or late.. 8 _____
Infrequently absent or late .... 6 ___6___
Occasionally absent or late .... 4 _____
Needs to improve attendance and punctuality.. 2 _____
Excessively absent or late .... 0 _____
INSTRUCTOR COMMENT:

ABILITY TO FOLLOW INSTRUCTIONS AND USE REFERENCE MATERIALS
Shows initiative in interpreting and following instructions and using references .... 8 _____
Follows instructions and uses references with no difficulty .... 6 ___6___
Usually follows instructions and uses references with little difficulty.................... 4 _____
Needs repeated detailed instructions .... 2 _____
Refuses to follow instructions or use reference materials .... 0 _____
INSTRUCTOR COMMENT: *You seem to have no difficulty following directions for even difficult and detailed activities.*

HUMAN RELATIONS SKILLS
Extremely tactful and understanding when dealing with people .... 8 ___8___
Usually poised, courteous, and tactful in dealing with people .... 6 _____
Tries to be compatible with people .... 4 _____
Needs to improve human relations skills .... 2 _____
Disruptive and uncooperative when dealing with people .... 0 _____
INSTRUCTOR COMMENT:

QUANTITY AND QUALITY OF WORK
Has an exceptional aptitude for doing neat, accurate work .... 8 _____
Does more than the required amount of neat, accurate work .... 6 _____
Does normal amount of acceptable work .... 4 ___4___
Needs assistance to do acceptable work .... 2 _____
Does little or no acceptable work.. 0 _____
INSTRUCTOR COMMENT: *You may wish to work on writing your numbers more clearly so that others can read them.*

TOTAL POINTS EARNED	32

A completed manager's weekly job performance evaluation is shown on the opposite page. Notice the five different evaluation criteria.

Attitude Toward Work. The activities you perform as manager are all necessary to the successful operation of your business. Your attitude will determine if you enjoy the task and if you will do it to the best of your ability.

Attendance and Punctuality. You must assume the responsibility for being on the job and on time each day. Being absent or late will require you to work faster to avoid detaining others who conduct business with you.

Ability to Follow Instructions and Use Reference Materials. The effective use of time during the simulation will depend upon your ability to follow instructions and use reference materials. Make sure you read directions carefully before you ask your Instructor for help.

Human Relations Skills. The interaction with other managers in the business community makes good human relations skills essential to the smooth operation and pleasant working environment of all businesses.

Quantity and Quality of Work. Your productivity will be measured by the quantity and quality of acceptable work performed. *Quantity* refers to the amount of work you produce, and *quality* refers to the neatness and accuracy of the work. Remember that both factors are important.

Total Points Earned. Look again at the illustration on the opposite page. The performance is rated on a point system. A rating of 8 means the performance is excellent. A rating of 6 means the performance is above average. A rating of 4 means the performance is average. A rating of 2 means the performance needs improvement. And a rating of 0 means the performance is unacceptable. The points earned are totaled at the end of each workweek.

©GETTY IMAGES/PHOTODISC

◆ HUMAN RELATIONS ON THE JOB

Human relations involve how well people get along in their personal contacts. Because employees often must work together as a team, it is very important that they maintain good human relations. Employees also must be able to interact effectively with customers. Think about your own community. How many jobs are available? Most openings are in service industries where workers are in constant contact with other employees and with the public.

Employees who achieve the greatest success on the job have learned to develop pleasing personality traits and work habits that encourage cooperation with others. Your success will depend on your ability to get along well with others. In addition, the work habits you form at school and on the job will determine whether you succeed or fail as a worker.

©GETTY IMAGES/PHOTODISC

Follow these steps when you evaluate human relations skills

1. Complete the human relations checklist on _page 307 in this Student Reference_ Book. Remember, in order to improve, you must first be honest with yourself.

2. Look at the back of the checklist sheet. Read Situation 1 and Situation 2. Answer the questions completely.

3. Choose a team leader when your Instructor assigns you to a group. Be prepared to discuss the human relations in action situations with the other team members and with your class.

WORK HABITS THAT ENCOURAGE COOPERATION

Congeniality	Sincerely enjoying being around other people.
Cooperativeness	Being a team player.
Dependability	Being trustworthy — having good attendance, getting to work on time, not "goofing off," and getting the job done.
Enthusiasm	Accepting work assignments with a pleasant attitude.
Honesty	Making sure you tell the truth at all times. And making sure you are not a thief— of time, of money, or of the company's property.
Initiative	Getting things done without being told what to do.
Loyalty	Speaking in a positive manner about your company.
Objectivity	Acting on facts without letting personal feelings get in the way.
Politeness	Saying "good morning," "please," and "thank you."
Productivity	Producing an acceptable quantity and quality of work.
Tact	Knowing what to say or do in a situation.
Tolerance	Recognizing and making allowances for the differences in people.

CHECKPOINT

Evaluating Job Performance

Answer the following questions.

1. A job performance evaluation is designed to help an employee identify _____ and _____ of his or her work performance.

2. A company's code of _____ may cover such topics as personal use of telephone and e-mail and theft of company property.

3. Recognizing and making allowances for the differences in people is called _____.

4. Dependability and initiative are _____ that encourage cooperation.

5. Productivity involves producing an acceptable _____ and _____ of work.

UNIT SUMMARY

1. Recruiting, hiring, and keeping good employees are responsibilities of all businesses.

2. People working for an organization, whether it is a large corporation or a small proprietorship, are part of a team.

3. For prospective employees, the first impression is frequently a piece of paper—a job application, a cover letter, or a resume.

4. The first step in preparing for work involves researching a prospective employer.

5. A resume should be brief but provide enough details for an employer to judge the applicant's qualifications.

6. All positions held should be listed on the resume beginning with the most recent.

7. The purpose of the letter of application is to attract the reader's attention and to introduce the resume.

8. A letter of application will make a better impression if the job applicant takes the initiative to contact the interviewer rather than asking the interviewer to contact him or her.

9. Employers judge a job application based on its completeness, accuracy, and neatness.

**LESSON 9•1
PREPARING
FOR WORK**

10. An employee's attitude toward work is one of the most important ingredients of job success.

11. A business cannot be successful and achieve its profit motive if the employees or their supervisors do not behave ethically.

12. A job performance evaluation is designed to help an employee identify his or her strengths and weaknesses.

13. Employees who achieve the greatest success have learned to develop pleasing personality traits and work habits that encourage cooperation with others.

**LESSON 9•2
EVALUATING JOB
PERFORMANCE**

Glossary

business ethics	rules of right and wrong about how employees and employers behave in the workplace
Employee's Withholding Allowance Certificate (W-4)	a form used by employers to determine the amount of income tax to withhold for the Internal Revenue Service
exemptions	the number of allowances an employee claims for self plus dependents
human relations	how well people get along in their personal contacts
job performance evaluation	an appraisal conducted by an employer of how well an employee performs his or her job
references	adults who know you well and who can verify your job performance
resume	a personal data sheet that summarizes the applicant's qualifications for a job

INTERNET EXPLORATIONS

Need help writing a resume? Want to practice your interviewing skills? Looking for a job? Try these web sites.

a. *www.all4resumes.com*
b. *www.careercity.com*
c. *www.careerperfect.com*
d. *www.headhunter.net*
e. *www.job.com*
f. *www.job-hunt.org*
g. *www.job-interview.net*
h. *www.job-interview-questions.com*
i. *www.jobs.com*
j. *www.jobweb.com*
k. *www.provenresumes.com*
l. *www.quintcareers.com*

Name	Evaluation

ACTIVITY 9•1 WRITING A RESUME AND LETTER OF APPLICATION

Directions: Use the outline below and on the back of this sheet to prepare a resume and a letter of application.

1. Turn to *page 286 in this Student Reference Book*. Complete the steps titled *Follow these steps when you prepare your resume.*

Devin Kuchynka
7450 Rushwood Lane
330-468-5861
dkuchynka@hotmail.com

OBJECTIVE

Seeking a management position that will provide experience in a post office.

EDUCATION

Nordonia High School, Macedonia Ohio will graduate June, 2010 Ranked 39th in class of 300 GPA 3.7 Business courses: Business Dynamics, Keyboarding & Microsoft Office Business skills: familiar with MS office

EXTRACURRICULAR ACTIVITIES AND HONORS

WORK EXPERIENCE

REFERENCES

Good references will be furnished upon request.

2. Turn to *page 287 in this Student Reference Book*. Complete the steps titled *Follow these steps when you prepare your letter of application.*

Devin Kuchynka
7950 Rushwood Lane
Sagamore Hills, OH 44067
e-mail dkuchynka@meanjeans.com
Phone 330-468-5861

June 15 , 20 07

Mr. Charles Vrabel, Principal
Nordonia High School Staff
Nordonia High School
8006 South Bedford Road
Macedonia, OH 44056

Dear Mr. Vrabel

I am a new sophomore at Nordonia High School with an excellent work ethic and a strong interest in a management position at Pettisville Post Office.

In the last year I have done very well academically at Nordonia High School and I would like to gain experience in the business world.

My goal is to obtain a management position at a business such as Pettisville Post Office, which will help me gain experience which I will use for the rest of my life.

Enclosed is my resume which includes my school achievements.

I will call this week to schedule an interview for this position.
Sincerely
Devin Kuchynka

Enclosure

Name	Evaluation

ACTIVITY 9•3 COMPLETING THE W-4

Directions: When you are hired as a manager in the model business community, you will complete the Employee's Withholding Allowance Certificate on the back of this sheet.

- Turn to *page 292 in this Student Reference Book*. Complete the steps titled *Follow these steps when you complete the Employee's Withholding Allowance Certificate (W-4).*

Mean Jeans Manufacturing Co.
45 Maple Street
Pettisville, OH 43553-0175

June 29, 20--

Mr./Ms.(Name of Student)
Street Address
City, State ZIPCODE

Dear Mr./Ms.(Name of Student):

Congratulations! Your application for employment has been reviewed, and you are indeed qualified for the position of manager. We are pleased that you chose employment within the model business community of Pettisville, Ohio.

Please report for work in your new management position on Monday, July 2, 20--. Your biweekly earnings will be $1,352. We will be closed on Wednesday, July 4, for the national holiday. However, you will be paid for that day.

Other fringe benefits you will enjoy include two weeks of paid vacation annually, an excellent health insurance policy, and a generous profit sharing program.

Please complete the Employee's Withholding Allowance Certificate (W-4) on the back of this sheet and give it to your Instructor.

We are looking forward to working with you soon. If you have any questions in the meantime, please call me.

Sincerely,

Jack Boyer

Jack Boyer, Manager

Enclosure (W-4)

NOTICE OF EMPLOYMENT

This notice is to inform you that the position you had available has been filled. The most qualified applicant for the position has been notified of the appointment. The following information is for your records:

NAME OF EMPLOYEE ___Kuchynka___ ___Devin___ ___L___
Last First Middle Initial

ADDRESS ___Rushwood Lane Sagamore Hills Ohio 44067___
Street City State ZIP Code

TELEPHONE NO. ___330-468-5861___ SOCIAL SECURITY NO. _____

MARITAL STATUS ___Single___ EXEMPTIONS ___zero___

POSITION ASSIGNED ___Manager___

DAILY WORK SCHEDULE ___8:00-12:00___ a.m. ___1:00-5:00___ p.m.

SALARY INFORMATION:

Date Scheduled to Report for Work ___July 2, 20--___

Hourly Rate ___$16.90___ Overtime Rate ___Time and one-half___

Health Insurance ___$49.00 to be deducted from each paycheck___

- - - - - - - - - - - - - - - Cut here and give Form W-4 to your employer. Keep the top part for your records. - - - - - - - - - - - - - - -

Form **W-4** Department of the Treasury Internal Revenue Service	**Employee's Withholding Allowance Certificate** ▶ Whether you are entitled to claim a certain number of allowances or exemptions from withholding is subject to review by the IRS. Your employer may be required to send a copy of this form to the IRS.	OMB No. 1545-0010 20--

1	Type or print your first name and middle initial	Last name		2	Your social security number

Home address (number and street or rural route)	3	☐ Single ☐ Married ☐ Married, but withhold at higher Single rate. **Note:** *If married, but legally separated, or spouse is a nonresident alien, check the Single box.*
City or town, state, and ZIP code	4	If your last name differs from that on your social security card, check here. **You must call 1-800-772-1213 for a new card** . . . ▶ ☐

5	Total number of allowances you are claiming (from line **H** above **OR** from the worksheet on page 2)	5	
6	Additional amount, if any, you want withheld from each paycheck	6	$
7	I claim exemption from withholding for 20--, and I certify that I meet **BOTH** of the following conditions for exemption:		

- Last year I had a right to a refund of **ALL** Federal income tax withheld because I had **NO** tax liability **AND**
- This year I expect a refund of **ALL** Federal income tax withheld because I expect to have **NO** tax liability.

If you meet both conditions, enter "EXEMPT" here . . . . ▶ | 7 |

Under penalties of perjury, I declare that I have examined this certificate and to the best of my knowledge and belief, it is true, correct, and complete.

Employee's signature
(Form is not valid
unless you sign it) ▶ _Devin Kuchynka_ Date ▶

8	Employer's name and address (Employer: Complete 8 and 10 only if sending to the IRS.)	9	Office code (optional)	10	Employer identification number

For Privacy Act and Paperwork Reduction Act Notice, see page 2. Cat. No. 10220Q Form **W-4** (2005)

Name		Evaluation

ACTIVITY 9•4 EVALUATING HUMAN RELATIONS SKILLS

Directions: *During the "Presimulation: Group Activity," you will evaluate your human relations skills. This checklist and the Human Relations in Action case studies on the back of this sheet will help you assess your personality traits and work habits and those of others. After you have completed the Human Relations activity on the back of this sheet, your Instructor will assign you to work with a group to discuss your answers.*

- Turn to page *298 in this Student Reference Book*. Complete the steps titled *Follow these steps when you evaluate human relations skills.*

HUMAN RELATIONS CHECKLIST	Always	Mostly	Sometimes	Rarely	Never
1. I show respect to people in authority, such as parents and supervisors.					
2. I tell the truth.					
3. I do not take things (even small items) that do not belong to me.					
4. I leave my personal problems at home when I am at work or school.					
5. I look at all sides of a problem before I form an opinion.					
6. I enjoy working with other people.					
7. I keep calm and give a soft response to an angry demand.					
8. I get things done without being told.					
9. I have excellent attendance at school or work.					
10. I arrive on time at school or work.					
11. I finish what I start.					
12. I am willing to try new ways of doing things.					
13. I do more than is required of me.					
14. I turn in my work on time.					
15. I respect the differences in others.					
16. I don't get frustrated easily.					
17. I don't blame others when I make a mistake.					
18. I work well under pressure.					
19. I am as careful with the property of others as I am with my own things.					
20. I like myself.					

HUMAN RELATIONS IN ACTION

SITUATION 1 YOU'RE RIGHT, YOU *HAVE* TOLD ME FOR THE LAST TIME!

Darren was hired as the office manager for a wholesale distributor, part of a large franchise operation. Mr. Copeland, the vice-president, constantly criticized the employees and frequently lost his temper. It wasn't long before Mr. Copeland began screaming at Darren every time something went wrong. One morning Mr. Copeland met Darren as he walked through his office door: "I've told you for the last time not to leave the office keys on your desk!" Darren replied, "You're right … you *HAVE* told me for the last time!" He then handed the keys to Mr. Copeland and walked out the door.

Do you think Darren did the right thing? Discuss the consequences of Darren's quitting the way he did.

_____

_____

_____

_____

_____

SITUATION 2 THE IRRITATED CASHIER

Mr. Steinberg decided to eat at the new fast food restaurant in town, the Top Burger Corral. After placing his order with the cashier, he realized he had a 50-cents-off coupon in his wallet. As the cashier was about to tell him the total of the order, Mr. Steinberg presented the coupon to the cashier and said, "I'm sorry, but could I change this order from a regular to a deluxe cheeseburger and a medium cola?" The cashier snatched the coupon out of Mr. Steinberg's hand and exclaimed in a shrill voice, "From now on, *PLEASE* tell me you have a coupon *BEFORE* you place your order!"

What do you think about how the cashier handled the situation? If you were the cashier's supervisor and overheard the interaction, how would you handle it?

_____

_____

_____

_____

_____

UNIT 9 • HUMAN RESOURCES IN BUSINESS

INVESTMENTS

At the turn of a new century, Bill Gates was declared the richest man in the world. You have probably heard of Bill Gates and his famous company, Microsoft. Perhaps you have not heard of the man who was declared the second richest man in the world in the year 2000, Warren Buffett. Buffett's net worth at that time was $36 billion. Interestingly, Warren Buffett did not get rich from selling a product. He amassed his fortune solely through stock market investments.

During the model business simulation, you will have an opportunity to see what it is like to buy into a real American business. Which business should you choose? Consider Warren Buffett's advice: "Never invest in a business you cannot understand." High school students have had a lot of success buying stocks in companies such as GAP, Wendy's, Nike, and Pepsi.

Your Instructor may also ask you to participate in or conduct a stockholders' meeting. If so, you will have an opportunity to see how business meetings are conducted and learn about the important role stockholders play in the decision-making process.

Unit Lessons

Lesson 10•1   **Purchasing Stocks**
Lesson 10•2   **Taking Part in Stockholders' Meetings**

Unit Activities

Activity 10•1   **Purchasing and Tracking Stocks**
Activity 10•2   **Voting by Proxy**

PURCHASING STOCKS

Investments are a way of saving for the future. An **investment** is money put to work to earn more money. You may be saving money now so you can buy a car to drive to school. Your parents may have investments so they can send you to college or retire from their jobs.

The stock market is a popular form of investment because stocks generally enjoy higher rates of return than other types of investments, such as savings accounts. When choosing an investment, remember that your rate of return will depend on the amount of risk you are willing to accept. Since the risk of losing your investment is greater with stocks than with other types of investments, you should carefully consider which business to buy. The following guidelines will help you decide which company is right for you.

©CORBIS

- Buy businesses that you understand.
- Buy businesses that are related to your interests or hobbies.
- Buy businesses that are the best in their industry.
- Buy businesses that have been around for a long time.
- Buy businesses that have repeat sales.
- Buy businesses that are large corporations.

Is the business a newcomer, or has it been around for several decades? Some of the strongest corporations in America have been in business for over a century. Is the product the company makes likely to be purchased again by the consumer? The toy that your little brother wants for his birthday may be popular now, but will it be a year from now? You might only purchase that toy once, but your shoes will have to be replaced over and over again. Consider also the size of the corporation. Large companies are more stable and less likely to fail than smaller firms.

After you have decided which company to purchase, you will find the stock's ticker symbol. A **ticker symbol** is the abbreviation for a business used by a stock exchange, such as NKE for Nike. You will then get a *stock quote* (the price for one share of stock).

Once you have decided on a company, found the ticker symbol, and have a quote, you will order shares from Nouveau Investment Company. The manager of Nouveau will give you a **stock certificate**, a printed form that shows ownership in a corporation. On July 20, you will receive another stock certificate—for the shares of stock you own in Mean Jeans Manufacturing Co., as shown in the illustration above. Always keep your stock certificates in a safe place. They are your proof of ownership.

It is important for an investor to track a stock's performance. Each time you check on your shares of stock, you will list the share price of your company and its increase or decrease on your New York Stock Exchange Guide.

The cash in your personal cash envelope represents savings that you may use to buy shares of stock from Nouveau Investment Company. Since you are purchasing this stock as a private citizen, not as a manager of a business, assume that this transaction is completed during your lunch hour.

Follow these steps when you order shares of stock

1. Choose a stock. If you have any difficulty finding the information you need, ask your Instructor for help.

If you are using a newspaper, find the financial section of a newspaper, such as
   a. The Wall Street Journal
   b. USA Today
   c. a local newspaper
   d. a metropolitan newspaper

If you are using the Internet, choose a web site that will give you a price quote, such as
   a. www.forbes.com
   b. www.morningstar.com
   c. www.nyse.com
   d. www.quicken.com

---

2. Find the stock's ticker symbol.

If you are using a newspaper, look for the company's ticker symbol. If it is not available, use the company name.

If you are using the Internet, use the symbol lookup feature on the web site. For example, Hilfiger keyed in the symbol lookup feature will show the ticker symbol TOM for the Tommy Hilfiger Corporation.

---

3. Get a stock quote for one share of stock (the last or closing price). Record the following information.
   • Name of the corporation whose stock you wish to purchase
   _____

   • Ticker symbol for the business, if available _____
   • Last or closing price (today's price per share) $_____

4. Remove your personal cash envelope from the Cash File. Count the cash. Record the total amount saved.
   TOTAL AMOUNT SAVED $_____

---

computationalresources

HOW TO COMPUTE COMMISSION

Example   Suppose you want to purchase 100 shares of Apple Computer, Inc. (AAPL). Apple stock is trading at $19.88 per share, and your broker's commission is $\frac{1}{2}$ of one percent (0.5% or 0.005) of the total sale. How much commission would you pay on the purchase?

$$\text{Commission} = (\text{Price per Share} \times \text{Number of Shares}) \times \text{Commission Rate}$$

$$x = (19.88 \times 100) \times 0.005$$

$$x = \$9.94$$

Solution   The commission on the stock purchase is $9.94.

5. Determine how many shares you can buy. Divide the total amount saved (recorded in Step 4) by the price per share (recorded in Step 3) to find the *maximum* number of shares that could be purchased with the money saved. Record your answer.

$_____$ (amount saved) ÷ $\$_____$ (price per share) = $_____$ (maximum number of shares)

The manager of Nouveau will add 6% sales tax and $\frac{1}{2}$% commission to the total cost of the shares, so you must buy fewer than the maximum number of shares. You have approximately $2,000 for your stock purchase. Keep at least $100 of your personal cash. (For instructions on how to compute a commission, refer to Computational Resources on the opposite page.)

6. Remove a half sheet of plain paper from your Supplies folder. Print the following information: your name, your *home address*, the name of the company whose stock you wish to purchase, and the ticker symbol for the stock.

7. Take the sheet of paper and go to Nouveau Investment Company. Tell the manager of Nouveau which stock you wish to purchase. Ask him or her to calculate the total cost for the number of shares. If the total cost of the shares is more than the amount you have saved, reduce the number of shares.

8. Decide how many shares you want to order. Record that number on the half sheet of paper. Sign your name at the bottom of the paper. Give the paper to the manager of Nouveau.

©CORBIS

9. Return to your place of business. In a few days, you will receive a confirmation letter from Nouveau Investment Company. It will tell you the date on which you will pay for the stock and receive your stock certificate.

10. Find your New York Stock Exchange Guide.

| *If you are using Instructor-supplied forms*, remove the New York Stock Exchange Guide from the Supplies folder. | *If you are printing your forms*, open the forms document on your computer. Find Unit 10 Investments. Print the New York Stock Exchange Guide. |

11. Record your name as manager, the name of the corporation whose stock you are following, and the stock ticker symbol. Then record today's date on the first line under the date column and the price you paid per share of stock under the Last/Closing Price column.

12. Place the New York Stock Exchange Guide in the Pending File. At two later dates, you will check on your shares of stock and then give the completed form to your Instructor.

Follow these steps when you check on your shares of stock

1. Remove from the Pending File your New York Stock Exchange Guide.

2. Use the financial section of a newspaper or the Internet to find the *closing* price of your stock.

3. On the New York Stock Exchange Guide, record today's date and the closing price per share.

4. Record the amount of the increase or decrease from the last price you received. For example, if Harley-Davidson, Inc. (HDI) sold for 48.50 per share on July 2 and sold for 49 per share on July 9, you would record +.50 (+$.50 per share) as the *increase*. If Harley-Davidson, Inc., sold for 49 on July 9 and 48.75 on July 16, you would record –.25 (–$.25 per share) as the *decrease*.

5. If you have checked on your shares of stock 3 times and the New York Stock Exchange Guide is now complete, take it to your Instructor. If you have *not* completed the New York Stock Exchange Guide, return it to the Pending File.

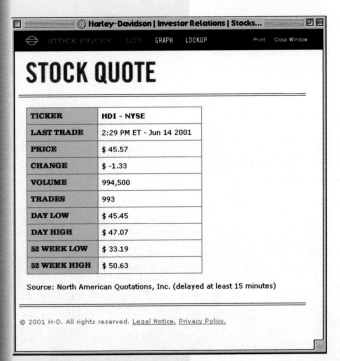

STOCK QUOTE

TICKER	HDI - NYSE
LAST TRADE	2:29 PM ET - Jun 14 2001
PRICE	$ 45.57
CHANGE	$ -1.33
VOLUME	994,500
TRADES	993
DAY LOW	$ 45.45
DAY HIGH	$ 47.07
52 WEEK LOW	$ 33.19
52 WEEK HIGH	$ 50.63

Source: North American Quotations, Inc. (delayed at least 15 minutes)

© 2001 H-D. All rights reserved. Legal Notice. Privacy Policy.

CHECKPOINT

Which stock is right for you?

Give an example of each of the following.

1. _____ A business that I understand.

2. _____ A business related to my interests or hobbies.

3. _____ A business that is the best in its industry.

4. _____ A business that has been around a long time.

5. _____ A business that has repeat sales.

6. _____ A business that is a large corporation.

TAKING PART IN STOCKHOLDERS' MEETINGS

People who own shares of stock in a corporation are called **stockholders** or shareholders. Each manager in the model business community owns shares of stock in Mean Jeans Manufacturing Co. and has a stock certificate showing his or her number of shares. As a stockholder, you are entitled to attend the annual stockholders' meeting.

Stockholders participate in the decisions of the company by voting with their shares of stock. A stockholder who is unable to attend the stockholders' meeting may vote by proxy. A **proxy** is a document giving permission for someone else to vote on behalf of the person signing the proxy. If you do not attend the stockholders' meeting, you should complete your proxy and return it to Mean Jeans by July 20.

This year's meeting has created a lot of interest. Mean Jeans is considering opening a new manufacturing facility in Mexico. The stockholders and employees of Mean Jeans are eager to hear about this bold move and want to know what impact it will have on the local operation of Mean Jeans.

©GETTY IMAGES/PHOTODISC

The board of directors of Mean Jeans has scheduled the annual meeting of stockholders for July 23. The **board of directors** of a corporation is made up of a group of people elected by the stockholders who make important decisions affecting the company.

Board members are elected at the annual stockholders' meeting. During this meeting, the company announces its projections for the coming year, such as its plans to expand the business or purchase new equipment. It also announces the dividend payment. A **dividend** is the division of profits of the business among the stockholders.

Financial statements for a public corporation like Mean Jeans are furnished to stockholders of the company. The balance sheet for Mean Jeans Manufacturing Co. illustrated on *page 316 in this Student Reference Book* shows the assets for the company total $17,827,220 as of June 30, 20––. The balance sheet also shows total liabilities of $11,959,150 and total stockholders' equity of $5,868,070.

UNIT 10 • INVESTMENTS

BALANCE SHEET FOR
MEAN JEANS MANUFACTURING CO.

MEAN JEANS MANUFACTURING CO.
BALANCE SHEET
As of June 30, 20––

ASSETS

CURRENT ASSETS

Cash and investments	$ 1,275,110	
Accounts receivable	5,216,385	
Inventory	6,335,510	
Prepaid items	172,525	
Total current assets		$12,999,530

PROPERTY AND EQUIPMENT

Land	$ 75,000	
Buildings	6,217,825	
Equipment	5,671,220	
	11,964,045	
Less: Accumulated depreciation	8,136,355	
Net book value		3,827,690

INTANGIBLES

Mean Jeans trademark		1,000,000
TOTAL ASSETS		**$17,827,220**

LIABILITIES

CURRENT LIABILITIES

Notes payable	$ 1,950,000	
Accounts payable	4,927,855	
Accrued taxes	525,500	
Total current liabilities		$ 7,403,355

LONG-TERM LIABILITIES

Real estate loan	$ 1,545,670	
Notes payable	3,010,125	
		4,555,795
TOTAL LIABILITIES		**$11,959,150**

STOCKHOLDERS' EQUITY

COMMON STOCK	$ 800,000	
RETAINED EARNINGS	$ 4,068,070	
Total stockholders' equity		5,868,070
TOTAL LIABILITIES AND STOCKHOLDERS' EQUITY		**$17,827,220**

STATEMENT OF INCOME FOR MEAN JEANS MANUFACTURING CO.

MEAN JEANS MANUFACTURING CO.
STATEMENT OF INCOME
For the year ended June 30, 20--

INCOME
Sales		$64,466,275

COST OF SALES
Beginning inventory	$ 6,176,620	
Purchases	15,989,755	
Freight	510,110	
Labor	30,195,265	
Other factory costs	4,236,780	
	57,108,530	
Less: Ending inventory	6,335,510	
Total cost of sales		50,773,020

GROSS PROFIT
		$13,693,255

GENERAL AND ADMINISTRATIVE EXPENSES
Administrative salaries	$ 925,160	
Selling expenses	4,279,435	
Depreciation	1,161,575	
Other administrative expenses	2,192,700	
Total general and administrative expenses		$ 8,558,870

INCOME FROM OPERATIONS
		$ 5,134,385

OTHER DEDUCTIONS
Interest		762,720

NET INCOME BEFORE FEDERAL INCOME TAX
		$ 4,371,665

PROVISION FOR FEDERAL INCOME TAX
		1,597,865

NET INCOME
		$ 2,773,800

©GETTY IMAGES/PHOTODISC

The statement of income for Mean Jeans illustrated on _page 317 in this Student Reference Book_ shows the net income for the company for the year ended June 30, 20-- totals $2,773,800. Be sure to familiarize yourself with these two financial statements before you attend the stockholders' meeting. Also, be prepared to speak out about how expansion of the business into Mexico will affect the company, its employees, and you as a stockholder.

Follow these steps if you will not attend the annual stockholders' meeting

1. Find your Mean Jeans forms. You will need a different stock certificate for each manager in your business.

If you are using Instructor-supplied forms, remove the following forms from your Supplies folder.
- 1 Notice of Annual Meeting of Stockholders
- 1 proxy card for each manager
- 1 Mean Jeans stock certificate for each manager

If you are printing your forms, open the forms document on your computer. Find Unit 10 Investments. Print the following forms.
- 1 Notice of Annual Meeting of Stockholders
- 1 proxy card for each manager
- 1 Mean Jeans Stock Certificate for each manager.

2. Read the Notice of Annual Meeting of Stockholders. Pay special attention to the purposes of the meeting.

3. Record the place and time of the stockholders' meeting on your appointment calendar.

4. Complete the stock certificate. Each manager should print his or her name on the line that begins with the words _This Certifies that_.

5. Find the total number of shares on the stock certificate. How many shares do you own? ___140___ shares

6. Complete the proxy card.
   a. In the top portion of the card, read Proposal 1. Place a ✔ in the box of your choice.
   b. In the top portion of the card, read Proposal 2. Place a ✔ in the box of your choice.
   c. In the middle portion of the card, write today's date.
   d. In the middle portion of the card, print your name and _home address_ on the 3 lines provided.
   e. In the middle portion of the card, write the number of shares that you own beside the words _NUMBER OF SHARES_.
   f. In the middle portion of the card, sign your name on either line beside _(SEAL)_.

7. Use scissors to cut along the dashed lines on the outside edges of the form. Do not cut through the middle of the form. Fold the proxy card along the dashed lines so that the Mean Jeans address shows. Tape the edges.

8. Write your name and *home address* on the 3 return address lines provided. Mail the proxy card. The addressee will pay the postage.

9. Place the notice and your stock certificate in the Office File.

Follow these steps if you are told to attend the annual stockholders' meeting

1. Find your Mean Jeans forms. You will need a different stock certificate for each manager in your business.

If you are using Instructor-supplied forms, remove the following forms from your Supplies folder.
- 1 Notice of Annual Meeting of Stockholders
- 1 Mean Jeans stock certificate for each manager

If you are printing your forms, open the forms document on your computer. Find Unit 10 Investments. Print the following forms.
- 1 Notice of Annual Meeting of Stockholders
- 1 Mean Jeans Stock Certificate for each manager

---

2. Read the Notice of Annual Meeting of Stockholders. Pay special attention to the purposes of the meeting.

3. Record the place and time of the stockholders' meeting on your appointment calendar.

4. Complete the stock certificate. Each manager should print his or her name on the line that begins with the words *This Certifies that*.

5. Find the total number of shares you own listed on the stock certificate. How many shares do you own? _____ shares

6. Place the notice and your stock certificate in the Pending File until the meeting is held.

©GETTY IMAGES/PHOTODISC

CHECKPOINT

Annual Stockholders' Meeting

Answer the following questions.

1. Stockholders may participate in the decisions of the company by attending the annual stockholders' meeting and voting with their _____.

2. A stockholder who is unable to attend the stockholders' meeting may vote by _____.

3. The members of a company's _____ of _____ make important decisions affecting the company.

4. During the annual stockholders' meeting, the company announces its projections for the coming year, such as its plans to _____ the business or purchase new _____.

5. A _____ is the division of profits of the business among the stockholders.

Doing Business on the 'Net

Trading Stocks Online

E*Trade.com is one of many web sites where individuals can purchase stocks online. This company advertises fees as low as $4.95 per trade. Buying stocks through companies like E*Trade and Charles Schwab allows investors to greatly reduce the amount of commissions charged by full-service brokers. Besides purchasing stocks, you can access E*Trade's site to

❑ research companies

❑ get financial advice

❑ use bill-pay services

❑ customize your own portfolio

Browse E*Trade's site at **www.etrade.com**. Access the Help menu and use their index and Glossary to answer the following questions. What is a mutual fund? What is a Roth IRA?

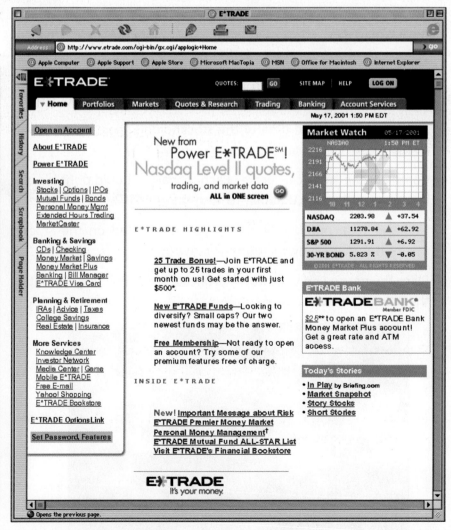

UNIT SUMMARY

1. Investments are a way of saving for the future.

2. The stock market is a popular form of investment because stocks generally enjoy higher rates of return than other types of investments.

3. Since the risk of losing your investment is greater with stocks than with other types of investments, you should carefully consider which business to buy.

4. When buying shares of stock, invest in businesses you understand that are related to your interests or hobbies.

5. Large companies are more stable and less likely to fail than smaller firms.

6. A stock quote is the price for one share of stock.

7. It is important for an investor to track a stock's performance.

8. All stockholders are entitled to attend the annual stockholders' meeting.

9. Stockholders may participate in the decisions of the company by voting with their shares of stock.

10. The election of the board of directors of a corporation is held during the company's annual stockholders' meeting.

11. A stockholder who is unable to attend the stockholders' meeting may vote by proxy.

12. During the annual stockholders' meeting, the company announces its projections for the coming year, such as its plans to expand the business or purchase new equipment.

13. Financial statements for a public corporation are furnished to stockholders of the company.

Glossary

board of directors	a group of people elected by the stockholders of a corporation who make important decisions affecting the company
dividend	the division of profits of a business among the stockholders
investment	money put to work to earn more money
proxy	a document giving permission for someone else to vote on behalf of the person signing the proxy
stock certificate	a printed form that shows ownership in a corporation
stockholder	a person who owns stock in a corporation (same as shareholder)
ticker symbol	the abbreviation for a business used by a stock exchange

INTERNET EXPLORATIONS

Many of America's largest corporations had humble beginnings. Businesses often start with an entrepreneur who has a creative idea on a shoestring budget.

Harland Sanders began his famous Kentucky Fried Chicken at the age of 65 with only $105, his first Social Security check. Grandma Bama started The Bama Companies during the Great Depression. She baked pies at Woolworth's by day, and she and her daughters made hundreds of pies each night that were delivered the next morning.

Many corporations include a history of the company's beginnings on their home pages. Browse the home pages of the businesses listed in Internet Explorations on *page 234 in this Student Reference Book*. The history of Bama follows (**www.bama.com**).

Company	The Bama Companies, Inc.
Product	bakery goods
Founder	Cornelia Alabama Marshall
Year Founded	1937
Headquarters	Tulsa, Oklahoma
Philosophy/Goals	consistent quality at competitive prices
Other Information	Bama also makes pies for McDonald's.

ACTIVITY 10•1 PURCHASING AND TRACKING STOCKS

Directions: *Assume you have $2,000 to spend purchasing shares of stocks. Choose 2 companies and spend $1,000 for shares of stock in each company. Then track each stock's performance for 3 days.*

Day 1

1. Select <u>2 stocks</u>. Turn to *page 312 in this Student Reference Book*. Find the steps titled *Follow these steps when you order shares of stock*. **Complete steps 1 and 2.**

2. **Complete step 3.** Use the line for Day 1 on the chart below for each of the stocks you have chosen.

3. Calculate the number of shares you can purchase for $1,000. <u>Do not round up</u>.

   Example: $1,000 ÷ $48.38 = 20.66 No. shares to order = 20

   Stock #1 $1,000 ÷ $_____ (price per share) = _____ no. of shares

   Stock #2 $1,000 ÷ $_____ (price per share) = _____ no. of shares

4. Record the number of shares to order for each stock on the chart below.

NEW YORK STOCK EXCHANGE GUIDE						
Name of Corporation	Symbol	No. of Shares	Day	Date	Closing	Change + or –
Home Depot	HD	20	1	6/27	48.38	
			2	6/28	48.06	−.32
			3	6/29	48.52	+.46
Name of Corporation	Symbol	No. of Shares	Day	Date	Closing	Change + or –
			1			
			2			
			3			
Name of Corporation	Symbol	No. of Shares	Day	Date	Closing	Change + or –
			1			
			2			
			3			

Day 2

5. On the next day your class meets, check on the share price of your stocks. Turn to *page 314 in this Student Reference Book*. Find the steps titled *Follow these steps when you check on your shares of stock*. **Complete step 2 and step 4.**

Day 3

6. Check on the share price of your stocks. Repeat step 5 above.

ACTIVITY 10•2 VOTING BY PROXY

Directions: *Assume you own 70 shares of stock in United Communications. On* **July 1**, *you received the Notice of Annual Meeting of Stockholders shown on the opposite page. Since you will be out of town on July 10, you decide to vote by proxy. Use the proxy card below to cast your votes.*

- Turn to *page 318 in this Student Reference Book*. Find the steps titled *Follow these steps if you will not attend the annual stockholders' meeting.* **Complete step 2 and step 6.**

PROXY CARD

UNITED COMMUNICATIONS • SOLICITED BY THE BOARD OF DIRECTORS

The undersigned hereby appoints Kenneth Howell and Carmen Rodriguez, and each of them with full power of substitution, to represent and vote the stock of the undersigned at the Annual Meeting of Stockholders of UNITED COMMUNICATIONS to be held on July 10, 20––, and at the adjournment thereof, as follows:

The Board of Directors recommends a vote "FOR" proposals 1 and 2.

1. Election of Directors
   ☐ **FOR** nominees listed below (except as marked to the contrary below)   ☐ **WITHOUT AUTHORITY**
   J. L. Bridges, S. P. Callaway, W. L. Dunaway, B. C. Eichler, S. L. Flythe, W. R. Frech, D. W. Garner, L. R. Hansen, P. A. Little, F. S. Minarovich, K. C. Miller, G. L. Teffeteller, and G. A. Zeigler
   Instruction: To withhold authority to vote for any individual nominee, write that nominee's name here:

   _____

2. Ratification of the appointment of Shapiro and Associates, P.C. as independent public accountants for the Company for the next fiscal year.
   ☐ **FOR**   ☐ **AGAINST**   ☐ **ABSTAIN**

3. In their discretion on such other matters as may properly come before the meeting or any adjournment thereof.

— — — — — — — — FOLD ALONG DASHED LINES WITH ADDRESS SHOWING. TAPE EDGES. MAIL. POSTAGE IS PREPAID. — — — — — — — —

This proxy will be voted as specified by the stockholder, BUT IF NO CHOICE IS SPECIFIED, IT WILL BE VOTED "FOR" PROPOSALS 1 and 2.

The undersigned acknowledges receipt of notice of said Annual Meeting and of the accompanying Proxy Statement dated June 15, 20 ––.

Dated _____ , 20 ––

_____

_____

_____

_____ (SEAL)

_____ (SEAL)

NUMBER OF SHARES _____

Please sign proxy exactly as your name appears hereon.

PLEASE MARK, DATE, SIGN, AND RETURN THIS PROXY PROMPTLY.

— — — — — — — — FOLD ALONG DASHED LINES WITH ADDRESS SHOWING. TAPE EDGES. MAIL. POSTAGE IS PREPAID. — — — — — — — —

NO POSTAGE
NECESSARY IF
MAILED IN THE
MEAN JEANS
BUSINESS
COMMUNITY

BUSINESS REPLY MAIL

FIRST-CLASS MAIL   PERMIT NO 0000   PETTISVILLE OH

POSTAGE WILL BE PAID BY ADDRESSEE

UNITED COMMUNICATIONS
INFORMATION CIRCLE
PETTISVILLE, OH 43553-0176

UNIT 10 • INVESTMENTS

INFORMATION CIRCLE • PETTISVILLE, OH 43553-0176

Notice of Annual Meeting of Stockholders
July 10, 20--

The Annual Meeting of Stockholders of UNITED COMMUNICATIONS will be held in the Fayette Building at the headquarters of the Company at Information Circle, Pettisville, Ohio, on Tuesday, July 10, 20--, at 2:30 p.m. for the following purposes.

1. To elect a Board of thirteen Directors of the Company. Nominees are J. L. Bridges, S. P. Callaway, W. L. Dunaway, B. C. Eichler, S. L. Flythe, W. R. Frech, D. W. Garner, L. R. Hansen, P. A. Little, F. S. Minarovich, K. C. Miller, G. L. Teffeteller, and G. A. Zeigler.

2. To consider and vote upon the ratification of the appointment of Shapiro and Associates, P.C., as independent public accountants for the Company for the next fiscal year.

3. To transact such other business as may properly come before the meeting or any adjournment thereof.

The Board of Directors has fixed the close of business on July 6, 20--, as the record date for the determination of stockholders entitled to notice of and to vote at this meeting of any adjournment thereof. The stock transfer books will not be closed.

The Proxy Card which accompanies this letter provides additional information relating to the above matters. If you cannot attend the stockholders' meeting, please cast your vote by completing the proxy card. Your proxy should be mailed to United Communications no later than Thursday, July 5.

By the order of the Board of Directors.

William Malone

William Malone
Secretary-Treasurer

July 2, 20--

PART 4

Presimulation: Group Activity

Becoming Familiar with the Mean Jeans Business Community Simulation

Becoming Familiar with Part 3 Reference Guide

Applying for Employment as a Business Manager

Obtaining Employment as a Business Manager

Participating in the Managers' Meeting

ALL PHOTOS THIS PAGE COURTESY MARIE WEEKS

PRESIMULATION: GROUP ACTIVITY

Before the Pettisville business community can begin operating, you must complete the Presimulation: Group Activity outlined in this section. This group activity is designed to prepare you for employment as manager of a Pettisville business. Your Instructor will tell you when to begin. Be sure to check off activities on each of the five checklists that begin on the next page.

The Presimulation: Group Activity is divided into five steps.

STEP 1 Becoming Familiar with the Mean Jeans Business Community Simulation

During the Presimulation: Group Activity, you will first become familiar with the parts of this *Student Reference Book*, with the model business community in general, and with the Mean Jeans Manufacturing Co.

STEP 2 Becoming Familiar with PART 3 Reference Guide

PART 3 Reference Guide in this *Student Reference Book* is the "how to" part of this simulation. It includes 10 units that provide step-by-step instructions for completing the *DAILY ACTIVITIES* outlined in the *Operations Manual* for your business. The lessons presented in PART 3 are important because they will prepare you for managing your business. Pay careful attention as your Instructor previews the lessons. You will be completing activities that will help you become familiar with the forms you will use before you begin your work as a business manager.

STEP 3 Applying for Employment as a Business Manager

Before you are hired, you will complete a job application to apply for a management position at one of the 15 businesses. Writing a resume and composing a letter of application are optional activities your Instructor may assign.

STEP 4 Obtaining Employment as a Business Manager

After you have been hired as a manager, you will complete the Employee's Withholding Allowance Certificate (W-4), and your Instructor will explain how you will be evaluated during the simulation. You will want to take this opportunity to become familiar with the *Operations Manual* for your business and find out about your company's business organization and finances. Your Instructor may also assign you a due date for the optional business plan report.

STEP 5 Participating in the Managers' Meeting

The last part of this Presimulation: Group Activity is the Managers' Meeting. You will prepare a presimulation report to provide the other managers with specific information about the operation of your business. Those listening to your report are potential customers. Your customers will want to know how your company interacts with the other businesses within the community.

BECOMING FAMILIAR WITH THE MEAN JEANS BUSINESS COMMUNITY SIMULATION

All page references refer to pages in this Student Reference Book.

■ **BECOME FAMILIAR WITH THE *STUDENT REFERENCE BOOK*.**

☑ Turn to the table of contents beginning on *page iii* . Look closely at the titles of the 5 parts.

■ **BECOME FAMILIAR WITH THE MODEL BUSINESS COMMUNITY.**

☑ Read the letter of welcome from Jerry Sherman, president of Pettisville Chamber of Commerce. (See *page 3*.)

■ **BECOME FAMILIAR WITH THE NAMES OF THE BUSINESSES OPERATING IN THE MODEL BUSINESS COMMUNITY.**

☑ Read the names of the 16 businesses listed in the Pettisville Business Community Directory on *page 4*.

■ **BECOME FAMILIAR WITH THE MODEL BUSINESS COMMUNITY IN GENERAL.**

☑ Read the information about the model business community (See *pages 5-10*). Your Instructor may also give a PowerPoint presentation about the model business community.

■ **BECOME FAMILIAR WITH MEAN JEANS MANUFACTURING CO.**

☑ Read the information about Mean Jeans Manufacturing Co. and the business community simulation. (See *pages 11-15*).

■ **BECOME FAMILIAR WITH PART 2 ORIENTATION TO THE 15 BUSINESSES.**

☑ Turn to PART 2, Orientation to the 15 Businesses, on *pages 16-47*. Read the information about the 15 businesses. Try to decide which business you would like to manage.

■ **BECOME FAMILIAR WITH BUSINESS ORGANIZATIONS AND FINANCIAL STATEMENTS FOR BUSINESSES.**

☑ Turn to PART 4, Business Organizations, beginning on *page 336*. Preview the information given there about business organizations and legal documents.

☑ Turn to PART 4, Financial Statements for Businesses, beginning on *page 345*. Preview the information given there about financial statements.

■ **BECOME FAMILIAR WITH PART 5 PRICE LISTS AND PERSONAL SUPPLIES.**

☑ Turn to PART 5, Price Lists and Personal Supplies, on *pages 350-380* . You will refer to these pages whenever you have questions regarding prices of items you purchase. The money is for your use when you conduct personal business during the simulation.

- -

BECOMING FAMILIAR WITH PART 3 REFERENCE GUIDE

Activities flagged with a ✪ *are essential but may be taught after the simulation begins.*
Activities flagged with a ✪ *MUST BE be completed before beginning the simulation.*

■ **BECOME FAMILIAR WITH WRITING CHECKS.**
- Preview Lesson 1.1: Writing Checks. (See *page 51*.)
- Answer the Checkpoint questions on *pages 53 and 56*.
- ✪ Complete Activity 1.1: Writing Checks. (See page 83.)

■ **BECOME FAMILIAR WITH POSTING TO A CASHBOOK.**
- Preview Lesson 1.2: Posting to a Cashbook. (See *page 57*.)
- Answer the Checkpoint questions on *page 64*.
- ✪ Complete Activity 1.2: Posting to a Cashbook. (See *page 87*.)

■ **BECOME FAMILIAR WITH MAKING BANK DEPOSITS.**
- Preview Lesson 1.3: Making Bank Deposits. (See *page 65*.)
- Answer the Checkpoint questions on *page 70*.
- ✪ Complete Activity 1.3: Writing Checks, Posting to a Cashbook, and Making Bank Deposits. (See *page 89*.)

■ **BECOME FAMILIAR WITH RECONCILING A BANK STATEMENT.**
- Preview Lesson 1.4: Reconciling a Bank Statement. (See *page 71*.)
- Answer the Checkpoint questions on *page 80*.
- ✪ Complete Activity 1.4: Reconciling a Bank Statement. (See *page 91*.)

■ **BECOME FAMILIAR WITH WRITING BUSINESS LETTERS.**
- Preview Lesson 2.1: Writing Business Letters. (See *page 94*.)
- Answer the Checkpoint questions on *pages 95, 98, and 100*.
- ✪ Complete Activity 2.1: Writing Business Letters. (See *page 111*.)

■ **BECOME FAMILIAR WITH USING TELEPHONE AND E-MAIL.**
- Preview Lesson 2.2: Using Telephone and E-mail. (See *page 101*.)
- Answer the Checkpoint questions on *pages 102 and 106*.
- Complete Activity 2.2: Using the Telephone. (See *page 113*.)
- Complete Activity 2.3: Using E-mail. (See *page 115*.)

■ **BECOME FAMILIAR WITH SPEAKING IN PUBLIC.**
You will preview Lesson 2.3 Speaking in Public (on *page 107*) and complete Activity 2.4 Speaking in Public (on *page 117*) when you participate in the Managers' Meeting.

■ **BECOME FAMILIAR WITH PREPARING TIME CARDS.**
- Preview Lesson 3.1: Preparing Time Cards. (See *page 120*.)
- Answer the Checkpoint questions on *page 123*.
- ✪ Complete Activity 3.1: Preparing Time Cards. (See *page 139*.)

PART 4 • PRESIMULATION: GROUP ACTIVITY

BECOME FAMILIAR WITH COMPLETING A PAYROLL REGISTER.

- Preview Lesson 3.2: Completing a Payroll Register. (See *page 124*.)
- Answer the Checkpoint questions on *page 130.*
- ✪ Complete Activity 3.2: Completing a Payroll Register. (See *page 141*.)

BECOME FAMILIAR WITH PAYING FEDERAL WITHHOLDING AND FICA TAXES.

- Preview Lesson 3.3: Paying Federal Withholding and FICA Taxes. (See *page 133*.)
- Answer the Checkpoint questions on *page 136*.
- Complete Activity 3.3: Paying Federal Withholding and FICA Taxes. (See page 143.)

BECOME FAMILIAR WITH PREPARING PURCHASE ORDERS.

- Preview Lesson 4.1: Preparing Purchase Orders. (See *page 146*.)
- Answer the Checkpoint questions on *page 154*.
- ✪ Complete Activity 4.1: Preparing a Purchase Order. (See *page 169*.)
- Complete Activity 4.2: Ordering Office Supplies. (See *page 171*.)

BECOME FAMILIAR WITH USING ITEM INVOICES.

- Preview Lesson 4.2: Using Item Invoices. (See *page 155*.)
- Answer the Checkpoint questions on *page 161*.
- ✪ Complete Activity 4.3: Invoicing and Shipping. (See *page 173*.)

BECOME FAMILIAR WITH USING SERVICE INVOICES.

- Preview Lesson 4.3: Using Service Invoices. (See *page 162*.)
- Answer the Checkpoint questions on *page 166*.
- Complete Activity 4.4: Preparing a Service Invoice. (See *page 175*.)

BECOME FAMILIAR WITH USING POSTAL SERVICES.

- Preview Lesson 5.1: Using Postal Services. (See *page 178*.)
- Answer the Checkpoint questions on *page 184*.
- Complete Activity 5.1: Using Postal Services. (See *page 199*.)

BECOME FAMILIAR WITH USING POSTAGE METERS.

- Preview Lesson 5.2: Using Postage Meters. (See *page 185*.)
- Answer the Checkpoint questions on *page 187*.
- Complete Activity 5.2: Using Postage Meters. (See *page 200*.)

BECOME FAMILIAR WITH USING FREIGHT SERVICES.

- Preview Lesson 5.3: Using Freight Services. (See *page 188*.)
- Answer the Checkpoint questions on *page 196*.
- Complete Activity 5.3: Shipping Via 18 Wheeler Truck Lines. (See *page 201*.)

BECOME FAMILIAR WITH USING PROMISSORY NOTES.

- Preview Lesson 6.1: Using Promissory Notes. (See *page 204*.)
- Answer the Checkpoint questions on *page 211*.
- Complete Activity 6.1: Completing Promissory Notes. (See *page 219*.)
- Complete Activity 6.2: Calculating Interest and Finding Maturity Dates. (See *page 220*.)

■ **BECOME FAMILIAR WITH PAYING MORTGAGE AND INSTALLMENT LOANS.**

- Preview Lesson 6.2: Paying Mortgage and Installment Loans. (See *page 212*.)
- Answer the Checkpoint questions on *page 216*.
- Complete Activity 6.3: Making Mortgage Loan Payments. (See *page 221*.)

■ **BECOME FAMILIAR WITH WRITING CLASSIFIED ADVERTISING.**

- Preview Lesson 7.1: Writing Classified Advertising. (See *page 224*.)
- Answer the Checkpoint questions on *page 226*.
- Complete Activity 7.1: Writing Want Ads. (See *page 235*.)
- Complete Activity 7.2 Calculating the Cost of Want Ads. (See *page 236*.)

■ **BECOME FAMILIAR WITH PREPARING DISPLAY ADVERTISING.**

- Preview Lesson 7.2: Preparing Display Advertising. (See *page 227*.)
- Answer the Checkpoint questions on *page 229*.
- Complete Activity 7.3: Preparing a Display Ad. (See *page 237*.)

■ **BECOME FAMILIAR WITH CREATING ELECTRONIC ADVERTISING.**

- Preview Lesson 7.3: Creating Electronic Advertising. (See *page 230*.)
- Answer the Checkpoint questions on *page 232*.
- Complete Activity 7.4: Creating Electronic Advertising. (See *page 239*.)

■ **BECOME FAMILIAR WITH PREPARING A PRESIMULATION REPORT.**

- You will preview Lesson 8.1 Preparing a Presimulation Report (on *page 242*) and complete Activity 8.1 Preparing a Presimulation Report (on *page 275*) when you participate in the Managers' Meeting.

■ **BECOME FAMILIAR WITH COMPILING AUDIT REPORTS.**

- Preview Lesson 8.2: Compiling Audit Reports. (See *page 245*.)
- Answer the Checkpoint questions on *page 248*.
- Complete Activity 8.2: Completing an Audit Summary. (See *page 277*.)

■ **BECOME FAMILIAR WITH WRITING A BUSINESS PLAN.**

- Preview Lesson 8.3: Writing a Business Plan. (See *page 249*.)
- Answer the Checkpoint questions on *page 267*.
- Complete Activity 8.3: Writing a Business Plan. (See *page 279*.)

■ **BECOME FAMILIAR WITH PREPARING FINANCIAL STATEMENTS.**

- Preview Lesson 8.4: Preparing Financial Statements. (See *page 268*.)
- Answer the Checkpoint questions on *page 272*.
- Complete Activity 8.4: Preparing Financial Statements. (See *page 281*.)

■ **BECOME FAMILIAR WITH PREPARING FOR WORK.**

☐ You will preview Lesson 9.1 Preparing for Work (on *page 284*) and complete Activity 9.1 Writing a Resume and Letter of Application (on *page 301*) and Activity 9.2 Completing a Job Application (on *page 303*) when you apply for a manager's position. You will complete Activity 9.3 Completing the W-4 (on *page 305*) when you obtain employment as a manager.

■ **BECOME FAMILIAR WITH EVALUATING JOB PERFORMANCE.**

☐ You will preview Lesson 9.2 Evaluating Job Performance (on *page 295*) and complete Activity 9.4 Evaluating Human Relations Skills (on *page 307*) when you obtain employment as a manager.

■ **BECOME FAMILIAR WITH PURCHASING STOCKS.**

☐
- Preview Lesson 10.1: Purchasing Stocks. (See *page 310*.)
- Answer the Checkpoint questions on *page 314*.
- Complete Activity 10.1: Purchasing and Tracking Stocks. (See *page 323*.)

■ **BECOME FAMILIAR WITH TAKING PART IN STOCKHOLDERS' MEETINGS.**

☐
- Preview Lesson 10.2: Taking Part in Stockholders' Meetings. (See *page 315*.)
- Answer the Checkpoint questions on *page 320*.
- Complete Activity 10.2: Voting by Proxy. (See *page 324*.)

APPLYING FOR EMPLOYMENT AS A BUSINESS MANAGER

■ **BECOME FAMILIAR WITH PREPARING FOR WORK.**

☐
- Preview Lesson 9.1: Preparing for Work. (See *page 284*.)
- Answer the Checkpoint questions on *page 294*.
- Complete Activity 9.1: Writing a Resume and Letter of Application. (See *page 301*.)
- ✪ Complete Activity 9.2: Completing a Job Application. (See *page 303*.)

OBTAINING EMPLOYMENT AS A BUSINESS MANAGER

■ **OBTAIN EMPLOYMENT AS MANAGER OF A PETTISVILLE BUSINESS.**

☐ Congratulations! Your application for employment has been reviewed, and you have been selected for the position of manager. Your Instructor will announce your appointment as manager of a Pettisville business. More than one manager may be appointed to a business.

■ **COMPLETE THE EMPLOYEE'S WITHHOLDING ALLOWANCE CERTIFICATE (W-4).**

 ☉ Complete Activity 9.3: Completing the W-4. (See *page 305*.)

■ **BECOME FAMILIAR WITH EVALUATING JOB PERFORMANCE.**

- Preview Lesson 9.2: Evaluating Job Performance. (See *page 295*.)
- Answer the Checkpoint questions on *page 298*.
- Complete Activity 9.4: Evaluating Human Relations Skills. (See *page 307*.)

■ **IDENTIFY THE *OPERATIONS MANUAL* FOR YOUR BUSINESS.**

Write your name on the line provided on the cover of the *Operations Manual* for your business.

■ **RECORD THE DUE DATE FOR YOUR BUSINESS PLAN (PROVIDED BY YOUR INSTRUCTOR).**

The business plan is an optional report. If your Instructor assigns the business plan, turn to *page 2* of your *Operations Manual*. Find the notation about your business plan at the bottom of the page. Record the due date.

■ **BECOME FAMILIAR WITH THE DAILY INSTRUCTIONS FOR YOUR COMPANY IN THE OPERATIONS MANUAL.**

Notice that the daily instructions for your company are divided into 6 parts. Locate the following.
- Information You'll Need to Know About (your company)
- Addresses You Will Need
- Financial Statements for (your company)
- Getting Ready to Do Business
- Responsibilities of the Manager(s) of (your business)
- Daily Activities for (your business)

■ **FIND OUT ABOUT YOUR SPECIFIC RESPONSIBILITIES AS MANAGER OF YOUR BUSINESS.**

Read the section titled RESPONSIBILITIES OF THE MANAGER(S) OF (YOUR BUSINESS) in your *Operations Manual*. **The importance of this section cannot be overemphasized.** When a customer comes to you or you receive mail, this is where you will go for help.

■ **IDENTIFY THE TYPE OF CALENDAR YOU WILL USE.**

One way for businesspersons to organize their work schedules is to keep an appointment calendar. You will want to use this tool to record upcoming appointments and to help you remember work that will be completed at a later date.

All activities for this simulation take place during the month of July. A July calendar is provided for your use in both an electronic and a paper version. Your Instructor will tell you which type of calendar to use.

■ FIND OUT HOW YOUR BUSINESS IS ORGANIZED.

- Read the information about how your business is organized beginning on <u>page 336</u>.
- Complete the steps titled *Follow these steps when you are told to find out about your business organization* on <u>page 343</u>.

■ FIND OUT HOW YOUR BUSINESS IS DOING FINANCIALLY.

- Read the information about financial statements beginning on <u>page 345</u>.
- Complete the steps titled *Follow these steps when you are told to find out how your business is doing financially* on <u>page 348</u>.

PARTICIPATING IN THE MANAGERS' MEETING

■ BECOME FAMILIAR WITH PREPARING A PRESIMULATION REPORT.

- Preview Lesson 8.1: Preparing a Presimulation Report. (See <u>page 242</u>.)
- Answer the Checkpoint questions on <u>page 244</u>.
- ✪ Activity 8.1: Preparing a Presimulation Report. (See <u>page 275</u>.)

■ BECOME FAMILIAR WITH SPEAKING IN PUBLIC.

- Preview Lesson 2.3: Speaking in Public. (See <u>page 107</u>.)
- Answer the Checkpoint questions on <u>page 108</u>.
- ✪ Complete Activity 2.4: Speaking in Public. (See <u>page 117</u>.)

■ PARTICIPATE IN THE MANAGERS' MEETING CONDUCTED BY YOUR INSTRUCTOR.

Your Instructor may give a *PowerPoint* presentation to introduce the Mean Jeans Manufacturing Co. It will describe the location, history, policies, and overall operations of the Mean Jeans Manufacturing Co.

Then, you and your fellow classmates will present your reports to introduce the remaining 15 businesses. Listen carefully to the reports. Remember, you will soon be doing business with these companies; and you will need to know how each business operates.

■ LEARN ABOUT ROUTINES YOU MUST FOLLOW EACH DAY.

Listen carefully as your Instructor discusses the routines you will be expected to follow each day the simulation is in operation.

**YOU ARE NOW READY TO BEGIN
THE "GETTING READY TO DO BUSINESS" ACTIVITIES
IN THE *OPERATIONS MANUAL* FOR YOUR PETTISVILLE BUSINESS.**

BUSINESS ORGANIZATIONS

Businesses may be organized in a number of different ways. An individual may own a business as a sole proprietor, a partner, a member of a limited liability company, or a stockholder in a corporation. Some businesses are owned by the government, such as the Pettisville Post Office.

In the Pettisville business community, two businesses are organized not to make a profit. Pettisville Post Office is a federal agency, and Lee Community Center is a nonprofit corporation. Nonprofit corporations include churches, charities, and businesses organized for public or mutual benefit, such as student organizations and political groups.

Some businesses are formed to offer services that cannot be provided by private corporations. Such a business is best operated under the control and supervision of the government. Pettisville's telephone service is provided by United Communications, a public utility that operates as a *controlled monopoly*, a business that operates without competition but is regulated by the government.

©GETTY IMAGES/PHOTODISC

TYPES OF BUSINESS ORGANIZATIONS

Sole Proprietorship. A *sole proprietorship* is a business owned by one person. It is the most common type of business ownership in the United States today. This type of ownership permits the owner to be his or her own boss and take sole responsibility for making decisions that affect the profits and losses of the company.

There are five sole proprietorships in the model business community.

- The Clothes Closet   Kimo Yonekura, Owner
- Passports-2-Go   Sidney Parker, Owner
- Popular Designs   Felicia Hernandez, Owner
- Taylor Office Supplies   Tom Taylor, Franchisor;
  Tom Williams, Franchisee
- The Towne Crier   Samantha Nichols, Owner

Tom Williams has organized his business, Taylor Office Supplies, as a sole proprietorship; but he is also operating as a franchisee. A *franchisee* is a person who receives permission from a parent company to sell its product or service. The *franchisor*, then, is the parent company of a franchise agreement that grants a person or group of people the right to sell its product or service.

Federal Agency. A *federal agency* is an administrative unit of the United States Government. Pettisville Post Office is a service organization that is not intended to make a profit.

Partnership. A *partnership* is a business owned by two or more people operating as co-owners and sharing profits or losses.

There are two partnerships in the model business community.

- Buckeye Equipment   Lawrence Avery and Guy (Buck) Burkholder, Owners
- Nouveau Investment Company   Pierre and Sonja Nouveau (brother and sister), Owners

Corporation. A *corporation* is a business made up of many owners but authorized by law to act as a single person. The owners of a corporation are called *stockholders* (people who own shares of stock in a corporation), but the company is actually managed by its board of directors. A corporation has perpetual life, which means it lives on even after stockholders have sold their investments. With a sole proprietorship or a partnership, the business is dissolved if an owner quits or dies.

Six corporations are operating within the model business community.

- 18 Wheeler Truck Lines
- The Denim Maker
- Lee Community Center
- Mean Jeans Manufacturing Co.
- Pettisville Bank
- United Communications

Of these six corporations, three are operating as public corporations. A *public corporation* is one that sells stock on the open market. The Denim Maker, Mean Jeans Manufacturing Co., and United Communications have publicly traded stocks. The remaining three companies are *private corporations*, which means that their stocks are not publicly traded on the stock market. Frequently, private corporations are family owned businesses.

Limited Liability Company. The newest form of business ownership, the *limited liability company (LLC)*, is managed by its members (owners) or by selected managers. It operates much like a partnership but enjoys the corporate advantages of limited liability. *Limited liability* means that the owners of the business are responsible for losses only up to the amount of their investments. The LLC is fairly easy to start and does not have the complicated government regulations of corporations. Many professional organizations, such as medical and legal offices, are organized as limited liability companies.

There are two limited liability companies operating within the model business community.

- Creative Advertising Agency   Jose Fernandez, Lawrence Marree, and Mary Ellen Newman, Members
- Hollywood & Vine Videos   Steve and Kathy Ripley, Members

❖ ADVANTAGES AND DISADVANTAGES OF BUSINESS OWNERSHIP

Not everyone is suited for business ownership. Often it is difficult to save enough money to start a business, and the responsibilities of business ownership are great. Before investing in a business, you should consider the advantages and disadvantages. The illustration on _page 339 in this Student Reference Book_ shows some of the advantages and disadvantages of each type of business ownership.

©GETTY IMAGES/PHOTODISC

It is easy to start a sole proprietorship, and the owner gets to keep all the profits. Owning a business can be a source of great pride, but being your own boss usually means that you work long hours and have a lot of responsibility. Often it is more difficult to raise capital if you are the only person making the investment. When obtaining a bank loan, it is not uncommon for a sole proprietor to be required to pledge personal assets, such as his or her home, to secure the loan. A sole proprietor also has a risk of personal loss. _Unlimited liability_ means that the owner must pay the debts of the business even if it means losing his or her home, car, or bank account.

It is also relatively easy to start a partnership. There are more sources of money since each partner may invest capital. And the partners bring to the business their own special skills to help manage the company. Because the investments and responsibilities are shared, then the profits must also be shared. The major threat for a partnership is personality conflicts among the partners. Any partner can act for the partnership, and it is difficult to have more than one boss. Like sole proprietorships, the partners also have unlimited liability for the debts of the business.

It is easier to raise money in a corporation because the business can sell its stock. Therefore, it is easy to change ownership—since all you have to do is sell the stock. Another major advantage of a corporation is that the owners have limited liability, which means they are not at risk of losing their personal assets. Corporations are more complicated to organize and usually require the help of attorneys and accountants. Corporations are also difficult to terminate, and the government more closely regulates them.

One of the strongest advantages of the limited liability company is what is known as "pass-through taxation." All earnings are passed through directly to the owners so that the company itself is not taxed. Another advantage is that owners are only liable up to the amount of their investments. And LLCs are generally free to establish any management structure agreed on by the members. Unlike a corporation,

©GETTY IMAGES/PHOTODISC

the LLC does not issue stock certificates. Sometimes businesses choose to retain profits for the growth of the company rather than divide earnings among the owners. However, the owners must pay taxes on earnings even if they choose not to keep the profits for themselves. Although the LLC is fairly easy to start, it does require that an articles of organization be filed with the state where the business is located.

Type of Ownership	Advantages	Disadvantages
Sole Proprietorship	Ease of start-up	Long hours and hard work
	Retention of profits	Limited investment capital
	Pride of ownership	Unlimited liability
Partnership	Ease of start-up	Shared profits
	Shared investment capital	Disagreements among partners
	Shared responsibilities	Unlimited liability
Corporation	More financial resources	Initial cost
	Easy to change ownership	Hard to start; hard to terminate
	Limited liability	Government regulations
Limited Liability Company	Pass-through taxation	No stock certificates issued
	Limited liability	Income is taxed even if not withdrawn
	Flexible management	Requires articles of organization

❖ LEGAL AGREEMENTS OF BUSINESSES

Sole proprietorships are simple to start. The only legal contract required may be a business license, which is a permit to operate a business.

Partnership Agreement. Although the law does not require a partnership to be based on a written agreement, it is best to visit an attorney and draw up a partnership agreement to reduce the possibility of future conflicts between the partners. The partnership agreement should include the name of the business; the duties and responsibilities of each partner; the division of profits, losses, and salaries; and a provision for how the partnership can be dissolved. The partnership agreement for Lopez Associates is illustrated on <u>page 340 in this Student Reference Book</u>.

Articles of Incorporation. The articles of incorporation is a corporate charter granting a business permission to operate as a corporation by the state where the business is incorporated. The articles of incorporation for Mean Jeans Manufacturing Co. is illustrated on <u>page 341 in this Student Reference Book</u>.

LOPEZ ASSOCIATES
PARTNERSHIP AGREEMENT

THIS AGREEMENT, made and entered into on the first day of April, 1985, between Caleb Hutchinson of Pettisville, Ohio, and Alan Crim of Pettisville, Ohio.

WITNESSETH.-- The above-named parties have this date formed a partnership for the purpose of engaging in commercial real estate under the following stipulations, which are a part of this contract:

FIRST.-- The partnership is to continue for a term of ten years from the above date.

SECOND.--The business shall be conducted under the firm name of LOPEZ ASSOCIATES, located at 1212 Oshkosh Boulevard, Pettisville, Ohio 43553-0177.

THIRD.--The investments are as follows: Caleb Hutchinson, Cash, $220,000; Alan Crim, Cash, $140,000.

FOURTH.--The profits or losses arising from the operation of the business are to be shared in proportion to each partner's investment.

FIFTH.--Each partner shall devote full time and attention to the operation of the partnership and shall engage in no other business without the written consent of the other partner.

SIXTH.--Proper accounts shall be kept of all transactions relating to the partnership. On a calendar year basis, the books will be closed and financial documents will be prepared by the CPA firm of Stewart, Stalvey & Co., or another accounting firm agreed upon by both partners.

SEVENTH.--Each partner is to receive a salary of $105,000 annually.

EIGHTH.--The duties of each partner shall be as follows: Caleb Hutchinson shall be responsible for sales, advertising, and customer service. Alan Crim shall be responsible for office management, banking, and bookkeeping. Any remaining duties shall be shared equally.

NINTH.--In case of death, incapacity, or withdrawal of one partner, the business is to be conducted for the rest of the fiscal year by the remaining partner and the profits or losses divided with the withdrawn partner according to the ratio of the time he was a partner during the year to the whole year. In case the partnership is dissolved or at the termination of this agreement, the assets, after the liabilities have been paid, are to be divided equally between the partners.

IN WITNESS HEREOF, the parties have set their hands and seals on the day and year written.

Signed _Caleb Hutchinson_ (Seal)   Date _April 1, 1985_

Signed _Alan Crim_ (Seal)   Date _April 1, 1985_

ARTICLES OF INCORPORATION
of
MEAN JEANS MANUFACTURING CO.
45 Maple Street, Pettisville, OH 43553-0175

WE, the undersigned, for the purpose of forming an Ohio corporation for profit, do hereby certify:

FIRST. – The name of the corporation is _____MEAN JEANS MANUFACTURING CO._____ .

SECOND. – The principal office of the corporation is located in _____Pettisville,_____

_____Fulton County, Ohio_____ .

THIRD. – The purpose of the corporation is _____to manufacture and sell jeans_____

and other denim clothing _____

_____ .

FOURTH. – The amount of the capital stock of the corporation is _____

_____Eight Hundred Thousand_____ dollars

_____($800,000)_____ to consist of _____Sixteen Thousand (16,000)_____ shares of

the par value of _____Fifty_____ dollars _____($50)_____ each.

FIFTH. – The existence and duration of the corporation is perpetual.

SIXTH. – The names and addresses of the directors of the corporation, who are also subscribers to these Articles of Incorporation, and the number of shares of common stock that each agrees to purchase, are as follows:

Brent Rychener, 405 Dame Street, Pettisville, Ohio	1,000 shares
Diane Diener, P.O. Box 18, Pettisville, Ohio	1,000 shares
Jack Boyer, 20 Willow Street, Pettisville, Ohio	500 shares

SEVENTH. – All of the undersigned are of full age, United States citizens, and residents of the state of Ohio.

IN WITNESS WHEREOF, we have made, subscribed and executed these Articles of Incorporation the _____first_____ day of _____July_____ in the year one thousand nine hundred and _____seventy-four_____

Brent Rychener	July 1, 1974
Diane Diener	July 1, 1974
Jack Boyer	July 1, 1974

LIMITED LIABILITY COMPANY
ARTICLES OF ORGANIZATION
of
MOUSE-N-LOUSE EXTERMINATOR SERVICE
7362 Cherokee Street
Wauseon, OH 43567-0005

FIRST. – The name of the limited liability company is _____.

_____ Mouse-N-Louse Exterminator Service _____.

SECOND. – The address of its registered office in the State of Ohio is _____.

109 Martin Luther King Jr. Drive _____.

in the City of _____ Pettisville _____ The name of its registered agent at such address is

Spencer Graybeal _____.

THIRD. – The limited liability company shall exist for the purpose of _____

the extermination of vermin _____.

FOURTH. – The life of the limited liability company shall be _____ perpetual _____.

FIFTH. – The company shall be managed by _____ three _____ member(s). The names and addresses of the members are:

Jeff Harrell, 7362 Cherokee Street, Wauseon, OH 43567-0005 _____

April Harrell, 7362 Cherokee Street, Wauseon, OH 43567-0005 _____

SIXTH. – The members have addressed additional matters in the attached three (3) pages.

SEVENTH. – Certificate of Acceptance of Appointment of Resident Agent:

I, _____ Spencer Graybeal _____ hereby accept appointment as Resident Agent for the above named limited liability company.

_____ *Spencer Graybeal* _____
Signature of Resident Agent

_____ *March 13, 1999* _____
Date

Articles of Organization. States require the members of a limited liability company to file an articles of organization with the secretary of state. The *articles of organization* provides the names and addresses of all the members of the business and grants permission for the business to operate as an LLC. The LLC should also write an operating agreement that describes in detail how the business will be operated. However, the operating agreement does not have to be filed with the secretary of state. The articles of organization for Mouse-n-Louse Exterminator Service is illustrated on *page 342 in this Student Reference Book*.

Follow these steps when you are told to find out about your business organization

For managers of partnerships (Buckeye Equipment and Nouveau Investment Company)

1. Turn to *page 6 in your Operations Manual*. Read the information about the company's partnership agreement.

2. Answer the following questions.
   How are profits divided between the partners?

   _____

   How long has the business been in operation?

   _____

For managers of corporations (18 Wheeler Truck Lines, The Denim Maker, Lee Community Center, Pettisville Bank, and United Communications)

1. Turn to *page 4, FINANCIAL STATEMENTS, in your Operations Manual*. Turn the pages until you find the ARTICLES OF INCORPORATION. Read the information about your corporation.

2. Answer the following questions.
   Who were the first directors or trustees of the corporation?

   _____

   How long has the corporation been in operation?

   _____

For managers of franchises (Taylor Office Supplies)

1. Turn to *page 5 in your Operations Manual*. Read the information on the FACT SHEET.

2. Answer the following questions.
   Who is the owner of the parent company (the franchisor)?

   _____

Who is the owner of the store in Pettisville, Ohio (the franchisee)?

_____

What percentage of gross sales does Tom Williams pay to Taylor Office Supplies (the franchisor) each month?

_____

For managers of sole proprietorships (The Clothes Closet, Passports-2-Go, Popular Designs, and The Towne Crier)

1. Turn to _page 5 in your Operations Manual_. Read the information on the FACT SHEET.

2. Answer the following questions.
   Who is the owner of the business?

   _____

   Describe the type of merchandise sold, services provided, and/or source of income for the business.

   _____

For managers of federal agencies (Pettisville Post Office)

1. Turn to _page 4 in your Operations Manual_. Read the information on the FACT SHEET.

2. Answer the following questions.
   What is the name and location of the office that takes care of the accounting?

   _____

   Approximately how much money was received by the post office last year from the sale of postage stamps, postal cards, envelopes, and services?

   _____

For managers of limited liability companies (Creative Advertising Agency and Hollywood & Vine Videos)

1. Turn to _page 4, FINANCIAL STATEMENTS in your Operations Manual_. Turn the pages until you find the ARTICLES OF ORGANIZATION. Read the information about your LLC.

2. Answer the following questions.
   Who are the members of your limited liability company?

   _____

   How long has the LLC been in operation?

   _____

Financial statements are like benchmarks. They measure the success of a business by answering some important questions: How much is this business worth? Is the business making a profit, or is it losing money? For that reason, they are very helpful to the business owner. But other people also need to examine a business's financial statements, such as the Internal Revenue Service and financial institutions that offer loans to businesses.

The balance sheet and statement of income are described below and on _pages 270-271 in this Student Reference Book_. You will also find a description of another type of financial statement, the cash flow statement, beginning on _page 269 in this Student Reference Book_.

Balance Sheet. The financial condition of the business is reflected on the company's balance sheet, which shows the wealth of the business. A _balance sheet_ is a financial statement that reports the assets, liabilities, and owner's equity of a business on a specific date. _Assets_ are items of value owned by a business, and _liabilities_ are amounts of money owed by a business. _Owner's equity_ is the amount of capital invested in the business by the owner or owners plus any earnings retained by the business. Another name for owner's equity is net worth. The "balance" in a balance sheet comes from the accounting equation shown below.

ASSETS = LIABILITIES + OWNER'S EQUITY

You don't have to own a business to prepare a balance sheet. Families and individuals should prepare their own balance sheets, too. Think about all the things you own—your clothes, car, CD player, etc. Add the value of each of your possessions, then subtract any monies you still owe on them; and you will determine your "owner's equity" or net worth.

You may see several categories of assets and liabilities on a balance sheet. Look at the illustration of the balance sheet for Lopez Associates on _page 346 in this Student Reference Book_. Notice that assets are divided into current assets, short-term investments, and fixed assets. Current assets are things owned that can be easily converted into cash, such as a checking account. Short-term investments also represent assets that could be converted into cash, such as stocks, bonds, and certificates of deposit. Fixed assets are things owned that could be sold but cannot be quickly converted into cash, such as property, furniture, and fixtures. The total assets for Lopez Associates are $22,491,125.

LOPEZ ASSOCIATES
BALANCE SHEET
As of June 30, 20—

ASSETS

Current Assets
Cash $ 122,035
Prepaid insurance   8,365
    Total Current Assets $ 130,400

Short-Term Investments
Certificates of deposit $ 800,000
    Total Short-Term Investments $800,000

Fixed Assets
Rental property $16,943,070
Other real estate   8,326,905
Furniture and fixtures   42,955
Automobiles   52,630
                                                  25,365,560
Less: Accumulated depreciation   3,804,835
    Net book value   21,560,725

TOTAL ASSETS $22,491,125

LIABILITIES

Current Liabilities
Accounts payable $141,915
Accrued taxes   16,930
    Total current liabilities $158,845

Long-Term Liabilities
Notes payable $ 52,185
Real estate loans   13,771,015
    Total long-term liabilities   13,823,200

TOTAL LIABILITIES $13,982,045

PARTNERS' EQUITY

Partners' Equity
Investment — Caleb Hutchinson $5,200,000
Investment — Alan Crim   3,309,080
    Total partners' equity   8,509,080

TOTAL LIABILITIES AND PARTNERS' EQUITY $22,491,125

LOPEZ ASSOCIATES
STATEMENT OF INCOME
For the year ended June 30, 20—

INCOME
Rental income	$1,482,685	
Real estate sales	3,922,465	
		$5,405,150

OPERATING EXPENSES
Partners' salaries	$ 210,000	
Salaries - other	175,000	
Real estate purchases	3,491,000	
Repairs and maintenance	372,620	
Advertising	18,800	
Insurance	30,500	
Office supplies	1,680	
Automobile	9,165	
Utilities	3,650	
Telephone	4,140	
Legal and accounting	4,800	
Depreciation	12,600	
Taxes	6,210	
Insurance	18,105	
Miscellaneous expense	840	
		4,359,110

INCOME FROM OPERATIONS   1,046,040

OTHER DEDUCTIONS
Interest		516,060

NET INCOME $ 529,980

Now look at the liabilities section for Lopez Associates. Current liabilities represent bills that are due within a short time, and long-term liabilities are loans that may be paid off over a period of years. Notice that the total assets ($22,491,125) equal the total of the liabilities ($13,982,045) plus the partners' equity ($8,509,080).

Statement of Income. The financial progress of the business is reflected on the company's statement of income. A *statement of income* shows the income, expenses, and profit or loss for the business. Companies find their income by adding the amount of their sales (called income or revenue) and subtracting their operating expenses. If sales are greater than expenses, then the company has made a profit. Likewise, if expenses are greater than sales, then the company has incurred a loss.

A statement of income may be prepared monthly, quarterly, or annually. Look at the statement of income for Lopez Associates on page 347 in this Student Reference Book, which was prepared at the end of the fiscal year. You will see that by subtracting the total expenses of $4,359,110 and interest of $516,060 from the total income of $5,405,150, Lopez obtained a net profit of $529,980 for the year.

> **Follow these steps when you are told to find out how your business is doing financially**

For managers of federal agencies (Pettisville Post Office)

Because Pettisville Post Office is an agency of the U.S. Government, all accounting records are kept in a data center. Since only cash records are maintained by this post office, no financial information is supplied here.

For managers of nonprofit corporations (Lee Community Center)

1. Turn to page 4 in your Operations Manual. Read the information on the STATEMENT OF CASH RECEIPTS AND DISBURSEMENTS for the year ended June 30.

2. Answer the following questions.
   What was the BEGINNING CASH BALANCE last year?

   _____

   What were the total receipts last year?

   _____

   What were the total disbursements (operating expenses) last year?

   _____

   What was the ENDING CASH BALANCE last year?

   _____

For managers of all other businesses

1. Turn to _page 4 in your Operations Manual_. Read the information on the BALANCE SHEET for the year ended June 30.

2. Answer the following questions.
   What is the value of your company's TOTAL ASSETS?

   _____

   What is the amount of your company's TOTAL LIABILITIES?

   _____

   What is the total of the owners' equity, partners' equity, stockholders' equity, or common stock and retained earnings?

   _____

3. Turn to _page 5 in your Operations Manual_. Read the information on the STATEMENT OF INCOME for the year ended June 30. Answer the following question.
   What was your company's NET INCOME last year?

   _____

©GETTY IMAGES/PHOTODISC

PART 5

Price Lists and Personal Supplies

Price Lists

Personal Money

Mean Jeans
Letterhead Stationery

18 WHEELER TRUCK LINES
Local Cartage Rates

WEIGHT POUNDS	CRATED PALLETIZED	NOT CRATED NOT PALLETIZED
70-100*	$ 14.30	$ 25.05
101-150	19.06	32.16
151-200	23.83	39.09
201-250	28.59	47.48
251-300	33.36	58.11
301-350	38.12	64.33
351-400	42.89	69.89
401-450	47.94	76.86
451-500	53.22	86.40
501-550	57.98	94.20
551-600	62.58	103.84
601-650	66.96	112.81
651-700	72.54	121.28
701-750	77.43	130.49
751-800	83.70	139.66
801-850	89.28	147.82
851-900	93.86	156.19
901-950	98.20	163.91
951-1000	102.40	168.77
1001-2000	190.60	288.46
2001-3000	285.90	385.32
3001-4000	381.20	475.65
4001-5000	476.50	565.90
5001-6000	571.80	666.84
6001-7000	667.10	755.10
7001-8000	762.40	851.43
8001-9000	857.70	943.70
9001-10,000	953.00	1,048.61
10,001-11,000	1,048.30	1,133.55
11,001-12,000	1,143.60	1,238.56
12,001+	**See note below.	**See note below.

* For shipments under 70 pounds, the minimum charge of $14.30 (crated/palletized) or $25.05 (not crated/not palletized) applies.

** For shipments over 12,000 pounds, call 18 Wheeler Truck Lines for current rates.

BUCKEYE EQUIPMENT

Custodial Supplies Price List

CATALOG NO.	QUANTITY	DESCRIPTION	RETAIL PRICE	WEIGHT LB.	OZ.
16-442	1 case	Carpet cleaner, traffic lane pretreatment spray, 4 one-gallon bottles per case	$ 53.35	34	0
18-501	1 case	Cleaner/degreaser, industrial strength, 8 one-gallon bottles per case	$124.80	71	2
24-772	1 only	Dust mop, 72-inch looped-end	$ 29.99	3	8
24-701	1 only	Floor brush, 36-inch length, two threaded handle holes	$ 16.99	4	0
24-688	1 case	Floor cleaner, industrial strength, 8 one-gallon bottles per case	$ 51.60	71	5
22-015	1 case	Glass cleaner, twelve 32-oz. bottles per case	$ 69.75	29	0
13-681	1 case	Hand soap, liquid, 2 one-gallon bottles per case	$ 37.60	17	0
13-522	1 case	Hand towels, bleached white C-fold, 250 towels per pack, 16 packs per case	$ 43.99	43	5
11-147	1 case	Insect spray, water-based, twelve 15-oz. aerosol cans per case	$ 55.40	16	0
24-534	1 only	Mop bucket, 44 quart, downward pressure wringer, 3" non-marking casters	$101.00	24	8
17-233	1 case	Polyliner bags, 20-32 gal., tear resistant, 300 bags per case	$ 69.70	27	8
23-099	1 case	Sponges, large cellulose, polywrapped, assorted sizes, 24 per case	$ 43.50	7	12
23-131	1 case	Steel wool pads, 16 pads per box, 12 boxes per case	$ 45.90	5	0
17-342	1 only	Wastebaskets, black molded plastic, 13-quart	$ 3.99	1	5
17-343	1 carton	Wastebaskets, black molded plastic, 13-quart, 10 per carton ($3.82 each)	$ 38.20	13	0
13-471	1 box	Work gloves, 13" long, superior chemical resistant, 12 pair per box	$ 39.60	5	0

NOTE: ALL MERCHANDISE IS NOT CRATED. All items except 5-gallon containers may be put together into one or more packages and shipped per customer's order. Shipping charges and 6% sales tax will be added to each order unless the customer has a sales tax certificate of exemption.

Equipment Price List and Rental Fees

CATALOG NO.	ITEM	DESCRIPTION	WEEKLY RENTAL FEE 1st Wk	2nd Wk	RETAIL PRICE	SHPG WEIGHT
7-1842	Air Compressor	5-1/2 HP, 60-gal. tank, 35.35 PSI, 19.28 CFM	$ 35.00	$ 25.00	$ 1,054.00	221*
9-2438	Conveyor (small)	36-inch overall width, 3" roller centers	$ 12.00	$ 8.00	$ 368.00	305*
9-2439	Conveyor (large)	30-inch overall width, 4" roller centers	$ 55.00	$ 35.00	$ 1,638.00	1,025*
2-1119	Dock Shelter	30" projection for use with 10' x 10' door	$ 33.00	$ 20.00	$ 980.00	330*
1-3221	Hand Truck, Light	Aluminum, load capacity up to 500 lbs.	$ 4.00	$ 3.00	$ 52.00	22
1-3222	Hand Truck, Medium-Duty	Sturdy frame, beveled noseplate, 450 lb. capacity	$ 6.00	$ 4.00	$ 93.00	35
1-3223	Hand Truck, Heavy-Duty	Quality steel frame, 700 lb. capacity, 60" height	$ 8.00	$ 6.00	$ 180.00	56
3-1268	Ladder, Rolling	Fold-n-store, 106" overall height	$ 16.00	$ 10.00	$ 499.00	101*
1-3229	Pallet Truck	21" x 36" fork width length, 5,500 lb. capacity	$ 16.00	$ 10.00	$ 468.00	170*
1-3236	Platform Truck	Stands 10" above floor, 36" x 72"	$ 10.00	$ 7.00	$ 291.00	130*
3-1261	Scaffolding	Base tower only, 8' x 8'	$ 8.00	$ 6.00	$ 184.00	65*
6-1414	Tractor, Garden	20 HP with 54" mower deck	$250.00	$150.00	$ 7,549.00	997*
6-1418	Tractor, Lawn	16 HP with hydrostatic transmission	$110.00	$ 67.00	$ 3,299.00	687*
6-1425	Tractor with Front Loader	45 HP diesel engine with 1,275 lb. loader	$800.00	$485.00	$24,265.00	5,075*
4-1781	Water Cooler	Two-faucet design with 5-gallon bottle, 5 oz. cups or cones	$ 10.00	7.00	$ 279.00	57*

*CRATED MERCHANDISE

NOTE: NOT CRATED items may be put together into one or more packages and shipped per customer's order. Shipping charges and 6% sales tax will be added to each order unless the customer has a sales tax certificate of exemption. RENTAL FEES include sales tax and shipping charges.

PRICE LIST
Denim Fashions

Catalog Number	Item	Supplier	Retail Price	Weight LB.	OZ.
AZ-843	Denim Jeans Boys' sizes	Garment Gallery	$29.95		12
AZ-845	Junior Jeans Girls' sizes	Garment Gallery	$29.95		12
AZ-847	Denim Jeans Men's sizes	Garment Gallery	$49.95	1	12
CA-584	Bib Overalls Boys' & Girls'	Garment Gallery	$44.95	1	9
CA-586	Bib Overalls Men's sizes	Garment Gallery	$60.95	2	1
FX-492	Denim Jackets Boys' & Girls'	Garment Gallery	$54.95	3	
FX-493	Denim Jackets Misses' sizes	Garment Gallery	$64.95	3	8
FX-494	Denim Jackets Men's sizes	Garment Gallery	$74.95	4	4
HD-100	Belts Sizes 22-48	Garment Gallery	$22.95		8
HD-200	Shop Aprons	Garment Gallery	$20.95	1	
HD-300	Bandanna Scarves	Mean Jeans	$ 7.50		3
JT-105	Baby Tees	Mean Jeans	$21.95		12
KL-265	Men's 5-Pocket Jeans	Mean Jeans	$59.95	1	14
LQ-100	Denim Jumper Girls' sizes	Mean Jeans	$35.95		13
LQ-200	Denim Jumper Juniors' & Misses'	Mean Jeans	$42.95	1	8
MN-400	Denim Shirts Boys' & Girls'	Mean Jeans	$24.95		7
MN-402	Denim Shirts Juniors' sizes	Mean Jeans	$31.95		14
MN-403	Denim Shirts Misses' & Men's	Mean Jeans	$40.95	1	9
PR-100	Designer Jeans	Mean Jeans	$89.95	1	9
PR-200	Designer Skirts Trouser Style	Mean Jeans	$71.95	1	15
SA-500	Jeans Jacket Boys' and girls'	Mean Jeans	$59.95	3	
SA-502	Jeans Jacket Juniors' sizes	Mean Jeans	$69.95	3	4
SA-508	Jeans Jacket Misses' sizes	Mean Jeans	$79.95	3	6
SA-510	Jeans Jacket Men's sizes	Mean Jeans	$88.95	4	4

NOTE:

All merchandise is **NOT CRATED**. Shipping charges and 6% sales tax will be added to each order unless the customer has a sales tax certificate of exemption.

ADVERTISING RATES CHART

NOTE: Fees for special services (such as art, layout, copy, camera work, and talent) are given in your Daily Activities. Fifteen percent (.15) commission and 6 percent (.06) sales tax should be added to service invoices.

The Towne Crier (Circulation: 12,000 weekly newspapers)

Display advertising rates:

Per column inch subject to usage discount** .... $ 5.00

Black + 1 color: (This flat color charge should be added to the price of column inches.) $100.00

4-color (This flat color charge should be added to the price of column inches.) $300.00

NOTE: There are 126 column inches per page and 252 column inches per double page of a 6-column newspaper.

Family Trends (Magazine subscribers: 370,000 nationally)

333 West Wind Avenue, Liberty Center, OH 43532-0666

Page ad:	Black and White	1-year contract, ad published monthly	per month $3,190
	Black and 1 color		per month $4,030
	4-color		per month $4,965

WADD-FM RADIO

30-second radio commercial .... $35 to $100*

1-minute radio commercial .... $63 to $180*

WAJO-TV

30-second television commercial .... $100 to $2,500*

1-minute television commercial .... $200 to $5,000*

Outdoor Advertising

Billboard (copy area 14' x 48') base monthly rate for 1 year .... $890 per month

1-week display is charged at 50% of monthly rate above $445

2-week display is charged at 70% of the monthly rate above $623

3-week display is charged at 90% of the monthly rate above $801

Electronic Scoreboard Advertising at Wildcat Stadium

30-second ad flashed on screen 1 time during 1 game .... $ 20

30-second ad flashed on screen 1 time per game for whole season $360

Printing Rates

Advertising Brochures (4-color)

Number of copies	500	1,000	—	—	—	—
8½" x 11" with 6-page folds	$650	$700	—	—	—	—

Single Sheets (fliers and poster paper signs)

Number of copies	500	1,000	2,000	3,000	5,000	10,000
8½" x 11" 20 lb. stock	$49	$56	$ 78	$100	$144	$254
14" x 18" poster paper 16 lb.***	$75	$93	$130	$167	$240	$420

* Rate is lowest from 7 a.m. to 12 noon on Sunday. Rate is highest from 8 p.m. to 11 p.m. Monday through Saturday.
** Usage discount: A full-page ad is $4.00 per column inch.
*** The printing rates do not cover the cost of $.22 per sheet of poster paper.

752 Gold Mine Lane • Pettisville, OH 43553-0176

PRICE LIST

CATALOG NUMBER	DESCRIPTION	WHOLESALE PRICE	SHIPPING WEIGHT
A640Q	army stretch denim, 12 oz.	$300.00	192 lbs.
B779U	blue and white hickory stripe, 10 oz.	$360.00	300 lbs.
A872T	blue brushed denim, 10 oz.	$340.00	300 lbs.
B644J	brown duck denim, 8 oz.	$360.00	320 lbs.
Q993X	check patterned denim, 6 oz.	$380.00	320 lbs.
F129S	classic red denim, 10 oz.	$375.00	300 lbs.
T495F	cotton indigo dobby stripe, 6 oz.	$289.00	220 lbs.
H849P	indigo cords, 14 oz.	$340.00	225 lbs.
H852P	indigo dyed denim, 10 oz.	$300.00	375 lbs.
R123B	lycra stretch, 12 oz.	$358.00	195 lbs.
Q991Z	plaid patterned denim, 6 oz.	$380.00	320 lbs.
U318V	ring-spun blue denim, 8 oz.	$350.00	306 lbs.
U320V	ring-spun cotton yarn, 6 oz.	$325.00	320 lbs.
W617D	silky chinos, 10 oz.	$400.00	198 lbs.
C844F	stone-washed denim, 14 oz.	$390.00	330 lbs.
Q992C	stretch stripe denim, 8 oz.	$390.00	320 lbs.
C849F	woodland camouflage denim, 14 oz.	$385.00	319 lbs.

NOTE: All merchandise is CRATED. All sales are WHOLESALE and not subject to sales tax. Shipping charges will be added to each order.

HOLLYWOOD & VINE VIDEOS

2501 Kneepatch Avenue • Pettisville, OH 43553-0175

PRICE LIST

NEW RELEASES – $4.00

Cat. No.	Title
22-400	A Difference of Taste
22-401	Flight of Night
22-402	Kiss the Baby
22-403	Magnificent Maggie
22-404	Subway in Paris

CLASSICS – $2.50

Cat. No.	Title
24-500	Casablanca
24-501	Doctor Zhivago
24-502	Gone with the Wind
24-503	Gunfight at the OK Corral
24-504	Little Women
24-505	Moby Dick

DRAMA – $2.50

Cat. No.	Title
28-700	12 Angry Men
28-701	The Caine Mutiny
28-702	Death of a Salesman
28-703	Fatal Vision
28-704	Rocky
28-705	Three Came Home

CHILDREN'S – $2.50

Cat. No.	Title
30-200	101 Dalmatians
30-201	Bambi
30-202	It's Magic, Charlie Brown
30-203	Peter Pan
30-204	Winnie the Pooh and Tigger Too

TRAINING – $10.00

Cat. No.	Title
40-600	Cardiopulmonary Resuscitation
40-601	Computer-Aided Manufacturing
40-602	Efficient Consumer Response
40-603	Ethics on the Job
40-604	Hazardous Waste Disposal
40-605	Interactive Marketing
40-606	International Business
40-607	Job Safety
40-608	Total Quality Management
40-609	Workplace Etiquette

HORROR – $2.50

Cat. No.	Title
50-300	Count Dracula
50-301	Dr. Jekyll and Mr. Hyde
50-302	Frankenstein
50-303	Friday the 13th
50-304	Psycho
50-305	Terror in the Haunted House

COMEDY – $2.50

Cat. No.	Title
53-400	Any Which Way You Can
53-401	Beetlejuice
53-402	Liar Liar
53-403	Pete 'N' Tillie
53-404	Return of the Killer Tomatoes
53-405	Runaway Bride
53-406	Smokey and the Bandit

NOTE: All videos except new releases are available for purchase at 10 times the rental rate. Videos are shipped via priority or express mail. The shipping weight on all videos is 1.5 pounds. Video rentals not returned within 3 days will incur an additional rental fee.

MEAN JEANS MANUFACTURING CO.
Price List

CATALOG NUMBER	DESCRIPTION	SHIPPING WEIGHT LB.	OZ.	UNIT WHOLESALE PRICE	SUGGESTED RETAIL PRICE
62-8274	Denim Designer Jeans by Hernandez Hernandez stretch jeans (all sizes) Hernandez designer items sold only to retailers	1	9	49.00	89.95

62-8296
62-8297
62-8298
	Denim Designer Skirts by Hernandez
	    A-line skirt, sizes S, M, L
	    Trouser-style denim skirt, sizes S, M, L
	    Wraparound skirt, sizes S, M, L
	Hernandez designer items sold only to retailers
			13
			14
			15
				37.00
				40.00
				35.00
					65.95
					71.95
					62.95

17-6244
17-6245
17-6246
	Western-Style Stretch Mean Jeans
	    Boys' sizes
	    Girls', Juniors', and Misses' sizes
	    Men's sizes
		
		1
		1
			12
			8
			12
				15.00
				20.00
				25.00
					26.95
					35.95
					44.95

27-6289
27-6290
	Bib Overalls
	    Boys' and Girls' sizes
	    Men's sizes
		1
		2
			9
			1
				23.00
				35.00
					41.95
					61.95

91-205
91-206
91-207
91-208
	Western-Style Mean Jeans Jacket
	    Boys' and Girls' sizes
	    Juniors' sizes
	    Misses' sizes
	    Men's sizes
		3
		3
		3
		4
			
			4
			6
			4
				37.00
				40.00
				45.00
				50.00
					59.95
					69.95
					79.95
					88.95

45-774
45-775
	Brushed Denim Jumper
	    Girls' sizes
	    Juniors' and Misses' sizes
		
		1
			13
			8
				21.00
				24.00
					35.95
					42.95

66-731
66-732
	Cowboy Denims with Stretch Bootlegs
	    Misses' sizes
	    Men's sizes
		1
		1
			9
			13
				29.00
				33.00
					51.95
					59.95

54-467	Western Leather Belt, waist sizes 20-50		8	18.00	31.95

23-456
23-457
23-458
	Relaxed Fit, 5-Pocket Jeans w/ Cargo Pockets
	    Boys' sizes
	    Juniors', Girls', and Misses' sizes
	    Men's sizes
		
		1
		1
			14
			10
			14
				20.00
				31.00
				34.00
					35.95
					52.95
					59.95

87-652
87-653
87-654
	Western-style Shirt
	    Boys' and Girls' sizes
	    Juniors' sizes
	    Misses' and Men's sizes
		
		1
			7
			14
			9
				13.00
				18.00
				23.00
					24.95
					31.95
					40.95

10-409	Bandanna Scarf—red, navy, green, and yellow		3	4.50	7.50
83-161	Baby Tees—blue, pink, and white (M, L, XL)		12	12.00	21.95

NOTE: ALL MERCHANDISE IS NOT CRATED. All items may be put together into one or more packages and shipped per customer's order. Shipping charges and 6% sales tax will be added to each order unless the customer has a sales tax certificate of exemption. WHOLESALE SALES are not subject to sales tax.

TRAVEL RATES AND FARES CHART

Car Rental Rates*

	COMPACT	MID-SIZE	FULL-SIZE
1-day rental	$ 60	$ 70	$ 80
1-week rental	$170	$185	$200
10-day rental	$200	$215	$230

*NOTE: Rates include unlimited mileage; insurance extra; sales tax not included.

Airline Reservations*

	COACH	FIRST-CLASS
Toledo to Atlanta	$309	$1,200
Toledo to Dallas	$328	$1,450
Toledo to New York City	$205	$1,050
Toledo to Paris	$692	$5,061

*NOTE: Fares are round trip, per-person; all taxes included.

Hotel Accommodations*

	SINGLE-ROOM	DOUBLE-ROOM
Atlanta, Galleria-Fulton	$119	$129
Cincinnati, Ashley Oaks Hotel	$ 85	$ 85
Dallas, Colonial Inn	$ 95	$ 99
New York City, Grand Marquis	$219	$229
Paris, Chateau-Bastille	$259	$265

*NOTE: Room rates are per-night, non-smoking; sales tax not included.

Group Travel Packages*

7-day, 6-night Alaskan Tour .... $2,295 per person
Accommodations at the Yukon Wilderness Lodge; includes buffet breakfast.

8-day, 7-night Hawaiian Paradise Tour .... $1,715 per person
Accommodations at the Lahaina Villas on Maui Island; includes continental breakfast.

6-day, 5-night Caribbean Cruise .... $ 829 per person
Single or double occupancy cabin on the Catalina cruise ship; includes all meals and entertainment.

*NOTE: All taxes included.

Passports-2-Go • 728 Blazer Avenue • Pettisville, OH 43553-0177
PHONE 419-555-0164 • FAX 419-555-0168
e-mail: s_parker@mjsemail.com

UNITED STATES POSTAL SERVICE
Chart of Postage, Fees, and Services*

FIRST-CLASS

LETTER RATES:
1st ounce	42¢
Each additional ounce up to 13 ounces	29¢

FOR PIECES OVER 13 OUNCES SEE FIRST-CLASS
ZONE RATED (PRIORITY) MAIL RATES

CARD RATES:
Single postal cards	23¢ each
Large postal cards	37¢ each

PERIODICALS APPLICATION FEES

Original Entry	$375.00
Additional Entry	$60.00
Reentry	$40.00
Registration for News Agents	$40.00

PERIODICALS (REGULAR)

Pound Rates (per pound or fraction)

Zone	Rate
Local	0.223
1 & 2	0.248
3	0.267
4	0.315
5	0.389
6	0.466
7	0.559
8	0.638

BULK RATE
CONSULT POSTMASTER

NOTE

*All rates and fees charged are fictitious and apply solely to the MEAN JEANS MANUFACTURING Co.—A Business Community Simulation.

SPECIAL SERVICES—
DOMESTIC MAIL ONLY
INSURANCE

For Coverage Against Loss or Damage
Fees (in addition to postage)

Liability		Fee
$0.01 to	$50	$1.30
50.01 to	100	2.20
100.01 to	200	3.20
200.01 to	300	4.20
300.01 to	400	5.20
400.01 to	500	6.20
500.01 to	600	7.20
600.01 to 5,000 ....$8.20 plus $1.00 for each $100 or		
(Maximum liability is $5,000.00)	fraction over $600 in declared value	

ADDITIONAL SERVICES

CERTIFIED MAIL	$2.30
(in addition to postage)	

CERTIFICATE OF MAILING	$0.90
(For Bulk mailings, see Postmaster)	

ADDITIONAL SERVICES FOR INSURED, CERTIFIED
AND REGISTERED MAIL

Restricted Delivery*	$3.50

Return Receipts*

Requested at time of mailing:

Showing to whom, when, and address where delivered	$1.75
Requested after mailing:	
Showing to whom and when delivered	$3.25

*Not available for mail insured for $20 or less.

COD

Consult Postmaster for fee and conditions of mailing.

UNITED STATES POSTAL SERVICE ZONE CHART

Origin 3-Digit: 435 • PETTISVILLE, OH

Use the first 3-digits of your destination ZIP code to determine the zone.

Destination ZIP Code	Zone	Destination ZIP Code	Zone	Destination ZIP Code	Zone	Destination ZIP Code	Zone
005	4	354	5	514	4	726..731	5
006..009	8	355..359	4	515..516	5	733	6
010..013	4	360..361	5	520..528	4	734..741	5
014..034	5	362	4	530..532	3	743..767	5
035..037	4	363..369	5	534..535	3	768..772	6
038..049	5	370..386	4	537..539	3	773..777	5
050..054	4	387	5	540	4	778..816	6
055	5	388	4	541..543	3	820..831	6
056..139	4	389..398	5	544..548	4	832..838	7
140..143	3	399	4	549	3	840..847	7
144..146	4	400..406	3	550..551	4	850	7
147	3	407..409	4	553..561	4	852..853	7
148..149	4	410..418	3	562	5	855..857	7
150..168	3	420..424	4	563..564	4	859..860	7
169..212	4	425..427	3	565..567	5	863..864	7
214	4	430..433	2	570..577	5	865	6
215	3	434..436	1*	580..587	5	870..875	6
216..249	4	437..438	2	588	6	877..879	6
250..253	3	439	3	590..595	6	880	7
254	4	440..449	2	596..599	7	881..885	6
255..268	3	450..452	3	600..611	3	889..891	7
270..293	4	453..455	2	612	4	893	7
294	5	456..457	3	613	3	894..895	8
295..298	4	458	2	614..616	4	897	8
299	5	459..464	3	617..619	3	898	7
300..303	4	465..468	2*	620	4	900..908	8
304	5	469	2	622..623	4	910..928	8
305..309	4	470..472	3	624	3	930..977	8
310	5	473	2	625..631	4	978..979	7
311	4	474..475	3	633..641	4	980..986	8
312..329	5	476..477	4	644..658	4	988..989	8
330..334	6	478..479	3	660..662	4	990..994	7
335..338	5	480..483	1*	664..681	5	995..999	8
339..341	6	484..491	2*	683..693	5		
342	5	492	1*	700..701	5		
344	5	493..495	2*	703..708	5		
346..347	5	496..497	3*	710..714	5		
349	6	498..509	4	716..722	5		
350..352	4	510..513	5	723..725	4		

*Indicates zones eligible for Intra-BMC Rates (Bulk Mail Center Rates)

STUDENT REFERENCE BOOK

UNITED STATES POSTAL SERVICE
Chart of Priority and Express Mail Rates

PRIORITY (FIRST-CLASS ZONE RATED MAIL)

Weight Not Over (lbs.)[1]	Local 1, 2, & 3	Zone 4	Zone 5	Zone 6	Zone 7	Zone 8
1	3.85	3.85	3.85	3.85	3.85	3.85
2	3.95	4.55	4.90	5.05	5.40	5.75
3	4.75	6.05	6.85	7.15	7.85	8.55
4	5.30	7.05	8.05	8.50	9.45	10.35
5	5.85	8.00	9.30	9.85	11.00	12.15
6	6.30	8.85	9.90	10.05	11.30	12.30
7	6.80	9.80	10.65	11.00	12.55	14.05
8	7.35	10.75	11.45	11.95	13.80	15.75
9	7.90	11.70	12.20	12.90	15.05	17.50
10	8.40	12.60	13.00	14.00	16.30	19.20
11	8.95	13.35	13.75	15.15	17.55	20.90
12	9.50	14.05	14.50	16.30	18.80	22.65
13	10.00	14.75	15.30	17.50	20.05	24.35
14	10.55	15.45	16.05	18.60	21.25	26.05
15	11.05	16.20	16.85	19.75	22.50	27.80
16	11.60	16.90	17.60	20.85	23.75	29.50
17	12.15	17.60	18.35	22.05	25.00	31.20
18	12.65	18.30	19.30	23.15	26.25	32.95
19	13.20	19.00	20.20	24.30	27.50	34.65
20	13.75	19.75	21.15	25.35	28.75	36.40
21	14.25	20.45	22.05	26.55	30.00	38.10
22	14.80	21.15	22.95	27.65	31.20	39.80
23	15.30	21.85	23.90	28.80	32.45	41.55
24	15.85	22.55	24.85	29.90	33.70	43.25
25	16.40	23.30	25.75	31.10	34.95	44.95
26	16.90	24.00	26.60	32.25	36.20	46.70
27	17.45	24.70	27.55	33.35	37.45	48.40
28	18.00	25.40	28.50	34.50	38.70	50.15
29	18.50	26.15	29.45	35.60	39.95	51.85
30	19.05	26.85	30.35	36.80	41.20	53.55
31	19.55	27.55	31.20	37.85	42.40	55.30
32	20.10	28.25	32.15	39.00	43.65	57.00
33	20.65	28.95	33.10	40.10	44.90	58.70
34	21.15	29.70	34.00	41.25	46.15	60.45
35	21.70	30.40	34.95	42.40	47.40	62.15
36	22.25	31.10	35.85	43.55	48.65	63.85
37	22.75	31.95	36.80	44.65	49.90	65.60
38	23.30	32.65	37.70	45.85	51.15	67.30
39	23.75	33.50	38.65	47.00	52.40	69.05
40	24.25	34.30	39.60	48.10	53.60	70.75
41	24.70	35.00	40.45	49.25	54.85	72.45
42	25.20	35.85	41.35	50.30	56.15	74.20
43	25.65	36.60	42.30	51.50	57.40	75.90
44	26.15	37.40	43.25	52.60	58.70	77.60
45	26.60	38.20	44.15	53.75	59.95	79.35
46	27.10	39.00	45.05	54.85	61.20	81.05
47	27.55	39.75	46.00	56.05	62.50	82.75
48	28.05	40.60	46.95	57.20	63.75	84.50
49	28.50	41.35	47.80	58.30	65.05	86.20
50	28.95	42.15	48.75	59.45	66.30	87.95
51	29.45	42.95	49.65	60.55	67.55	89.65
52	29.90	43.75	50.60	61.75	68.80	91.35
53	30.40	44.50	51.50	62.85	70.05	93.10
54	30.85	45.25	52.45	63.95	71.30	94.80
55	31.35	46.10	53.40	65.05	72.50	96.50
56	31.80	46.85	54.25	66.25	73.75	98.25
57	32.30	47.65	55.15	67.35	75.00	99.95
58	32.75	48.45	56.10	68.50	76.25	101.65
59	33.25	49.25	57.05	69.60	77.50	103.40
60	33.70	50.00	58.00	70.80	78.75	105.10
61	34.20	50.85	58.85	71.95	80.00	106.85
62	34.65	51.55	59.80	73.05	81.25	108.55
63	35.15	52.40	60.75	74.20	82.50	110.25
64	35.60	53.20	61.70	75.35	83.70	112.00
65	36.10	53.90	62.50	76.45	84.95	113.70
66	36.55	54.75	63.45	77.55	86.20	115.40
67	37.05	55.60	64.40	78.70	87.45	117.15
68	37.50	56.30	65.35	79.80	88.70	118.85
69	38.00	57.10	66.25	81.00	89.95	120.55
70	38.45	57.95	67.15	82.10	91.20	122.30

EXPRESS MAIL

Weight Not Over (lbs.)	Same Day Airport[1]	Custom Designed	Next Day & Second Day PO to PO	Next Day & Second Day PO to Addressee
1/2[2]	———	10.70	10.40	13.65
1	———	14.90	14.60	17.85
2	———	14.90	14.60	17.85
3	———	18.10	17.80	21.05
4	———	21.25	20.95	24.20
5	———	24.35	24.05	27.30
6	———	27.45	27.15	30.40
7	———	30.50	30.20	33.45
8	———	31.80	31.50	34.75
9	———	33.25	32.95	36.20
10	———	34.55	34.25	37.50
11	———	36.25	35.95	39.20
12	———	38.90	38.60	41.85
13	———	40.80	40.50	43.75
14	———	41.85	41.55	44.80
15	———	43.15	42.85	46.10
16	———	44.70	44.40	47.65
17	———	46.20	45.90	49.15
18	———	47.60	47.30	50.55
19	———	49.05	48.75	52.00
20	———	50.50	50.20	53.45
21	———	51.95	51.65	54.90
22	———	53.40	53.10	56.35
23	———	54.90	54.60	57.85
24	———	56.30	56.00	59.25
25	———	57.70	57.40	60.65
26	———	59.20	58.90	62.15
27	———	60.60	60.30	63.55
28	———	62.10	61.80	65.05
29	———	63.55	63.25	66.50
30	———	65.00	64.70	67.95
31	———	66.45	66.15	69.40
32	———	67.95	67.65	70.90
33	———	69.30	69.00	72.25
34	———	70.85	70.55	73.80
35	———	72.20	71.90	75.15
36	———	73.75	73.45	76.70
37	———	75.40	75.10	78.35
38	———	77.20	76.90	80.15
39	———	78.95	78.65	81.90
40	———	80.75	80.45	83.70
41	———	82.55	82.25	85.50
42	———	84.40	84.10	87.35
43	———	86.10	85.80	89.05
44	———	87.85	87.55	90.80
45	———	89.45	89.15	92.40
46	———	90.80	90.50	93.75
47	———	92.45	92.15	95.40
48	———	93.90	93.60	96.85
49	———	95.30	95.00	98.25
50	———	96.80	96.50	99.75
51	———	98.40	98.10	101.35
52	———	99.80	99.50	102.75
53	———	101.35	101.05	104.30
54	———	102.80	102.50	105.75
55	———	104.30	104.00	107.25
56	———	105.85	105.55	108.80
57	———	107.30	107.00	110.25
58	———	108.85	108.55	111.80
59	———	110.45	110.15	113.40
60	———	112.20	111.90	115.15
61	———	114.10	113.80	117.05
62	———	115.85	115.55	118.80
63	———	117.55	117.25	120.50
64	———	119.50	119.20	122.45
65	———	121.20	120.90	124.15
66	———	123.10	122.80	126.05
67	———	124.80	124.50	127.75
68	———	126.70	126.40	129.65
69	———	128.45	128.15	131.40
70	———	130.25	129.95	133.20

[1] Parcels that weigh less than 15 pounds but measure more than 84 inches combined length and girth are charged the applicable rate for a 15-pound parcel.

[2] The 1-pound rate is charged for matter sent in a flat-rate envelope provided by the USPS, regardless of the weight of the piece.

[1] Same Day Airport Service is currently suspended.

[2] The 1/2-pound rate is charged for matter sent in an Express Mail flat-rate envelope provided by the USPS, regardless of the actual weight of the piece.

UNITED STATES POSTAL SERVICE
International Parcel Post Rates

RATE TABLES: Parcel Post— Air (All Countries)

Weight Not Over[3] (lb.)	Group 1[2] Canada	Group 2 Mexico	Group 3	Group 4 Japan	Group 5 China	Group 6	Group 7	Group 8	Group 9	Group 10	Group 11	Group 12	Group 13
1	13.25	13.00	16.00	16.25	15.25	14.00	16.50	12.50	14.50	16.00	18.00	14.00	17.00
2	13.25	15.50	20.00	20.50	19.75	15.50	19.00	16.00	18.75	18.50	22.00	15.50	19.00
3	14.25	17.75	24.00	24.50	24.50	17.50	21.75	20.00	23.25	21.50	26.00	17.25	22.00
4	15.50	20.25	28.00	29.00	29.75	20.25	24.50	24.25	26.75	24.00	30.00	19.25	25.00
5	16.75	23.00	32.00	33.50	35.00	22.75	27.25	28.75	32.75	26.50	34.00	21.25	28.00
6	17.85	25.00	35.00	36.80	39.25	25.65	30.25	32.65	36.50	29.50	37.50	23.75	31.25
7	18.95	27.00	38.00	40.10	43.50	28.55	33.25	36.55	40.40	32.50	41.00	26.25	34.50
8	20.05	29.00	41.00	43.40	47.75	31.45	36.25	40.45	44.30	35.50	44.50	28.75	37.75
9	21.15	31.00	44.00	46.70	52.00	34.35	39.25	44.35	48.20	38.50	48.00	31.25	41.00
10	22.25	33.00	47.00	50.00	56.25	37.25	42.25	48.25	52.10	41.50	51.50	33.75	44.25
11	23.35	35.00	50.00	53.30	60.50	40.15	45.25	52.15	56.00	44.50	55.00	36.25	47.50
12	24.45	37.00	53.00	56.60	64.75	43.05	48.25	56.05	59.90	47.50	58.50	38.75	50.75
13	25.55	39.00	56.00	59.90	69.00	45.95	51.25	59.95	63.80	50.50	62.00	41.25	54.00
14	26.65	41.00	59.00	63.20	73.25	48.85	54.25	63.85	67.70	53.50	65.50	43.75	57.25
15	27.75	43.00	62.00	66.50	77.50	51.75	57.25	67.75	71.60	56.50	69.00	46.25	60.50
16	28.85	45.00	65.00	69.80	81.75	54.65	60.25	71.65	75.50	59.50	72.50	48.75	63.75
17	29.95	47.00	68.00	73.10	86.00	57.55	63.25	75.55	79.40	62.50	76.00	51.25	67.00
18	31.05	49.00	71.00	76.40	90.25	60.45	66.25	79.45	83.30	65.50	79.50	53.75	70.25
19	32.15	51.00	74.00	79.70	94.50	63.35	69.25	83.35	87.20	68.50	83.00	56.25	73.50
20	33.25	53.00	77.00	83.00	98.75	66.25	72.25	87.25	91.10	71.50	86.50	58.75	76.75
21	34.35	55.00	80.00	86.30	103.00	69.15	75.25	91.15	95.00	74.50	90.00	61.25	80.00
22	35.45	57.00	83.00	89.60	107.25	72.05	78.25	95.05	98.90	77.50	93.50	63.75	83.25
23	36.55	59.00	86.00	92.90	111.50	74.95	81.25	98.95	102.80	80.50	97.00	66.25	86.50
24	37.65	61.00	89.00	96.20	115.75	77.85	84.25	102.85	106.70	83.50	100.50	68.75	89.75
25	38.75	63.00	92.00	99.50	120.00	80.75	87.25	106.75	110.60	86.50	104.00	71.25	93.00
26	39.85	65.00	95.00	102.80	124.25	83.65	90.25	110.65	114.50	89.50	107.50	73.75	96.25
27	40.95	67.00	98.00	106.10	128.50	86.55	93.25	114.55	118.40	92.50	111.00	76.25	99.50
28	42.05	69.00	101.00	109.40	132.75	89.45	96.25	118.45	122.30	95.50	114.50	78.75	102.75
29	43.15	71.00	104.00	112.70	137.00	92.35	99.25	122.35	126.20	98.50	118.00	81.25	106.00
30	44.25	73.00	107.00	116.00	141.25	95.25	102.25	126.25	130.10	101.50	121.50	83.75	109.25
31	45.35	75.00	110.00	119.30	145.50	98.15	105.25	130.15	134.00	104.50	125.00	86.25	112.50
32	46.45	77.00	113.00	122.60	149.75	101.05	108.25	134.05	137.90	107.50	128.50	88.75	115.75
33	47.55	79.00	116.00	125.90	154.00	103.95	111.25	137.95	141.80	110.50	132.00	91.25	119.00
34	48.65	81.00	119.00	129.20	158.25	106.85	114.25	141.85	145.70	113.50	135.50	93.75	122.25
35	49.75	83.00	122.00	132.50	162.50	109.75	117.25	145.75	149.60	116.50	139.00	96.25	125.50
36	50.85	85.00	125.00	135.80	166.75	112.65	120.25	149.65	153.50	119.50	142.50	98.75	128.75
37	51.95	87.00	128.00	139.10	171.00	115.55	123.25	153.55	157.40	122.50	146.00	101.25	132.00
38	53.05	89.00	131.00	142.40	175.25	118.45	126.25	157.45	161.30	125.50	149.50	103.75	135.25
39	54.15	91.00	134.00	145.70	179.50	121.35	129.25	161.35	165.20	128.50	153.00	106.25	138.50
40	55.25	93.00	137.00	149.00	183.75	124.25	132.25	165.25	169.10	131.50	156.50	108.75	141.75
41	56.35	95.00	140.00	152.30	188.00	127.15	135.25	169.15	173.00	134.50	160.00	111.25	145.00
42	57.45	97.00	143.00	155.60	192.25	130.05	138.25	173.05	176.90	137.50	163.50	113.75	148.25
43	58.55	99.00	146.00	158.90	196.50	132.95	141.25	176.95	180.80	140.50	167.00	116.25	151.50
44	59.65	101.00	149.00	162.20	200.75	135.85	144.25	180.85	184.70	143.50	170.50	118.75	154.75
Each add'l lb. or fraction[3]	1.10	2.00	3.00	3.30	4.25	2.90	3.00	3.90	3.90	3.00	3.50	2.50	3.25

[1] See the "Air Mail Parcel Post Rate Group" column in the Country Listing for each country's rate group.
[2] Canada: Minimum parcel weight is 1 pound; maximum parcel weight is 66 pounds, but only 22 pounds for parcels addressed to members of the Canadian Armed forces based outside Canada (CFPOs).
[3] See the "EMS Max. Weight Limit" column in the Country Listing for each country's maximum weight limit.

COUNTRY LISTING

COUNTRY NAME	EMS Rate Group	EMS Max. Weight Limit (lb.)	Airmail Parcel Post Rate Group	Economy (Surface) Parcel Post Rate Group	Parcel Post Max. Weight (lb.)	Parcel Post Insurance Indemnity Limit ($)	Letter-post Rate Group	GXG Rate Group
China	5	66	5	5	70	1130	5*	4
Denmark	7	66	6	6	66 Air 70 Econ.	5000	3*	6
Egypt	11	44	11	11	66	1685	5	7
Finland	7	66	6	6	66 Air 70 Econ.	5000	3*	6
France (includes Corsica & Monaco)	6	66	6	6	66	5000	3*	3
Indonesia (includes East Timor)	8	22	8	8	44	-----	5	4
Italy	7	66	6	6	66 Air 44 Econ.	5000 Air 2200 Econ.	3	3
Japan	4	66	4	4	66	5000	4*	-----
New Zealand (includes Cook Islands and Niue)	8	44	8	8	66	980	4*	4
Portugal (includes Azores and Madeira Islands)	7	66	7	7	66	5000	3*	6
Russia	7	44	7	7	44	5000	5	8
Sweden	7	66	7	7	66 Air 44 Econ.	5000 Air 1350 Econ.	3*	6
Ukraine	7	44	7	7	22	5000	5	8

STUDENT REFERENCE BOOK

TAYLOR OFFICE SUPPLIES

Office Supplies Price List

CATALOG NO.	QTY.	DESCRIPTION	SUGGESTED RETAIL PRICE
PZ-8311	1 bottle	Correction fluid, tapered brush in spill-resistant bottle	$1.89
SS-9753	1 box	Envelopes #10, 4-1/8" x 9-1/2", 500 per box	$15.30
SQ-4473	1 box	Garment tags, black ink on white stock, 500 per box	$20.00
RT-5674	1 set	Highlighters, 4-color set	$3.55
RH-3899	1 pkg.	Note pads, self-stick, 3" x 3", 12 pads per pkg.	$10.95
HA-4120	1 pkg.	Paper clips, 10 boxes of 1000 per pkg., 1-1/4 " long	$2.99
UL-1982	1 case	Paper for computers (laser), 24 lb. stock, 10 reams per case	$84.90
VR-3890	1 only	Pen, ballpoint, ultra-fine point, retractable	$1.29
NQ-6590	1 book	Receipts for money, NCR paper, consecutively numbered	$13.99
IN-3575	1 box	Rubber bands, 1-lb. box, assorted sizes	$3.99
YH-0845	1 only	Rubber cement, 4-oz. jar with brush attached, metal cap	$1.45
SA-3134	1 pkg.	Sales order forms, 3-part snap-off style, 250 sets per box, NCR paper	$46.25
XP-5332	1 box	Staples, standard for office stapler, 5,000 staples per box	$1.25
RI-1532	1 only	Tape dispenser for 1" to 3/4-inch tape widths, rubberized base	$5.63
PN-2244	1 roll	Tape for package sealing, 28-lb.-per-inch tensile strength	$1.51

Furniture and Equipment Price List

CATALOG NO.	QTY.	DESCRIPTION	SUGGESTED RETAIL PRICE	SHIPPING WEIGHT LB.	OZ.
TS-9334	1 only	Cash register, electronic, 10 departments	$ 219.00	52	6
K6-6015	1 only	CD player, portable	$ 69.00	3	6
06-5000	1 only	Chair, ergonomically designed, with casters	$ 329.00	32	13
06-6120	1 only	Chair mat for high-pile carpeting, 48" x 60"	$ 99.00	26	8
UB-1606	1 only	Clock, wall mounted, battery operated, quartz	$ 52.00	2	12
HN-3161	1 only	Clothing rack, w/ 12 hangers, heavy-gauge steel (enamel)	$ 309.00	48	4
ME-3005	1 only	Copier, desktop, up to 12 copies per minute	$1,395.00	70	8
SC-2905	1 only	Desk, executive, 30" x 60" with four drawers	$ 559.00	180	14
SR-2473	1 only	Fax machine, 10-page document feeder	$ 129.00	15	0
06-4319	1 only	File cabinet, 4 drawer, 26-1/2" deep, full suspension	$ 222.00	117	0
K6-9315	1 only	Lamp, desk, fluorescent, brass with walnut grain trim	$ 79.00	8	6
HN-4332	1 only	Paper shredder, high volume	$ 228.00	22	2
PT-2972	1 only	Safe, insulated, 2 cubic feet, 1 shelf, 18" x 20" x 26"	$ 495.00	204	0
HN-3141	1 only	Scanner, color, flatbed, 12" x 4" x 20"	$ 249.00	8	0
KI-6440	1 only	Time clock with automatic ribbon reversal	$ 399.00	27	6

NOTE: ALL MERCHANDISE IS NOT CRATED. All items may be boxed individually and then put together in one or more packages and shipped per customer's order. Shipping charges and 6% sales tax will be added to each order unless the customer has a sales tax certificate of exemption.

Information Circle Mall
P. O. Box 276
Pettisville, OH 43553-0176

The
TOWNE CRIER

RATES CHART

FOR YOUR INFORMATION

Frequency of publication ....weekly

Circulation 12,000

COLUMN INCH DATA

- a 6-column newspaper has 126 column inches per page
- a double page has 252 column inches

NEWSPAPER RATES

Newsstand price..$1.00

Annual subscription rate (52 issues)...$50.00

DISPLAY ADVERTISING ADS

21-column inch ad (black & white) @ $5.00 per column inch
    (subject to usage discount)...$105.00

Full-page ad (black & white) 126 columns @ $4.00 per column inch.........................$504.00

Black + 1 color $100.00
    Flat 1-color charge is added for each color to the price of column inches

4-color..$300.00
    Flat 4-color charge is added to the price of column inches

CLASSIFIED (WANT AD) RATES

Per word charge, 1-issue appearance..25¢

Per word charge, 2-issue appearance..45¢

Per word charge, 3-issue appearance..65¢

Per word charge, 4-issue appearance..85¢

Minimum charge for a want ad...$3.00

UNITED COMMUNICATIONS • TELEPHONE EQUIPMENT

Name	Description	Purchase Price	Installation Charge
PLUTO, MODEL 3600	Enhanced convenience allows both hands on the wheel while driving. Three dedicated "Hot Keys" provide one-button access to your most frequently called numbers. The phone book stores up to 99 of the most frequently dialed numbers. Credit card dialing allows you to store credit card and pager numbers. *There will be a service charge of $16.00 per phone per month.*	$189.95	$52.00 per phone
VENUS, MODEL 3700	Take your world with you! The Venus slips easily into your pocket. The advanced sleek styling makes it convenient to carry and convenient to use. You'll love its quick, easy charging and long talk time. *There will be a service charge of $16.00 per phone per month.*	$199.95	
SATURN, MODEL 3800	The large bright display on this model makes reading easy. You can recharge the battery in less than four hours, which gives you up to 100 minutes of talk time before recharging. This model has security features that allow you to lock your phone. *There will be a service charge of $16.00 per phone per month.*	$264.95	
NEPTUNE, MODEL 3900	The Neptune is the thinnest and lightest weight of our cellular phones. It features easy-to-use large keys that are soft to the touch and a full-color display for easy reading! *There will be a service charge of $16.00 per phone per month.*	$159.95	
THE COPPER CONNECTION I, MODEL CC-I	The Model CC-I provides an integrated access device (IAD) designed for small businesses. It combines data and voice traffic onto a single DSL line. Regular phones, fax machines, key systems, and PCs plug into the system for telephone and high-speed Internet access. *There will be a service charge of $51.00 per month.*		$65.00 per system
THE COPPER CONNECTION II, MODEL CC-II	The Model CC-II with its Voiceover DSL provides an integrated access device (IAD) designed especially for medium- to large-size businesses. Users have continuous availability to the Internet and private business networks with a line speed up to 3Mbps on a single copper pair. *There will be a service charge of $153.00 per month.*		$95.00 per system

NAME OF BUSINESS	MONTHLY CHARGES*	
18 WHEELER TRUCK LINES	Local Service ....$ 290.00 Directory Advertising 45.00	Cellular Service ....80.00 Long Distance..............329.00
BUCKEYE EQUIPMENT	Local Service ....630.00 Directory Advertising 105.00	Cellular Service ....64.00 Paging Service 28.00
THE CLOTHES CLOSET	Local Service 58.00	Directory Advertising 15.00
CREATIVE ADVERTISING AGENCY	Local Service ....945.00 DSL Lines 102.00	Directory Advertising ....125.00 Internet Access 22.00
THE DENIM MAKER	Local Service ....1,260.00 Desktop Fax 216.00	Cellular Service 128.00
HOLLYWOOD & VINE VIDEOS	Local Service ....58.00 Internet Access...................22.00	Directory Advertising 23.00
LEE COMMUNITY CENTER	Local Service 116.00	Long Distance..............182.00
MEAN JEANS MANUFACTURING CO.	Local Service ....1,890.00 Managed Security Service ...82.00	DSL Lines.....................204.00 Shared Web Hosting 399.00
NOUVEAU INVESTMENT COMPANY	Local Service ....290.00 Shared Web Hosting 199.00	Directory Advertising 108.00
PASSPORTS-2-GO	Local Service ....174.00 DSL Lines 51.00	Directory Advertising ....105.00 Internet Access 22.00
PETTISVILLE BANK	Local Service ....945.00 Desktop Fax 36.00	Directory Advertising ....108.00 Web Site Builder 25.00
PETTISVILLE POST OFFICE	Local Service ....174.00 Paging Service 18.00	Internet Access 22.00
POPULAR DESIGNS	Local Service ....58.00 Internet Access...................22.00	Directory Advertising ....146.00 Shared Web Hosting 199.00
TAYLOR OFFICE SUPPLIES	Local Service ....630.00 Cellular Service 48.00	Directory Advertising 45.00
THE TOWNE CRIER	Local Service ....630.00 DSL Lines 51.00	Cellular Service ....135.00 Paging Service 158.00

*Long Distance Service is not included in the monthly charges listed. 6% sales tax and 2% federal tax are calculated on the total bill.